The Book of
Football
Quotations

Phil Shaw is a sports journalist who has written for the *Daily Telegraph, Independent, Guardian, Observer, Scotland on Sunday* and *Time Out*. He has compiled eight editions of *The Book of Football Quotations* over the past 25 years, the first five in collaboration with the late Peter Ball. Among the major sporting events on which he has reported are five World Cups and four European Championships. A self-confessed professional Yorkshireman, Phil now lives in Staffordshire with his wife, son and daughter.

The Book of Football Quotations

Phil Shaw

EBURY
PRESS

1 3 5 7 9 10 8 6 4 2

Published in 2008 by Ebury Press, an imprint of Ebury Publishing
A Random House Group Company

The Random House Group Limited Reg. No. 954009

Addresses for companies within the Random House Group can be found at
www.randomhouse.co.uk

A CIP catalogue record for this book is available from the British Library

The Random House Group Limited supports The Forest Stewardship Council (FSC),
the leading international forest certification organisation. All our titles that are
printed on Greenpeace approved FSC certified paper carry the FSC logo.
Our paper procurement policy can be found at www.rbooks.co.uk/environment

Mixed Sources
Product group from well-managed
forests and other controlled sources
www.fsc.org Cert no. TT-COC-2139
© 1996 Forest Stewardship Council

Designed and set by seagulls.net

Printed in the UK by CPI Mackays, Chatham, ME5 8TD

ISBN 9780091923334

To buy books by your favourite authors and register for offers visit www.rbooks.co.uk

CONTENTS

ACKNOWLEDGEMENTS

All journalists who have stood outside a stadium in the cold and damp, be it Old Trafford or Vale Park, waiting to elicit some precious 'nannies' (nanny goats: quotes) from determinedly tight-lipped managers and players can take my admiration and gratitude as read.

Special thanks go to Chris Davies, Andy Hunter, Hyder Jawad, John Keith, Tony Leighton, Kevin McCarra, Kenny MacDonald, Glenn Moore, Ged Scott, Janine Self, Martin Smith, Danny Taylor, Sam Wallace and Henry Winter for their interest and input into this edition.

Thanks also to Andrew Goodfellow of Ebury Press for keeping alive a project conceived by Roddy Bloomfield and the late Peter Ball a quarter of a century ago; to my family, Julie, Ellie and Joe, for their love and support; and to my parents, Roy and Gwen, for indulging my football obsession too many years ago.

INTRODUCTION

Dour Yorkshiremen. Humourless Germans. Rhythmic Jamaicans. Tight-fisted Scots. Oh, and sophisticated Swedes. To these stereotypes, trotted out daily in the media and in the 'real world', can be added The Thick Footballer.

It has long been widely accepted that the game's main practitioners, especially the players, are brainless, monosyllabic morons. Around 40 years ago there was a sketch, in *Monty Python's Flying Circus* I believe, in which a player plainly based on George Best answered every question put to him with 'I'm opening a boutique, Brian.'

Little has changed, it seems. When the producer of the film *Bend It Like Beckham* announced (jokingly, it transpired) at the British Comedy Awards in 2002 that she had received a congratulatory letter from the England captain himself, a voice called out, to smug titters from the assembled scribes and comics: 'Can he write?'

Such episodes remind me of a radio interview I did in the course of publicising the first edition of *The Book of Football Quotations*, in 1984. My interrogator, a plummy BBC veteran, was incredulous that anyone should have attempted what myself and my co-compiler, Peter Ball, had done. Having clearly not taken a moment to study the erudition and wit on display within its pages, he wondered aloud how we had contrived to make such a sturdy volume out of 'sick as a parrot' and 'over the moon' utterances.

While it was never our mission to rectify the sweeping generalisation about the intelligence of football folk, it has, over the course of seven previous editions, been a pleasing by-product. There are, of course, many footballers whose brains are to be found only in their feet, which in turn are often in their mouths. But to suggest it is a defining personality trait of an entire profession betrays ignorance bordering on snobbery and is not borne out by my experiences as a sports journalist over the past 30 years.

But why has the notion arisen? One reason is that players and managers are frequently interviewed within seconds or minutes of finishing a match, when their adrenalin is still pumping furiously. Microphones are thrust in their faces and they are asked 'how it felt' to score the winner or to lose in the last minute. The question invites, nay demands, a stock answer, but if the response starts with 'obviously', whose fault is that?

That's why, incidentally, *The Book of Football Quotations* has tended to resist pressure from various publishers, not to mention reviewers, to include more Colemanballs – the slips of the tongue that have been such a source of merriment to readers of *Private Eye*. Sneering at other people's mistakes under pressure has never seemed particularly amusing to this dour Yorkshireman, unless it produces an image or wordplay that is funny in its own right.

Another factor that has led to the perception of footballers being capable only of inanities is the sheer ridiculousness of trying to capture the essence of the sport in words. The wonderfully unpredictable nature of football means that participants and watchers (among whom I include the media, however dispassionate they may strive to be) are often plunged into the depths of despair or propelled to great emotional heights in the space of seconds.

How to articulate and encapsulate such extremes is a task with which the most exceptional wordsmiths, men and women of the chattering classes, can struggle, even with the comparative luxury of an hour to go before deadline. Yet we expect a member of the clattering classes, or a manager whose job may have been on the line, to come up with bons mots.

In the circumstances, there is something brilliantly succinct and all-encompassing about a reply like Alex Ferguson's to the TV interviewer who collared him immediately after Manchester United turned defeat into victory in the European Cup final with two implausibly late goals: 'Football,' he said, shaking his head and breaking into a grin. 'Bloody hell.'

Footballers do not, it is true, tend to be well educated, often having devoted themselves to the sport at the expense of academic learning before they reach puberty. Their intelligence develops in a different way from ordinary mortals, but it is there none-the-less, expressed in the humour of the dressing room, which is often scalpel-sharp and savagely witty, rather than in correct syntax or grammar. An interview with an experienced pro with a fund of anecdotes can be as entertaining as seeing a top comedian. And managers may tell you they will let their players do the talking but cannot help filling your notebook or tape.

The book was Peter Ball's idea. Peter, who was then my sports editor at *Time Out* and later worked for the *Guardian*, the *Observer*, *The Times* and Dublin's *Sunday Tribune*, would literally surround himself with massive piles of newspapers and magazines. He particularly liked *Sports Illustrated*'s 'They Said

It' section, which was the inspiration for the first-ever 'Quotes of the Week' column which I started in the *Independent* in 1986.

Every December, Peter and I trawled through this newsprint mountain and produced a 'Quotes of the Year' spread. A common feature nowadays, it had previously been found solely in the *Guardian*, where my colleague Frank Keating could claim to be the father of a cottage industry.

Peter was as keen on the polished prose he found in football literature (which is often lazily or snootily dismissed as 'not as good as cricket's', despite the evidence to the contrary produced by Brian Glanville, John Moynihan, Hugh McIlvanney, Brian James, James Lawton et al) as the off-the-cuff quips by the Shanklys, Dochertys, Cloughs or Atkinsons. Anything that made 'Bally' smile or snarl, whether a bizarre verbal flight or a cold, hard put-down, would make the cut.

My more anal approach to quote-collecting, which betrayed my past incarnation as a GLC clerk and librarian, entailed clipping them throughout the year instead of the annual needle-in-haystack search. We shared equal billing in what became a solo venture after Peter died of leukaemia in 1997.

The book was launched at a time when football was in decline, yet reviewers, from the *Sun* to the *Field*, were almost all positive or enthusiastic. It endured during the 'boom' years leading up to the millennium. Now, although 'bust' is always lurking like a ticket tout outside a big match, talking a good game is a more apt expression than ever. Speaking to the press (dailies, evenings, Sundays, local), and TV (satellite and terrestrial), and radio (local, national and commercial), and websites, and so on, is acknowledged as part of the job, be it the player, manager, chairman, groundsman, tea lady, supporters' representative or referee. There has never been so much source material to choose from.

My role is to scan the myriad press interviews, homing in on anything in inverted commas. Programme columns, letters pages and the burgeoning number of books offer rich pickings, as do press conferences, commentaries and what we still call 'terrace' humour. I also look for anything pithy said about the game by pop singers, soap actors and film stars, politicians, cricketers or vicars. Having collected great carrier-bagfuls of cuttings (my typically low-tech idea of a database), the task then is to seek out quotations that will have a life beyond the week in which they appear and to juxtapose them with remarks that provide a different, perhaps ironic twist.

My preference is for the punchy one-liner that makes me chuckle or think. Profane or profound, hilarious or humbug, the best quotations have a certain rhythm to them (it did not surprise me when a football bard approached me recently about the possibility of doing a Two Ronnies-style routine at various literary and poetry festivals, which would draw heavily on the book).

I am invariably asked which is my favourite, but that could be any one of a couple of dozen from down the decades, depending on my mood on the day in question. I have phases where neat, finely honed epigrams seem better than anything, and others where I prefer the stream of semi-consciousness (cf. Colin Murphy).

This book tries to cover all bases – I believe it will prove equally useful as a reference work or something to peruse while seated in the smallest room in the house – and is updated here to include everything from Jose Mourinho's provocative broadsides and the madcap utterances of Ian Holloway to the Beckhams' adventures in a far-away galaxy and Leeds United's spectacular fall to earth.

This, the eighth edition, combines the classics with around 2,000 new entries of comparable quality. TV scriptwriters would kill for a line like Paul Jewell's when the then Wigan Athletic manager was asked at what point he stopped fretting over relegation and started dreaming of Europe: 'After about 10 pints.' But the book was never just about the humour of the game. There's eloquence, too, as Derek Dougan proved after serving as a pall-bearer at George Best's funeral. 'He carried us for so long. It was an honour to carry him,' said Best's former Northern Ireland team-mate, his words gaining poignancy from his own subsequent death.

If pushed to nominate the quotes that always make me smile, I return to two in particular. One is by Joe Royle, then the manager of Oldham, after Paul Warhurst had been sent off. As we hacks clamoured for his view, which we hoped would be suitably outraged, Royle declared, without missing a beat: 'The ref says it was for foul and abusive language, but the lad swears blind he never said anything.'

I despised Margaret Thatcher's politics, and still do, but I thank her profusely for her reply when, attending the Ipswich–Arsenal FA Cup final of 1978 as leader of the opposition, she was asked who her man of the match was. Not realising that there had been a programme change which meant David Geddis had played instead of Trevor Whymark, she opined with that regal authority we came to know so well: 'I thought the Ipswich no. 10, Whymark, played particularly well.'

Even then, you see, the Iron Lady only had eyes for No. 10. But please, don't quote me on that.

one

PLAYERS: PRESENT

FREDDY ADU

A blind man on a galloping horse could see his talent. He's a little Fabergé egg, a God-given talent.
RAY HUDSON, former coach to DC United of Washington, after Adu's Major League Soccer debut at 14 years old, 2004

DARREN ANDERTON

Anderton wins England fitness fight.
'HEADLINE you will never see', Football365 website, 1999

NICOLAS ANELKA

He didn't deal with the transfer business as well as he should but he was badly advised. As the boss [Arsene Wenger] said: 'He's not bad, he's just young.'
LEE DIXON, Arsenal defender, on Anelka's exit from Highbury, 1999

[David] Dein bought me for £500,000 and sold me for 44 times as much, so he has made a huge profit. And he still tried to block things. This man thinks only about money.
ANELKA, 1999

I'm no longer part of Arsenal. To hell with the English people.
ANELKA, 1999

I think he's confused. He lives in a world of his own and he'll have to get out of it.
VICENTE DEL BOSQUE as Anelka's stay at Real Madrid turned sour, 2000

We used to have romantic nights in, watching films – with his agent. We only ever went out to Tesco. It was embarrassing – I'd get dressed up for a lovely night out and end up at the seafood counter.
BETH MOUTREY, Anelka's ex-girlfriend, 2003

MICHAEL BALLACK

I'm a footballer, not a social historian.
BALLACK when asked what impact staging the World Cup had made on Germany, 2006

Michael didn't want to learn a new language or a new culture, but a new currency.
ULI HOENESS, Bayern Munich general manager, on the midfielder's move to Chelsea, 2006

NICK BARMBY

Are we talking about a change of religion here, or just a change of football club?
GERARD HOULLIER, Liverpool manager, when asked whether Barmby 'might have to become a recluse' after moving from Everton, 2000

FABIEN BARTHEZ

The man with whom most French women would like to spend their holidays.
RESULT of opinion poll in Paris Match magazine, 1998

Barthez sat in my office smoking during the second half. He comes off for ill health and puts a fag in his mouth. Is that not ironic? It's a no-smoking area, too.
GORDON STRACHAN, Southampton manager, after the Manchester United keeper was substituted, 2003

JOEY BARTON

I thought his bum cheeks looked very pert. Nice and tight, no cellulite. If anyone's offended by that they should go and see a doctor.
IAN HOLLOWAY, Plymouth manager, after Manchester City midfielder Barton bared his backside following a game at Everton, 2006

JAMES BEATTIE

[Glenn] Hoddle said I had no future at Southampton and agreed to sell me to Crystal Palace. Apart from that, we got on great.
JAMES BEATTIE, Southampton and England striker, 2003

DAVID BECKHAM

He is making his mark on the school sportswise and never shows any sign of this going to his head – congratulations, David.
EXTRACT from 11-year-old Beckham's school report, 1986

When they picked teams at school, I was always the last chosen. I used to get booted everywhere because I was really little. I didn't have many friends really.
BECKHAM, 2002

My wife picked me out of a football-sticker album and I chose her from a music video off the television.
BECKHAM in the book My Side, *2003*

I was with David that fateful night he first saw the Spice Girls on telly and said: 'See that girl who can't dance or sing, I'm going to marry her.'
GARY NEVILLE, best man at Beckham's wedding, 2003

Beckham's silly little, smart little kick at his Argentinian opponent was what is wrong with the national character. This Gaultier-saronged, Posh-Spiced, Cooled Britannia, look-at-me, what-a-lad, loadsamoney, sex-and-shopping, fame-schooled, daytime-TV, over-coiffed twerp did not, of course, mean any harm.
DAILY TELEGRAPH leader article after Beckham's sending-off v Argentina, World Cup finals, 1998

Posh Spice is pregnant. At least that's one time David Beckham has stayed on long enough.
BRADLEY WALSH, host-comedian on TV's National Lottery Show, *1998*

I think the majority of people in Britain dislike me.
BECKHAM, interviewed by Alan Hansen on the TV documentary The Football Millionaires, *1999*

Nobody should ever underestimate David Beckham. The lad has balls.
At times I have disagreed with decisions he has taken off the field but he
has a stubbornness that cannot be broken, and he will make up his own mind,
whatever Alex Ferguson might think.
ALEX FERGUSON, in his autobiography, 1999

People say you get married and spend the rest of your life in the kitchen, but
my life is not like that. I'm not very domesticated – I don't even know how to
turn on the washing machine and I have no intention of ever bloody learning.
David does all that.
VICTORIA BECKHAM, David's pop-star wife, 1999

*We don't really have many rows.
We're quite childlike.*
VICTORIA, 1999

They are precisely the kind of people one would dread having as neighbours.
They have lots of money but no class and no idea how to behave.
*DAME BARBARA CARTLAND on hearing that the Beckhams planned to move near her,
1999*

The face of an angel and the bum of a Greek god. Rumour has it that his
tackle is enough to not only take your breath away but possibly do you serious
damage.
ATTITUDE, gay magazine, naming Beckham top of its 'fantasy' players, 1999

Whether it's men or women who fancy you, it's nice to be liked.
BECKHAM in OK! magazine on going to gay bars with his wife, 2000

He walks around the kitchen going: 'I'm a gay icon, I'm a gay icon.' When I
try to say 'So am I' he just goes: 'But they love me more.'
VICTORIA, 2000

I'm partial to a bit of Beckham… I prefer him with his cropped hair – it makes
him a little more rough and ready.
BOY GEORGE, gay pop singer and DJ, 2000

I saw some rock 'n' roll T-shirts in Los Angeles which had been customised with sequins. They were $250 each, which I thought was far too expensive, so I didn't buy one. The next day David was in the same shop with my sister and bought 12.
VICTORIA in OK! *magazine, 1999*

Beckham can't kick with his left foot. He can't head a ball, can't tackle and doesn't score many goals. Apart from that, he's all right.
GEORGE BEST, 2000

He's a really intelligent person. He's really deep, which I like.
VICTORIA, 2000

It's a sign of the times when Beckham has to be guarded against muggers [in Rio de Janeiro] because he's brandishing a £40,000 necklace, the big girl's blouse. I'd been in the game 20 years before I was earning that kind of dosh in a calendar year, but there he is wearing that amount around his neck.
ALAN HUDSON, former England midfielder, 2000

Is he the guy that wears his wife's G-string? I've got a message for him: 'Get out of those G-strings as quick as you can.'
MIKE TYSON, American boxer, 2000

It was a joke. I mean, as if he'd wear my knickers, come on.
VICTORIA, 2000

I feel sorry for Becks. He must come home and shut the door and say to Victoria: 'What the fuck did you say today?'
NOEL GALLAGHER of Oasis during the 'thong' episode, 2000

Posh Spice needs publicity desperately for her career. It is her oxygen. But for Beckham it is cyanide.
JOHNNY GILES, ex-Leeds and Manchester United midfielder, in his Daily Express *column, 2000*

David is an animal in bed. Some woman asked me in an interview: 'Are you so thin because you shag all day?' And I said: 'Actually, yes.'
VICTORIA, 2000

I've read it, cover to cover.
It's got some nice pictures.

VICTORIA on a biography of her husband, 2000

This is what I do when I'm bored – new tattoos, new cars, new watches.
BECKHAM, 2000

Football is such a male environment, but the fact that he is so prepared to be involved with his baby [Brooklyn] really matters to all the young men who want to be affectionate to theirs but have had no role models.
PROFESSOR ANTHONY CLARE, psychiatrist, 2000

People like Beckham make a far better role model [than Mike Tyson]. He shops for nice clothes, has a gentle character and he loves his child.
JULIE BINDEL, Justice for Women spokesperson, 2000

One's colleagues form their own opinion. They think: 'Why's he always at the fashion show in London?' Within the team, that can be damaging. Why are his five Ferraris always in the paper? He deserves 10 Ferraris but they shouldn't always be in the press. On the field I have no advice for him – he's a wonderful footballer.
LOTHAR MATTHAUS, former Germany captain, 2000

Football has become a religion and to be up to date we have to share the feelings of millions of people who admire this man.
CHAN THEERAPUNYO, Buddhist monk, after unveiling a gold statue of Beckham in a Thai temple, 2000

Being thick isn't an affliction if you're a footballer because your brains need to be in your feet. Beckham works hard, he's brave and he's a superb crosser. He treats a football like he does his wife – lovingly, with caresses.
BRIAN CLOUGH, 2000

He's not going to sit down in interviews and start using really long words, because he is just not interested. Also, David is quite shy and I think people don't realise the difference between being shy and being thick.
VICTORIA, 2000

Do you fancy me or something?
BECKHAM to a male reporter who asked about his 'Mohawk' haircut, 2001

David Beckham will not be asked to take a turn in the black chair on *Mastermind*, but I doubt whether I'd be wanted there either. David's not thick, just a normal guy having to put up with a lot of shit thrown at him by people who don't even know his personality.
JAAP STAM, Manchester United colleague, in Head To Head, *the book which preceded his sudden transfer to Lazio, 2001*

[Beckham] has an almost Garbo-like frozen facial perfection.
JULIE BURCHILL in the book Burchill on Beckham, *2001*

A man who has done nothing. Anyone can wear clothes but not quite as badly as him. He looks embarrassed about every single thing he puts on. His hairdos start out as some radical idea but end up as a horrific compromise, usually around the back.
JOHN LYDON, aka Johnny Rotten of the Sex Pistols, 2002

He's extremely good-looking, isn't he? And so noble. I think he's wonderful, especially when you consider what a brat he used to be.
DORIS LESSING, 83-year-old novelist, 2002

They are Mr and Mrs Everyday who suddenly got famous.
DAVID FURNISH, Elton John's partner, 2002

He's very good-looking and very rich, he's a fantastic footballer with an attractive wife and a lovely child. He has what everyone wants, which is why everyone hates him.
ROBBIE WILLIAMS, pop singer, 2002

He represents something for every woman – father, husband, footballer, icon. In a word he's the ultimate hero.
MARIE O'RIORDAN, editor of Marie Claire, *on her decision to make Beckham the first man ever to appear on its cover, 2002*

The first man on the cover of *Marie Claire*. I was touched.
BECKHAM, 2002

Don't cry for me, England! The Empire, the Queen, London Bridge trembles. Once it was the hand of Diego Armando Maradona, now it is the foot of Aldo Duscher. Duscher is a national hero. If Beckham – Sad Spice – is out of the World Cup so much the better for us!
REPORT in Argentina's Ole *newspaper after Beckham suffered a broken bone in his foot in a challenge by Deportivo La Coruna's Argentinian defender Duscher, 2002*

There is nothing more important than the state of David Beckham's foot.
TONY BLAIR MP, Prime Minister, 2002

Normally when you swap shirts they are soaked in sweat, but Beckham's smelt only of perfume. Either he protects himself against BO or he sweats cologne
RONALDO, Brazil striker, after the World Cup quarter-final win over England, 2002

I stayed at hotels where Beckham stayed. I checked toilets he might have used, took photos of them and licked them. I'm definitely going to England and if I meet his wife, I will ask her to leave him.
TAEKO, Japanese woman, quoted in the Shukan Post, *2002*

It's not easy when someone pulls your ponytail.
BECKHAM on being provoked on the pitch, 2003

At least his hair is OK.
DAVID JAMES, England goalkeeper, after Beckham, sporting a 'corn-braid' style, sustained a hand injury v South Africa, 2003

The moment he changes his hairstyle I have to get mine done the same. I'm not exactly ecstatic.
ANDY HARMER, professional lookalike, after Beckham adopted the braided look, 2003

The Blackest White Man in Britain
HEADLINE in Time *magazine on Beckham's braids and penchant for 'bling' fashions, 2003*

The gaffer had had enough. I'd grown up as a person and he didn't seem to like what I'd become. Now it looked like he'd seen enough of me as a player as well.
BECKHAM on being relegated to United's bench, in the book My Side, *2003*

The world worships him but 20 Beckhams would not make one Emre or Hakan Suker.
ALPAY OZALAN, Turkey defender, after a fracas with the England captain, 2003

The trouble is that he is a pony without a trick.

BRIAN CLOUGH, 2003

What do you buy David Beckham? He's the guy who has everything, so I might just stick myself in a box with a bow on it and leap out naked. He did ask for a briefcase to keep his laptop in. He's very intelligent when it comes to computers – much more so than me.
VICTORIA, before Christmas, 2003

We went away to Elton John's place for a week and I remember not showing any emotion at all.
BECKHAM on how he knew he was 'depressed', 2003

After training, he'd always be practising, practising, practising. But his life changed when he met his wife. She's in pop and David got another image. He's developed this 'fashion thing'. I saw his transition to a different person.
SIR ALEX FERGUSON, 2003

I'm not the world's best talker, not at least until I know someone well.
BECKHAM in the book My Side, *2003*

Beckham should guide Posh in the direction of a singing coach because she's nowhere near as good at her job as he is at his.
BRIAN CLOUGH, 2003

The ladies think he's a nice-looking young man. From what I've seen, though, he has always lived perfectly.
SVEN-GÖRAN ERIKSSON, England manager, 2003

Maybe we're like a big brother and smaller brother. It's very, very difficult not to like David Beckham. It's impossible. I don't think he can have enemies anywhere.
ERIKSSON, 2003

I'm sure there are lots of people out there who'd love to feel how soft his skin is. His skin is like our baby's.
VICTORIA claiming her husband was a fan of a face cream she was endorsing, 2003

The way I and my family have been treated is an absolute disgrace because at the end of the day I'm a nice person and a loving husband and father.
BECKHAM complaining of press reports alleging affairs with Rebecca Loos and Sarah Marbeck, 2004

As far as the tabloids are concerned, David Beckham is the new Princess Diana. This was the biggest kiss-and-tell ever.
MAX CLIFFORD, publicist, on Loos's claims, 2004

I will not let that tart ruin my marriage.

VICTORIA on Loos, 2004

Sleeping with David was a momentous day for me, not just a one-night stand. This is probably the most famous father, family man and husband in the world and he changed my life. When we made love David told me: 'I know what we're doing is wrong, but I can't help it.' I looked down and there was David Beckham kissing my breasts! David Beckham!
SARAH MARBECK, alleging a sexual liaison (which Beckham denied) during United's 2001 tour of Singapore, 2004

He has a very nice, toned, athletic body and he's well endowed. You might say he's a very genetically blessed man. Even his feet are gorgeous.
MARBECK, as above

I've no idea how long it lasted. When you're in bed with David Beckham you're not looking at the clock, believe me.
SARAH MARBECK, as above

The scandal may add something extra to the Beckham brand because most football fans expect a bit of sex, drugs and rock 'n' roll in the sport. To them, what he has allegedly done is within the limits of acceptable behaviour.
MATTHEW OSMAN, sponsorship and marketing consultant, on the claims of affairs, 2004

It's impossible to trust people. I don't like it being like that – I'm not that sort of person. But I've been made into that kind because there have been so many things and people who sold lies on me. We could be suing people every week. Every day there's a different story that's not true.
BECKHAM on the TV documentary A Footballer's Story, *2006*

Me and David have always been very compatible. We're going to get old together. We have a laugh. We got into bed together the other night, he put on the TV, and what's he watching? *Ground Force.* I said to him: 'But I heard you're really into porn.'
VICTORIA on her husband's alleged adultery, 2004

He's done nothing wrong. He's not the sort of man who goes out and gets drunk, has loads of women round him and stays out all night. That's not him.
VICTORIA in an interview with Marie Claire *magazine, 2004*

If we split up now I'll have to marry David Blaine or Daniel Bedingfield.
VICTORIA on her 'DB' tattoo after the allegations of Beckham's affairs, 2004

Much as it pains a feminist such as myself, Beckham has been grotesquely, massively, pussy-whipped by his talentless ambition-hound of a wife.
JULIE BURCHILL, journalist, in the Guardian, *2004*

She has everything except looks.
JORDAN, model and TV personality, 2004

[Beckham] has managed single-handedly to change male behaviour globally, and for the better.
DR ANDREW PARKER, Warwick University sociology lecturer, in One David Beckham: Celebrity, Masculinity and the Soccerati, *a research paper, 2002*

Beckham seems to scare the pants off macho men because he shows he's hurt when he feels it.
JENNI MURRAY, presenter of BBC Radio 4's Woman's Hour, *after the 'flying boot' incident, 2003*

I don't like the Beckhams and the way they prance around.
PETER HOWSON, official war artist, 2003

Don't forget to take your Preparation H out there with you. You spend more time sitting on that bench than you do playing. Piles will be next.
VICTORIA to David, as quoted in My Side, *on his being relegated to substitute when United played Real Madrid, 2003*

Beckham has transcended the classic footballing context. He is an integral part of showbusiness. But unlike Anna Kournikova, he does the business on the pitch.
MARCEL DESAILLY, Chelsea and France defender, 2003

Beckham is more of a pop star than a footballer.

PELE, 2003

I can totally understand the way the manager thought. When you're a footballer, traditionally all you're meant to think about is football, but I need other things outside of football as well. This is me. This is the way I am.
BECKHAM on whether the 'distractions' of fashion and global branding accounted for Ferguson's change of opinion on him, 2003

Becks hasn't changed since I've known him. He's always been a flash Cockney git.
RYAN GIGGS, United colleague, 2003

Throughout the Far East the adoration extended to him is a heady brew of sexual longing and a need for a blond messiah.
WILL SELF, author and journalist, on Beckham's promotional trip to Japan, 2003

We have this traditional kind of food in England called pie and mash. It's a meat pie and mashed potato. I think it's disgusting but David loves it.
VICTORIA to the Japanese press, 2003

We need to sign players the coach wants, not ones who appear in *Hello!* magazine.
ARTUR BALDASANO, candidate for the Real Madrid presidency, 2004

I feel like a piece of meat.
BECKHAM during transfer negotiations between United and Real, 2003

Perhaps as a pro-Europe gesture, we could give David Beckham to the Spanish in exchange for keeping Gibraltar.
LETTER to The Times, 2003

It won't take too long for the defenders in that Spanish League to work him out.

BRIAN CLOUGH after Beckham joined Real, 2003

He wouldn't get into our local park team, never mind Real Madrid.
DON PRICE, Manchester City Supporters' Association official, 2003

David wanted to come from the theatre of dreams to the team of dreams.
FLORENTINO PEREZ, president of Real Madrid, 2003

I'm so glad there will now be two good-looking guys at Real. I've felt so lonely in such an ugly team.
ROBERTO CARLOS, Brazilian defender, 2003

People love me because of football. To me, merchandising is an extra and derives from the fact that I'm a footballer. It doesn't interfere with my football.
BECKHAM at Real, 2003

I'm really happy to receive the OBE and it's a great honour. The Queen said it was great for her to be giving me the award, and it's an honour to be with Her Majesty, obviously. I'm very honoured to be given this honour.
BECKHAM at Buckingham Palace, 2003

At the age of 28, to be known as Sir David Beckham is some achievement.
ROBERTO CARLOS after Beckham was made an OBE, 2003

He wouldn't have been the player I'd have gone for. I'm not interested in how many shirts you sell.
JOHN TOSHACK, former Real Madrid coach, 2004

[As a player] he may not be the perfect lover, but he's an ideal husband. He pushes the Hoover around, cooks up romantic dinners and never falls asleep on you.
JUANMA TRUEBA, Spanish journalist, in AS newspaper, on Beckham's strong start in La Liga, 2003

The only footballer in the world that doesn't need to beat a man to play well.
HUGO GATTI, Madrid-based journalist and former Argentina goalkeeper, 2003

Beckham has a special hinge in his ankle which lets him place the ball wherever he wants.

ROBERTO PALOMAR, Spanish journalist, in Marca *newspaper, 2003*

It's not the penalty spot's fault if Beckham wants to impersonate Jonny Wilkinson. It seems one person had a particular problem with the spot but none of the others. Everyone can draw their own conclusions.
WILLIAM GAILLARD, UEFA director of communications, after the England captain skied his shoot-out penalty over the bar v Portugal, European Championship quarter-final, 2004

I've recently had to explain some things to my son [Brooklyn] about winning and losing. He has just started playing football and wants to score in every match. He even has to win arcade games. I've been telling him you can't win everything. Maybe after what happened this time, he will have to explain it back to me.
BECKHAM after blazing his kick over the bar as England went out on penalties, 2004

I don't know what it is about David Beckham and kicking.
SERENA WILLIAMS, American tennis player at Wimbledon, after Beckham's second penalty miss of the European finals, 2004

His passing was so accurate, as if he had a hand instead of a foot. We do miss him, despite what some may think.
MIKAEL SILVESTRE, Manchester United defender, 2004

I'm sure some people think I have not got the brains to be that clever, but I do.
BECKHAM on fouling Wales's Ben Thatcher to ensure he would be suspended while recovering from injury, 2004

Why do people criticise his intelligence when he can do miraculous things with a ball?
SHANIA TWAIN, American country-pop singer, 2003

He's the most famous athlete in the world (except in the USA)
HEADLINE on profile of Beckham in USA Today, 2003

I think of my horse, Tamarillo, as David Beckham. He's obsessed with his looks and would love a diamond earring.
WILLIAM FOX-PITT, British Olympic showjumper, 2004

Sir David Beckham? You're having a laugh. He's just a good footballer with a famous bird.
IAN HOLLOWAY, Plymouth manager, on reports that Beckham might be knighted, 2006

[Victoria] is very thin. I leaned forward to kiss her but there is so little of her, I almost missed.
DAVID CAMERON MP, leader of the Conservative party, on meeting Mrs Beckham at a pre-World Cup party, 2006

He [Steve McClaren] just said he had other ideas and wanted to move on. He said: 'You're one of the casualties.' There was no shouting, no crying. Not on the phone to the manager anyway.
BECKHAM on being dropped by England after the World Cup, 2006

The best part for me was the [singing of the US] national anthem. I got goose bumps. I love LA. It's a great place to live.
BECKHAM after playing against LA Galaxy for Real Madrid two years before agreeing to join them, 2005

She can't act. She can't sing. She can't dance. What can she do, except be Posh? The one thing you can say for her is that there's no one else out there who could be a better Posh.
FRANK BAUER, head of the Bauer-Griffin photo agency in LA, on paparazzi interest in Victoria's arrival in California, 2007

He is the greatest icon on the planet, the greatest catwalk model there is. And yet he has been an anti-diva. He was the most galactic of galacticos off the pitch, but the greatest of earthlings when he stepped on to it.
EL PAIS, Spanish newspaper, after Beckham bowed out of Real Madrid by helping them win the Spanish title, 2007

Beckham is not joining the Los Angeles Galaxy as an athlete, but as an advertising campaign. His job here is not to win, but to give his sport one last chance to work in the biggest place where it doesn't. His success will be defined not by corner-kicks, but by converts.
BILL PLASCHKE, sports writer, in the LA Times, *2007*

The craziness around him gets bigger and bigger, but he focuses on what he's best at: playing football.
ALEXI LALAS, president of LA Galaxy, 2007

I'm here to play foot... [Stops mid-word] ..er, soccer. I'll get used to that at some point. Sorry.

BECKHAM to the media on being unveiled as a Galaxy player, 2007

People [in LA] probably think we'll win my first game 10–0. But I'm not a player who'll run past six men or score four goals. My game is about working hard and being a team player.
BECKHAM, 2007

The Senate announced today that they've doubled the reward for information that could lead to the capture of Osama Bin Laden to $50m. Sounds a lot until you realise that we here in LA have paid $250m for David Beckham.
JAY LENO, American satirist and broadcaster, on The Tonight Show, *2007*

CRAIG BELLAMY

He is a hard man to love, but maybe one day I'll learn to love him.
GRAEME SOUNESS, Newcastle manager, before loaning the Wales striker to Celtic, 2005

He says he's a Red but they all say that when they sign, don't they?

STEVEN GERRARD, Liverpool captain, after Bellamy's arrival, 2006

Has no one learned the lesson about signing him? If only [Liverpool manager] Rafa Benitez had rung me, I'd have told him exactly what he was like.
ALAN SHEARER, former Newcastle team-mate, on reports that the Tyneside club might re-sign Bellamy, 2007

TAL BEN HAIM

I've been told I'm a big man and I think that says a lot. I can't even spell the word 'fear'.
BEN HAIM, Bolton and Israel defender, 2007

MARC BIRCHAM

My wife said I looked good in hoops. And after QPR there weren't that many options.
BIRCHAM, Canada midfielder, on exchanging the London club's blue and white hoops for Yeovil's green and white, 2007

GEORGE BOATENG

George's English is so good you forget he is Dutch. We gather round talking about foreigners in the English game and he is sitting there agreeing with us.
GARETH SOUTHGATE, Aston Villa captain, on his midfield colleague, 2000

JAY BOTHROYD

Let's blow smoke up Jay Bothroyd's arse for a change.
MICK McCARTHY, Wolves manager, calling for praise for his maligned striker after his winner v West Bromwich, 2007

KHALID BOUHLAROUZ

He likes to get right up your backside and make you turn the other way.
PAUL MERSON, TV pundit and former England player, on Chelsea's Dutch defender, 2006

LEE BOWYER

Q: What's the first film you remember watching?
A: *The Goonies* when I was off sick from school. These days the first video I play would be *The Krays.*
BOWYER in Leeds United club magazine questionnaire, 1999

He seemed to have lap dancing on his mind, not affray. He seemed to have girls on his mind, not grievous bodily harm.
DESMOND DE SILVA, Bowyer's counsel, summing up during the trial of Bowyer and Jonathan Woodgate on charges of assaulting an Asian student, 2001

Having been acquitted of both charges, I was hoping to put this matter behind me. Now the club appear to be victimising me and forcing me out.
BOWYER after he was found not guilty but fined by Leeds, 2001

I'm not saying that how a man plays on a football pitch is the best indicator of guilt or innocence in such a serious case. But to me, Lee performed as if he were innocent and the jury found him innocent, yet the public is critical. Why? Because it has pre-judged the issue.
PETER RIDSDALE, Leeds chairman, on Bowyer's good playing form while in the dock, 2002

I always found him a cheery lad, especially when I brought him up some pie and mash from London.
TERRY VENABLES, Leeds manager, 2003

Bowyer used my face as a skating rink.
GERADO, Malaga player, after Bowyer stamped on him in a UEFA Cup tie v Leeds, 2003

Lee seems a very quiet lad and, from what I have learned, what has happened in the past has been out of character.
SIR BOBBY ROBSON, Newcastle manager, on signing Bowyer, 2003

Bowyer is an obnoxious twerp. Sir Bobby Robson isn't. So why sign him?
MICHAEL PARKINSON, Daily Telegraph *columnist, 2003*

I'm no racist. I never have been and never will be one.
BOWYER, declaring his support for Keep Racism Out of Football, 2003

GIANLUIGI BUFFON

You score goals as a kid. Then you grow up stupid and become a goalkeeper.
BUFFON, Juventus and Italy goalkeeper, 2004

JIMMY BULLARD

He covered so much ground I thought we had twins on the pitch.
CHRIS COLEMAN, Fulham manager, on his midfield signing from Wigan, 2006

NICKY BUTT

It was animalistic behaviour. You're meant to play by kicking the ball, not people's heads.
KEW JALIENS, AZ Alkmaar player, after a clash with the Newcastle midfielder in a UEFA Cup tie, 2007

HENRI CAMARA

The day I get my bearings back in front of goal, people won't be talking about Thierry Henry any more.
CAMARA, Wolves' Senegalese striker, 2004

SOL CAMPBELL

Big Sol never says a word. When we play Spurs and I have a go at him, it's like talking to the deaf and dumb.
IAN WRIGHT, Arsenal striker, 1998

Ask him what he's doing and he'll always say: 'Chilling.'
LES FERDINAND, former Tottenham team-mate, 2001

People think they know me but they don't. They think: 'Oh, he's a quiet little boy.'
CAMPBELL, a year after switching from Tottenham to Arsenal, 2002

All artists have their own quirky little ways. I like to be the tiger roaming the jungle or the eagle soaring the skies.
CAMPBELL, 2002

Sol is a tortured soul.
KELLY HOPPEN, interior designer and ex-girlfriend, after Campbell went AWOL after being substituted by Arsenal, 2006

ROBERTO CARLOS

I studied him after the whistle in the World Cup final. Walking around the pitch like he was in his local park. He wasn't waving flags, crying or kissing his boots. You could see what he's about. 'This is what I expect, this is what I deserve.'
ROY KEANE on the Brazil wing-back, 2002

JAMIE CARRAGHER

He had a big mouth – about the only thing about him that was big.
LIZ TRAILL, nightclub stripper, after Carragher went naked at Liverpool's Christmas party, 1998

I'm going to start a competition with my 10-month-old son to see who can start walking first.
CARRAGHER after sustaining a broken leg playing for Liverpool at Blackburn, 2003

Carragher is 10 times a better defender than I could ever be. If we look at the Liverpool greats over the years, he's up there with the best.
ALAN HANSEN, former Liverpool captain, after his old club beat Chelsea to reach the Champions' League final, 2005

We all dream of a team of Carraghers.
SONG by Liverpool fans to tune of 'Yellow Submarine', 2005

People call me a 'classic scally' and I take that as a compliment.
CARRAGHER, 2005

I'm the kind of player that trains well every day. Do I sound like a teacher's pet?
CARRAGHER, 2006

PETR CECH

Q: Is there any music you like from the Czech Republic?
A: There's a group named Support Lesbians who are one of my favourites.
CECH, Chelsea and Czech Republic goalkeeper, in an Observer music magazine interview, 2006

DJIBRIL CISSE

I would like to be a woman, though I don't know why.
DJIBRIL CISSE, France striker, on owning a Jean Paul Gaultier dress, 2003

ANDY COLE

It always amazes me when people say: 'All he can do is score goals.' It's the most famous quote in football.
ALEX FERGUSON after Manchester United paid Newcastle £7m for Cole, 1995

He needs too many chances to score a goal.
GLENN HODDLE, England manager, 1998

His comments are diabolical and disrespectful. Is he a man or a mouse?
COLE replying to Hoddle, 1998

It wasn't a criticism, but an observation.
HODDLE, by now Tottenham manager, after Cole scored Blackburn's winner against Spurs in the Worthington Cup final, 2002

He raps the way he talks, and if you've ever heard him talk, you don't want to hear him rap.
NEIL McCORMICK, Daily Telegraph rock critic, after Cole released a single, 1999

Andy Cole should stick to playing football and driving his Ferrari.

BOBBY ROBSON, Newcastle manager, after Cole criticised Alan Shearer, 1999

ASHLEY COLE

I wouldn't play for Arsenal again even for £200,000 a week.
COLE after the then Arsenal defender was found to have had illegal talks with Chelsea, 2005. Six weeks later he re-signed for Arsenal for a reported £70,000 a week

If people come to your window and talk to your wife every night, you can't accept it without asking what's happening.
ARSENE WENGER, Arsenal manager, on the 'tapping up' of Cole by Chelsea, 2005

When I heard the figure of £55k I nearly swerved off the road. I yelled down the phone: 'He's taking the piss, Jonathan [Barnett, Cole's agent]'. I was so incensed, I was trembling with anger.
COLE on how he heard Arsenal would not meet his demand for a wage of £60,000 a week, from the book My Defence, *2006*

People think I'm a greedy pig. But it's nothing like that. I am genuine. I want to win things and play for the club I'm at. It's never been about money. For me it's about respect.
COLE on being dubbed 'Cashley' by Arsenal fans after joining Chelsea, 2006

JOE COLE

The older players all love him. When we took him to Newcastle before he broke into the side, they started singing his name as he boarded the coach.
HARRY REDKNAPP, West Ham manager, 1998

When Joe first came to Chelsea he would turn away in disappointment if West Ham had lost. I would smile.
FRANK LAMPARD, Chelsea and former West Ham colleague, 2006

PAUL CONNOLLY

What a complete chicken nugget with double barbecue sauce he is.
IAN HOLLOWAY, Plymouth Argyle manager, on the defender, 2006

HERNAN CRESPO

I wanted to be a garbage collector. Ours would drive past my house with his horse and cart, and I loved that.
CRESPO, Chelsea and Argentina striker, on his boyhood ambitions, 2003

PETER CROUCH

A lovely big bag of bones.
DAVID O'LEARY, Aston Villa manager, on his 6ft 7in striker, 2004

He's big, he's red, his feet stick out the bed, Peter Crouch, Peter Crouch.
SONG by Liverpool supporters, 2005

If you say you do not like Crouch that means you do not know a lot about football.
RAFAEL BENITEZ, Liverpool manager, 2005

A basketball player.
ARSENE WENGER, Arsenal manager, 2006

How do you defend against the Eiffel Tower?
JELLE GOES, Estonia coach, after Crouch's headed goal against his team, 2007

CARLO CUDICINI

Cudicini is like a rabbit with headlights.
DAVE BASSETT, Sky pundit, on the Chelsea goalkeeper, 2006

ARAJAN DE ZEEUW

He's really strong, never gives up. I could do with him in the whips' office.
TONY BLAIR MP, Prime Minister, naming Wigan's Dutch captain as one of his favourite modern players, 2005

EL HADJI DIOUF

Michael Owen has already nicknamed me Dioufy. It happened quite naturally one day in training.
DIOUF, Senegal striker, after joining Liverpool, 2002

He wouldn't have dared to behave the way he did outside a stadium. If he insulted me like that in the street, I'd have laid into him.
DIOUF after spitting at a Celtic fan who patted his head during a UEFA Cup game, 2003

Sometimes when I need to dive to get a penalty it's because, for me, the best footballer is one who is very clever.
DIOUF, by now with Bolton, 2007

PAOLO DI CANIO

Paolo often storms off the training pitch in the middle of a game if something doesn't go right. Maybe it's the Italian way, or more likely he is a nutter.
NEIL RUDDOCK, West Ham colleague, 1999

He's a smashing professional and a leader. He's like Bobby Moore in that respect, though he wouldn't have made it into Bobby's drinking school.
HARRY REDKNAPP, West Ham manager, 2000

Does this man not know the meaning of cretin or moron? He clearly doesn't. A cretin suffers from a thyroid deficiency. It comes from an 18th-century French word and was initially directed at people living in the valleys of the Alps and the Pyrenees.
DAVID JAMES, Aston Villa goalkeeper, on criticism from Di Canio, 2000. Within a year the pair were West Ham team-mates

There would have to be a bubonic plague for me to pick Di Canio.
GIOVANNI TRAPATTONI, Italy coach, 2000

I want to finish each game sweating and bleeding.
DI CANIO, 2000

What fascinates me – and this is probably where Mussolini and I are very different – is the way he was able to go against his morals to achieve his goals.
DI CANIO on his admiration for the late Italian fascist leader, 2000

I'm so exciting – every time I play, the fans want to have sex with me.
DI CANIO, 2000

The man who comes to take care of my piranhas told me that if I left West Ham he would kill all my fish.
DI CANIO after a projected move to Manchester United collapsed, 2002

How could anyone think the team would be better off without me?
DI CANIO when Glenn Roeder dropped him at West Ham, 2003

The salute gives legitimacy to fascism, a murderous and tyrannical ideology.
I take my hat off to Di Canio the footballer but Di Canio the fascist is a
disgrace.
*ENZO FOSCHI, Italian centre-left politician, after Di Canio made a fascist salute after
scoring for Lazio in the Rome derby, 2005*

I'm a fascist, not a racist. I give the straight-arm salute because it's a salute
from a *camerata* to *camerati* (members of Benito Mussolini's fascist
movement).
*DI CANIO on being fined £10,000 by the Italian FA for his actions while playing for Lazio v
Livorno, 2005*

He's not a big man and he's not a big player.
ERIC CANTONA, 2004

DANIELE DI ROSSI

I've left him to boil in his own soup. He's a fantastic guy but he must change
his computer chip.
*MARCELLO LIPPI, Italy coach, on the midfielder's red card for elbowing an American player,
World Cup finals, 2006*

DIDIER DROGBA

A fighter – the kind of player you could go to every war with.
JOSE MOURINHO, Chelsea manager, on his Ivory Coast striker, 2006

Sometimes I dive.
DROGBA admitting he went down easily when tackled, 2006

Drogba – the strength of a bull but the pain threshold of a lamb.
CLIVE TYLDESLEY, ITV commentator, on his tendency to go to ground, 2007

JERZY DUDEK

He looked like a starfish with jelly legs.
BRUCE GROBBELAAR, Liverpool goalkeeper in 1984 European Cup final, on Dudek's
copying his wobbly-leg routine during the Champions' League final shoot-out v Milan, 2005

DAMIEN DUFF

When I leave Duff out of the side, my 84-year-old mother rings to ask me
why. She kills me for it.
CLAUDIO RANIERI, Chelsea manager, 2003

Chelsea haven't bought duff at all.
SIR BOBBY ROBSON, Newcastle manager, on the quality of Chelsea's signings after a side
including Duff beat his team 5–0, 2003

KIERON DYER

I haven't got a clue about the exact number of women I had – four or five
maybe. But I regret it deeply.
DYER, Newcastle midfielder, on tabloid claims of an eventful holiday in Ayia Napa, 2000

We were driving back from Birmingham when Kieron suddenly shouted: 'Stop
the bus! I've left my diamond earring in the dressing room.' Can you imagine
in my playing days a player telling Bill Shankly: 'Stop the bus, Bill, I've left me
earring in the dressing room.'
SIR BOBBY ROBSON, Newcastle manager, 2003

PAUL EVANS

He was gnawing away like a puppy on a sock.
CHRIS MORGAN, Sheffield United captain, alleging that Nottingham Forest's Evans bit him
on the ankle, 2005

PATRICE EVRA

I haven't got used to English life. The food is truly disastrous and it rains all the time.
PATRICE EVRA, Manchester United and France defender, 2006

CESC FABREGAS

We even watched him in training. How did I do that? With a hat and moustache.
ARSENE WENGER on Arsenal's teenaged prodigy from Spain, 2004

RIO FERDINAND

When I hear about a defender who is good on the ball, I think: 'Oh Christ.'
JACK CHARLTON, ex-England defender, when Ferdinand left West Ham for Leeds, 2000

No one is worth £18m for just kicking a ball around a pitch.
DAVID O'LEARY, Leeds manager, on his British-record outlay for Ferdinand, 2000

It's an obscene amount of money and people will say nobody's worth that, but he is
JONATHAN WOODGATE, new Leeds team-mate, 2000

Rio has fantastic ball skills. This, of course, is fine by us. As is the sight of his sexy, sweaty body every Saturday afternoon.
ATTITUDE, gay magazine, naming the England defender as one of its top 'fantasy' players, 1999

I just can't get my head round the idea that someone has a five-year contract, and after 18 months he thinks: 'Well, that was very nice of you, thanks very much, but I want to move on.'
TERRY VENABLES, Leeds manager, before Ferdinand joined Manchester United for £29.1m, 2002

It was wicked meeting Nelson Mandela.
FERDINAND with the England squad in South Africa, 2003

If something wrong happened, I'm sure it's based on a misunderstanding.
I found him to be an incredible professional. If you asked me to name five
players as role models, he'd be among them.
*CARLOS QUEIROZ, Real Madrid and former Manchester United coach, after Ferdinand
missed a drug test, 2003*

Having known Rio very well, I'm sure he's not a drug-taker. But he is a
forgetful lad. If he'd been caught doing drugs, I'd have said give him three
years.
HARRY REDKNAPP, Portsmouth and former West Ham manager, 2003

We were always going to call our son Rio, although perhaps the timing wasn't
right. On the other hand it was quite fitting because he was a week late.
*HENNING BERG, former United defender, talking about a new baby soon after Ferdinand's
missed test, 2003*

I'm beginning to realise what it's like being in the public eye. It's not for me.
FERDINAND during his eight-month ban for missing the test, 2004

LUIS FIGO

Which player would I pay to watch? I like what is beautiful. I would pay to see
Figo, not Beckham. Even if they are both effective, I take more pleasure from
watching the first.
THIERRY HENRY, 2003

You could put Figo in a phone booth with 11 opponents and he would find
his way to the door. He'd beat them all and dribble his way out.
CARLOS QUEIROZ, Real Madrid coach, 2003

DIEGO FORLAN

One Sally Gunnell, there's only one Sally Gunnell.
*SONG by Manchester City fans as Diego Forlan warmed up during the derby with United,
2004*

BEN FOSTER

Not so long ago he was working in the kitchen as a chef, so he has the hunger.
ADRIAN BOOTHROYD, Watford manager on his on-loan goalkeeper, 2006

ROBBIE FOWLER

When you come from a council estate in Liverpool, how you come across is important. You don't want to be seen as a biff – some busy bollocks like Gary Neville, or someone who has sold his soul like [David] Beckham.
FOWLER on his Toxteth roots, 2005

If Razor had hit me properly, I don't think I'd be here to talk about it.
FOWLER after an airport fracas with Neil 'Razor' Ruddock following a Liverpool trip to Russia, 1995

I never saw the incident, just a trail of blood going through the green exit at Customs.
STAN COLLYMORE, Liverpool colleague of Fowler and Ruddock, 1995

I never do anyone any harm. Deep down I'm a quiet lad, believe it or not.
FOWLER after England colleague Graeme Le Saux alleged he made homophobic taunts during a Chelsea v Liverpool match, 1999

A killer with a fantastic left foot, who always picks the shortest route to goal.
JAAP STAM, Manchester United defender, 2000

You could run a university course on how to score goals, based on his finishing.
DAVID O'LEARY, Leeds manager, 2002

RICHARD KEYS: Is there anything you've learned about Robbie from working with him that the rest of us wouldn't have seen?
RIO FERDINAND: Well, if you see his ears close up, they're quite small.
EXCHANGE on Sky as Fowler's injured Leeds colleague acted as summariser, 2002

I went over to see Robbie and his wife in Liverpool. I risked getting my tyres and wheels nicked to speak to him.
KEVIN KEEGAN, Manchester City manager, in an aside that provoked anger on Merseyside, 2003

God played here 1993–2001, 2006–07
SLOGAN on T-shirt with an 'Anfield Heritage Plaque' design after Fowler's second spell at Liverpool, 2007

BRAD FRIEDEL

Friedel must have got changed in a phone box today. When he takes his jersey off there'll probably be a blue shirt with an 'S' on it.
GORDON STRACHAN, Southampton manager, frustrated by Blackburn's American keeper, 2003

AL-SAADI GADDAFI

Even at twice his current speed he would still be twice as slow as slow itself.
LA REPUBLICA, Italian newspaper, after the Libyan leader's son made a debut of 20 minutes and three touches for Perugia v Juventus, 2004

STEVEN GERRARD

It was so weird. Liverpool were 3–0 down at half-time, just like we were all those years ago and Steven psyched the boys up just like he did this time. We went on to win 4–3.
STEVEN MONAGHAN, teacher and coach when Gerrard led Cardinal Heenan Catholic High School to a cup final victory at 11, after the Champions' League final, 2005

People say you don't reach your peak until you're around 27. In that case Steven is going to be universe-class, never mind world-class by then.
ROBBIE FOWLER on his Liverpool and England colleague, then aged 21, 2001

You only need eight more men with him in your side.
NEIL WARNOCK, Sheffield United manager, after Gerrard's display in the Worthington Cup semi-finals, 2003

It's the cup with the big ears and I slept with it after the match.
GERRARD, Liverpool captain, after their European Cup triumph in Istanbul, 2005

We were having breakfast at the training ground when news came that he was staying, and I spat my cornflakes out all over the table.
JAMIE CARRAGHER, Liverpool team-mate, after Gerrard ended speculation about a move to Real Madrid or Chelsea by re-signing for the club, 2005

RYAN GIGGS

When Ryan was 13 he was the only one I felt was a certainty to make it. I remember saying to Bobby Charlton: 'You must come and see this kid.'
FERGUSON before Giggs, 33, captained Manchester United in the FA Cup final, 2007

I admire his pace and skills. I'd only look that fast if you stuck me in the 1958 FA Cup final.
RICK HOLDEN, Manchester City winger, 1993

Giggs was a big problem to us, but the biggest is that he does not have a German passport.
BERTI VOGTS, Germany coach, 1995

I'd said we would win but your talent overwhelmed my mind.

URI GELLER, self-professed psychic and Reading fan, to Giggs after Manchester United's FA Cup win against his team, 1996

I remember when I first saw him. He was 13 and he just floated over the ground like a cocker spaniel chasing a piece of silver paper in the wind.
ALEX FERGUSON, 1997

He gives defenders twisted blood.

GARY PALLISTER, Manchester United colleague, 1997

Teenagers probably look at Becks and other younger players. I'm the wrinklies' favourite these days.
GIGGS at 28, 2002

OWEN HARGREAVES

Football is not some concert where you pick your favourite songs.
OLIVER KAHN, Bayern Munich goalkeeper, after Hargreaves said he wanted to join Manchester United, 2006

JOHN HARTSON

With my ability I'd have played for a top foreign side or Manchester United or Liverpool if I'd gone through my career a stone and a half lighter... But there's plenty of slim, fit footballers who'd swap for my 50 caps, 200 goals and £20m of transfers.
HARTSON at West Bromwich Albion, 2006

Before our five-a-side in training one day, John yelled: 'Let's have Wales v The Rest.' Someone shouted: 'But you're the only Welshman here.' He said: 'Yeah, me against you fucking lot.' That's him.
TERRY WESTLEY, Hartson's former manager at Luton, 1997

When I saw the pictures of what I did I was ashamed. The worst thing was when people phoned my missus, who's six months pregnant, and said: 'What's it like living with a lunatic?'
HARTSON, after kicking West Ham colleague Eyal Berkovic in the head during training, 1998

I've always been an aggressive player, kicking and clattering people and being kicked myself. If I try to play tippy-tappy stuff I end up having a stinker. I have to hate the centre-half.
HARTSON, Celtic striker, 2004

If you're a striker who plays for the Old Firm, if you're not scoring 20 goals a season, you're not doing your job properly.
HARTSON, 2005

JIMMY FLOYD HASSELBAINK

I asked for his shirt and he said: 'You deserve it.' I probably did – it's not often you get elbowed by someone like him.
MARK HOTTE, Scarborough defender, after Hasselbaink helped Chelsea beat the non-leaguers 1–0 in the FA Cup, 2004

You're just a fat Eddie Murphy.
SONG by Newcastle fans to Middlesbrough's Hasselbaink, 2005

STEPHANE HENCHOZ

Henchoz spat at me. It wasn't the way to behave, but then he's not English, is he, so you expect one or two things like that.
NEIL WARNOCK, Sheffield United manager, on a post-match clash with Liverpool's Swiss defender, 2003

THIERRY HENRY

Arsenal will be in my blood as well as my heart. I said I was going to be a Gunner for life and I didn't lie because when you are a Gunner you will always be a Gunner.
HENRY on leaving Arsenal for Barcelona, 2007

Henry plays like he's a Brazilian.
ROBERTO CARLOS, Real Madrid and Brazil defender, 2004

I remember the very first day and people laughing when Arsene Wenger said he wanted me to lead the attack. I was pretty dubious myself. I looked at him with my eyes wide open in surprise.
HENRY, 2003

If there's a 50–50 ball and it's Thierry Henry, it will be 60–40 in his favour because of his sheer speed.
KASEY KELLER, former Tottenham goalkeeper, recalling how he ended up pulling down the Frenchman and conceding a penalty during a match v Arsenal, 2003

I don't understand how any defender in the world can cope with Thierry. In training I make sure I go on the opposite wing to him, just to get away from him. In matches, I just give the ball to him and [Robert] Pires and let them run at defenders. Next thing you know it's in the net.
ASHLEY COLE, Arsenal colleague, 2003

I have to kick a ball around the home. Even in the narrow corridor at my house, I'm always trying to dribble past my friends. I once broke a glass but one breakage in five years isn't bad.
HENRY, 2003

The only way to stop Henry is with an AK47.

GRAEME SOUNESS, Blackburn manager, 2003

REPORTER: How do you stop Henry?
EDDIE GRAY: Punch him and knock him out.
EXCHANGE at Leeds caretaker-manager's press briefing after Henry scored four in Arsenal's 5–0 win, 2004

Stubborn, committed, honest – maybe a bit too much. Arrogant? Maybe, I don't know. Sometimes, when you are honest with people, they say you're a bit up yourself.
HENRY describing himself, 2004

I've never thought of myself as a star. The word disturbs me.
HENRY after his Barca debut, 2007

EMILE HESKEY

5–1, even Heskey scored.
SONG by England fans to their German hosts during the World Cup, 2006

Emile could probably pick up Gareth Southgate and throw him the length of the pitch, yet he has developed the art of dropping like a sack of spuds whenever he is touched.
JOHN GREGORY, Aston Villa manager, 1999

Nobody likes to get that sort of criticism. But I'm pleased he got it because I tried all my career to get away crowds to give me stick and I was never good enough. I'd have loved to have 40,000 people baying for my blood. It was my lifetime ambition to have an away crowd boo me like that, but generally they didn't even know I was playing.
MARTIN O'NEILL, Leicester manager, after Heskey was jeered at Leeds, 1999

Soccer isn't ballet. If Heskey doesn't like getting kicked, he should play the piano.
JOVAN TANASIJEVIC, Yugoslavia Under 21 defender, 2000

He's a skilful big lump.
STEVE BRUCE, Birmingham manager, on his club-record £6.25m signing, 2005

DAVID JAMES

It's not nice going into the supermarket and the woman at the till is thinking: 'Dodgy keeper.'
JAMES, then playing erratically in goal for Liverpool, 1997

I am this super-human person. If you like, I feel invincible.
JAMES, then with West Ham, 2003

Q: What's the difference between Jesus and David James?
A: Jesus saves.
ELWIN COCKETT, West Ham club chaplain, in his Christmas message to the fans, 2002

As soon as the ball is in the net, you're thinking: 'Shit.' It's a sickening feeling.
JAMES after criticism of his goalkeeping for England, 2004

MARIO JARDEL

I don't know what you say to your mates after that. When they ask: 'What did you do in the game?' and you say: 'I fell like a big Jessie.'
GORDON STRACHAN, Southampton manager, after his defender Michael Svensson was sent off following a theatrical tumble by Bolton striker Jardel, 2003

ANDY JOHNSON

You only need to breathe on Andy for him to go down.
NEIL WARNOCK, former Sheffield United manager, in Made In Sheffield, *2007*

SETH JOHNSON

It's not my fault they paid me that money. If someone offers it to you, what are you supposed to do – turn it down and say 'no thanks'?
JOHNSON, Derby midfielder, on being jeered by Leeds fans for the £37,000-a-week wage he had reputedly commanded at Elland Road, 2005

KAKA

I belong to Jesus
SLOGAN on the Brazilian's undershirt after he helped Milan beat Liverpool, Champions' League final, 2007

NWANKWO KANU

He's tall, he's black, he's had a heart attack, Kanu, Kanu.
SONG by Arsenal fans in homage to Kanu, who had endured coronary problems, 2000

I am a Nigerian and I will remain a Nigerian until the day I die.
KANU, 2003

ROBBIE KEANE

I will accept full responsibility for not signing him. If Coventry win the title and he gets Footballer of the Year I'll bare my backside in the Co-op window.
JOHN GREGORY, Aston Villa manager, after declining to meet Wolves' valuation, 1999

If we could have got him for £500,000 and played him in our reserves for a couple of seasons, we might have been interested.
ALEX FERGUSON after the Republic of Ireland striker joined Coventry from Wolves for £6m, 1999

When I was a kid I always watched Italian football on TV. Playing in the back streets of Dublin, I always pretended I was playing for Inter.
KEANE claiming lifelong passion for his new club, 2000

I don't have a girlfriend at the moment. I'm engaged to Inter Milan.
KEANE shortly before being sold to Leeds, 2000

PADDY KENNY

Paddy was in the wrong place at the wrong time. Judging by the photos he was also with someone hungrier than him.
NEIL WARNOCK, Sheffield United manager, after his goalkeeper's eyebrow was bitten off in a fight at Ziggy's Curry House in Halifax, 2007

HARRY KEWELL

Harry's too famous up here [in Yorkshire]. You can't go out for a meal without people interfering. It's better in London, where people are only bothered if you're a Hollywood star.
SHEREE MURPHY, Kewell's partner and Emmerdale actress, in an interview with Loaded magazine, 2000

I thought he was cute but I never got any vibes. But we had a kiss and I thought: 'Oh my God!'
MURPHY on the start of her relationship with the Australian, 1999

If Harry misses a goal, I hear: 'You're keeping him up too long. Stop shagging him.'
MURPHY, 2000

I see people who are rated world-class and he does much more. He can do everything – run, head, shoot. And he's brave. Apart from that, he has got nothing.
GORDON STRACHAN, Coventry manager, 2001

I've achieved nothing, I've won nothing – that's why I'm here.
KEWELL on joining Liverpool from Leeds, 2003

FRANK LAMPARD

I laugh when I see I'm an 'ex-West Ham favourite'. Bollocks! I was never a favourite. They booed me for years.
LAMPARD, Chelsea and ex-Hammers midfielder, 2006

There are very few midfielders today who can play 130 Premiership matches in a row. But there are freaks and that's freakish.
SIR ALEX FERGUSON, Manchester United manager, on Lampard's 'amazing statistic', 2005

I told my players Frank Lampard has got 17 goals from midfield this season, but they just said: 'Perhaps that's why he's on 150 grand a week.'
HARRY REDKNAPP, Portsmouth manager, 2007

The girls like Lampsy. If I was that way, I'd see something in him.
JOHN TERRY, Chelsea and England captain, when asked to nominate the best-looking Chelsea player, 2007

HENRIK LARSSON

He has improved so much as a player, maybe because he has cut off his dreadlocks. He is more aerodynamic.
WIM JANSEN, Celtic manager, 2001

Before a game, I always tell myself that it will hurt and it should hurt. I know I am bloody strong, stronger than them. Even if it hurts, it is going to hurt them even more.
LARSSON, Celtic and Sweden striker, 2003

JENS LEHMANN

I have to accept that there are people who don't have a clue about football.
LEHMANN, Arsenal goalkeeper, on critics who argued he was the team's weak link, 2004

NEIL LENNON

He has failed in the face of a hoax threat by some clown with a 10p piece.
KENNY McCLINTON, Protestant pastor, after the Celtic midfielder pulled out of a Northern Ireland match because of a death threat by a caller claiming to represent the Loyalist Volunteer Force, 2002

I've a tiny wee daughter who knows nothing about this. It's time for me to say enough's enough.
LENNON after deciding not to play for Northern Ireland again, 2002

MARCO MATERAZZI

Marco is not the villain he is made out to be. He is a great player and a lovely, gentle and tender father.
GIUSEPPE MATERAZZI, the Italy defender's father, on the clash between his son and Zinedine Zidane that led to the France midfielder's sending-off, World Cup final, 2006

Zidane did wrong and he knows it. But Materazzi is a sickness. His sort should not exist.
LILIAN THURAM, France defender, 2006

LIONEL MESSI

Messi does things with the ball that defy the laws of physics. The only other player I've seen do such things is Maradona.
ENRIQUE DOMINGUEZ, Barcelona youth coach, on the Argentinian prodigy, 2004

How do you say 'cheating' in Catalan? Can Messi be suspended for acting? Barcelona is a cultural city with many great theatres and this boy has learned play-acting very well.
JOSE MOURINHO, Chelsea manager, after facing Barcelona, 2006

I owe Barcelona everything because they paid for my growth-hormone treatment.

MESSI, 2007. He was below average weight and height on arrival in Catalonia

DANNY MILLS

The oldest 24-year-old I've ever met. He wears pyjamas, slippers, everything your granddad would wear.
RIO FERDINAND, Mills's Leeds and England colleague, 2002

CLINTON MORRISON

Sometimes you spit in the air and it comes back at you.
GERARD HOULLIER, Liverpool manager, after the Crystal Palace striker had criticised his team, who then beat the Londoners 5–0 in the Worthington Cup semi-final, 2001

I'd been ill and hadn't trained for a week. Plus I was out of the side for three weeks before that. So I wasn't sharp. I got cramp before half-time as well. But I'm not one to make excuses.
MORRISON, then with Birmingham, on his disappointing display at Palace, 2005

ADRIAN MUTU

Mutu should drink a dozen bottles of wine a night instead of taking drugs.
VIO GANEA, Wolves and Romania striker after his compatriot tested positive for cocaine, 2004

Coke-snorting Mutu sucked my blood says Transylvanian tart
HEADLINE in the Sun, 2004

PAVEL NEDVED

Nedved's deceptively quick, even when he's completely stationary.
RUSSELL OSMAN, Eurosport TV pundit and former England defender, 2004

SZILARD NEMETH

The only forward in the country whose Christian name is also an amphibian anagram.
PEN PICTURE of Middlesbrough's Slovakian striker in the West Brom programme, 2002

GARY NEVILLE

Being a robot devoid of passion and spirit is obviously the way forward for the modern footballer.
NEVILLE on being fined for celebrating a Manchester United goal in front of Liverpool fans, 2006

What I know for certain is that I'd rather have Gary Neville in my team than some kind of cold fish.
SIR ALEX FERGUSON, 2006

If he was an inch taller he'd be the best centre-half in Britain. His father is 6ft 2in – I'd check the milkman.
ALEX FERGUSON on Manchester United's 5ft 11in defender, 1996

Dear Gary, How many caps have you got for England? How many do you think you deserve? Answer – fucking none. Lots of love, Noel.
MESSAGE by Noel Gallagher, Oasis guitarist and Manchester City fan, on a guitar Neville donated to a charity auction, 2001

Gary Neville is a really good-looking bloke. And just doesn't know it. Good-looking in a Robert De Niro sort of way – hard face, bent nose and stuff.
WILLIAM HUNT, Savile Row tailor, 2005

DAVID NORRIS

I reckon he tackles his girlfriend before they eat their tea. The lads tell me he met her in a nightclub, where he crunched her and liked the fact she got up so fast.
IAN HOLLOWAY, Plymouth Argyle manager, on his club's combative midfielder, 2007

NYRON NOSWORTHY

Now that Nos has switched to centre-back, he has much less time on the ball. Which is best for all concerned.
ROY KEANE, Sunderland manager, on the former full-back's positional switch, 2007

ANDREW O'BRIEN

Andrew's not got an ounce of fat on him, he's solid muscle. He's also got a big hooter. Some strikers he marks go off with broken elbows.
PAUL JEWELL, Bradford City manager, on his central defender, 1999

JOHN O'SHEA

I nut-megged Luis Figo
SLOGAN on T-shirt sent to O'Shea by a Manchester United fan after the defender played the ball through the Real Madrid star's legs, 2003

MICHAEL OWEN

I'm not sure whether he is a natural goal-scorer.
GLENN HODDLE, England coach, 1998

He showed the sureness of a surgeon in every movement, the high-speed precision of a computer in every touch and the ambition of a thief in the final shot.
JORGE VALDANO, former Real Madrid and Argentina striker, after Owen scored for England v Argentina, World Cup finals, 1998

Some people think he gets away with a lot because he is the boy wonder, Mr Squeaky Clean.
JOHN GREGORY, Aston Villa manager, 1999

In this country everyone seems to believe the Boy Wonder can do no wrong, and I find the hype that surrounds him a bit over the top. He scores a few goals and all of a sudden the newspapers scream that Milan want to buy him for £25m. That's absolute rubbish and I'm sure he knows it.
JAAP STAM, Manchester United defender, in Head To Head, *2001*

He has got this enigma around him.
GABBY LOGAN, ITV football presenter, on Channel 4's 100 Greatest World Cup Moments, *2002*

I'm a football fan now. In the papers this morning they said a nation's thoughts were on Michael Owen's groin. I thought: 'Me too!'
GRAHAM NORTON, gay talk-show host, during the World Cup finals, 2002

Michael Owen: Weapon of Manc Destruction
SLOGAN on Liverpool fans' banner at Worthington Cup final v Manchester United, 2003

I'm not a tights wearer. Maybe in my own household but not on the pitch.
OWEN after declining to wear leggings in the freezing temperature of Ukraine when playing for Real Madrid against Dinamo Kiev, 2004

Geordio Galactico.
FREDDY SHEPHERD, Newcastle chairman, after signing Owen from Real, 2005

OWEN: I've worked my nuts off to get back.
INTERVIEWER: How are you feeling now?
OWEN: My groin's a bit sore.
EXCHANGE in TV interview when Owen returned to Newcastle's side after injury, 2007

KEVIN PHILLIPS

He was so keen to join us at the hotel that he almost got there early enough to meet the last squad going home.
KEVIN KEEGAN, England manager, 1999

ROBERT PIRES

Does he do it on purpose? Only God will be able to decide.
ARSENE WENGER, Arsenal manager, after Portsmouth accused Pires of diving to earn a penalty, 2003

Sometimes when you play against these types of players, it's as if they have it in their contracts that you're not allowed to tackle them.
PHIL NEVILLE, Everton defender, after the Frenchman accused him of trying to injure him, 2005

JOSE ANTONIO REYES

There were only three tackles on him. That hardly constitutes the Texas Chainsaw Massacre.
SIR ALEX FERGUSON on the perception of the Spanish attacker as a 'victim' because of his treatment when Manchester United ended Arsenal's 49-match unbeaten run, 2005

Despite global warming, England is still not warm enough for him.
ARSENE WENGER on Reyes's loan exile in Spain, 2007

RIVALDO

How do you stop Rivaldo? You try to buy him the day before you play him.
ARSENE WENGER, Arsenal manager, 1999

Q: Who would Rivaldo choose to be World Player of the Year for 1999?
A: Rivaldo.
Q: Why?
A: Because I'm the best player.
RIVALDO, Barcelona and Brazil, in World Soccer *interview, 2000*

ARJEN ROBBEN

We love Robben – just like the Scousers
SLOGAN on a Chelsea supporter's T-shirt at Liverpool, 2005

LAURENT ROBERT

You always say something good about players who leave. Robert is leaving.
Good.
FREDDY SHEPHERD, Newcastle chairman, on the French forward's departure for
Portsmouth, 2005

JASON ROBERTS

We're talking about a person who spelt his name wrong on the transfer request.
GARY MEGSON, West Bromwich Albion manager, 2003

He's like a second wife.
BENNI McCARTHY, Blackburn striker, on his partnership with Roberts, 2006

PAUL ROBINSON

I thought: 'That's a sweet connection, I never even felt it touch my foot.'
Then I looked round and it's in the back of the net.
ROBINSON, England goalkeeper, on missing his kick to concede an own goal by Gary Neville v
Croatia, 2006

ROMARIO

God created me to delight people with my goals.
ROMARIO, Brazil striker, 1994

Romario is arrogant and petty-minded, and without his football he would be
a criminal.
DELMA KATZ, mother of the Brazilian striker's girlfriend, 1995

RONALDINHO

Any player who doesn't really want to come to Manchester United needs his head examining...To me United is above any club in the world.
ROY KEANE after Ronaldinho, the Brazil striker, chose Barcelona instead of United, 2003

Ronaldinho does incredible things in training. One day they'll come off in a match and the stadium will collapse.
LUIS GARCIA, Liverpool player and former Barcelona colleague, 2004

Not only am I as happy as I look, but I go out looking for happiness. My childhood taught me that.
RONALDINHO, 2005

I don't honestly think I'm the best player in the world. Sometimes I don't even think I'm the best at Barca.
RONALDINHO, 2006

Ronaldinho is the kind of player who makes kids' dream. They're not going to walk around with [Marcel] Desailly or [Didier] Deschamps on their shirts, are they?
ERIC CANTONA, 2005

Ronaldinho – Our Cilla wants her teeth back
BANNER at Liverpool v Barcelona match, 2007

RONALDO

I want to go down in the history of world football. I want to mark an era, to be a different player, to score special goals. Just to be a good player is not enough.
RONALDO before becoming the top scorer in the World Cup finals, 2002

The wunderkind controlled the chaotic, bouncing ball with a gentle but firm touch. And, as only the best strikers can, he poked the precocious orb with pace and a pocketful of surprise past the sturdy figure of Rustu Recber.
FIFA WEBSITE describes Ronaldo's winner v Turkey, World Cup semi-finals, 2002

After what happened to me in 1998, and all the injuries of the past four years, every time I step on the pitch and every time I score is a victory.
RONALDO after scoring both goals in Brazil's 2–0 defeat of Germany, World Cup final, 2002

He arrived like a king and leaves like a thief.
CORRIERE DELLO SPORT, Italian sports newspaper, on Ronaldo's move from Inter Milan to Real Madrid, 2002

I play much better if I have sex before a game. I have to have sex three times a week.
RONALDO, 2004

CRISTIANO RONALDO

There have been a few players described as the new George Best over the years, but this is the first time it's been a compliment to me.
GEORGE BEST, 2004

I always had the belief that if you put five men in front of me, I could go past them all.
RONALDO, Manchester United and Portugal winger, 2004

His tricks annoy people. One day someone will hurt Cristiano Ronaldo properly and he will be out for a long time.
GEORGE BOATENG, Middlesbrough midfielder, 2005

When they get back to Man United's training ground, I wouldn't be surprised if Rooney doesn't stick one on him.
ALAN SHEARER, BBC TV pundit, on Ronaldo's apparent role in Rooney's dismissal playing for England v Portugal, World Cup finals, 2006

Maybe some people don't like me. Maybe it's because I'm too good for them.
RONALDO after allegations of diving, 2007

Maybe it's a difficult childhood, no education.
JOSE MOURINHO, Chelsea manager, alleging a lack of maturity in his compatriot, 2007

It's really below the belt to bring class into it. Ronaldo has principles, which is why he hasn't responded. Other people are educated but have no principles.
SIR ALEX FERGUSON defends his player, 2007

His strokes of artistry put paint on the canvas.
FERGUSON when Ronaldo was crowned Footballer of the Year, 2007

Nothing can stop him. Probably the only way to do it is to kill him.
PATRICE EVRA, United team-mate, 2007

Cristiano is the only one with a personal mirror in the dressing room. He spends hours doing his hair and putting on his gel.
EVRA, 2007

WAYNE ROONEY

I had two obsessions [as a child] – football and Ninja Turtles... We copied [the Ninja moves] off the TV until we got them perfect and if anybody else wanted to be Raphael I used to sit on them until they gave in. I rated Raphael up there alongside Alan Shearer.
ROONEY quoted in England's Hero *by Sue Evison, 2004*

I asked their manager, Big Neville: 'Who's the little fella?' He looked at me and groaned: 'We've only just signed him. Leave him alone.' I said: 'Leave him alone? You must be joking.'
BOB PENDLETON, Everton scout, on how he spotted Rooney playing for Copplehouse Juniors in the Walton & Kirkdale Junior League, 2003

Wayne would be there at seven in the morning, just kicking a ball. My Granny Mavis didn't think it was funny. She'd yell 'Wa-ay-ne' and he'd get a slap. Sometimes it would be me or one of the others, but we'd tell her it was Wayne.
THOMAS ROONEY, Tranmere player and Wayne's cousin, on life in a Croxteth council estate, 2003

I came home and said to my dad: 'Are we Irish?' 'How do I know?' he replied.
ROONEY in My Story So Far, *2006*

I did a radio interview and I tried to play down Rooney, but how can you play down the greatest thing around in football?
BILL KENWRIGHT, Everton deputy chairman, on their 16-year-old striker, 2002

There's too much fantasy in this lad's story for one of my theatre shows. A boy who sits muttering in his monosyllabic way when the microphones are there can go out and bring 50,000 men to their feet in joy.
KENWRIGHT, 2003

To Charlotte, I shagged you on 28 Dec, loads of love, Wayne Rooney
AUTOGRAPHED NOTE to prostitute Charlotte Glover, 2002

It [visiting prostitutes] was all a bit of a laugh and happened before me and Coleen [McLoughlin] had become serious... But I do deeply regret it.
ROONEY in My Story So Far, *2006*

We have to look after Wayne and that includes every Evertonian. If you see him out in the street, send him home. Sir Alex Ferguson used to offer £100 to anyone telling him where his young stars were. I might do the same.
DAVID MOYES, Everton manager, 2002

I suspect he hasn't had many positive experiences with older male figures. I want him to turn 30 and be able to say to himself: 'David Moyes was all right for me.'
MOYES, 2003

One of the last street footballers, part of a dying breed.
MOYES, 2003

I'm more scared of my mum than of Sven-Göran Eriksson. She'd always give me a clip round the ear if she thought I wasn't doing right.
ROONEY quoted in England's Hero *by Sue Evison, 2004*

You look into his eyes and he looks 17 but if you look at him from behind and at the way he plays, you'd think he was 32.
DAVID JAMES, England team-mate, 2003

My old mate Colin Harvey, who coaches the kids at Everton, is not one to go overboard. He described Kenny Dalglish as 'all right', but Rooney as 'a good player'.
PETER REID, Leeds United caretaker-manager, 2003

If [Rooney] thinks he's got pressure now, things are going to get 10 times worse.
GEORGE BEST, 2003

Is he as good as me? Don't be silly!
BEST, 2004

Rooney has a man's body on a teenager's head.
GEORGE GRAHAM, TV pundit and former Arsenal and Leeds manager, 2003

After that incredible first goal against Arsenal, when Arsene Wenger was talking to the world's media about his special talent, Wayne was already out on his BMX bike, meeting his mates outside the local chip shop. He even ended up kicking a ball against a wall with them.
PAUL STRETFORD, Rooney's agent, 2003

All people could talk about was that his tie was undone and he was chewing gum. There was very little celebration and a lot of sneering, but it didn't affect him or hurt him one iota.
STRETFORD after Rooney was criticised for his dress and attitude on BBC TV's Sports Personality of the Year *show, 2003*

I ran from the top of the house, through the garden and down the slope which goes down to Long Island Sound. I screamed across the bay: 'Rooooooneyyyyyy!' Everyone for miles around must've thought, 'What's that madman up to?' Then I ran all the way back up the stairs. It was like being a kid again.
BILL KENWRIGHT on the moment Rooney became England's youngest-ever scorer, 2003

It's hard for a Scotsman to say, but I was supporting England. And when Wayne nearly scored, I jumped out of my seat.
DAVID MOYES after Rooney scored for England v Turkey, 2003

We would never sell Wayne Rooney. That would never come about, because any club would have to pay a king's ransom for a player like him. All I can say is I haven't had one phone call about him.
KENWRIGHT, 2004

Wayne Rooney – Talented and Spirited Sweetie
HEADLINE in Le Monde, French newspaper, 2004

Wayne's the antithesis of Beckham. He'll never wear a sarong out in Liverpool, for example.
DAVE BARRACLOUGH, designer of Rooney's clothing line, 2004

He's incredible – I don't remember anyone making such an impact on a tournament since Pele in 1958.
SVEN GÖRAN ERIKSSON, Rooney's manager with England, at the European Championship finals, 2004

Rooney and Pele? They're different. One's white and one's black. Rooney is a big-game player but Pele was a one-off. There won't be another like him in 1,000 years.
LUIZ FELIPE SCOLARI, Portugal and former Brazil coach, after England's Sven-Göran Eriksson likened Rooney's impact to the teenaged Pele, European Championship finals, 2004

He's about as attractive as a clenched fist.

GERMAINE GREER, writer, broadcaster and feminist, 2004

He's not just a footballer. He's so damned strong he'd make a great removal man as well.
MICHEL SALGADO, Spain defender, 2004

I like to play with a little bit of temper.
ROONEY, 2004

When I scored my first goal for England, I was so excited I didn't know what to do or where to run. David [Beckham] just pointed and said: 'Well, the England fans are that way, mate.'
ROONEY, 2004

Wayne Rooney is the new Harry Potter. With his magic, his nose for the ball, his speed and his tactical awareness, he has that robust aspect and boyish face that make him the new English idol... He is the best-seller at Euro 2004.
AS, Spanish newspaper, 2004

People laugh when I tell them my name. I was renting a video and the lad in the shop cracked up when he heard it. He shouted to his mate: 'Come here, I've got Wayne Rooney in the shop.' But it's never been easy. My dad's name is Mickey Rooney so you can imagine the stick I got as a kid.
WAYNE ROONEY, plasterer in the West Midlands, 2004

Rooney is a throwback to the street players who used to come out of places like inner-city Glasgow. He's an old-fashioned footballer with modern sensibilities.
ERIC HARRISON, former head of Manchester United's youth academy, 2004

I sat next to Rebekah Wade [editor of the *Sun*] at a party for Max Clifford's birthday and we were discussing Hillsborough. She didn't know much about it, and why should she? Wayne Rooney at 18 ought to know more because there isn't a footballing kid of 18 in Liverpool that doesn't know exactly what happened at Hillsborough.
DEREK HATTON, broadcaster, Everton fan and former Liverpool councillor, after Rooney sold his 'story' to the Sun, *2004*

Once a Blue, Always a Blue
SLOGAN on T-shirt worn by Rooney beneath his Everton top after scoring in the FA Youth Cup final, 2002

Once a Blue, Always a Red
SLOGAN on T-shirts on sale outside Old Trafford, 2007

Could've been a God but chose to be a Devil
GRAFFITI outside Goodison Park the day Rooney joined United, 2004

Rooney has signed a deal to do five books. That's an awful lot of crayons.
JOHNNIE WALKER, Radio 2 DJ, 2006

We were shite and I was shite.
ROONEY in his book My Story So Far *on his display v Sunderland, 2006*

I not only like to have the TV and light on to help me sleep, but also a vacuum cleaner. Failing that, a fan or a hair-dryer. I've ruined so many hair-dryers by letting them burn out. So far I haven't set fire to anywhere.
ROONEY, 2006

LOUIS SAHA

He's got pace and intelligence. It's like finding a beautiful woman with money.
TERRY BURTON, Wimbledon manager, on Fulham's French striker, 2001

ROBBIE SAVAGE

I'm not everybody's cup of tea.
SAVAGE when playing for Birmingham, 2004

He looks as if he should be surfing in California, and if there's one thing that annoys me about him, it's that tan. We haven't been to Barbados lately, so he must have been on the sun bed. As we approach February, I like players to have that drained, pale look that I've always had at that stage of the season.
MARTIN O'NEILL, Leicester manager, 2000

Outside Leicester, everyone hates him, but he's a folk hero here. There's more meat on a toothpick and to see him with his clothes off, you wonder where he gets all his energy from... Even when he has had a poor game he thinks he should be man of the match. He's always saying: 'Didn't you think I was great today?'
ALAN BIRCHENALL, Leicester public-relations officer and ex-striker, 2000

If brains were chocolate, he wouldn't have enough to fill a Smartie.
BIRCHENALL, 2000

I'm a bit anxious. I think every other manager out there hates me.
SAVAGE on pleading with Leicester chairman John Elsom to give manager Peter Taylor more time to stop a bad run, 2001

Robbie had to come off with cramp – in his hair.
STEVE BRUCE, Birmingham manager, on his long-haired midfielder, 2003

All they see is the hair and someone getting stuck in.
SAVAGE on why opposition fans dislike him, 2004

He's a drama queen who likes a lot of attention. He has built a reputation for putting it about, yet as soon as he gets a bad tackle he starts moaning about it.
LAWRIE SANCHEZ, Northern Ireland manager, when Savage threatened to retire from international football after his sending-off for Wales v Northern Ireland, 2004

Here's one for Mr and Mrs Robbie Savage. You do know he's gay?
ROBBIE WILLIAMS, pop singer, during a concert attended by the midfielder, 2006

PAUL SCHOLES

He's not under-rated. Every top club in Europe knows about him. We have always had players linked with moves abroad but Paul doesn't fit into that. No chance. Oldham Athletic maybe. He's a big Oldham fan.
SIR ALEX FERGUSON, 2003

One of the best football brains Manchester United have ever had.
FERGUSON, 1999

One of the top three players in the world, certainly one of the most complete, yet he has never even won the PFA player of the year. He's not fashionable. He doesn't have the image to suit certain people. If England won Euro 2004 and he scored six goals, they'd still give it to someone else.
GARY NEVILLE, Manchester United and England team-mate, 2004

The one player who can do everything. He can defend and attack, pass the ball, dribble and though he's small, there's no better header of the ball. The best player available to England.
LAURENT BLANC, former United colleague, before Scholes's international retirement, 2004

I'm sure if he was 6ft 2in, he'd be the best player in the world.
RAY WILKINS, Millwall coach and ex-United player, on the 'wonderful, world-class' Scholes before the FA Cup final, 2004

Ask Patrick [Vieira] which midfielder he most dislikes playing against and he will tell you: Paul Scholes. No one else. He's always moving, creating. He's the best player I've seen since coming to England.
THIERRY HENRY, Arsenal striker, 2004

The best midfielder in the world. He's what the rest of us aspire to. He can do everything: tackle, pass, score goals.
EDGAR DAVIDS, Juventus and Netherlands midfielder, 2003

Like Kenny Dalglish, his brain is quicker than 99 per cent of footballers. And like Kenny, he has eyes in the back of his head.
ERIC HARRISON, the United youth coach who nurtured the young Scholes, 2003

They [Scholes and Wayne Rooney] batter the ball in training. Gary Neville was having a piss one day, 45 yards away by a fence. Scholes whacked him right in the arse.
SIR ALEX FERGUSON, 2004

Scholes is nasty and I like that in him. You need that if you play in the centre of the park.
ROY KEANE, Sunderland manager, working as TV summariser, 2006

Scholesy sees things before they actually happen.

MICHAEL CARRICK, United team-mate, 2007

TEDDY SHERINGHAM

When he played for me at Nottingham Forest he was the slowest player in the squad – perhaps due to all those nightclubs he kept telling me he didn't frequent.
BRIAN CLOUGH after Sheringham was named Footballer of the Year, 2001

Clough called me Edward. I told him I preferred to be called Teddy. He said: 'Right you are, Edward.'
SHERINGHAM, 2001

ALAN SMITH

One club I would never consider joining is Manchester United.
ALAN SMITH, Leeds striker, on the Soccer AM *programme, 2002*

Not a lot of people would have been brave enough to make this step.
SMITH on his move from Leeds to Manchester United, 2004

If we'd stayed up, I'd have cut off both my legs rather than leave Leeds.
SMITH, 2004

I've learned that you never say never.
SMITH, 2005

Usually it pisses me off when the press say things like that. But it was so absurd it actually made me laugh.
DIDO, pop singer, on being romantically linked to Smith, 2004

When I looked down, the leg was pointing one way and the ankle was pointing towards Hong Kong. So I knew I was in serious trouble.
SMITH after suffering a broken leg and dislocated ankle playing for Manchester United at Liverpool, 2006

IBRAHIMA SONKO

Anyone brave enough to meet him down a dark alley should be armed with a big chunk of Kryptonite.
WALLY DOWNES, Reading assistant manager, after the defender received death threats following a collision which injured Chelsea goalkeeper Carlo Cudicini, 2006

THOMAS SORENSEN

I'm just as good as Peter Schmeichel, but I'm more modest by nature.
SORENSEN, Sunderland and Denmark goalkeeper, 2000

GARY SPEED

We can't replace Gary Speed. Where do you get an experienced player like him with a left foot and a head?
SIR BOBBY ROBSON, Newcastle manager, 2004

STEVEN TAYLOR

It's a long time since I've seen a player who you feel would kick his granny to win. It's lovely, though not for the granny.
GLENN ROEDER, Newcastle manager, on the club's young defender, 2006

JOHN TERRY

When I'm driving in to the game I always count the lamp-posts on the way to Stamford Bridge. Also, I always put the tape three times round my shin pads. And there's certain toilets in the dressing room I won't use. In the morning of a match I won't have a cup of tea or anything else to drink when I get out of bed.
TERRY, Chelsea captain, on his superstitions, 2004

John's an extra-terrestrial. I think he's from Mars. He's like ET and needs to phone home.
CLAUDIO RANIERI, Chelsea manager, on his England defender, 2003

He'd be worth a minimum of £50m on the market... If every 10 years we produce a John Terry, then the work of the Academy is done.
JOSE MOURINHO, Chelsea manager, on his captain, 2005

It was important to have John Terry and Frank Lampard on your side... When I say breakfast is at 9 o'clock and Terry and Lampard are in at 9.10 then everyone thinks they can do the same. But they don't so they were very good allies for me.
MOURINHO, 2005

CARLOS TEVEZ

Football's equivalent of a murderer out on bail.
NEIL WARNOCK, former Sheffield United manager, in Made In Sheffield, *2007. Warnock's team were relegated after Tevez's winner at Manchester United for West Ham, who had been fined rather being docked points for irregularities concerning the Argentinian's transfer*

I just couldn't train in a Brazil shirt. It was like asking an Englishman to wear a German shirt.
TEVEZ on the punishment devised by West Ham team-mates after he was sent off v Sheffield United, 2006

BEN THATCHER

What do you have to do to get a red card? Kill someone?
HARRY REDKNAPP, Portsmouth manager, after the Manchester City defender elbowed Pedro Mendes, 2006

FRANCESCO TOTTI

I don't recognise myself from the television images... I want to make it clear that the true Francesco Totti is not the one on that video.
TOTTI after the Italian schemer was caught on camera spitting at a Denmark player, European Championship finals, 2004

Holy Madonna of Divine Love, I ask you to forgive me and never to leave me.
TOTTI in message attached to his Italy shirt and left at a shrine near Rome after his expulsion from the finals, 2004

Every player has some genius, but there's only one Van Gogh and there's nobody like Totti.
GIOVANNI TRAPATTONI, Italy coach, 2004

ANDY VAN DER MEYDE

I'm not saying Van der Meyde is a bad winger. He just can't cross the ball.
JOHAN CRUYFF, Dutch TV summariser and former Netherlands captain, on the national team's winger, 2004

RUUD VAN NISTELROOY

You get the impression that if United won 5–0 and Van Nistelrooy didn't score, he would sulk on the way home. That's why he is where he is.
GARETH SOUTHGATE, Middlesbrough defender, 2004

What a player. Even when he farts he seems to score.
ALESSANDRO DEL PIERO, Juventus striker, on his Manchester United counterpart, 2003

You can't compare me to Van Nistelrooy. He's far better than I am. Maybe I could beat him at arm-wrestling.
JAMES BEATTIE, Southampton striker, 2003

In years to come, we could well be unveiling a statue of him at Old Trafford. That's how good he is.
SIR ALEX FERGUSON, 2003

You see Thierry Henry and it's beautiful. You see me and it's not classic.
VAN NISTELROOY, 2004

Ruud's game is all about finishing. He never scores from outside the 18-yard box and never takes free kicks. It's rare to see him trying his luck from distance. He's strong and uses his body well to shield the ball, but unlike Thierry [Henry] he can't run 100 metres in eight seconds. Thierry is a tough all-round athlete whereas Ruud doesn't take as much part in the collective play.
LOUIS SAHA, Van Nistelrooy's club colleague and France team-mate of Henry's, 2004

Why would any club want to sell Van Nistelrooy?
DICK ADVOCAAT, Netherlands coach, on speculation that United had received an offer from Real Madrid, 2004

When United lose, I feel solely responsible. Things get too much for me. My brain will go mad. I have a storm in my head and the noise is deafening. At times I just feel numb.
VAN NISTELROOY, 2004

When he stops playing football, he can go into acting.
LAUREN, Arsenal defender, on Van Nistelrooy's alleged part in the sending-off of Patrick Vieira, 2003

JUAN SEBASTIAN VERON

Listen, you've all been going on about fucking Veron. He's a fucking great player. You are fucking idiots.
SIR ALEX FERGUSON to reporters who questioned the impact of Manchester United's £28m Argentinian, 2002

Criticism doesn't bother me. I don't read newspapers or watch sports programmes on TV. Lately I've been busy watching *Teletubbies*.
VERON, 2002

NEMANJA VIDIC

Q: What's the strangest aspect of English culture you've noticed?
A: Driving on the left and tea with milk.
VIDIC, Manchester United and Serbia defender, 2007

PATRICK VIEIRA

Vieira was bragging about all the things he'd done in Senegal. I said to him: 'If you're so fucking worried about Senegal, why didn't you play for them?'
ROY KEANE looks back to a tunnel fracas before an Arsenal v Manchester United game, 2006

What I did was unforgivable, mainly because I'm a role model. My brother is a teacher. If one of his pupils spits at another, he can't tell him not to do it. The kids will just turn round and say: 'Your brother does exactly the same.' But the thing that pisses me off is the £45,000 fine. Coming from where I do, I know the value of money. To my family that is a phenomenal sum.

VIEIRA after being fined for spitting in retaliation to West Ham's Neil Ruddock, 1999

Pat's a great friend. When Everton were playing Arsenal last season, he called my wife and told her to get some ice packs ready because I would come back seriously bruised.

OLIVIER DACOURT, Leeds and ex-Everton midfielder, 2000

There are players who have no interest in playing the game properly. They are just trying to upset Patrick. There are certain managers who encourage this.

ARSENE WENGER, Vieira's manager at Arsenal, after he was sent off for the second time in three days, 2000

I'm amazed how big Patrick's elbows are. They can reach players 10 yards away. Let's just give him a 15-game ban and get it over and done with.

WENGER, 2002

Patrick would love to have come here last year, but they wouldn't let him. Players always want to play for a bigger club.

SIR ALEX FERGUSON, Manchester United manager, 2002

What has Patrick done? He has been suspended for two games and fined £20,000 for not walking off the pitch quickly enough. What speed do you have to walk at when you've been sent off? In which rule is that written?

WENGER on Vieira's punishment from the FA for flicking a kick at Manchester United's Ruud Van Nistelrooy, 2003

Every Sunday morning I feel like a true Englishman. I take the full English breakfast – and I eat everything – and I read all the papers.

VIERA before playing for France v England, 2004

It was eight weeks of torture. I felt like the fire brigade on Guy Fawkes night.

DAVID DEIN, Arsenal vice-chairman, on the protracted saga of Real Madrid's interest in Vieira, 2004

THEO WALCOTT

I didn't watch the England–Argentina match in 1998. I can't remember why not. It may have been past my bedtime.
WALCOTT, 17-year-old Arsenal striker, on being named in England's World Cup squad, 2006

PAULO WANCHOPE

Paulo was way out of order, but I deny I ever called him a 'poof'. I'd never use that kind of language, even if it were justified.
JIM SMITH, Derby manager, on a heated row with the Costa Rican striker after he was substituted, 1997

SANDER WESTERVELD

The goalkeeping strip is dreadful. It is a blue shirt with green shorts and green socks. I am very cocky and vain. A keeper needs charisma and that's impossible wearing green pants. I want blue pants and white socks.
SANDER WESTERVELD, Dutch keeper, on joining Liverpool, 1999

JONATHAN WOODGATE

I got a lot of deserved stick but there were some nasty things said about me by people who had never met me and didn't know me. I resented that because I'm not like they said... I think I'm a half-decent lad. I'm not an arrogant prick like some footballers.
WOODGATE after joining Newcastle, 2004

I go to clubs. I'm a young lad, aren't I? I'm not going to live like a monk, as David O'Leary says. It's just natural but you have to know when to stop.
WOODGATE shortly before the assault of student Sarfraz Najeib which led to his conviction for affray, 1999

Q: Which programme would you bother to record if you were going out?
A: I don't watch much TV. Probably *Crimewatch*.
WOODGATE in a questionnaire in the Leeds programme shortly before the incidents that led to his trial, 1999

Q: Who would you definitely not invite on a night out?
A: I know the first person I would invite, and that's Woody.
HARRY KEWELL, Leeds team-mate, in the club magazine shortly before Woodgate's arrest, 1999

He has a heart of gold but is as daft as a brush.

DAVID O'LEARY, Leeds manager, after the defender was charged, 2001

Jonathan is full of remorse for the shame he has brought on the club, his family and himself. I believe he will end up being a better person.
PETER RIDSDALE, Leeds chairman, after he was found guilty, 2002

We were going to build a team around him… To this day he doesn't look right in black and white.
PAUL ROBINSON, Leeds goalkeeper, after Woodgate was sold to Newcastle, 2003

He's a beautiful boy, you know.
SIR BOBBY ROBSON, Newcastle manager, 2004

I wish I was brainier than I am. I'm not saying I'm thick but I wish I'd learned more at school, instead of messing about.
WOODGATE, 2004

ALAN WRIGHT

I got the ball and the crowd started singing: 'One Ronnie Corbett, there's only one Ronnie Corbett!'
ALAN WRIGHT, diminutive Aston Villa defender, 2000

SHAUN WRIGHT-PHILLIPS

I'll have to turbo-charge my Zimmer frame.
DAVID EYRES, 41-year-old Oldham midfielder, on the prospect of facing Wright-Phillips in an FA Cup tie v Manchester City, 2005

ABEL XAVIER

When I went blond the manager [Walter Smith] wrote to me and said: 'Hey man, what have you done?'
ABEL XAVIER, Everton defender, with Portugal at the European Championship finals, 2000

SERGEN YALCIN

The things I do best in life? Playing football, sex, swimming, driving and betting on horses. Actually I'm fed up with sex. Looking at betting bulletins and playing football are more important to me.
YALCIN, Besiktas and Turkey striker, 2003

DWIGHT YORKE

If that lad makes a First Division footballer, my name is Mao Tse Tung.
TOMMY DOCHERTY, former manager, on the then Aston Villa striker while working as a radio pundit, 1991

I think he's an idiot…It's a shame I'm having his kid really.
JORDAN, model, accusing Yorke of treating her 'like dirt' during her pregnancy with their child, 2002

Sir Alex is 60 and I'm sure that when he was a player they used to settle down to family life much earlier, but I've never felt it was the right thing for me to do. When I left I was exactly the same person he bought – a single man who likes to enjoy life. He knew what he was buying into.
YORKE, Blackburn and former Manchester United striker, 2003

two

PLAYERS: PAST

TONY ADAMS

My next guest has fulfilled every schoolboy's dream. He's won the Double, he's captained England and he's driven a car into a wall at very high speed. Ladies and gentlemen, Tony Adams!
SANJEEV BHASKAR, comic actor, on the spoof TV chat show The Kumars at No. 42, *2003*

For Tony to admit he is an alcoholic took an awful lot of bottle.
IAN WRIGHT, Arsenal and England team-mate, 1996

When he was sent to prison [for drink-driving], he whispered to me: 'I have done wrong and I'm going to take my punishment. I don't want to appeal.' That's Tony. If you're in a battle on the pitch, he's the first bloke you'd want on your side.
DAVID O'LEARY, former Arsenal colleague, 1995

I was never too aware of his problems with booze, but he was still a hell of a player when he had them.
ALAN SHEARER, Newcastle opponent and England colleague, 1998

I haven't pissed the bed for two and a half years.
ADAMS on recovering from alcoholism, 1999

[Adams] is getting ready for a new career as a traffic policeman. He was always ace at putting his hands up, indicating offside, even before the other team had kicked off. Now he is perfecting his pointing-hand routine, indicating where his team-mates should be for his next pass, before he belts it into the stand.
HUNTER DAVIES, Tottenham fan, in his New Statesman *column, 1999*

Manager of Arsenal? Give us a break. It's very demanding being a manager. I need a life first. I fancy a bit of skiing and painting.
ADAMS, 1999

An actor friend has got a big part in *Henry V*, and he said: 'Tone, I've got a block about learning all these lines.' I told him: 'Do it the way I work. Start with the first one and take it from there. Eventually you'll get to the end, just like I get to the end of the season.'
ADAMS with a new twist on taking each game as it comes, 2000

It would be nice not having to spend Christmas Day in a hotel.

ADAMS contemplating retirement, 2002

The greatest Arsenal man of all time. As a player, he goes beyond Liam Brady, Alex James, Joe Mercer or Frank McLintock. I don't think anyone has represented the club from the age of 17 to 35 and sustained all the injuries he's had, while half the time fighting for his own soul. Only those close to him knew how bad it was.

BOB WILSON, goalkeeper with Arsenal's 1971 Double-winning side and club goalkeeping coach, after Adams led them to League and FA Cup success, 2002

SAM ALLARDYCE

Sam was a ball-playing defender. If he wasn't with the ball, he was playing with your balls.

DAVE BASSETT, TV pundit and former manager, 2006

OSSIE ARDILES

I will never return to play in England, even if they gave me all the money in the world.

OSSIE ARDILES, Argentinian former Tottenham midfielder, during the Falklands conflict, June 1982

I can't wait to get back. Every night I go to bed dreaming of Wembley.

ARDILES, December 1982

JEFF ASTLE

Jeff had this window- and office-cleaning business. His slogan was: 'We never miss a corner.'

FRANK SKINNER, comedian and West Bromwich Albion fan, after the death of Astle, who was renowned for his heading, 2003

ROBERTO BAGGIO

The Divine Pony Tail
SLOGAN on Italian fans' banner, World Cup finals, 1994

ALAN BALL

As I was running towards the German goal, Alan Ball was shouting: 'Hursty, Hursty, give me the ball!' I said to myself: 'Sod you, Bally. I'm on a hat-trick.'
SIR GEOFF HURST recalling England's 1966 triumph, 1999

The only thing that stops me being a world-class player is that I don't score enough goals.
BALL, 1972

My ambition is to meet Prince Charles. I call him 'King'.

BALL, 1979

Jim Baxter drove him mad calling him Jimmy Clitheroe but Bally couldn't get near enough to him to do anything about it.
BILLY BREMNER, former Scotland captain, recalling his country's 1967 defeat of world champions England, 1992. Clitheroe was a high-voiced comic actor

I didn't need telling when I hadn't played as well as I'd have liked, but my dad told me all the same. I also didn't need him to tell me when I'd played well. And he never did.
BALL on the influence of his late father, Alan Ball Snr, 2005

GORDON BANKS

At that moment I hated Gordon Banks more than any man in soccer. But when I cooled down I had to applaud him with my heart for the greatest save I had ever seen.
PELE after Banks saved his header, Brazil v England, World Cup finals, 1970

JOHN BARNES

Coming from Jamaica, I am blessed with rhythm.
BARNES in The Autobiography, *1999*

Having a priest cane him every weekend... I thought: 'That'll be good for him.'
COLONEL KEN BARNES on his son's upbringing, 1988

Revenge does not feature in my psyche. The black community loves how Ian Wright reacts, the way he flings out a fist or mouths off... I'm different.
BARNES in his autobiography, 1999

I've never seen a better eater: Indian, Chinese, Mexican. You serve it and 'Digger' will see it off.
PETER BEARDSLEY, Liverpool and England colleague, 1988

There's no one I've ever met through football who I would class as a friend, but Jamie [Redknapp] comes closest.
BARNES in his autobiography, 1999

WARREN BARTON

The best-dressed footballer I've ever seen. Even in training – we're all in tracksuits and he arrives in shirt, trousers and shoes. And his hair's lovely. We call him The Dog, as in the dog's bollocks.
ROBERT LEE, Newcastle midfielder, on his defensive colleague, 1996

DAVID BATTY

Batty would probably get himself booked playing Handel's Largo.
DAVID LACEY reporting in the Guardian *on a Charity Shield match between Leeds and Liverpool in which Batty was cautioned, 1992*

Batty and Le Saux there, arguing over who has the sillier name.
RORY BREMNER as Des Lynam on his Channel 4 show, after the two Blackburn players traded punches in Moscow, 1995

JIM BAXTER

He was a magician on the park. He could have put a size-five football in an egg cup.
SIR ALEX FERGUSON on the late Baxter, 2006

Slim Jim had everything required of a great Scottish footballer. Outrageously skilled, totally irresponsible, supremely arrogant and thick as mince.
ALASTAIR MACSPORRAN, columnist, in the fanzine The Absolute Game, *1990*

PETER BEARDSLEY

The bottom line is that Beardsley comes from God.
ANDY ROXBURGH, Scotland manager, after Beardsley's winner for England, 1988

He's the only player who, when he's on TV, Daleks hide behind the sofa.
NICK HANCOCK, compere, on TV's They Think It's All Over, *1995*

Christ, he looks like a thin Ann Widdecombe.
NICKY CLARKE, hairstylist, 2001

FRANZ BECKENBAUER

Tell the Kraut to get his ass up front. We don't pay a million for a guy to hang around on defense.
NEW YORK COSMOS executive on the former West Germany captain's deep-lying role, 1977

COLIN BELL

He didn't seem to grasp his own freakish strength. I said to him: 'You're a great header of the ball, you have a terrific shot, and you're the best, most powerful runner in the business. Every time you walk off the pitch unable to say you were streets ahead of the other 21 players, you have failed.'
MALCOLM ALLISON, Bell's coach at Manchester City, 1968

DENNIS BERGKAMP

Intelligence and class. There's always a brain behind what he does, and his technique allows him to do what he sees and decides to do.
ARSENE WENGER, Arsenal manager, summing up the Dutch striker on his retirement, 2006

I never believed in star status. To me that means Rolex watches, gold chains and flashy cars. I hate all those.
BERGKAMP on joining Arsenal, 1995

If he thinks he's going to set the world alight he can forget it. When the fog, ice and cold arrive, he won't want to know.
ALAN SUGAR, Tottenham chairman, after Bergkamp's £7.25m move to Arsenal, 1995

Dennis is such a nice man, such a tremendous gentleman with such a lovely family. It's going to be very hard for me to kick him.
TONY ADAMS before England v Netherlands, European Championship finals, 1996

I've heard it said that he is aloof, but he has a British sense of humour and gives as good as he gets. He is also a prankster and can't keep his hands off other players' laces and clothes.
STEVE BOULD, Arsenal colleague, 1997

If he were in *Star Trek*, he'd be the best player in whatever solar system he was in.
IAN WRIGHT, Arsenal team-mate, 1997

If Ryan Giggs is worth £20m, Dennis Bergkamp is worth £100m.
MARCO VAN BASTEN, Holland coach, 2005

EYAL BERKOVIC

Eyal is a professional and clearly wants to earn as much money as possible. But he is Jewish and I am Scottish so it will be difficult for us to reach a financial agreement.
GRAEME SOUNESS, Blackburn manager, on the possibility of the Israeli's loan from Celtic becoming a permanent transfer, 2001

GEORGE BEST

When I die, they won't remember who I dated, the fights and the car crashes because they're not important. They will remember the football.
BEST shortly before his death, 2005

Unquestionably the greatest player of all time.
SIR ALEX FERGUSON, 2002

There are times when you want to wring his neck. He hangs on to the ball when other players have found better positions. Then out of the blue he does something which wins the match. Then you know you're in the presence of someone special.
PAT CRERAND, Manchester United team-mate, 1970

Best makes a greater appeal to the senses than the other two [Stanley Matthews and Tom Finney]. His movements are quicker, lighter, more balletic... And with it all, there is his utter disregard for physical danger... He has ice in his veins, warmth in his heart, and timing and balance in his feet.
DANNY BLANCHFLOWER, former Northern Ireland captain, in David Meek's book
Anatomy of a Football Star: George Best, *1970*

PARKINSON: What was the nearest to kick-off that you made love?
BEST: Er... I think it was half-time actually.
EXCHANGE on Michael Parkinson's BBC TV chat show, 1980s

I don't drink every day but when I do it's usually for four or five days on the trot. I've got a drink problem.
GEORGE BEST, 1979

I might go to Alcoholics Anonymous but I think it would be difficult for me to be anonymous.
BEST, 1980

Well, he has a drink problem, hasn't he?

DON MEGSON, Bournemouth manager, on why he left Best out of his team, 1983

Well, I suppose that's the knighthood fucked.
BEST at Southwark Crown Court, waiting to be sentenced after being found guilty of assaulting a policeman, 1984

We had our problems with the wee feller, but I prefer to remember his genius.
SIR MATT BUSBY, 1988

If you'd given me a choice between beating four defenders and smashing in a goal from 30 yards or going to bed with Miss World, it would have been difficult. Luckily, I had both. It's just that you do one of those things in front of 50,000 people.
BEST, 1991

One day they might even say I was another Ryan Giggs.
BEST, 1992

I always had a reputation for going missing – Miss England, Miss United Kingdom, Miss World...
BEST, 1992

I spent a lot of my money on booze, birds and fast cars. The rest I squandered.

BEST, 1992

People say he wasted his career. Nonsense. He was hunted down by defenders for 11 seasons starting at 17. He paid his dues all right.
DAVID MEEK, journalist who covered Manchester United for four decades, 1995

Jesus, I was quick! I'd forgotten I was that fast.
BEST watching old footage of himself in action, 1996

It's a pleasure for me to be standing up here. It's a pleasure to be standing up.
BEST, accepting the Footballer of the Century award, 1999

If I was reincarnated I'd come back as George Best, because he was a genius and had all them women and drank all that wine.
BARRY FRY, Peterborough manager and teenaged Old Trafford colleague, 1999

He was Roy of the Rovers on the field, but sadly Roy of the Ravers off it.
DESCRIPTION of Best on International Hall of Fame website, 2000

He has three problems: he is famous, he is rich and he is Irish. Not a good combination.
PETER STRINGFELLOW, nightclub owner, 2000

It was typical of me to be finishing a long and distinguished drinking career just as the government is planning to open pubs 24 hours a day.
BEST trying the give up alcohol, 2001

In her youth the Queen was quite a stunner. Who knows what might have happened if I'd met her in Tramp in my heyday.
BEST during the Queen's Golden Jubilee celebrations, 2002

I celebrated my 56th birthday with a banana and honey milkshake. A new liver would have been a nice present.
BEST, 2002

He's a totally different person now. The lovely side was always there, which is why I married him. It's just that I've got it all the time now.
ALEX BEST, Best's wife, before his liver-transplant operation, 2002

On the field, fantastic. Off it, nightmare, sometimes. I wanted to strangle him but he always said: 'Boss, I'll make it up to you. I'll win the game for you tonight.' And he always did.
MILAN MANDARIC, Portsmouth chairman, on his time as owner of Best's US club San Jose Earthquakes, 2003

George once turned down trifle because it had sherry in it. I trusted he had sent his demons packing, but whenever the going is good George grows restless.
MICHAEL PARKINSON, writer, broadcaster and friend of Best's, 2003

He seems to be on a mission to self-destruct and it's getting worse.
ALEX BEST after he resumed drinking following the liver transplant, 2003

George shouldn't be criticised for going back on the booze. Alcoholism is a disease and he should have our sympathy.
BRIAN CLOUGH, who also had a liver transplant, 2003

I'm furious that anyone served him. Why couldn't they simply have said: 'You're a valued customer but please don't ask us for a drink.' It's like giving a loaded gun to someone who's suicidal.
PHIL HUGHES, Best's agent, when he resumed drinking, 2003

Our talking point this morning is George Best, his liver transplant and the booze culture in football. Don't forget – the best caller wins a crate of John Smith's bitter.
ALAN BRAZIL, Talk Radio chat-show host and former Manchester United striker, 2002

They said Bestie was roaring drunk on the Parkinson show, but Oliver Reed phoned the BBC to say: 'He looks all right to me.'
FRANK WORTHINGTON, after-dinner speaker and former England striker, 2003

In 1969 I gave up alcohol and women. It was the worst 20 minutes of my life.
BEST, 2003

So this movie you star in, *The Life Story of George Best*. Tell us what it's about.
GEORGE GAVIN, Sky sport presenter, to Best, 2003

I love the simple life and being on my own. The only thing I want out of our marriage is our dogs.

BEST on splitting with Alex, 2003

Now I truly believe he wanted to be caught with another woman so he had the excuse to leave me and continue his love affair with the bottle. Alcohol is the only thing he's ever really loved.
ALEX BEST on estrangement from George, 2003

I know George has told her she's the most beautiful girl he has ever met. But it's the same old George rubbish when he wants to woo you. He's very, very good at it.
ALEX BEST on George's relationship with divorcee Gina Devivo, 2003

The only thing I have in common with George Best is that we come from the same place, played for the same club and were discovered by the same man.
NORMAN WHITESIDE, former United and Northern Ireland forward, 2003

One of the few fellas I know that does *The Times* crossword.
PAT CRERAND, former United team-mate, 2004

People seem to believe I have a death wish. Sometimes I think they sit around hoping that I'll die. I bet the obituary is already written.
BEST, 2003

People always say I shouldn't be burning the candle at both ends. Maybe because they haven't got a big enough candle.
BEST, 2003

George always got annoyed at celebrities who refused to talk to people in the street, or the pub. They bloody well put us here, he'd say; give something back. So he'd take a drink off them.
ALEX BEST, by now his ex-wife, 2005

Once that [being the best at football] passed, he had to be the best at drinking and at keeping bars open. Preferably the dirtiest bars: if you had a line of pubs, wine bars, gastropubs in any street, you knew you'd find George in the filthiest old man's pub with the sticky carpet.
ALEX BEST, 2005

Years later I asked him to stand in front of me so I could see his face. He wondered why and I told him: 'Because for years all I saw was your arse disappearing down the touchline.'
GRAHAM WILLIAMS, the West Bromwich Albion full-back who faced the 17-year-old debutant Best, 2005

I used to talk to him in New York when we were both playing in America. I told him, 'You're not a European. You're a Latin. A Brazilian.'
PELE on Best's death, 2005

It's very sad that he has gone. The good thing is that he lived 100 years in his 59 years.
BARRY McGUIGAN, former world champion boxer and fellow Northern Irishman, 2005

Shevchenko £50m. Ronaldinho £80m. George Best priceless.

MESSAGE on a card attached to a floral tribute, 2005

He carried us for so long. It was an honour to carry him.
DEREK DOUGAN, Northern Ireland team-mate and a pall-bearer at Best's funeral, 2005

Doctors are supposed never to get too close to their patients. It's not easy when that patient is George Best.
PROFESSOR ROGER WILLIAMS, 2005

GARRY BIRTLES

People used to say that if I'd shot John Lennon, he'd still be alive today.
BIRTLES, former England striker, on his long goalless run at Manchester United, 2004

DANNY BLANCHFLOWER

In a poor side Danny is an expensive luxury. That's why I dropped him when we had a poor team. But in a good side as Spurs are now he is a wonderful asset through his unorthodox approach and marvellous ball skill.
BILL NICHOLSON, Tottenham's Double-winning manager, on his captain in Julian Holland's book Spurs – The Double, *1961*

MARK BOSNICH

That's why Fergie didn't like me. He wanted all communists in his team.
BOSNICH, former United goalkeeper under Sir Alex Ferguson and 'big fan of Margaret Thatcher', 2005

STAN BOWLES

If Stan could pass a betting shop the way he can pass a ball he'd have no worries.
ERNIE TAGG, Crewe manager, who launched the compulsive gambler on a career which earned him England caps, 1974

I was invited to appear on the Kilroy show. The subject was gambling addicts, though I'm not sure what it had to do with me. I declined and spent the day at Sandown Races.
BOWLES, 2003

BILLY BREMNER

I'm no angel, but I've never kicked anyone deliberately.
BREMNER, Leeds captain, 1967

10st of Barbed Wire
HEADLINE on Sunday Times profile, 1970

TREVOR BROOKING

Floats like a butterfly and stings like one, too.
BRIAN CLOUGH, Nottingham Forest manager, before Brooking headed West Ham's winner in the FA Cup final v Arsenal, 1980

STEVE BULL

People say his first touch isn't good, but he usually scores with his second.
GRAHAM TURNER, Wolves manager, 1988

He's so single-minded in front of goal. I've known some greedy players – I remember wrestling for the ball with Gavin Peacock, who's in Christians In Sport, for heaven's sake, when Newcastle had a penalty and I was on a hat-trick – but Bully takes the biscuit.
DAVID KELLY, Wolves striker, 1994

CRAIG BURLEY

Q: Most embarrassing moment?
A: Trying to follow Craig Burley's instructions on the park when he didn't have his teeth in, and getting it hopelessly wrong.
MALKY MACKAY, Norwich defender, on his former Celtic colleague, 2001

TERRY BUTCHER

I haven't had the chance to kick a Celtic player for many years.
TERRY BUTCHER, former Rangers captain, on playing in the Old Firm Veterans' Challenge, 2001

ERIC CANTONA

1966 was a great year for English football. Eric was born
NIKE advertising slogan, 1994

1995 was a great year for English football. Eric was banned.
SLOGAN on T-shirts sold at Manchester City, Leeds, Liverpool, etc., after Cantona was suspended for nine months after launching a 'kung-fu' kick on an abusive fan, 1995

He gave interviews on art, philosophy and politics. A natural room-mate for David Batty, I thought immediately.
HOWARD WILKINSON, Leeds manager, in Managing to Succeed: My Life in Football Management, *with David Walker, 1992*

Eric likes to do what he likes, when he likes, because he likes it – and then fuck off. We'd all want a bit of that.
WILKINSON after offloading the Frenchman to Manchester United, 1993

Rimbaud wanted to write about everything, to seek flashes of inspiration, to enjoy different ideas and live with different philosophies. He had the spontaneity of a child, and I believe in that. He was a pioneer, but the torch he lit was picked up by others, like Jim Morrison. I believe that, even in football, I should live as instinctively as that.
CANTONA early in his time at Manchester United, 1993

Cantona will let you down at the highest level. He let Leeds down against Rangers, twice, and in the big games, against Inter Milan or whoever, he will go missing. He's a cry baby when the going gets tough.
GEORGE GRAHAM, Arsenal manager, 1994

Just as I can bring happiness to people with my spontaneity, my instinctiveness, so there are always going to be dark shadows, black stains.
CANTONA, 1994

When Eric feels an injustice, he has to prove to the whole world that he's been wronged. He can't control his temper. That's just part of his game.
ALEX FERGUSON after Cantona was sent off in a friendly v Rangers, 1994

I just yelled: 'Off you go, Cantona – it's an early shower for you.'
MATTHEW SIMMONS, Crystal Palace fan, explaining what he had said to provoke Cantona's 'kung-fu' assault, 1995

Pressure is no excuse. I would take any amount of personal abuse for £10,000 a week [Cantona's reputed salary].
SIR STANLEY MATTHEWS after the Selhurst Park incident, 1995

I'd have cut his balls off.

BRIAN CLOUGH after Cantona's fracas at Crystal Palace, 1995

My initial feeling was to let him go. I couldn't imagine his playing for the club again... My wife Cath said: 'You can't let him off. Never let it be said that you put winning the championship above doing the right thing.'
ALEX FERGUSON, in his diary A Year in the Life, 1995

'Well played, my son. That's something I've wanted to do for years.'
JOHN FASHANU, former England striker, recalling his reaction to Cantona's 'kung-fu' leap, 2003

I'd have wanted him hung, drawn and quartered, William Wallace business, tear out his insides.
IAN WRIGHT, former England striker, on the Palace fan attacked by Cantona, in Black Flash: A Century of Black Footballers, *BBC TV documentary, 2003*

I told him: 'Eric, you can't go to court like that' [wearing a shirt unbuttoned to his chest]. He says: 'I am Cantona. I can go as I want.' So he got into the dock and he got 14 days in prison. I thought: 'Oh my God, it must be the shirt.'
PAUL INCE, former United team-mate, recalling the 1995 incident, 2004

I'd give all the champagne I've ever drunk to have played alongside him in a big European match at Old Trafford.
GEORGE BEST, 1997

Cantona is a great player, but only in the context of English football.
ROBERT LOUIS-DREYFUS, Marseilles president, 1997

For my next film role I would love to play a psychopath or an unpleasant person.

CANTONA, 2000

I might have said that, but on the whole I talk a lot of rubbish.
CANTONA on reports that he was about to return to football as a coach, 2003

I do not support France. I am French but I'm not interested in France.
CANTONA, 2004

I should have been born English. When I hear 'God Save the Queen' it can make me cry, much more than when I hear 'La Marseillaise'.
CANTONA, 2005

TONY CASCARINO

When I arrived at Marseilles, [president] Bernard Tapie said to me: 'I didn't like Lee Chapman or Mark Hateley. I like players like Chris Waddle.' I thought: 'Oh shit, what am I doing here?'
CASCARINO, former Republic of Ireland striker, on his spell in France, 2001

LEE CHAPMAN

Footballers are supposed to look like Billy the Fish out of *Viz*, aren't they? Well, I've never looked like that. I've never even had a mullet.
CHAPMAN, former Leeds and Arsenal striker, 2000

JOHN CHARLES

John always looked like a Greek god. He could have been a boxer, a rugby player. He could have been anything.
TERRY MEDWIN, former Wales team-mate, after Charles's death, 2004

He'd have been on £50,000 a week now. No one would have been earning more.
HAROLD WILLIAMS, former Leeds team-mate, 2001

John was never interested in money. He thought you lived on fresh air.
GLENDA CHARLES, his second wife, 2002

If you had 22 players of John's character on the pitch, you wouldn't need a referee, only a timekeeper.
CLIVE THOMAS, former international referee and fellow Welshman, after Charles's death, 2004

BOBBY CHARLTON

Trumpets sound
Doves take flight
Lisa Stansfield sings
And Bobby Charlton's haircut forms the five Olympic rings
HOVIS PRESLEY, Bolton poet, on Manchester's bid to stage the Olympics, from the anthology Poetic Off Licence, 2005

The fact that they accused Bobby Charlton of sheltering me while I 'stole' a bracelet proves I'm innocent. Bobby has never done a dishonest thing in his life.
BOBBY MOORE, England captain and colleague, after the 'jewel theft' incident in Bogota, 1970

Bobby deserves to keep the record. He was a much better player than me and scored far better goals.
GARY LINEKER on retiring from international football one goal short of Charlton's England record, 1992

The Prince of Wales's visit is big news here but Mr Charlton's was even bigger.
SPOKESMAN for the British Embassy in Morocco, 1995

I sent my son to one of his schools of excellence and he came back bald.
GEORGE BEST, former Manchester United team-mate, on TV's Mrs Merton Show, 1996

We just don't get on. Our kid was a much better player than me but I'm a much better bloke.
JACK CHARLTON, 1998

Robert 'Bobby' Charlton was forward for the British team at the '66 and '67 World Cups.
PELE'S website, 2002

I just couldn't get on with Bobby Charlton. When I first went to Old Trafford, I thought he was a god. Later, I couldn't stand the sight of him.
GEORGE BEST, 2003

STEVE CLARIDGE

I've got a morbid obsession with football. Have done for 20 years.
CLARIDGE, 39-year-old striker, before playing his 1,000th professional match, for Bournemouth, 2006

Once I went training with £4,500 in my pocket and then ran out of petrol on the way home because I'd spent it all betting on horses. I had to hitch a lift.
CLARIDGE admitting to being serial gambler, 1996

BRIAN CLOUGH

I got one or two goals a season, give or take the odd 30.
CLOUGH aged 69 on TV documentary Local Heroes, 2004

The only thing I enjoyed during my six years at Middlesbrough was scoring goals. From Saturday to Saturday I was very unhappy. My ability was never utilised, by me or the management. Only goals kept me sane. That was my only pleasure.
CLOUGH, 1973

NIGEL CLOUGH

He's not joining Pisa for the simple and most important reason that his mother decided that days ago.
BRIAN CLOUGH after speculation that his son was Italy-bound, 1988

GEORGE COHEN

We used to say of George Cohen: 'He's hit more photographers than Frank Sinatra.' Usually he would hit his cross into the crowd, or into the photographers.
BOBBY ROBSON, former Fulham team-mate, in his book Time On the Grass, *1982*

EDDIE COLMAN

When he waggled his hips he made the stanchions in the grandstand sway.
HARRY GREGG, Manchester United goalkeeper, on the colleague nicknamed 'Snakehips' who perished in the Munich disaster, 1958

STAN COLLYMORE

He had everything Thierry Henry has got and more.
JOHN GREGORY, Collymore's former manager at Aston Villa, 2004

I'm no angel but I think I'm more misunderstood than anything else. I think I'm a pretty interesting bloke.
COLLYMORE, then with Liverpool, 1997

I regard Aston Villa as my club. If some Villa fans are worried that I might be trouble, then I think they've got it wrong. The Liverpool experience has matured me.
COLLYMORE on starting a controversial spell with Villa, 1997

I've ridiculed him, I've tried to love him and I've told him what a great player he is. I've said to him: 'I wish I was you, Stan. I wish I was on the money you're earning. I wish I had your lifestyle. And most of all, I wish I had your talent because with it, I'd have been the first name in the England team.'
GREGORY as Collymore suffered clinical depression, 1999

Some days he could climb Everest, others he can't even climb out of bed.
GREGORY on his striker's continuing illness, 1999

I find it difficult to understand how someone in Stan's position, with the talent and money he has, is stressed. I wonder how a 29-year-old at Rochdale, in the last three months of his contract, with a wife and three kids, copes with stress.
GREGORY, 1999

You can't be sure he will ever be taken on by a club anywhere. Unless it's some Outer Mongolian outfit that has been locked away from news, television and society for 10 years.
EDITORIAL in Nottingham Post after Collymore declined to rejoin Forest, 1999

At school Stan would have been the boy who ate worms. Weird but nice.
NEIL RUDDOCK, former Liverpool colleague, 2000

At the end of the day I haven't killed anybody. A million players have done it [letting off a fire-extinguisher in a hotel lobby] and a million more will do it in the future.
COLLYMORE on hitting the headlines following a prank on a Spanish break with his new club, Leicester, 2000

When I retire I want to work in the cinema and television. I want to be the first black James Bond.
COLLYMORE, 2001. He soon retired and became a match summariser on radio

It was very exciting to walk into a club and there was Chris Evans and Emma Bunton.
COLLYMORE recalling how he went clubbing in London while a Liverpool player, 2004

There really is no upside to being caught dogging.

COLLYMORE *on being exposed as a 'dogger' who watched others having sex in cars at* Cannock Chase, Staffordshire, 2004

I went looking for extreme forms of gratification to replicate the buzz I'd had as a footballer.
COLLYMORE *on why he went dogging, 2006*

CHARLIE COOKE

When he sold you a dummy you had to pay to get back in the ground.
JIM BAXTER, Scotland team-mate, on the Chelsea winger, 1976

JIM CRAIG

When Billy McNeill [Celtic's captain in 1967] was recovering from a heart operation, I called to see how he was and his eight-year-old grandson James picked up the phone. He asked who I was and when I told him he snapped back: 'You're the guy that gave away the penalty in Lisbon.'
CRAIG, a member of Celtic's European Cup-winning side of '67, 2003

KENNY DALGLISH

Is he better in midfield or up front? Och, just let him on the park.
JOCK STEIN, Dalglish's former Celtic manager, 1977

He would make a perfect trades-union official.
GRAEME SOUNESS, former Liverpool colleague, in No Half Measures, *1985*

The way he sticks out his arms and legs represents plain obstruction. He's supposed to be one of the best screeners of the ball in the game. I say that's rubbish – too many refs can't see that he's breaking the law.
CLIVE 'THE BOOK' THOMAS, Football League referee, 1984

When he scored...he had a better smile than Clark Gable. Beautiful teeth, arms wide, that's how he celebrated. He wasn't that big but he had a huge arse. It came down below his knees, and that's where he got his strength from.
BRIAN CLOUGH, former managerial adversary, 1995

The best player this club has signed this century.

JOHN SMITH, Liverpool chairman, 1986

Few great players make the transition into management. The reason is that great players are normally like soloists in an orchestra. They perform alone and tend to look down on those of lesser ability. That was never Kenny. He was like a conductor who brought others into play. He understood that not everyone was blessed with the greatest skill. He had patience, both as a player and a manager.
BOB PAISLEY, the manager who bought Dalglish for Liverpool, 1991

DIXIE DEAN

He belongs in the company of the supremely great, like Shakespeare, Rembrandt and Beethoven.
BILL SHANKLY honouring the legendary Everton centre-forward at a dinner hours before Dean died at the Mersey derby, 1980

KAZIMIERZ DEYNA

Deyna's on a different wavelength. He is tuned into Radio Four and the rest of the Manchester City side are on Radio Luxembourg.
ALAN DURBAN, Stoke City manager, on the Poland midfielder, 1979

JULIAN DICKS

Rumour has it that when Dicks moved to Liverpool he picked up the No. 23 shirt because it said Fowler on it.
KEVIN BALDWIN, author, This Supporting Life: How To Be a Real Fan, *1995*

ALFREDO DI STEFANO

One of the greatest, if not the greatest footballer I had ever seen. At that time
[the 1950s] we had forwards and defenders doing separate jobs, but he did
everything.
*MATT BUSBY, Manchester United manager, on the Real Madrid centre-forward, in Motson
and Rowlinson,* The European Cup 1955–80, *1980*

TOMMY DOCHERTY

I once told Tommy that if we had five Bill Shanklys and five Tommy
Dochertys, plus a goalkeeper, we'd beat the world. Tommy said: 'If there were
five Bill Shanklys and five Tommy Dochertys, we wouldn't need a goalkeeper.'
BILL SHANKLY reminisces about his successor in the Preston team, quoted in John Keith's
Shanks For the Memory, *1998*

ROBBIE EARLE

The Jamaica boys have always said that my best foot is my head and Nike
should sponsor my haircuts as well as my boots.
*EARLE, Wimbledon and Jamaica midfielder, recalls his headed goal at the World Cup finals,
in* One Love, *with Daniel Davies, 1998*

One afternoon in hospital I was told I had picked up an infection again.
By this time I had lost four stone. My breathing was irregular, I was in agony.
If somebody had told me that death was the best choice, I'd have accepted it –
anything to take away the pain.
EARLE on the injury that ended his career, 2000

DUNCAN EDWARDS

*Duncan was the only player that
made me feel inferior.*
SIR BOBBY CHARLTON, former Manchester United team-mate, 2006

The Kohinoor diamond among our crown jewels. Even when he'd won his first England cap, and was still eligible for our youth team, he used to love turning out at a lower level. He remained an unspoiled boy to the end, his head the same size it had been from the start.
JIMMY MURPHY, Matt Busby's No. 2 at Manchester United, after Edwards died from injuries sustained in the Munich disaster, 1958

People still haven't forgotten. Strangers come up and tell me: 'He were a good 'un.'
ANNE EDWARDS, mother of Duncan, 35 years after his death, 1993

STEFAN EFFENBERG

He looked like a picture of an angel blowing a trumpet.
FRANZ BECKENBAUER, Bayern Munich president, on the ex-Bayern midfielder's heavyweight appearance after he joined Wolfsburg, 2002

JOHN FASHANU

When I saw my face I felt like the Elephant Man. Fashanu was not playing with due care and attention.
GARY MABBUTT, Tottenham defender, after sustaining a broken jaw from the Wimbledon striker's elbow, 1993

People ask what John Fashanu can bring to Northampton Town. In a word, glamour.
FASHANU before his attempt to take over the club failed, 2001

LES FERDINAND

He loved sex but he always checked the football scores on Teletext first.
EVA DIJKSTRA, model, on the England striker, 1996

ALEX FERGUSON

I scored 45 goals in 51 games for Dunfermline one season [1965–66].
Modesty forbids me broadcasting it, of course, but I may have mentioned it to
[Ruud] Van Nistelrooy and [Ole Gunnar] Solskjaer. They're fed up of listening
to me, in fact.
FERGUSON, by now Sir Alex, recalling his playing days, 2004

DUNCAN FERGUSON

I stepped forward and I collided with [John] McStay. Subsequently he fell to
the ground.
*FERGUSON appealing against conviction for assault while playing for Rangers against Raith
Rovers, 1995*

I can drink like a chimney.

FERGUSON, quoted by Rangers team-mate John Brown in Blue Grit, *1995*

TV just asked permission to interview Dunc. I said yes, but don't hold your
breath. I'm just glad the refs can't understand a word he's saying to them.
JOE ROYLE, Ferguson's first manager at Everton, 1995

He has never achieved anything near what he could have done. I said to him
time and again: 'The game means far too much to me; I know that. But it
means fuck all to you.'
JIM McLEAN, Ferguson's first manager at Dundee United, 2003

TOM FINNEY

Tommy was grizzly strong and could run for a week. I'd have played him in an
overcoat. There'd have been four men marking him at the kick-in. When I told
people in Scotland that England were coming up with a winger better than
Stanley Matthews, they laughed at me. They weren't bloody laughing when
Big Georgie Young was running all over Hampden looking for Tommy Finney.
BILL SHANKLY recalls his former Preston team-mate, 1972

MARC-VIVIEN FOE

At half-time his last words were: 'Boys, we must win this match, even if it means dying on the pitch.' And he was the victim. It's terrible.
RIGOBERT SONG, Cameroon captain, on his 'brother', who collapsed and died during a Confederations Cup semi-final in France, 2003

TREVOR FRANCIS

He told me he had a system for taking penalties. I don't know what it is but it's obviously bloody useless.
JIM SMITH, QPR manager, after Francis's second successive miss from the spot, 1988

PAUL GASCOIGNE

For most players, the pressure is in the 90 minutes on the pitch and they have 22½ hours to relax. For Gazza it was the other way round.
TONY DORIGO, former England team-mate, in Channel 4's documentary Inside the Mind of Paul Gascoigne, *2003*

[Gascoigne] wasted the gifts he was blessed with and doesn't have an excuse.
BRIAN CLOUGH in Cloughie: Walking On Water, *2002*

George Best without brains.
STAN SEYMOUR, Newcastle chairman, 1988

He is accused of being arrogant, unable to cope with the press and a boozer. Sounds like he's got a chance to me.
GEORGE BEST, 1988

He can be a loony with a fast mouth. He's either going to be one of the greats or finish up at 40 bitter about wasting such talent.
JOHN BAILEY, former Newcastle colleague, 1988

Paul Gascoigne has done more for Mars Bars than anyone since Marianne Faithfull.
PATRICK BARCLAY, football writer, the Independent, *1988*

If he were a Brazilian or an Argentinian, you would kiss his shoes.

ARTHUR COX, Derby manager, after Gascoigne had inspired Tottenham to victory over his team, 1990

Fierce and comic, formidable and vulnerable, urchin-like and waif-like, a strong head and torso with comparatively frail-looking breakable legs, strange-eyed, pink-faced, fair-haired, tense and upright, a priapic monolith in the Mediterranean sun – a marvellous equivocal sight.

KARL MILLER, writer, in London Review of Books, 1990

Before Paul Gascoigne, did anyone ever become a national hero and a dead-cert millionaire by crying? Fabulous. Weep and the world weeps with you.

SALMAN RUSHDIE, novelist and writer, in the Independent on Sunday, 1990

I'm extremely grateful to Gazza because at least now people are going to spell my name properly.

BAMBER GASCOIGNE, former University Challenge presenter, 1990

Literally the most famous and probably the most popular person in Britain today.

TERRY WOGAN, introducing Gascoigne on his TV chat show, 1990

I'm no poof, that's for sure.

GASCOIGNE on Wogan, 1990

Comparing Gascoigne with Pele is like comparing Rolf Harris to Rembrandt.

RODNEY MARSH, former England striker, 1990

Always seems to be about two stone overweight.

PROGRAMME pen-picture of Gascoigne, Republic of Ireland v England, 1990

A dog of war with the face of a child.

GIANNI AGNELLI, Juventus president, admiring Gascoigne during England's World Cup run, 1990

Sometimes I think I'm playing in the wrong era.
GASCOIGNE on being targeted by opponents, 1990

Coping with the language shouldn't prove a problem. I can't even speak English yet.

GASCOIGNE after agreeing to move to Lazio, 1991

I'm very pleased for Paul but it's like watching your mother-in-law drive off a cliff in your new car.
TERRY VENABLES, Tottenham manager, after Gazza finally joined Lazio, 1992

You'll have to excuse Gazza. He's got a very small vocabulary.
LAWRIE McMENEMY, England assistant manager, after the player had said 'Fuck off Norway' on television, 1992

He wears a No. 10 jersey. I thought it was his position, but it turns out to be his IQ.
GEORGE BEST, 1993

He's an intelligent boy who likes people to think he's stupid. He doesn't have a bad bone in his body but he does some stupid, ridiculous things. That's what makes him so interesting.
ALLY McCOIST, Rangers colleague, 1996

They [the schoolboys] asked me things like: 'How big are Gazza's balls?'
VINNIE JONES after addressing the boys of Eton College, 1996

If he farts in front of the Queen, we get blemished.
PAUL McGAUGHEY, Adidas spokesman, on the risks of a sponsorship deal, 1996

Gazza is no longer a fat, drunken imbecile. He is, in fact, a football genius.
EDITORIAL in the Daily Mirror headed 'Mr Paul Gascoigne: An Apology' after his solo goal v Scotland, 1996

He's a fantastic player when he isn't drunk.
BRIAN LAUDRUP, Rangers team-mate, 1997

I respect him. He goes up to journalists and says: 'Fuck off!'
DANNY BAKER, broadcaster and writer, 1997

God gave him this enormous footballing talent but took his brains out to even things up.
TONY BANKS MP, Labour, Minister for Sport, 1997

Gazza reminds me of Marilyn Monroe. She wasn't the greatest actress in the world, but she was a star and you didn't mind if she was late.
MICHAEL CAINE, actor, 1998

Once you've played in the same side as Gazza, you fall in love with him because of the sort of person and player he is.
DAVID BECKHAM, England colleague, 1998

He was charming, he was funny... Literally, he was an angel.
SHERYL GASCOIGNE, ex-wife, on when she first met him, 1999

I knew managing him would have been no joy ride, but the hazards that went with the talent would never have put me off.
SIR ALEX FERGUSON recalling a thwarted bid to sign Gazza, 1999

Q: *When do you think you peaked?* A: *In two years' time.*

GASCOIGNE in interview on Sky's Soccer AM, *1999*

At his peak, Gazza was phenomenal, the best player I've seen in this country. Becks is a great player but he isn't fit to lace Gazza's boots.
PAUL MERSON, Aston Villa midfielder, 1999

Is there anything I'd like to change? Oh yes. I'd like to change the family's bank account numbers and that tackle I did [on Nottingham Forest's Gary Charles] at Wembley in the 1991 FA Cup final.
GASCOIGNE in TV interview by ex-Rangers colleague Ally McCoist, 1999

I didn't play many games for Middlesbrough towards the end of the season –
or at the start or in the middle.
GASCOIGNE, 2000

I enjoy a glass of wine but I'm not a great drinker. I can't handle my drink
brilliantly, that's all.
GASCOIGNE, 2000

People think Paul and I have a father-and-son relationship. Well, I've got two
sons and I have never felt like hitting them, but I have certainly felt like
smacking him.
WALTER SMITH, his manager at Everton and Rangers, 2000

Probably the kindest man I've met in football.
ROBBIE MUSTOE, Middlesbrough player, 2000

We would like him to be our spiritual leader.
ZONG BOHONG, coach to Chinese club Gansu, on signing Gascoigne, 2003

There's a little man in my head saying: 'Have a drink, have a drink.' You
cannot get him out of your head, especially when there's only you and him.
GASCOIGNE after returning from China, 2003

There's been suicide thoughts, I don't mind admitting that. I don't want any
sympathy. I honestly thought I couldn't live without a drink.
GASCOIGNE, 2004

I have been spat at and hit on planes loads of times, but nobody said a word
because it was First Class and it was Paul.
SHERYL GASCOIGNE, ex-wife, calling his autobiography 'a catalogue of half-truths', 2004

My daughters told me I shouldn't write a book about a man who had beaten
his wife.
HUNTER DAVIES, writer, after collaborating on Gascoigne's autobiography, 2004

Beating up my wife is the only thing I really regret big time. It's not right for a man to hit a woman. I make no excuses, but it was not a regular occurrence… I had a lot of shit in my head and sometimes I took it out on the person I loved, which was Sheryl.
GASCOIGNE, 2004

I have never seen Chris Evans or Danny Baker drunk. I have only seen Jimmy ['Five Bellies'] Gardner drunk twice in 10 years. They were all too busy keeping an eye on me.
GASCOIGNE, 2004

I thought he [Glenn Hoddle] said: 'Do you want to visit a brewery?'
GASCOIGNE on why he jumped at the chance to visit faith healer Eileen Drewery, quoted in his autobiography, 2004

A lost spirit, endlessly wandering up and down the hotel corridors.
TERRY BUTCHER, former England captain, recalling Gascoigne's inability to sleep, 2003

The warm human being will come out and it will blossom.
TONY ADAMS, former England colleague, predicting a happier future for Gascoigne, 2003

Gazza is the only member of our coaching staff who could afford lobster, but that's what he had and it has done for him.
STEVE EVANS, Boston United manager, after his new player-coach suffered stomach trouble, 2004

I like the solitude of writing.
GASCOIGNE on the possibility of producing a novel, 2005

I've got the full set of problems. It's not just the booze, it's the panic attacks, bipolar disorder, the purging – it's everything I have to deal with every day. For me to be alive it proves there really is a God.
GASCOIGNE, 2005

JOHNNY GILES

I thought he was miles better than [Billy] Bremner. A better passer, shrewder, more devious and harder when he wanted to be.
STEVE PERRYMAN, Tottenham captain, in A Man For All Seasons, *1985*

Giles was the man everybody wanted to sort out. He was extremely adept at escaping bookings. He would be furthest away when anything went off. And he was nearly always the instigator.
TERRY CONROY, former Republic of Ireland team-mate and Stoke adversary, 2002

DAVID GINOLA

Frog on the Tyne
HEADLINE in Daily Star after Newcastle signed the Frenchman, 1995

Men will love his skills and women his looks. He could end up being popular enough to replace Robbie Williams in Take That.
CHRIS WADDLE, former England midfielder, 1995

I'm told he ran up the tunnel and dived into the bath.

JOE ROYLE, Everton manager, alleging Ginola went to ground too easily, 1995

It was beautiful. The sensitivity from everyone he met in Birmingham really impressed David.
CHANTEL STANLEY, Ginola's agent, on his reception after leaving Tottenham for Aston Villa, 2000

He hasn't played many matches and he missed pre-season [training]. So it's possible that he is carrying a little extra timber.
JOHN GREGORY, Villa manager, sparking a row with Ginola over his weight, 2001

ANDY GORAM

When is Andy Goram going to piss off and stop annoying us with his bloody wonder saves? Yours in victimisation.
LETTER to the Celtic fanzine Not the View, 1997

ANDY GRAY

You're from Drumchapel, laddie. What do you know about prawn cocktails? You'll have soup like the rest of us.
JOCK STEIN, Scotland manager, to Gray after he tried to order from the menu on a trip abroad, 1979

His style is more suited to rugby union.

UDO LATTEK, Bayern Munich coach, on the Everton striker who became a TV pundit, 1985

EDDIE GRAY

When he plays on snow, he doesn't leave any footprints.
DON REVIE on the Leeds and Scotland midfielder, 1970

JIMMY GREAVES

He was always very calm, very collected, and, where scoring goals was concerned, he was a Picasso.
CLIVE ALLEN, Tottenham striker, in There's Only One Clive Allen, *1987*

Q: Who was the biggest influence on your career?
A: IAN ST JOHN: Bill Shankly.
A: JIMMY GREAVES: Vladimir Smirnoff.
INTERVIEW with Saint and Greavsie in Loaded *magazine, 1995*

HARRY GREGG

Somewhere in there, the grace of a ballet dancer joins with the strength of an SAS squaddie, the dignity of an ancient king, the nerve of a bomb disposal officer.
EAMON DUNPHY, journalist and former Republic of Ireland player, 1983

RUUD GULLIT

JIMMY GREAVES: 'E's a Moroccan or something, isn't 'e?
IAN ST JOHN: Moluccan.
GREAVES: Yeah, Moluccan, that's it. Well, blimey, 'e can't 'alf play a bit.
EXCHANGE on ITV's Saint & Greavsie, *1988*

If all else fails you could wait for the first corner kick and use his dreadlocks to tie him to a post.
VINNIE JONES, Wimbledon midfielder, 1988

Watching Ruud was like watching an 18-year-old play in a game for 12-year-olds.
GLENN HODDLE, Chelsea manager, on Gullit's English debut, 1995

My pot-bellied pigs don't squeal as much as him.
VINNIE JONES after being sent off for fouling the Dutchman, 1995

BRUCE GROBBELAAR

Football teams are a balance of road sweepers and violinists. Bruce is a lead violinist.
LAWRIE McMENEMY, Southampton manager, signing the Liverpool goalkeeper, 1994

I'd rather have Grobbelaar trying to throw a game than Dave Beasant trying to win one.
CALLER to Six-O-Six radio phone-in after Grobbelaar's arrest on match-fixing charges, 1994

GHEORGHE HAGI

He's a brilliant player but we're no' getting all psychedelic about him.
ANDY ROXBURGH, Scotland coach, on the Romanian playmaker, 1991

ALAN HANSEN

A good skipper, but he could have been a really great one if he had been a bit more extrovert.
BOB PAISLEY, former Liverpool manager, 1989

He looks like a pissed vampire.
CHRIS DONALD, editor of Viz *magazine, 1994*

RON HARRIS

I like to think that I've something else to offer apart from being a bit of a butcher.
HARRIS, Chelsea captain, 1979

COLIN HENDRY

He's not happy unless he has been kicked in the bollocks three times during training.
GRAEME LE SAUX, Blackburn team-mate, 1997

JIMMY HILL

If he can find a ground where he scored a league goal, I'll meet him there.
BRIAN CLOUGH replying to Hill's challenge to debate, 1979

GLENN HODDLE

Hoddle a luxury? It's the bad players who are a luxury.
DANNY BLANCHFLOWER, predecessor in Tottenham's midfield, 1981

I hear Glenn has found God. That must have been one hell of a pass.
JASPER CARROTT, comedian, 1988

MARK HUGHES

A warrior you could trust with your life.
ALEX FERGUSON in the David Meek and Mark Hughes book, Hugesie: The Red Dragon, *1994*

My fondest memory of him is his passport picture, which was a Panini sticker of himself.

MICHAEL DUBERRY, Reading defender and ex-Chelsea colleague of Hughes, 2007

He was a horrendous trainer. The worst I've seen. The ball would go everywhere. I couldn't believe it was Mark Hughes. But in a game he was brilliant. He would never give the ball away.
CRAIG BELLAMY, Wales striker, recalls playing with his national manager, 2004

ROGER HUNT

Yes, he misses a few. But he gets in the right places to miss them.
BILL SHANKLY, the England forward's manager at Liverpool, 1966

NORMAN HUNTER

Norman bites yer legs
BANNER by Leeds fans honouring the hard-tackling defender, 1972

TERRY HURLOCK

The only footballer I've ever seen who could play properly while drunk.
FRANK MALONEY, boxing promoter and Millwall supporter, on the former Millwall and Rangers midfielder, 2004

GEOFF HURST

Q: In your heart of hearts would you like to see another player score a World Cup final hat-trick?
A: No. That hat-trick and the win itself have transformed my life.
HURST in an interview with the Independent, *2006*

I wanted to play for England and score three goals in the World Cup final like Geoff Hurst in 1966. I used to pray for that every night. That's why I no longer believe in God. He let me down.
HUGH GRANT, screen actor and Fulham fan, 2002

Deep down all the lads will be keeping a sort of score in their heads. Every time they jump for the ball and get it they'll be chalking it down, 'Three to me, one to Geoff Hurst,' or whatever. Despite what the boss says, he is special. Nicking the ball off a player like that, beating him in the tackle, is something you'll always remember. Magic!
PAUL PRICE, captain of Midland side Tividale, before FA Cup tie v Telford, where Hurst was player-manager; from Journey to Wembley, *by Brian James, 1977*

DAVID ICKE

David Icke says he is here to save the world. Well, he saved bugger all when he played in goal for Coventry.
JASPER CARROTT, comedian, 1992

PAUL INCE

Incey's always banging on about the past. In training the other day he tried a bicycle kick which went 20 feet over the bar. He just turned to us all and went: 'Ooh, did that once in the San Siro.' We told him to belt up.
MATT MURRAY, Wolves goalkeeper, 2003

When a player is at his peak, he feels as if he can climb Everest in his slippers. That's what he was like.
ALEX FERGUSON, Ince's manager at Manchester United, 1997

Paul Ince wants everyone to call him Guv'nor but we call him Incey.
LEE SHARPE, United colleague, 1995

At United, everyone called me Guv. I hope it'll be the same here.
INCE on arriving for training at Inter Milan after leaving Old Trafford, 1995

All this 'Guv'nor' nonsense should have been left in his toy-box.
SIR ALEX FERGUSON in his autobiography, 1999

L'assino della Settimana (Donkey of the week)
GUERIN SPORTIVO magazine, Italy, 1995

After Bobby Moore, I'm probably the greatest player to come out of West Ham, which is to their credit.
INCE, 2001

DENIS IRWIN

Denis's dress sense scares me. When I'm that old, I hope I don't go down that road.
SHAUN NEWTON, Wolves winger, on his veteran team-mate, 2003

LEIGHTON JAMES

Your pace is very deceptive, son. You're even slower than you look.
TOMMY DOCHERTY, Derby manager, to the Welsh winger, 1977

MAURICE JOHNSTON

I didn't do it [sign the Catholic Johnston for the traditionally Protestant Rangers] to be a revolutionary. I did it because he was a bloody good player.
GRAEME SOUNESS, Blackburn and former Rangers manager, 2002

Scottish football was rocked to its pre-cast concrete foundations when Rangers finally broke with 100 years of tradition and bought a player from FC Nantes for the first time in their history.
THE ABSOLUTE GAME, *Scottish football fanzine, after Johnston spurned a return to Celtic and joined Rangers, 1989*

JIMMY JOHNSTONE

Bless him. What would he be earning today? What's Beckham on? Double it.
TERRY COOPER, former opponent with Leeds and England, pondering the terminally ill ex-Celtic and Scotland winger's worth in the modern game, in the documentary film Lord of the Wing, *2004*

We spent three hours one night drinking, talking, singing. He said he wished the evening would never end. When we put him in a cab, I said: 'Treat this guy good, he's like Jesus Christ.' The driver said: 'He's better than that!'
ROBERT DUVALL, American film actor, as above, 2004

We always had this little pact whereby I'd say to him, particularly over at the Jungle side of Celtic Park, 'Jimmy, if you go by me, keep going,' because he had this terrible habit of coming back and beating you three or four times. I'd say: 'Keep going, cos if you come back I'm going to have to do something about it.'
JOHN GREIG, former Rangers defender, as above, 2004

Just as well you've no' got a touch like [Celtic defender] Bobo Balde or you'd go straight through that window.
GORDON STRACHAN, Celtic manager, to Johnstone as he controlled his wheelchair with his left foot because of motor neurone disease, 2006

VINNIE JONES

I like to upset anybody I play against.
JONES, Wimbledon midfielder, 1988

He's incredibly loyal. Ask him to jump off the stand roof and he'll do it. But he's as thick as two short planks. He always grabbed the quiz book on our coach trips so he could ask the questions. That way he didn't have to answer.
ARNIE REED, physiotherapist at Jones's first club, Wealdstone, 1988

Vinnie is a once-in-a-lifetime human being.

SAM HAMMAM, Wimbledon chairman, after selling Jones to Leeds, 1989

In Don Revie's day he wouldn't have got through the door, let alone pulled on a Leeds shirt.
JOHNNY GILES, former Leeds midfielder, 1989

I've been trying to be a footballer and that isn't me. I got a bit carried away with the *Wogan* show and all that.
JONES, 1990

At half-time on my Wimbledon debut our old kit-man, Sid, came round with the tea. I asked him how I was doing and he said: 'I'm 85 and if you gave me the No. 4 shirt I'd do better.'
JONES, 1991

George Orwell said that political speech was the defence of the indefensible. Michael Heseltine is the Vinnie Jones of the indefensible.
ALLISON PEARSON, Observer television reviewer, 1995

My career has been like the migrating woodcock. You've got all the shooters and storms trying to whack you down, but in the end you just want to get to new fields.
JONES, 1995

I'm still on the transfer list but Alex Ferguson has yet to take the hint.
JONES, 1996

Vinnie admits he threw a piece of toast at Gary Lineker. What he didn't say was that it was still in the toaster.
TONY BANKS MP, Labour, on Radio 4's News Quiz, 1997

Vinnie is a natural [as an actor]. People have knocked him all his life but they are just bitter and twisted. He can do anything. If he goes on to manage England one day, I wouldn't be surprised.
JOHN HARTSON, former colleague in the Wales team, 2000

You wouldn't know in our house whether I was a dustman or a movie star. There's no conversation about it.
JONES, 2000

I can't keep up this hard image. I must be the nicest person I know.
JONES, 2000

I've seen that advert with Giggsy wearing an apron and holding a feather duster and I wouldn't do that. I might have done it a few years ago for a few quid. I've been in some fucking ridiculous pictures, I can tell you.
JONES, 2002

I like autobiographies. Sports ones are interesting. You might be surprised that I like a bit of poetry, too. I don't have any books on it, but I do like it.
JONES, 2002

ROY KEANE

Roy will be the hardest to replace. Forget the playing part, it's the spiritual and emotional thing he gives you. In his will to win, he's an absolute beast of a man.
SIR ALEX FERGUSON, 2005

Nicknamed Damien, after the character in *The Omen*. He's mad but he's funny too.
RYAN GIGGS, 1994

Young Keane shouldn't screw up his privileged position at Old Trafford for the sake of a few thousand extra quid he might make abroad. It's tempting – 60 grand a week after tax, and a four-year contract. But I reckon that on top of what he has got already, he'd have to live until he's 634 to spend that lot.
BRIAN CLOUGH, who had brought Keane to England by signing him for Nottingham Forest from Cobh Ramblers, 1999

If I was in management now and had the money to take my pick of any player, anywhere, if I could have the best at Arsenal, Leeds, Chelsea or Real Madrid, I'd take Keane.
BRIAN CLOUGH, 1999

He was very, very drunk and as aggressive as you can possibly imagine. He had evil in his eyes and he gave me a good kick – I'll have a bruise.
LEANNE CAREY, Australian tourist, alleging a wine-bar assault by Keane as United players celebrated winning the championship, 1999

If that is not a sending-off offence, what is? What do we need to see, a leg with blood dripping off the stump?
PETER WILLIS, president of the Referees' Association, after Keane was sent off in the Charity Shield, 2000

I'm a great admirer of Roy Keane. He has been there, done it and still wants to do it. I don't like Manchester United but to be mentioned in the same breath as him is great.
STEVEN GERRARD, Liverpool midfielder, 2000

I'd never put Keane in the real hard-man bracket. He's more of the roll-up-your-sleeves leader every team wishes they had. He doesn't care who you are or what you've done in the game or in the last five minutes. If you're not pulling your weight he'll bawl you out in front of 50,000 fans.
IAN WRIGHT, former Arsenal and England striker, 1999

We all bang on about how much players earn these days but Keane is worth every penny of the £54,000 a week or whatever he gets. I know it's a few bob more than me, give or take 49 grand.
DEAN WINDASS, Bradford City midfielder, 2000

As if cutting Haaland in half wasn't bad enough, Keane then swoops over him like Dracula. All he needed was the black cloak.
BRIAN CLOUGH after Keane was sent off in the Manchester derby, 2001

I'm sick and tired of hearing commentators telling us how much running Keane does in a match, how he covers every blade of grass. He's entitled to be fresher than most because he has so much time off – eight red cards and that long injury lay-off, which was his fault, incidentally, and not Alf-Inge Haaland's. He's had more than enough rest through the suspensions alone. He's had more holidays than Judith Chalmers.
CLOUGH, 2001

I'll have to see whether any of Keane's studs are still in there.
ALF-INGE HAALAND, Manchester City midfielder, before a scan on his knee, 2002

On the field [Keane] is a major asset. Off it he's quite unassuming, an ordinary lad. He'll say 'What are you all doing tonight?' and he'll come to the pictures or whatever. What you see on the pitch is a usually extravagant character but he's not like that off it.

MICK McCARTHY, Republic of Ireland manager, before leaving for the World Cup finals, 2002

As he waded in with one expletive after another, I asked myself if this was my captain. Was this a man who could serve Ireland as a role model for our children? The answer was no.

McCARTHY after banishing Keane from the squad in Japan, 2002

Roy Keane has no manners. There's never any reason not to be polite, even with people you don't like.

GEORGE BEST, former Manchester United player, after the falling out between Keane and McCarthy, 2002

Sanity is more important.

KEANE after being banished from the Irish World Cup squad in Japan after a row with McCarthy, 2002

Oh, I'd have sent him home all right, but I'd have shot him first.

BRIAN CLOUGH after Keane's expulsion by McCarthy, 2002

The people of Ireland may forgive him but I never will. He is a disgrace to his country.

JACK CHARLTON, former Republic manager, 2002

Roy Keane and Michael Collins: Two great Cork leaders shot in the back

SLOGAN on a pro-Keane T-shirt sold in Ireland after the World Cup, 2002. Collins was an IRA leader in the first half of the 20th century

He slides into the all-time list of Irish heroes somewhere just below Oliver Cromwell.

MATT GRAY, undergraduate journalist, reviewing Keane's book in Oxford Student, 2002

I've made mistakes. I was naïve and probably drank too much.
KEANE in his controversial autobiography, 2002

Socialising with Roy was always a pleasure – until that one drink too many.
NED KELLY, former head of security at United, in his memoir The Untold Story, *2003*

I'm surprised he did a book in the first place. He'd be the first to give someone stick in the dressing room if they had done something similar.
DENIS IRWIN, former United and Ireland colleague, now with Wolves, 2002

I'd rather buy a Bob the Builder CD for my two-year-old son.

JASON McATEER, former Ireland team-mate, on Keane's book, 2002. Within days, Keane was sent off for elbowing the Sunderland midfielder in the face

I only ever hit Roy the once. He got up so I couldn't have hit him that hard.
BRIAN CLOUGH, 2003

People ask where my competitive streak comes from. It's fear. I have a big fear of failure.
KEANE, 2003

A lot of people think I'm a traitor. I can't worry about that. I believe I've given good service. All I'd ask is to be judged on what I did on the pitch in my 58 matches for Ireland, not on what I said in an interview.
KEANE after quitting international football, 2003

There isn't a person in the game who has Roy's mental toughness. Patrick Vieira is influential at Arsenal, but he can't compare with Keane in terms of mental strength and pride. Roy is more driven – just when you think he hasn't got anything more, he gives it.
SIR ALEX FERGUSON, 2003

Alex Ferguson is Manchester United. His mentality is in the team and Roy Keane is an expression of this. Keane is Ferguson as a player.
CLAUDIO RANIERI, Chelsea manager, 2003

I see certain players and the way they are after games – win or lose they can be dead relaxed. If we do win on Sunday it will be great, but I'll be thinking about Wednesday very quickly.
KEANE, 2003

There was no malice in the incident. It's not Roy's style to do anything like that.
FERGUSON after Keane was sent off for 'stamping' against Porto, 2004

I'm not in this game to be popular. I like pushing myself and the people around me hard, but there seems to be problem with that in the modern day.
KEANE after signing for Celtic, 2005

KEVIN KEEGAN

The only thing I fear is missing an open goal in front of the Kop. I'd die if that happened. My eyes water when they sing 'You'll Never Walk Alone'. I've actually been crying while playing.
KEEGAN at Liverpool, 1974

Kevin Keegan is the Julie Andrews of football.

DUNCAN McKENZIE, playing contemporary of Keegan's, 1981

To call Keegan a superstar is stretching a point. As a player he's not fit to lace my boots.
GEORGE BEST, 1982

Keegan isn't fit to lace Best's drinks.
JOHN ROBERTS, football writer, in the Daily Mail, 1982

MARTIN KEOWN

Martin Keown's up everybody's backside.
TREVOR BROOKING on Match of the Day, 1996

JURGEN KLINSMANN

Me dive? Never. I always go straight for goal.
KLINSMANN rebutting charges of diving, World Cup finals, 1994

I was watching Germany and got up to make a cup of tea. I bumped into the telly and Klinsmann fell over.
FRANK SKINNER, comedian, 1994

MICHAEL LAUDRUP

There's not a lot you can do to stop him, short of sending a couple of guys in balaclavas with baseball bats round to knock on his door.
JIM DUFFY, Hibernian manager, when Laudrup was with Rangers, 1997

DENIS LAW

Denis was in the class of Alfredo Di Stefano because he could do everything, organise a side and score goals... Matt Busby knew how important he was – when Denis was doubtful [due to injury] the boss would practically be on his hands and knees hoping he would play.
HARRY GREGG, Manchester United goalkeeper, in the Motson-Rowlinson book The European Cup 1955–80, *1980*

FRANK LEBOEUF

I am very happy at Chelsea, but I don't want to be the club cretin.
LEBOEUF, French defender, claiming he was under-paid, 1999

The fella's got no spine, backbone, no bottle. He's a classic example of the foreign player who is ruining our game.
RON HARRIS, former Chelsea hard man, 1999

I know they are after me. They think I am temperamental just because I am French and because I am a world champion.
LEBOEUF claiming a vendetta against him and other foreign players, 2000

ROB LEE

I told him Newcastle was nearer to London than Middlesbrough and he believed me.

KEVIN KEEGAN, Newcastle manager, on how he lured Londoner Lee to Tyneside rather than Teesside, 1995

GRAEME LE SAUX

I've been slaughtered for reading the *Guardian*. In most walks of life, that would be respected, differences valued. I took stick from the lads and often it was upsetting. But I stuck it out when I had plenty of opportunities to fit in with the sheep.

GRAEME LE SAUX, Blackburn and England defender, 1995

No one cares whether or not Le Saux is gay. It is the fact that he openly admits to reading the *Guardian* that makes him the most reviled man in football.

PIERS MORGAN, editor of the Mirror, *after Le Saux alleged that England colleague Robbie Fowler called him a 'poof' during a Chelsea v Liverpool match, 1999*

Le Saux is vilified for a secret much more shameful than being a homosexual. For Le Saux is middle class.

IAN HISLOP, satirical journalist, 1999

MATTHEW LE TISSIER

You're never sure you want him playing for you, but you're sure you don't want him playing against you.

DARIO GRADI, Crewe manager, on the Southampton midfielder, 1995

The one thing I'd like to rid myself of is the word 'but'. You know: 'He's a great player, but…' or 'So much skill, but…'

LE TISSIER, 1997

Q: Have your years of playing football affecting your body?
A: No – it was McDonald's that did that.
Q: Any pre-match rituals?
A: I used to yawn a lot.
LE TISSIER answering a questionnaire on his website, 2003

GARY LINEKER

Conjugate the verb 'done great': I done great. He done great. We done great.
They done great. The boy Lineker done great.
LETTER to the Guardian *after TV pundit Mike Channon referred to the England striker as 'the boy Lineker' during the World Cup finals, 1986*

I'm rather a boring sort of person.
LINEKER on Desert Island Discs, *1990*

My record, averaging a goal every two games, sounds good, but that's only
one goal every three hours. Most of the time I'm frustrated, pissed off, waiting
for the right ball.
LINEKER, 1992

He had no feel for the game, no passion, and that's why, now that he has
retired, he's best keeping out of football.
VINNIE JONES, former opponent, 1994

Too good to be true.
ALEX FERGUSON, Manchester United manager, 1996

It's not deliberate. I don't think anyone would contrive an image as sickly
sweet as mine.
LINEKER, by now presenting Match of the Day, *2000*

He's a bit of a babe.
BOY GEORGE, gay pop singer and DJ, 2000

It's more likely that you'll see Gary selling the *Big Issue* than managing England.
JON HOLMES, Lineker's agent, when the TV presenter was touted as a possible successor to Sven-Göran Eriksson, 2004

DIEGO MARADONA

At the time I called it the Hand of God. Bollocks! It was the Hand of Diego!
MARADONA on his controversial goal for Argentina v England at the 1986 World Cup finals, 2005

A little bit the hand of God, a little the head of Diego.
MARADONA describing his 'volleyball' goal against England in the World Cup, 1986

Next you'll be saying I should ask a defender's permission before I dribble round him.
MARADONA to a World Soccer *reporter who asked whether he should have owned up to the handball, 1986*

Reidy [Peter Reid] might've taken Maradona down on the halfway line if he'd realised what was going to happen. Everyone would now like him to have taken him down.
BRYAN ROBSON, former England captain, recalling Maradona's dribble and scoring shot in the 'Hand of God' game, 2006

Pele had nearly everything. Maradona has everything. He works harder, does more and is more skilful. Trouble is he'll be remembered for another reason – he bends the rules to suit himself.
SIR ALF RAMSEY after Maradona's 'Hand of God' goal , 1986

The best one-footed player since Puskas.
SIR STANLEY MATTHEWS, 1986

I was dancing in a disco when this very small, fat man approached and started hugging me. I thought it was a fan, but then his bodyguard came over. Then I recognised him.
RUUD GULLIT, Netherlands captain, on meeting Maradona, 1988

His left foot is like a hand.
OSSIE ARDILES, former Argentina player, 1994

FIFA cut off my legs just when I had the chance to prove to my daughters that I could play with 20-year-olds.
MARADONA leaving the World Cup finals after failing a drugs test, 1994

I was, I am and I always will be a drug addict. A person who gets involved in drugs has to fight it every day.
MARADONA signing up to an Argentinian government anti-drugs campaign, 1996

For me, he was the perfect footballer. Pele was a better team player, but I believe Maradona was better than anyone who has played football on this planet.
GLENN HODDLE, England coach, 1998

The best player I ever played against. The ball belonged to Maradona. He always fought for his team, too, on and off the pitch.
LOTHAR MATTHAUS, former Germany captain, 2000

I've been to the Vatican and seen the gold ceilings. And then I hear the Pope saying that the church was concerned about poor kids. So? Sell the ceilings! You've got nothing going for you. You were only a goalkeeper.
MARADONA on Pope John Paul, 2003

I saw Maradona do things in practice and in matches I'd never dreamed of. There are many who can score, pass and assist but the way he did all three was unique. People talk about Pele but I've never seen him do anything Maradona did.
GIANFRANCO ZOLA, former Chelsea and Italy striker, on partnering the Argentinian at Napoli, 2004

If Jesus stumbled, then why shouldn't I as well?
MARADONA on his Argentinian TV chat show The Night of 10, *recalling his descent into drugs and obesity, 2005*

For this whole being-alive thing, I can only thank the two beards: God and Fidel.

MARADONA on his debt to God and Cuba's President Castro in his autobiography El Diego, *2004*

As far as we know, corpses can't speak.
MARADONA calling a Buenos Aires radio station after reports of his death, 2007

LOTHAR MATTHAUS

The Germans have five million registered footballers and yet they select a 39-year-old.
ARSENE WENGER, Arsenal manager, at Euro 2000

STANLEY MATTHEWS

George Best and David Beckham rolled into one.
KENNETH WOLSTENHOLME, former TV commentator, on Matthews's death, 2000

If I had to get 'stuck in' to get through a game I'm afraid my career would have ended long ago.
MATTHEWS, then 45, in The Stanley Matthews Story, *1960*

Last night I had the strangest dream
I've never had before
Stan Matthews on the wing for Stoke
At the age of 84.
SONG on a Keele University students' rag record, 1964

Stan was unique. He never went for 50–50 balls, didn't score many goals and was not good in the air. But on his days he was unplayable. He beat fellows so easily, with such pace and balance, often taking on four or five at a time.
JOE MERCER, former England team-mate, 1970

You usually knew how he'd beat you, but you couldn't do anything about it.
DANNY BLANCHFLOWER, former Tottenham captain, 1970

I never gave many fouls away. The most was when I played for Huddersfield against Stanley Matthews in his comeback game for Stoke City. I coughed twice and the referee blew.
RAY WILSON, England's World Cup-winning left-back, in Martin Tyler, Boys of 66, *1981*

Stan used to put the ball on my centre parting. They don't do that any more.
TOMMY LAWTON, former England centre-forward, 1985

He cut his partners out of the game. If you passed to him, you'd never see the ball again.
RAY BOWDEN, Matthews's first international partner in 1934, in Michael George's book
Sportsmen of Cornwall, *1986*

His name is symbolic of the beauty of the game, his fame timeless. A magical player, of the people, for the people.
INSCRIPTION on a statue of Matthews in Hanley, his birthplace, 1987

The maestro appears to be dribbling towards Millets but could easily swerve across the street to Woolworths.
GUINNESS FOOTBALL ENCYCLOPAEDIA, *ed. Graham Hart, describing the statue, 1991*

I'm not a scientist. I'm not a poet. I'm not a writer. But of course I am very honoured.

MATTHEWS accepting an honorary degree from Keele University, 1987

I don't know whether I was all that good. I never saw myself play, so how do I know?
MATTHEWS on his 80th birthday, 1995

I'm no hero. Doctors and nurses are heroes. Surgeons, people like that. We had a real hero born right here in Stoke-on-Trent: Reginald Mitchell, who designed the Spitfire. He saved Britain. Now that's what I call a hero.
SIR STAN, 1995

They cheer now when they win a corner. If I only got a corner, I didn't think I'd done my job very well.
MATTHEWS, 1997

Grabbing hold of Stan to try to stop him was fatal because he knew then that he'd got you. He'd often beat a full-back, wait for him to recover and then beat him again. It was never for show, but for the ruthlessly simple expedient of demoralising the opponent.

JIMMY ARMFIELD, former Blackpool colleague, on Matthews's death, 2000

Stan never looked as though he was enjoying himself. He always had a serious expression on his face because he was so focused on his game.

KEN ASTON, former World Cup referee, 2000

He never criticised the modern game, never said that the players weren't as good as in his day.

PETER COATES, Stoke City director, 2000

GARY McALLISTER

We were hovering above Wembley in a helicopter and I was listening to the match on headphones. As McAllister put the ball down for the penalty, I said: 'One, two, three, move!' The ball moved away from his foot and he missed. The hate letters I got from Scotland!

URI GELLER, 'psychic' entertainer, on the penalty save by England's David Seaman from Scotland captain McAllister during the European Championship finals, 1996

I know there are far more important things in life than football, but if you cut me open and looked inside right now it wouldn't be a pretty sight. I don't know if I can sink any lower.

McALLISTER after his penalty miss, 1996

FRANK McAVENNIE

Oh my God – this guy looks like a clown. If his catchphrase is 'Where's the burds?' then my answer has to be 'in hiding' because he's revolting.

JORDAN, model and TV personality, on the former Scotland striker, 2003

JASON McATEER

I'm nicknamed Trigger [after the *Only Fools and Horses* character] because, basically, I'm thick. It came about in my Liverpool days when I was in a pizza restaurant. The waitress asked if I wanted my pizza cut into four pieces or eight. I said four because there was no way I could eat eight pieces.
McATEER, Sunderland and Republic of Ireland player, 2003

ALLY McCOIST

He's handsome, he's rich, he's funny and he's happy. My envy knows no bounds.

BILLY CONNOLLY, comedian, in the foreword to Ally McCoist: My Story, *1992*

DAVID MURRAY: Nice to see you could make it, Mr McCoist.
McCOIST: Ah come on. This is the earliest I've been late in ages.
EXCHANGE between the Rangers chairman and the striker at a Burns Night supper, 1994. McCoist was legendary for poor timekeeping

I met Michael Jackson backstage at the Tokyo Dome in '93, but to be honest, meeting Ally McCoist was a bigger buzz.
ALAN McGEE, Creation Records label owner, 1995

Q: If you were to have a tattoo, what would it be?
A: Probably a tattoo of Ally McCoist's face and I'll leave it to your imagination where I'd have it. It would be payback for the 1989 League Cup final, when he dived. I hadn't even tackled him, but he fooled the referee and won a penalty.
WILLIE MILLER, former Aberdeen captain, in a newspaper interview, 2003

Cor! He's stunning – absolutely gorgeous... He can share my bed any time. We can count sheep. Perfect. 10/10.
JORDAN, model and TV personality, 2003

PAUL McGRATH

One of the all-time greats – someone to compare with Bobby Moore.
JACK CHARLTON, McGrath's Republic of Ireland manager and former defensive partner to Moore with England, 1995

COLIN McGLASHAN

Tell him he's Pele and get him back on.
JOHN LAMBIE, Partick Thistle manager, on being told that concussed striker McGlashan did not know who he was, 1993

STEVE McMANAMAN

They compare Steve McManaman to Steve Heighway. He's nothing like him but I can see why – it's because he's a bit different.
KEVIN KEEGAN, England manager and former team-mate of Heighway's, 2000

BILLY McNEILL

There's only one King Billy, that's McNeill.
SONG in praise of the 1967 European Cup-winning captain, by Celtic fans to the tune of 'She'll Be Coming Round The Mountain', 2003

Billy sets a high standard of conduct for all of us, and this is the main reason why you do not see any long-haired wonders walking through the doors at Celtic Park... Professional football is our business. We feel we do not have to look like a crowd of discotheque drop-outs to attract attention.
BOBBY MURDOCH, Celtic and Scotland colleague, in All the Way With Celtic, *1970*

PAUL McSTAY

McStay for Rangers? Sounds a fair swap to me.
LETTER to Sunday Mail *after reports that Rangers coveted Celtic's captain, 1992*

PAUL MERSON

My addictions are always there, waiting for me. They're doing press-ups outside my door.
MERSON, Aston Villa midfielder, on his fight against alcoholism, gambling addiction and drug abuse, 1999

The last thing a policeman said to me when I left the cell was: 'People would give their right arm to be like you.' I said: 'I'd give my right arm just to be normal.'
MERSON, by now with Walsall, on being detained for five hours for allegedly assaulting his wife, 2003

Gambling has beat me, spanked me all over the place. This is one of the biggest killers in the world. Every day it would go through my head about committing suicide.
MERSON, 2003

MIRANDINHA

TRAINER: How are you feeling?
MIRANDINHA: I'm very well, thank you, how are you?
EXCHANGE as Newcastle's Brazilian striker lay injured soon after his arrival in England, 1987

BOBBY MOORE

The slowest player I ever played with, without question, but no one ever ran him.
JACK CHARLTON, Moore's defensive partner in England's World Cup-winning side, 2006

There should be a law against him. He knows what's happening 20 minutes before anyone else.
JOCK STEIN, Celtic manager, 1969

Someone would come and kick a lump out of him, and he'd play as though he hadn't noticed. But 10 minutes later, whoof! He had a great 'golden boy' image, Moore. But he was hard.
GEOFF HURST, former West Ham and England colleague, in Brian James' Journey to Wembley, *1977*

Bobby would never take a liberty, let alone a bracelet.
JIMMY GREAVES, friend and ex-England team-mate, after Moore's arrest for alleged theft of jewellery in Bogota, 1970

The worst businessman in the world, listening to the wrong people.

JIMMY TARBUCK, comedian and friend of Moore's, 2006

Bobby wasn't a criminal himself. But he was friends with a lot of them – or they were friends with him.
ROB JENKINS, West Ham physio during the 1960s, on Moore's alleged underworld connections, 2006

STAN MORTENSEN

They'll probably call it the Matthews funeral.
MATTHEW ENGEL, Guardian journalist, after Mortensen's death, 1991. Mortensen scored a hat-trick in 'the Matthews final' of 1953

REMI MOSES

Half a million for Remi Moses? You could get the original Moses and the tablets for that price.
TOMMY DOCHERTY, former Manchester United manager, after Ron Atkinson took Moses from West Bromwich to Old Trafford, 1982

PAT NEVIN

Being a footballer is what I do. It's not what I am.
PAT NEVIN, former Scotland winger, 1997

STEVE NICOL

The most complete player in British football, the best two-footed player in the game, but not exactly a deep thinker.
MARK LAWRENSON, former Liverpool team-mate, 1988

CHARLIE NICHOLAS

We talked about football but all he really wanted to talk about was sex... I hear he's not been scoring many goals lately, but all I can tell you is he certainly scored a hat-trick with me that night.
THEREZA BAZAR, pop singer with Dollar, 1988

It was like buying a Van Gogh and sticking it away in a bank vault.

BRIAN CLOUGH on Nicholas's spell in Arsenal Reserves, 1987

People reckoned I spent all my time in Stringfellow's but I never went there that much. I preferred Tramp.
CHARLIE NICHOLAS on his spell with Arsenal, 1995

MARTIN O'NEILL

O'NEILL: Why am I playing for the second team?
BRIAN CLOUGH: Because you're too good for the thirds.
EXCHANGE between Nottingham Forest player and manager circa 1980, recalled by O'Neill, 2004

A good player but a pain the arse.
BRIAN CLOUGH in his autobiography, 2002

PETER OSGOOD

I am a pagan god.
FIRST SENTENCE of the former Chelsea, Southampton and England striker's autobiography, 2002

MARC OVERMARS

A couple of players stood up and told Overmars he had been jumping out of tackles for too long, as if he had a pole vault up his backside.
ALAN SMITH, former Arsenal player, revealing heated scenes in his old club's dressing room after defeat by Coventry, 2000

STUART PEARCE

I went to have a look at him playing for Wealdstone on a stinking night at Yeovil. After eight minutes he put in a thundering tackle and the Yeovil winger landed in my wife's lap. I said to her: 'That's it. I've seen enough. We're going home.'
BOBBY GOULD recalling how he signed Pearce for Coventry, 1991

Who needs Johnny Rotten when you can have Psycho?

STEVE DOUBLE, FA media officer, on the ovation for Pearce after he introduced the Sex Pistols' reunion show, 1996

Two days after a hamstring strain that would have kept anyone else out for a fortnight, on a freezing day when we were all training in bobble hats and gloves, he emerged, running out of the mist, wearing nothing but a pair of underpants and a towel wrapped round his head. That's why they call him Psycho.
KEVIN KEEGAN, Manchester City manager, after Pearce's last playing season ended in promotion to the Premiership, 2002

I'm getting to the age where a nice tea and scone are right up my street. I'll take the missus out and we'll find a quaint tea-room somewhere.
STUART PEARCE on retiring from football shortly before his 40th birthday, 2002

PELE

How do you spell Pele? G–O–D.
HEADLINE in the Sunday Times *after Brazil's World Cup success, 1970*

Pele does everything superbly, with the possible exception of taking a dive in an opponent's penalty area. He has to learn about that art, though with his skills I can't think why he bothers to lower himself and start acting.
MARTIN PETERS, England midfielder, 1970

I go much faster Than those who run Without thinking.

POEM by Pele, from My Life and the Beautiful Game, *1977*

I had the pleasure of being in Pele's company more than once, and if there was ever a World Drinking XI, he would get the No.10 shirt.
ALAN HUDSON, former England midfielder, 1996

Football is like music, where there is Beethoven and the rest. In football, there is Pele and the rest.
PELE on the decision by FIFA, football's world governing body, to split a player-of-the-century award between himself and Diego Maradona, 2001

People say 'Pele! Pele! Pele!' all over the world but no one remembers Edson. Edson is the person who has the feelings, who has the family and works hard. Pele is the idol. Pele doesn't die. Pele will never die and will go on for ever. But Edson is a normal person who is going to die one day, and the people forget that.
PELE, real name Edson Arantes de Nascimento, 2003

Pele knows nothing about the game. He's done nothing as a coach and his analysis is always wrong. If you want to win a title, do the opposite of what Pele says.
LUIZ FELIPE SCOLARI, Brazil coach, on winning the World Cup after criticism by Pele, 2002

Even if you tried to create the ideal footballer on a computer, there could never be another like Pele.
SCOLARI, 2004

Nowadays a player given a yellow card is scared to get sent off. In my day you didn't have this. That's why if I was playing today I wouldn't have scored 1,200 goals, I would have scored 2,400 – double the amount – because there is better protection.
PELE, 2003

Pele is the John Lennon of football. He's still the benchmark.

NOEL GALLAGHER, member of Oasis and Manchester City fan, 2006

Pele is well known for the shit he talks. Nobody should take him seriously. I don't want to end up a bitter old man like him who talks only bollocks.
RONALDO, Brazil striker, after Pele criticised him, 2006

MARTIN PETERS

Martin Peters is a player 10 years ahead of his time.
ALF RAMSEY, England manager, 1968

He's the one who's 10 years ahead of his time so we've got to wait for him to come good.
MALCOLM ALLISON, Manchester City manager and TV World Cup panellist, 1970

EMMANUEL PETIT

He's tall, he's quick, his name's a porno flick, Emmanuel, Emmanuel.
SONG by Arsenal fans in praise of Petit, 1999

I was delighted to see *American Beauty* get some Oscars. At times I felt my life was being projected on the screen.
PETIT, Barcelona midfielder, 2000

MICHEL PLATINI

I bought him for the price of a piece of bread. But the bread came liberally spread in *pate de foie gras.*
GIANNI AGNELLI, Juventus president, on signing the French international, 2002

FERENC PUSKAS

His shooting was unbelievable and his left foot was like a hand. He could do anything with it. In the showers he would even juggle with the soap.
FRANCISCO GENTO, Real Madrid colleague, in Motson and Rowlinson, The European Cup 1955–80, *1980*

The Indian ambassador said: 'Inocencio, haven't Real Madrid paid too much for the Englishman [David Beckham]?' The Hungarian ambassador told me: 'He's hardly Puskas.' I replied: 'Puskas was better but sold fewer shirts in India.'
INOCENCIO ARIAS, Spain's ambassador to the United Nations, 2003

He had a seventh sense for football. Offer him 1,000 solutions and he'd pick the 1,001st.
NANDOR HIDEGKUTI, team-mate in the great Hungary side of the 1950s, after Puskas's death, 2006

NIALL QUINN

Anyone who uses the word 'quintessentially' during a half-time talk is talking crap.
MICK McCARTHY, Republic of Ireland manager, after Quinn made a suggestion during an international match, 1998

In Ireland he is known as Sheikh Quinn because he's got nearly as many racehorses as the Aga Khan. I always knew he'd be rich and famous so I'm pleased he still says hello to me. When I finish in football, I can proudly boast that I've roomed with Niall Quinn.
DAVID O'LEARY, former Arsenal and Republic of Ireland team-mate, 1999

LUCAS RADEBE

What are you doing here? *(To aides)* This is my hero. I call him 'Big Tree'.
NELSON MANDELA, former president of South Africa, after meeting Radebe at a civic reception in Leeds (when he thought he was in Liverpool), 2001

I love the club, place, the vibe. But when I leave I have to be able to walk.
RADEBE after serious injuries forced his retirement at Leeds, 2005

FABRIZIO RAVANELLI

During the match he insulted me 150,000 times.
MARCEL DESAILLY, Chelsea defender, after rowing with the Italian striker during and after a match at Derby, 2001

I started the shirt-lifting thing and I'm still the best at it.
RAVANELLI struggling with colloquialisms at Derby, 2002

CYRILLE REGIS

I know Cyrille has found God. Now I want him to find the devil.
RON ATKINSON, Aston Villa manager, 1992

JOHN ROBERTSON

He was a very unattractive young man. If ever I felt off colour I'd sit next to him because compared with this fat, dumpy lad I was Errol Flynn. But give him the ball and a yard of grass and he was an artist.
BRIAN CLOUGH, the Scotland winger's former manager at Nottingham Forest, 1990

BRYAN ROBSON

I wish I was England coach because I'd teach Bryan Robson not to kick and foul people when things go wrong.
BRIAN CLOUGH, Nottingham Forest manager, 1983

England's Captain Marvel.
BOBBY ROBSON, England manager, 1989

Some said his bravery bordered on stupidity, but without that courage he would have been just another good player.
BOBBY ROBSON in Against All Odds, *1990*

NEIL RUDDOCK

Hearing Ruddock claiming to be a nice guy was shocking. Some people behave like monsters and the next day say they're not guilty.
ARSENE WENGER, Arsenal manager, after the clash with Patrick Vieira, 1999

IAN RUSH

Painful to watch, but beautiful.
DAVID PLEAT, Luton manager, after Rush scored five for Liverpool against his team, 1983

If I was really unhappy I would rather go home and play for Flint Town United.
RUSH, struggling to settle in Italy with Juventus, 1988

Sometimes I think people don't realise that Wales exists as a country. Pele has picked Gary Lineker in his list of the 125 greatest living footballers. Having played with Lineker and Ian Rush, I can tell you Rushie was twice the player.
NEVILLE SOUTHALL, former Everton and Wales goalkeeper, 2004

JOHN SCALES

His team-mates started to call him Gigolo. Unfortunately, it took me a while to cotton on to the full significance of the nickname.
ALEX BEST, former girlfriend of Scales and ex-wife of George Best, 2005

PETER SCHMEICHEL

Schmeichel was towering over me and the other players were covering their eyes. I was looking up and thinking: 'If he does hit me, I'm dead.'
SIR ALEX FERGUSON, the Dane's former manager, recalling a dressing-room clash, 2006

Peter returns, but the operation has not worked because he still won't admit it when he has made a mistake.
BRIAN McCLAIR, Manchester United colleague, in his diary in United Magazine, *1995*

His sheer presence frightens opponents. In one match recently, Spurs hit the bar twice and I'm sure it was because they were trying to avoid him.
RUUD GULLIT, Chelsea player-manager, 1997

DAVID SEAMAN

Q: Why is Nayim the most virile player in Europe?
A: Because he can lob Seaman from 50 yards.
JOKE by Tottenham fans after the ex-Spurs player Nayim scored from long range to clinch the Cup-Winners' Cup for Zaragoza against Arsenal, 1995

After the Nayim goal in Paris, people thought it was funny to totter backwards like I did that night and pretend to watch a ball dipping over their heads.
SEAMAN, 1997

That David Seaman is a handsome young man but he spends too much time looking in his mirror rather than at the ball. You can't keep goal with hair like that.
BRIAN CLOUGH *on the England keeper's ponytail, 2000*

I'd like to think that no professional stylist would do this for him. It's kitsch, but surely not deliberately so.
NICKY CLARKE, *celebrity hairdresser, on Seaman's ponytail, 2001*

I've told him to cut off his ponytail. It makes him less aerodynamic.

ARSENE WENGER, *Arsenal manager, 2002*

David Seaman looked a broken man afterwards. I told him: 'If you go on thinking about that goal, you'll break yourself down. You must stop it. It's over. You saved us in Germany and in other games here, so you shouldn't think about it any more.'
SVEN-GÖRAN ERIKSSON *after Seaman let a long-range free-kick drift over him for Brazil's winner v England, World Cup finals, 2002*

I haven't seen [Ronaldinho's] winner yet. It's not that I'm avoiding it, just that my little girl has been watching *Teletubbies* all the time.
SEAMAN *after arriving home from England's exit, 2002*

A great ability of Seaman's, one I lacked, was his knack of calming people down… The big smile and the arm round the shoulder providing a steadying influence on his team-mates.
PETER SCHMEICHEL, *Seaman's predecessor in Manchester City's goal, 2004*

I've always thought it a travesty that people talk of 'the famous Arsenal back four'. It should be 'the famous back five'.
SCHMEICHEL *on Seaman's sudden retirement, 2004*

ALAN SHEARER

In terms of bringing charisma to the club, Eric [Cantona] had an impact Shearer could never have matched. Yet in the long term, Shearer could have won us the European Cup. I think he was the missing ingredient for us in Europe.
SIR ALEX FERGUSON, Manchester United manager, on being spurned by the young Shearer, 2003

A person you'd be delighted to have as your son.
KENNY DALGLISH, his Blackburn manager, 1992

Alan is old beyond his ears, like 23 going on 50. His favourite record is 'Sailing' by Rod Stewart. Makes me feel like slapping him round the face and saying: 'Get a grip on yourself!'
GRAEME LE SAUX, Blackburn colleague, 1994

Sunday 31 July: I manage to venture out of the house to turn the sprinkler on the lawn and then on to the local garden centre with [daughter] Chloe to feed the ducks.
SHEARER in Diary of a Season: The Inside Story of a Champion Year, *1995*

I don't what I'd have done if I hadn't become a footballer. At school I put down 'dustbin man' on a careers questionnaire, but my dad made me change it to 'joiner'.
SHEARER, 1998

Alan Shearer is boring. We call him Mary Poppins.

FREDDY SHEPHERD, Newcastle director, secretly recorded by a News of the World *reporter, 1998*

I love playing against Alan. It's always a tough, fully committed, passionate, no-diving, no-cheating, English-style game between the two of us, which supporters love to watch.
TONY ADAMS, Arsenal captain, 1999

I went on the bench and didn't moan or groan. Mind you, I did the following day.
SHEARER after Ruud Gullit relegated him to substitute v Sunderland, 1999

Shearer has always been the favourite, always picked, chosen son of all our national managers during the 1990s. It is an issue which bugs me. You are supposed to pick the best 11, not shape every strategy around a supposed golden boy.
ANDY COLE, fellow England striker, in his autobiography, 1999

I see I've been used again to help sell somebody's book. Alex Ferguson, Graham Kelly and now Andy Cole have all had a pop in print at yours truly. Glad to have been of assistance, Andy.
SHEARER in his Newcastle programme column, 1999

I remember Ray Harford when he was Blackburn manager telling me how Bill Nicholson, the great Spurs manager, walked his daughter down the aisle in floods of tears on her wedding day. He found himself asking: 'Where have all the years gone?' He had missed seeing her grow up because of his involvement in football. I don't want that to happen to me.
SHEARER announcing his international retirement, 2000

The truth was that Alan's game really had fallen away. I sat him down and we had long, intense chats. I told him bluntly he had stopped doing the things that made him a genuine great. Some people told me Newcastle expected him to do too much, but I told them – and Alan – he wasn't doing half enough. His whole movement had stopped and he was just wearily going through the motions.
BOBBY ROBSON, Newcastle manager, 2000

A lot of players are born with natural skill. I wasn't one of them.

SHEARER, 2003

I looked him in the face and told him: 'You're the most overrated player I've ever seen.' He didn't reply. Maybe that's why they call him Mary Poppins; because he's always so innocent.
RUUD GULLIT recalling his time as Shearer's manager at Newcastle, 2004

[Shearer] has said he'll quit, but listen: I said I loved my wife when I left her this morning. Wait until tomorrow. Things change.
FREDDY SHEPHERD, Newcastle chairman, before Shearer decided to delay his retirement for a year, 2005

They should have pensioned off Alan Shearer 18 months ago. Bambi in roller boots, that's what I call him.
SID WADDELL, darts commentator and Newcastle fan, 2006

TOMMY SMITH

With 11 Tommy Smiths you would not only win the European Cup, you would fancy your chances against the whole Russian Army.
MARTIN BUCHAN, Manchester United captain, 1977

OLE GUNNAR SOLSKJAER

He's the best substitute in the world. If I ever feel guilty about the teams I pick, it invariably centres round him because he really deserves better. But the fact is that he's better than anyone at the club as a sub. He can come on and find the flow easily.
ALEX FERGUSON after the Norwegian scored four for Manchester United in an 18-minute cameo at Nottingham Forest, 1999

I was only on for 10 minutes.
SOLSKJAER playing down his European Cup-winning goal of 1999 on his retirement, 2007

GRAEME SOUNESS

If he was a chocolate drop, he'd eat himself.
ARCHIE GEMMILL, Scotland team-mate, 1978

He's the nastiest, most ruthless man in soccer. Don Revie's bunch of assassins at Leeds were bad enough, but there is a streak in Souness that puts him top of the list.
FRANK WORTHINGTON, widely travelled striker, 1984

They serve a drink in Glasgow called the Souness – one half and you're off.
TOMMY DOCHERTY after Souness attracted red cards with Rangers, 1988

I wouldn't go so far as to say he's a complete nutcase, but he comes very close.
TERRY YORATH, former midfield adversary, 1993

GARETH SOUTHGATE

I've only taken one penalty before, for Crystal Palace at Ipswich when it was 2–2 in the 89th minute. I hit the post and we went down that year. But I think I would be far more comfortable now than I was then.
SOUTHGATE, England defender, tempts fate before his decisive miss in the shoot-out v Germany, European Championship semi-final, 1996

Why didn't you just belt the ball?
BARBARA SOUTHGATE to her son after his infamous miss, 1996

I'm sure that people will always say: 'He's the idiot who missed that penalty.'
SOUTHGATE, 1997

Q: One wish?
A: Apart from world peace, a long, injury-free career.
SOUTHGATE in a Villa programme questionnaire, 1995

The worst part is that Gareth is such a nice guy. You never normally hear him utter a single swear word.
DAVID JAMES, Villa goalkeeper, after Southgate was fined £5,000 by the FA for verbal abuse of referee Jeff Winter, 1999

NOBBY STILES

Andy Lochhead was streaking towards goal when Nobby clipped him from behind. Out came my book and Stiles, full of apologies, pleaded: 'It's the floodlights, ref. They shine in my contact lenses and I can't see a thing.' As I was writing, Nobby leaned over and said: 'You spell it with an "I" not a "Y".'
PAT PARTRIDGE. Football League referee, in Oh, Ref!, *1979*

GORDON STRACHAN

A lot of the time he was playing from memory – but my God, what a memory.
RON ATKINSON, Manchester United manager, on Strachan's comeback after injury, 1985

He can destroy at once the big tough guys in the dressing room with one lash of his coruscating tongue. That's why he earned the nickname 'King Tongue'.
HOWARD WILKINSON, Leeds manager, in Managing to Succeed: My Life in Football Management, *1992*

There's nobody fitter at his age, except maybe Racquel Welch.
RON ATKINSON, Coventry manager, on Strachan's form at 39, 1995

MICKEY THOMAS

I don't mind Roy Keane making £60,000 a week. I was making the same when I was playing. The only difference is that I was printing my own.
THOMAS, former Manchester United midfielder with a conviction for counterfeiting currency, 2002

BERT TRAUTMANN

What manner of man is Trautmann? He is of the Nordic type, with blond hair, keen grey eyes, a gentle manner, a charming smile and a deceptive air of indolence in repose. But a steely look can come into those grey eyes; the thrust of a panther's spring into those clean, straight limbs; and few can pass with such lightning rapidity from complete immobility to energetic action. In straightforwardness and clean living he is a model for any young boy.
H.D. DAVIES, Guardian *football writer, on Manchester City's German goalkeeper in the* Boy's Own Paper, *1957*

MARCO VAN BASTEN

Orrible Little Basten
HEADLINE in the Sun *after the striker's hat-trick, Netherlands v England, European Championship finals, 1988*

Marco played football like a ballerina, like Rudolf Nureyev with a colossal body, but eventually his ankle wouldn't stand the strain.
RENE MARTI, Swiss surgeon who treated van Basten before his retirement, 1995

TERRY VENABLES

A clever, cocky player – arrogant, but then he was good.
MICK PEJIC, ex-Stoke and England defender, 1989

BERTI VOGTS

A team of 11 Berti Vogtses would be unbeatable.
KEVIN KEEGAN after playing for England against the West Germany defender, 1975

CHRIS WADDLE

For a defender, Waddle running at you is the worst sight in football.
ALAN HANSEN, 1993

PAUL WARHURST

The lad was sent off for foul and abusive language but he swears blind he didn't say a word.
JOE ROYLE, Oldham manager, after Warhurst's dismissal v Notts County, 1990

RAY WILKINS

He can't run, can't tackle and can't head a ball. The only time he gets forward is to toss the coin.
TOMMY DOCHERTY, on the midfielder dubbed 'The Crab' by Ron Atkinson, 1981

He played the game in the Liverpool fashion and I could never understand why he was criticised for that.
TREVOR BROOKING, former England midfielder, in his book 100 Great British Footballers, *1988.*

DENNIS WISE

I remember a game against him for Liverpool at Chelsea when he grabbed my tit. When I got changed, I had five finger marks around the nipple, like a love bite. That took some explaining to me missus.
JASON McATEER, Sunderland midfielder, before facing Wise in an FA Cup semi-final v Millwall, 2004

Monster, monster shocked.
ERIC HALL, Wise's agent, on his client's three-month jail sentence for assault, 1995

Monster, monster happy.
ERIC HALL after Wise's sentence was suspended, 1995

I'm not the sort of person you want around if you want peace and order in your life.
WISE in his autobiography, 1999

Wisey is one of those little big men in the mould of Billy Bremner. Five foot nothing off the pitch, ten feet tall on it.
VINNIE JONES, former Wimbledon team-mate, 2000

Whatever player he's up against, he tries to wind them up. If he fouls you he normally picks you up, but the referee doesn't see what he picks you up by.
RYAN GIGGS, Manchester United opponent, 2000

Ninety-five per cent of my language problems are the fault of that stupid little midget.
GIANFRANCO ZOLA on his former Chelsea team-mate, 2003

FRANK WORTHINGTON

The way he is losing his hair he'll be the first bald guy ever to do impressions of Elvis Presley.
GRAEME SOUNESS, Scotland midfielder, 1984

IAN WRIGHT

On his first day at Palace he told me he wanted to play for England, a bold statement for someone who had just walked in off a building site.
STEVE COPPELL, Crystal Palace manager, 1993

I just wish the record was going to someone else. I don't have a very high opinion of Ian Wright.
JOAN BASTIN, widow of Cliff Bastin, before Wright broke his all-time Arsenal scoring record, 1997

My surname's blinding for the press. Some of the headlines write themselves.
WRIGHT, 1998

To be quite honest I have always considered Wright to be a bit of an idiot.
PETER SCHMEICHEL, former adversary, in his autobiography, 1999

He would torment me the whole game. He was a right handful. Apart from being a nightmare to defend against, he gives it loads whenever he comes near you. I used to get him and Mark Bright running past me saying: 'Do you know where your missus was last night? We do – and she makes a great breakfast.'
NEIL RUDDOCK, former Liverpool and Tottenham defender, 2000

RON YEATS

He's a colossus. Come outside and I'll give you a walk round him.
BILL SHANKLY, Liverpool manager, to reporters after signing the 6ft 2in, 14-stone centre-half, 1961

With him at centre-half we could play Arthur Askey in goal.
SHANKLY, 1962

TONY YEBOAH

The third goal was in the net in the time it takes a snowflake to melt on a hot stove.
HOWARD WILKINSON, Leeds manager, on the Ghanaian's hat-trick v Ipswich, 1995

Sometimes, when I score, I can't even explain to myself how I did it.
YEBOAH, 1995

ZINEDINE ZIDANE

He proved in the final that he is not a god. He is merely a superman.
ROLAN COURBIS, Zidane's early mentor, after the France captain was sent off for butting Italy's Marco Materazzi in the World Cup final, 2006

When we don't know what to do, we give it to him and he works something out.
BIXENTE LIZARAZU, France defender, 2000

Sometimes you just want to stop playing just to watch him.
CHRISTOPHE DUGARRY, France colleague, 2000

Nobody knows whether Zidane is an angel or a demon. He smiles like Saint Teresa and grimaces like a serial killer.
JEAN-LOUIS MURAT, French rock singer, 2004

I was lucky to come from a difficult area. It teaches you not just about football but also about life. There were lots of kids from different races and poor families. People had to struggle to get through the day. Music was important. Football was the easy part.
ZIDANE, 2004

My father was my inspiration. He taught us that an immigrant must work twice as hard as anybody else; that he must never give up.
ZIDANE, whose Algerian father was a warehouseman in Marseilles, 2004

The No. 1 player ever in Europe, with Franz Beckenbauer second for his defending and creating and then Johan Cruyff, who was not easy to defend against. When Zidane gets the ball, it's very difficult to stop him.
SVEN-GÖRAN ERIKSSON, England coach, 2004

Zidane appeared and left Beckham in his underwear.
MARCA, Spanish newspaper, after the Frenchman's two late goals stunned England and his Real Madrid colleague, 2004

They say an unmade bed is art. But what Zidane does, that's art.
GORDON STRACHAN, former Scotland captain, working as a TV summariser, European Championship finals, 2004

The best of the best, as a human being and a player. He has a really big heart and you never hear anything bad about him.
PATRICK VIEIRA, France team-mate, 2004

Zidane plays as if he has silk gloves on each foot.
ALFREDO DI STEFANO, Real Madrid predecessor, 2005

He does things with his feet that others can't do with their hands.
THIERRY HENRY, France team-mate, 2006

What [Marco Materazzi] said was very personal. He insulted my mother, my sister, my whole family, and he did it not once, twice, but three times. I'd rather have been punched in the face than hear those insults. The third time it was too much. I'm a man first and foremost.
ZIDANE on what made him snap and assault Italy's Materazzi in the World Cup final, 2006

I did not call Zidane a terrorist. I'm ignorant; I don't even know what the word means. It was an insult like you hear dozens of times. I certainly didn't mention Zidane's mother – for me, a mother is sacred.
MARCO MATERAZZI, Italy defender, on what he said to provoke Zidane into butting him, 2006

A man, the son of Algerian immigrants, placed on a pinnacle by a whole country, whose fairy story was admired by the whole world, became with one gesture a bad example to thousands of children in the housing estates who dream of being a future Zizou.
EDITORIAL in Le Monde, *2006*

GIANFRANCO ZOLA

The moment I turned up for training and saw Zola, I knew it was time to go.
JOHN SPENCER, Scotland striker, on the Italian's impact at Chelsea, 1997

One hundred and sixty-eight centimetres of sheer fantasy.
PROGRAMME pen-picture, England v Italy, 1997

I'm not a grandfather yet.
ZOLA after his first Serie A goal in eight years, for Cagliari, 2005

three

CLUBS

ARSENAL

One–nil to the Arsenal, and that's how we like it.
GEORGE ALLISON, Arsenal manager, playing himself in the crime-thriller film The Arsenal Stadium Mystery, *1939*

You'll have to watch these Trojans. They don't play your game – they play an attacking game.
ALLISON giving a team talk in The Arsenal Stadium Mystery, *1939*

Only people who will not spend big money on transfers need apply.
ADVERTISEMENT for post of Arsenal secretary-manager in Athletic News, *1925. Herbert Chapman got the job*

Bill Shankly didn't really give Arsenal any credit. He said: 'They're nothing to beat, these Cockneys from London.'
PETER THOMPSON, former Liverpool winger, on his manager's team talk before Arsenal won the FA Cup in 1971 to complete their first Double, in David Tossell's Seventy-One Guns, *2002*

If [Osvaldo] Ardiles had gone to Arsenal they would have had him marking the opposing goalkeeper or something.
DANNY BLANCHFLOWER, former Tottenham captain, 1981

Boring, boring Arsenal.
CHANT by opposition fans, adopted with irony by Arsenal supporters as their team took the championship, 1991

I didn't want to play another 300 games with mediocre players and be up against it. I wanted the ball to be up the opposing end so I could get my cigars out at the back.
TONY ADAMS, Arsenal captain, on the importance of bringing in Dennis Bergkamp and others, 1995

At some clubs success is accidental. At Arsenal it is compulsory.
ARSENE WENGER, manager, on his first Premiership and FA Cup Double, 1998

When Arsenal aren't doing well in a game they turn it into a battle to try to make the opposition lose their concentration...The number of fights involving Arsenal is more than Wimbledon in their heyday.
ALEX FERGUSON, Manchester United manager, 1999

Being a Gunner is a happiness and a joy I can hardly begin to believe.

FREDDIE LJUNGBERG, Swedish midfielder, after Arsenal won the League and FA Cup Double, 2002

We give people what they like to see – pace, commitment, attacking football – and sometimes if we go overboard, I'm sorry.
WENGER on his team's red-card tally, 2002

We should not have reacted like we did. But I find the sensitivity of this country very selective. Suddenly the whole of England is so shocked, as if there's never any violence in your society.
WENGER after Arsenal incurred FA charges following the 'Battle of Old Trafford', 2003

You [the media] have the right to say Arsenal are a dirty team and should have been fined £700,000. But you will never, ever find anyone in my club that I told to go out and kick someone to win the game. If you find him, introduce him to me and I will face him.
WENGER after the FA punished several Arsenal players following the United game, 2003

I have read that Arsenal did a deal [with the FA] and I think that was the suspicion throughout the country. They've been doing deals for years. We hope we win titles without anybody's help.
SIR ALEX FERGUSON claiming the punishments for Arsenal were not strong enough, 2003

Even if you hang us, it is not enough for some people. They want us hung twice, and in Hyde Park, in front of the whole country.
WENGER responding to Ferguson, 2003

What Arsenal players did [at Old Trafford] last season was the worst thing I've seen in this sport. They're a mob – they get away with murder.
FERGUSON during the build-up to Arsenal's visit to United, 2004

That's what children do, throw food. That's not fighting. We were real men. We'd have chinned them.
GEORGE BEST after Arsenal players allegedly threw pizza at Ferguson, 2004

If you look at our red cards, it's mostly a case of provocation. You can say that winding someone up is clever but you'll never convince me it's fair. Unfortunately it has worked for 52 players.
WENGER after Arsenal passed the half-century for dismissals under him, 2003

It's amazing how a team can go from the most boring to the most exciting in the league. This is the closest I have seen to the Dutch concept of Total Football. They can all play one-touch stuff, and if you have that throughout your side, it's unstoppable.
DENNIS BERGKAMP, Arsenal's former Netherlands striker, after Premiership title success, 2004

Arsenal caress a football the way I dreamed of caressing Marilyn Monroe.
BRIAN CLOUGH, 2004

Arsenal are nothing short of incredible. They could have been nearly as good as us.
CLOUGH after Arsenal beat Nottingham Forest's 42-match unbeaten record, 2004

They're the worst losers of all time. They don't know how to lose. Maybe it's just Manchester United. They don't lose many games to other teams.
SIR ALEX FERGUSON, 2005

When you work on the training ground every day, you don't notice where they're from. I don't even know where I'm from.
WENGER after Arsenal's XI and substitutes contained no British players, 2005

Our objective is to keep Arsenal English, but with a lot of foreign players.
PETER HILL-WOOD, chairman, after American interest in buying the club, 2007

ASTON VILLA

Big clubs do get the decisions [from referees]. I'm not moaning about that –
I just want to make Aston Villa a big club so we get them too.
MARTIN O'NEILL, Villa manager, 2007

REPORTER: Doug Ellis has had 10 managers at Villa since you've been at
United.
FERGUSON: That averages out at a year and a half per manager. You'll never
get continuity like that.
EXCHANGE at Sir Alex Ferguson's press briefing before Manchester United v Villa, 2003

There's an aura about this club, a sense of history and tradition. Even the
name is beautifully symmetrical, with five letters in each word.
JOHN GREGORY, Villa manager, 1998

To compete week in, week out against the Man Us, Arsenals, Liverpools and
Chelseas says a lot about the little team from Birmingham that plays so big!
PROGRAMME for New York city tournament featuring Villa, 1999

Too many of us are content to play in the comfort zone. It doesn't hurt
enough if we lose. I have never heard a cross word in training, let alone seen a
punch-up. At Arsenal, something kicked off every week.
PAUL MERSON, Villa midfielder, 2000

*We were wimpish. And wanky, like
that character says on* Men Behaving
Badly. *Have you seen that?*
GREGORY to the media after Villa's Worthington Cup semi-final loss to Leicester, 2000

Gene Simmons constantly reminds us that Kiss were one of the biggest groups
in the world. This is like being reminded that Aston Villa won the European
Cup in 1982. You can only wonder what kind of world it was that allowed
such a thing to happen.
DAVID HEPWORTH, rock journalist, in Word magazine, 2006

BARCELONA

It's true what they say. Barcelona is more than a football club.
THIERRY HENRY when 25,000 Catalans turned out to welcome him to the club after his transfer from Arsenal, 2007

Barcelona is the best club in the world but a dreadful place to be. They never let you forget you're a South American and a spot on the face of humanity.
DIEGO MARADONA, ex-Barcelona player, 2001

BARNET

Barnet has been a big part of my life. I took a second mortgage to save them. I gave them my testimonial money. I got arrested driving the tractor on Christmas Day to flatten the pitch, and when I told the policeman I was the manager, he said: 'Oh yeah, and I'm George Best.'
BARRY FRY after leaving the Barnet manager's job for Southend, 1993

BARRY TOWN

Thank God for Barry Town
HEADLINE in Swiss tabloid Blick, hailing the Welsh Premier League's bottom club as the only one in Europe worse than Grasshopper Zurich, 2003

BIRMINGHAM CITY

Q: What attracted you to Birmingham City?
A: Nothing. I was told by my boss [David Sullivan] to come here.
KARREN BRADY, managing director, in interview with King's Heath Concorde FC fanzine, 1993

When I arrived there were 47 players, and it was 49 a week later when I found two more in a cupboard.
TREVOR FRANCIS on taking over as Birmingham manager from Barry Fry, 1999

I'd have to be mad to want to come to Birmingham. I'm only here because Deportivo [La Coruna] made it happen and my wife forced me.
WALTER PANDIANI, Uruguayan striker, on loan from Spain to St Andrew's, 2005

BLACKBURN ROVERS

All hail, ye gallant Rover lads!
Etonians thought you were but cads
They've found at football game their dads
By meeting Blackburn Rovers.
SONG by Blackburn supporters before the FA Cup final, 1882. Old Etonians won 1–0

It always seems to be pitch dark by 3.30pm in Blackburn. There is no language school, no fitness centre. And if you want to go shopping, there is nothing to buy. When I see the way people live up here, I realise how lucky I am.
STEPHANE HENCHOZ, Swiss defender, looking back on his spell with Blackburn, 1999

Eriksson obviously fancied the sunshine more than the cobbled streets and flat caps.
TONY PARKES, regular Blackburn caretaker-manager, after Sven-Göran Eriksson rejected Rovers to remain in Italy, 1997

During the afternoon it rained only in Blackburn's stadium. Our kit man saw it. There must be a micro climate here.
JOSE MOURINHO, Chelsea manager, 2005

It's obviously not our dream to have to go to Blackburn. It's hardly the most fantastic place touristically.
ARSENE WENGER as Arsenal faced an FA Cup replay at Ewood Park, 2007

BURNLEY

They have the potential to be a sleeping giant.
CHRIS WADDLE on becoming player-manager, 1997

A motley crew of ageing pros, stage-struck lads and inadequates who would struggle to get a game for Holby City.
STAN TERNENT, recalling the squad he inherited in 1998 on becoming Burnley manager, 2003

CARDIFF CITY

The only way you can see Cardiff is as another Barcelona. Yes, Barcelona is a football club, but it is also something that brings all the Catalan people together. Except Cardiff is more.
SAM HAMMAM, Cardiff City owner, 2002

We play orgy football. The other team know they're going to get it, but they don't know from who or from where.
HAMMAM, 2006

CARLISLE UNITED

We have a 10-year plan to reach the Premiership. So now we're a year ahead of schedule.
MICHAEL KNIGHTON, Carlisle chairman, celebrating promotion to the Second Division, 1995. They were relegated a year later

If that's not entertainment, I'm a banana.
KNIGHTON after the club escaped relegation from the Football League with a last-gasp goal by goalkeeper Jimmy Glass, quoted in Glass's book One Hit Wonder, *2004*

CELTIC

We don't just want to win the European Cup. We want to do it playing good football, to make neutrals glad we won it, pleased to remember how we did it.
JOCK STEIN, Celtic manager, before the victory v Inter Milan in Lisbon, 1967

The chairman, Robert Kelly, was the brain that fashioned the organisation with Jock Stein at its head. If he had a weakness it was his obsession with the players of the past and especially the great Celtic team before the First World War. The accolade was put on the trip [from Lisbon] when he declared solemnly and it seemed with some pain: 'This was the greatest Celtic team of all time.' He might have expanded the adjective to Scottish or even British and nobody would have questioned his judgement.
JOHN RAFFERTY, football writer for the Scotsman, *on the 1967 European Cup winners in the book* We'll Support You Evermore, *1976*

I can still remember it exactly as it was. And they can't take that feeling away from you. It was the most wonderfullest feeling in my life. I'll never ever, ever, ever forget it.
JIMMY JOHNSTONE, Celtic winger in the '67 final, in the documentary film Lord of the Wing, *2004*

Winning the European Cup might have been for Scotland but it definitely wasn't for Britain. It was for Celtic.
BILLY McNEILL, captain of the 1967 'Lisbon Lions', 1995

There's nothing worse than sitting in the dressing room at Celtic Park after a defeat, not a word being said, listening to them going mental next door.
ALLY McCOIST, Rangers striker, 1994

Are they really any better than the Coventrys and Southamptons of this world?
MARTIN EDWARDS, Manchester United chairman, on reports that Celtic wanted to join the English Premiership, 1997

Celtic are a big team in a crap league and understandably they want to move to a bigger stage.
XAVIER WIGGINS, Wimbledon supporters' spokesman, on speculation that the Glasgow club planned to take over the Dons, 1997

There's a culture at Celtic whereby if anything goes against them, a conspiracy theory comes out.
JOHN YORKSTON, Dunfermline chairman, after a Celtic player accused the Fife side of 'lying down' in a 6–1 defeat by Rangers, 2003

Are you Rangers in disguise?
SONG by FC Copenhagen fans when their team led Celtic 3–0, 2006

CHARLTON ATHLETIC

Strange how a ground can catch hold of you. I came past The Valley tonight and found myself staring at it. All those memories! We had to go back, didn't we?
ROGER ALWEN, Charlton chairman, announcing their return 'home', 1989

Unmatched by the record of any club in the British Isles, cradle of Association Football, or Soccer, the history of Charlton Athletic, one of the most sensational aggregations of the booting game ever to essay an invasion of the United States and Canada, is truly monumental in athletic annals.
PROGRAMME notes, Illinois All Stars v Charlton, in Chicago, 1937

CHELSEA

It's impossible to match Chelsea's spending power – unless we find oil at Highbury.
ARSENE WENGER, Arsenal manager, as Roman Abramovich financed massive spending at Stamford Bridge, 2005

Chelsea are the most unusual of clubs. They have never done what every other club was doing at the same time as every other club was doing it.
RALPH FINN, author, A History of Chelsea FC, 1969

I hate Chelsea. They stand for everything I hate in football, with their showbiz supporters. They come out looking more like the [dance troupe] Young Generation than a football team.
TERRY COLLIER, played by James Bolam, in the TV sit-com Whatever Happened to the Likely Lads? by Dick Clement and Ian La Frenais, 1974

Commodore already sponsors Tessa Sanderson, Chelsea FC and a football team, Bayern Munich.
COMPUTER GUARDIAN, 1988

When I left Chelsea before, I said I would have parachuted out of a snake's backside to get away, but circumstances change.
GRAEME LE SAUX on returning to Chelsea from Blackburn, 1997

When I first heard about Viagra I thought it was a new player Chelsea had bought.

TONY BANKS MP, Labour, Minister for Sport and Chelsea fan, 1998

Obviously there's a language barrier. The majority of the lads speak Italian, but there's a few who don't.
DENNIS WISE, Chelsea captain, 2000

When the first overseas players came we produced this book of Cockney rhyming slang. Luca [Vialli] and Ruud [Gullit] were fascinated and took it home to study. One day we were in a team meeting and Ruud suddenly said: 'I am a grave-digger...and a very rich one.'
WISE, 2000

We're a Continental team playing in English football.
COLIN HUTCHINSON, Chelsea managing director, 2000

Chelsea are the Foreign Legion. They may play in the English league but they are no longer an English club. Sometimes there is not one Englishman in the team. I don't like it at all. I can't understand how the fans accept that.
JOHAN CRUYFF, Dutchman and former Barcelona player and coach, 2000

Chelsea is a very nice, beautiful, great club, but something is missing. Only small things need to be done to make this a top, top, top European club. It is a top club, but not a top, top, top club.
JIMMY FLOYD HASSELBAINK, Chelsea striker, 2002

Chelsea are a financially doped club. They have enhancement of performances because their financial resources are unlimited. It's not healthy for the market. If they see Steven Gerrard or Rio Ferdinand, they say: 'How much are you on? We'll offer you twice as much.'
ARSENE WENGER, 2005

Frankly, I'm amazed this could have happened in a hotel in the centre of London. They seem to think they are above everything.
WENGER on Chelsea's 'tapping up' of Arsenal's Ashley Cole, 2005

Chelsea now welcome black supporters, employ black stewards and have the most diverse team in the Premiership. If you'd told me that was going to happen when I played at Stamford Bridge in 1987, I'd have called you a liar.
GARTH CROOKS, BBC TV football reporter and former Tottenham player, 2005

It was incredible going into the Chelsea dressing room to swap shirts. It's bigger than my house.
DICKSON ETUHU, Norwich midfielder, after FA Cup defeat at Stamford Bridge, 2007

I guess when you've invested £500m it's a fantastic season to win the League Cup.
RICK PARRY, Liverpool chief executive, after they beat Chelsea to reach the Champions' League final, 2007

It looks like there's one rule in football that it is forbidden to give a penalty against Manchester United and another to give none in favour of Chelsea.
JOSE MOURINHO, 2007

Chelsea will never be as big a club as Man United. United have a history and charisma that can't be bought.
BRYAN ROBSON, former United captain, 2007

Liverpool fans can continue to chant 'No history' at us, but we continue to make it.
MOURINHO, 2007

COVENTRY CITY

If the *Titanic* had been painted sky blue it would never have sunk.
BRYAN RICHARDSON, Coventry chairman, after another escape from relegation, 1997

We should rename ourselves Coventry Houdini.

MIKE McGINNITY, Coventry vice-chairman, 1997

There is something curious about the relationship between Coventry and Villa. We don't particularly dislike them. But blimey, do they hate us.
JOHN GREGORY, Aston Villa manager, 2000

COWDENBEATH

Why the nickname 'Blue Brazil'? Easy. Cowden play in blue and have the same debt as a Third World country.
BIG BOB, Cowdenbeath diehard, quoted in Ronald Ferguson's Black Diamonds and the Blue Brazil, *1993*

CRYSTAL PALACE

It's like one of those fairytales where you see a beautiful castle but when you get inside you discover years of decay. The princess, which is the players, is asleep. I'm trying to wake her but it takes more than one kiss.
ALAN SMITH, Crystal Palace manager, 2000

I always thought Palace were a bit flighty, bit flash, lacking in substance – a legacy of Terry Venables and Malcolm Allison. In human form we were the *Fast Show* character – a little bit tasty, a little bit 'whoooar', a little bit 'wayyy'.
SIMON JORDAN, Palace chairman, 2005

DARLINGTON

Darlington will become the most successful club in England.
GEORGE REYNOLDS, millionaire chairman, 2000

DERBY COUNTY

Whichever teams win the league championship in the next 20 years, and I hope teams like Rochdale and Halifax will be among them, none of them will have as hard a job as we had. We did it with 12 players. Those London bums can't explain it.
BRIAN CLOUGH, Derby manager, after their title success, 1972

DONCASTER BELLES

Some of them came over like lager louts. I kept wondering how they could be so unprofessional.
GILL WYLIE, Arsenal ladies captain, on their rivals' performance in a TV documentary, 1995

DUNFERMLINE ATHLETIC

Towards the end I thought about bringing on my subs, Torvill and Dean.
TERRY BUTCHER, Motherwell manager, criticising Dunfermline's plastic pitch, 2005

EVERTON

When you play against the smaller clubs at Anfield you know the game will be narrow.
RAFAEL BENITEZ, Liverpool manager, after a derby draw, 2007

Benitez is in a minority of one in believing Everton is a small club. Somehow we expect more of a Liverpool manager.
KEITH WYNESS, Everton chief executive, 2007

PRINCESS MARGARET: But Mr Labone, where is Everton?
BRIAN LABONE: In Liverpool, Ma'am.
PRINCESS MARGARET: Of course, we had your first team here last year.
BILL SHANKLY , Liverpool manager, story of FA Cup final, 1966

If anyone ever mentions the Everton 'School of Soccer Science' to me again, well, I'm sorry, I just don't see it.
ROY EVANS, Liverpool manager, after bruising derby draw, 1995

I was told I was going to be the first of many big-money signings. Someone was telling fibs.
JOHN COLLINS, Everton midfielder, 1999

I soon got out of the habit of studying the top end of the league table.
WALTER SMITH, Everton manager, on the difference with his previous club, Rangers, 1999

We're going to make sure that everybody has to have haggis and porridge in the canteen from now on.
SMITH on the club's Scottish enclave, 1999

I went on to play for other clubs, and though I always wanted to win, losing never really seemed to hurt any more.
KEVIN RATCLIFFE, Everton captain of the 1980s, in Becky Tallentire's book Still Talking Blue, *2002*

I've always believed that the folk on the streets of Liverpool support Everton. That's why this is the People's Club.
DAVID MOYES on joining Everton from Preston as manager, 2002

EXETER CITY

I haven't felt this bad since I killed a man.
URI GELLER, Exeter City co-chairman and former Israeli soldier, after relegation from the
Football League, 2003

FULHAM

We've got a long-term plan for this club and apart from the results it's going
well.
ERNIE CLAY, Fulham chairman, 1980

REPORTER: Are funds available for new signings?
IAN BRANFOOT: Oh, yes. About £2.54.
EXCHANGE at the Fulham manager's post-match press conference in the pre-Fayed era, 1994

I am going to make Fulham the Manchester United of the South.
MOHAMED AL FAYED, Harrods owner, on buying the then third-tier club, 1997

When I joined Fulham, in '97, we didn't even have enough bloody kit. I
couldn't get my shorts on for my debut. They were all too small, so we had to
snip the sides with scissors. That's how far away we were from being a proper
Premier League club.
CHRIS COLEMAN, Real Sociedad coach and former Fulham player and manager, 2007

GILLINGHAM

The possibility of a European Super League in years to come makes
Gillingham a prime location for a club to play in this competition, with its
proximity to the Channel Tunnel and to Europe.
PAUL SCALLY, Gillingham chairman, 2000

GRIMSBY TOWN

It's a hard place to come for a southern team. You can dress well and have all
the nice watches in the world, but that won't buy you a result at Grimsby.
ALAN SMITH, Crystal Palace manager, at Grimsby, 2000

Last time Grimsby were top of the First Division, dinosaurs roamed the earth.

LENNIE LAWRENCE, Grimsby manager, 2001

When I came here my agent told me it was a good club and this and that. I found out it was exactly the opposite.
MARCEL CAS, Dutch midfielder, on being released by Grimsby, 2004

HARTLEPOOL UNITED

The listening bank refused to listen and the bank that likes to say yes said no.
GARRY GIBSON, Hartlepool chairman, after receiving a winding-up petition from the Inland Revenue, 1993

Since Hartlepool last scored you could have watched all three *Godfather* movies, waded through every technicolour moment of *Gone With the Wind*, and still had time to settle down to a two-hour episode of *Inspector Morse*.
HARTLEPOOL MAIL on the club's record-breaking run without a goal, 1993

HEART OF MIDLOTHIAN

[Vladimir] Romanov used to be a Soviet naval commander. He thinks he can run Heart of Midlothian as a Soviet submarine.
GEORGE FOULKES, former Hearts chairman, on Lithuanian owner Vladimir Romanov, 2006

It's better than *Celebrity Big Brother*.
JAMIE McALLISTER, Bristol City and ex-Hearts defender, as upheavals at Tynecastle coincided with allegations of racism to Indian actress Shilpa Shetty on the TV show, 2007

We feared the worst. We got it.
REPORT on the club website after Hearts lost 5–0 at Celtic, 2007

JUVENTUS

People ask whether I like to see a Juve victory or the better team win. I'm lucky – the two often coincide.
GIANNI AGNELLI, Juventus president, 2001

KILMARNOCK

Scorer for Kilmarnock, number 16 Dick Turpin.
TANNOY ANNOUNCER at Motherwell alleging robbery after Killie's Rhian Dodds scored a last-minute winner against the run of play, 2007

LEEDS UNITED

You Get Nowt for Being Second

TITLE of Billy Bremner book, 1969. Leeds finished runners-up five times during Bremner's time as player

I didn't used to be frightened on the football pitch. But I was always relieved to get off in one piece, particularly during those mid- and late 1960s when the likes of Leeds United were kicking anything that moved.
JIMMY GREAVES, former Tottenham striker, in This One's On Me, *1979*

Leeds [under Don Revie] would try to win by fair means or foul…They were too good to do things like that and should have won more than they did. They were a magnificent side, a team made in heaven.
FRANK McLINTOCK, former Arsenal captain, in David Tossell's book Seventy-One Guns, *2002*

If I try something a bit saucy, the Dutch and Belgians I play with shout 'Hard luck' or 'Try again' if it doesn't come off. At Leeds I'd turn round and there'd be someone with a fist up, threatening to chin me. One of my own team-mates!
DUNCAN McKENZIE, Leeds striker of the immediate post-Revie era, during his time with Anderlecht, 1976

There's a stereotype that goes with a lot of clubs. Spurs are called stylish, West Ham is the academy, Arsenal are resilient. But Leeds are always seen as cynical and intimidating. It becomes a tired cliché.
HOWARD WILKINSON, Leeds manager, 1991

I think this is the most wonderful place in Europe.
TONY YEBOAH, Leeds Ghanaian striker, 1995

Q: Do you know about Leeds's history and tradition?
A: Oh yes, I'm very familiar with John Smith's and Tetley's.
Q: I meant the Don Revie era.
A: Yes I know. It was a joke.
ALF-INGE HAALAND, Norway midfielder, in a radio interview on joining Leeds, 1997

There was a time when nobody could stand Leeds United.

DAVID O'LEARY, Leeds manager, 1999

My babies trust me because I am their friend. They know they are safe in my hands.
O'LEARY after his youthful side won 5–1 at Portsmouth, FA Cup, 1999

Q: Which team's results do you look for first?
A: Leeds United, Leeds Reserves, Leeds youth team, Leeds Permanent Building Society pub team, Leeds & Holbeck pub team, Leeds ice hockey team, East Leeds chess under-19s, South Leeds over-19 poker team, anyone with Leeds in their name. And Middlesbrough.
JOANATHAN WOODGATE, Teesside-born Leeds defender, in magazine questionnaire, 1999

People hate Manchester United because they are so successful. People will hate us in a few years because we shall be winning everything.
WOODGATE, 1999

Leeds reminded me of the poor Englishmen who invented football 15 centuries ago when they cut off a Viking's head, put it in a bag and started to kick it around; as awkward and primitive as that.
REPORT in Marca, Spanish newspaper, after Leeds drew 0–0 with Valencia, Champions' League semi-final, 2001

The only people we haven't upset lately are NATO.
DAVID O'LEARY after UEFA suspended Lee Bowyer on the eve of a Champions' League semi-final in Valencia, 2001

Those Leeds guys are simply out of this world. The energy just rushes through them. And their fans are just as aggressive as the team.
ROBERT PIRES, Arsenal and France midfielder, 2002

We are a club that panics very quickly. We went to Newcastle last month and we were top of the Premiership, but the mood was as if we were bottom and looking for a win.
O'LEARY after a run of bad results saw Leeds slide, 2002

From being the second-favourite club of many people, we seem to have become the most hated club in the country.
O'LEARY after the end of the Bowyer-Woodgate trial, 2002

These two players let down Leeds United and the way they carried on was disgraceful. Whatever the court decided, they were guilty in my eyes of failing to exercise control, lacking responsibility and of failing to behave as professional footballers should. What did they think they were doing, boozed up and running through the streets? Was it not inviting trouble?
O'LEARY, 2002

It would have been better for the club if they had both gone inside. The law of the land had to sort it out, but after the courts had dealt with it, we got the backlash.
O'LEARY, 2002

One boozy night has brought this club down.
O'LEARY as Leeds's form slumped soon after the Bowyer-Woodgate trial, 2002

I'm still lighting my candles and my mum's in danger of burning down the church.
O'LEARY, a practising Catholic, praying for a change in Leeds's fortunes, 2002

Leeds footballers wearing gloves isn't a fashion statement. It's so they don't leave any fingerprints.
LETTER to the Daily Mail shortly after the trial and a disciplinary crisis at the club, 2002

He wants to play for a bigger and better club.
PINA ZAHAVI, Rio Ferdinand's agent, on the Leeds captain's desire to move to Manchester United, 2002

We've got to work twice as hard as other clubs to get some good news. I've never known another club that so many people have such a negative image of, for reasons that are difficult to put a finger on.
PETER RIDSDALE, Leeds chairman, on employing the PR consultant Max Clifford, 2002

It wasn't me that ran up a debt of £40m, £50m, £60m or £80m. I didn't force them to sign one player. I nominated players and the club sorted out the wages.
O'LEARY after resurfacing at Aston Villa, 2003

They reacted like a gambler on a losing streak in a Las Vegas casino. They went out and gambled more. It was a triumph of vanity over sanity. The whole future of the club has been put in jeopardy to fund a dash for glory.
DR BILL GERRARD, sports finance specialist, on Leeds's mounting debts and failure to reach the Champions' League, 2003

It's like mortgaging your house and then blowing all the money on a holiday.

DR GERRARD on the £60m 'securitisation' loan that was 'crippling' the club, 2003

We were paying one player more than Sheffield United were paying their entire squad.
GERALD KRASNER, Leeds chairman, after drastic cuts in the club's wage bill, 2004

Post-war Iraq is being better run than Leeds
HEADLINE in the News of the World, *2003*

There are very few variables to get wrong, yet many people seem to have conspired to make a hash of it.
TREVOR BIRCH, post-Ridsdale chief executive at Leeds, 2003

I've never known a club like it. If it can go wrong, it will go wrong.
KEVIN BLACKWELL, manager, after ex-Leeds player Jody Morris's late equaliser for Millwall, 2004

You wonder how someone could have come up with a plan straight out of *Blackadder*. You can see Baldrick: 'I've got a cunning plan that'll take us further into debt.'
BLACKWELL on the Ridsdale era, 2005

Right now we're at the bottom of our cycle but Leeds United are still one of the big six clubs. The small clubs can have their day in the sun but eventually they go back where they came from. Leeds will always be a big club.
KEN BATES, Leeds chairman, on taking the club into administration after relegation to the third tier, 2007

2004 Premiership.
2005 Championship.
2007 Sinkingship.
2008 Abandonship.

SLOGAN on T-shirt worn by Leeds fans after 15 points were deducted for breaching Football League insolvency rules, 2007

LEICESTER CITY

The players work hard in training – and so they should considering what they are paid – but then only three people and five cabbages are watching them.
DAVE BASSETT, Leicester manager, facing relegation from the Premiership, 2002

Wouldn't it be great to go to a club that's boring, where nothing happens?
MICKY ADAMS, resigning as Leicester manager after a spell in which the club went into administration, were promoted and relegated and endured the La Manga sex scandal, 2004

LEYTON ORIENT

Drugs? Who needs 'em? Just come to Leyton Orient. In celebration, we're going to drink from the elixir of life, here at Brisbane Road, centre of the universe.

BARRY HEARN, Orient chairman, after his team reached the Third Division play-off final (which they lost), 2001

LIVERPOOL

Liverpool FC is more than just a football club. It's a feeling.
RAFAEL BENITEZ, Liverpool manager, 2004

Yes, there are two great teams on Merseyside. Liverpool and Liverpool Reserves.
BILL SHANKLY, Liverpool manager, 1965

I want to build a team that's invincible, so they'll have to send a team from Mars to beat us.
SHANKLY, 1971

Liverpool are the most uncomplicated side in the world. They all drive forward when they've got the ball, and they all get behind it when they haven't.
JOE MERCER, former Manchester City manager, 1973

My idea was to build Liverpool into a bastion of invincibility. Napoleon had that idea. He wanted to conquer the bloody world. I wanted Liverpool to be untouchable, to build the club up and up until everyone would have to submit.
SHANKLY, a year after he retired, 1975

Mind you, I've been here during the bad times too. One year we came second.

BOB PAISLEY, Shankly's successor, 1979

A lot of teams beat us, do a lap of honour and don't stop running. They live too long on one good result. I remember Jimmy Adamson crowing after Burnley beat us that his players were in a different league. At the end of the season they were.
PAISLEY, 1979

We do things together. I'd walk into the toughest dockside pub in the world with this lot. Because you know that if things got tough, nobody would 'bottle' it and scoot off.
EMLYN HUGHES, Liverpool captain, in Brian James's Journey to Wembley, *1977*

For those of you watching in black and white, Liverpool are the team with the ball.
JOKE by Liverpool fans, quoted in Brian Barwick and Gerald Sinstadt, The Great Derbies: Everton v Liverpool, *1988*

As we all knew would happen when Ian Rush went abroad, Liverpool have fallen to pieces.
TED CROKER, FA secretary, as Kenny Dalglish's side advanced to league title, 1988

People should ask where were the wonder boys of Liverpool. Why didn't they turn it on when things started to go against them? They're good, but not that good.
LAWRIE SANCHEZ, Wimbledon match-winner, after the underdogs' FA Cup final win, 1988

I thought there might be eight goals but I never expected we'd get four of them.
DAVE LANCASTER, Chesterfield player, after 4–4 draw at Anfield during Liverpool's decline, 1992

We're an old-fashioned football club, not a quoted plc, and we don't pay dividends to shareholders. We are here for one reason: to win trophies.
PETER ROBINSON, Liverpool chief executive, 1996

The gaffer sent me to see whether I could spot a weakness and I found one. The half-time tea is too milky.
KEVIN SUMMERFIELD, Shrewsbury coach, after seeing his club's next FA Cup opponents beat Leeds 5–0, 1996

We were playing for history tonight. For immortality. What these players have achieved is unique.
GERARD HOULLIER, Liverpool manager, after his side beat Alaves of Spain 5–4 to win the UEFA Cup and complete a Treble, 2001

People say we're not pretty to watch but I'll tell you something: winning's pretty.
HOULLIER, 2002

I was only a kid the last time Liverpool won the league. In fact I think I was still an Everton fan.
MICHAEL OWEN, Liverpool striker, 2002

Liverpool–Manchester United games are fantastic. It doesn't matter if you were playing tiddlywinks, it would be really competitive.
SIR ALEX FERGUSON, 2003

I can't stand Liverpool. I can't stand Liverpool people. I can't stand anything to do with them.
GARY NEVILLE, Manchester United defender, 1999

You have to realise that, even by British standards, Liverpool are unique. You are not playing for yourself. You're playing for an ideal.
CRAIG JOHNSTON, former Liverpool player, 2003

That was the worst I've seen since I left the club, and that was 14 years ago.
ALAN HANSEN, former Liverpool captain, after a defeat at Southampton, 2004

It wasn't just the best comeback in a European Cup final; it wasn't just the best comeback I've seen in football; it was the best comeback I've seen in sport anywhere in the world.
HANSEN on the recovery from 3–0 down to beat Milan on penalties in the Champions' League final, 2005

Football is made up of subjective feeling, and in that Anfield is unbeatable. Put a shit hanging from a stick in the middle of a passionate, crazy stadium and some people will tell you it's a work of art. It's not – it's a shit hanging from a stick.
JORGE VALDANO, sporting director of Real Madrid, alleging a lack of style in Liverpool, 2007

Two finals in three years – not bad for a little club.
STEVEN GERRARD, Liverpool captain, after winning a Champions' League semi-final against Chelsea, whose manager Jose Mourinho had called them 'a little club', 2007

LOS ANGELES GALAXY

The Galaxy are looked on as the jewel in the crown of Major League Soccer. All this leads to the race to become the first MLS super club, an American team to compete with Real Madrid and Manchester United.
ALEXI LALAS, Galaxy president, after signing David Beckham, 2007

We have a good name but we need a more legendary, traditional look. We decided it was time we started thinking how we create a world brand. David Beckham will obviously help enormously with that.
TIM LEIWEKE, president of the Galaxy's parent company, on plans to change the club's colours and crest, 2007

David Beckham is a Beverly Hills star in a skid row team.

PAUL HAYWARD, Daily Mail chief sports writer, as the former England captain's new team struggled, 2007

MANCHESTER CITY

A Thai chairman and a Swedish manager. It could only happen at Manchester City.
GRAHAM TAYLOR, former England manager, in his Daily Telegraph column after former Thailand Prime Minister Thaksin Shinawatra recruited Sven-Göran Eriksson after his takeover of City, 2007

What's let us down this year is being good consistently. We are consistent but inconsistent. Inconsistently consistent.
DAVID JAMES, City goalkeeper, 2005

Check out the details about Manchester's second-largest club.
BLURB on the dustcover of Manchester City FC: An A to Z, by Dean Hayes, 1995

There are three types of Oxo cubes. Light brown for chicken stock. Dark brown for beef stock. And light blue for laughing stock.
TOMMY DOCHERTY, former manager of neighbouring United, 1988

1976 was a strange year for English football – City won a trophy
SLOGAN on T-shirts sold outside Old Trafford, 1995

Seeing 42 players coming towards me I felt like the garrison commander at Rorke's Drift when the Zulus came pouring over the hill.
ALAN BALL, City manager, on the size of his new squad, 1995

Watching City is probably the best laxative you can have.

PHIL NEAL, City caretaker-manager, after they lost a 2–0 lead before beating Bradford City, 1996

May I wish Joe Royle well in a task equivalent to nailing jelly to a ceiling.
LETTER to the Manchester Evening News Pink after Royle became manager, 1998

The worse City play, the better the crowds are. It's as though the fans feel the team needs them. The other factor is that we are not United. Their fans are the most horrible in the world, as everybody knows.
DAVE WALLACE, editor of Manchester City fanzine King of the Kippax, 1999

I really felt things had changed for City when we beat Gillingham on penalties in the Second Division play-off final after being 2–0 down going into stoppage time. But then I'm an emotional person. I might have kicked a few full-backs in my time but I always sent them flowers afterwards.
MIKE SUMMERBEE, former City winger, on promotion to the Premiership, 2000

To score four goals when you are playing like pigs in labour is fantastic.
JOE ROYLE, City manager, after 4–1 win at Blackburn took them into the Premiership, 2000

They're my old club and I hate to speak badly of them, but they are crap.
RODNEY MARSH as City went straight back down, 2001

Coming to Manchester City is, if anything, more exciting than being at Real Madrid.

STEVE McMANAMAN, England midfielder, 2003

Manchester City are a springboard for me... I'm ready to play for a big club again and have no preference.
NICOLAS ANELKA, City striker and former Real Madrid and Arsenal player, 2004

We can't keep gambling on players who have scored six goals in the Pontins League or in Belgium.
JOEY BARTON, City midfielder, 2007

I don't think we should be talking about trophies. We need to be very realistic.
SVEN-GÖRAN ERIKSSON after his first pre-season friendly as City manager, 2007

MANCHESTER UNITED

I remember Alex Ferguson telling me when I first signed: 'You won't believe what it's like to play for Man United.' And I was like, 'Yeah, yeah, yeah.' But he was right.
TEDDY SHERINGHAM, West Ham and former Manchester United striker, 2006

The road back may be long and hard, but with the memory of those who died at Munich, of their stirring achievements and wonderful sportsmanship ever with us, Manchester United will rise again.
H.P. HARDMAN, chairman, in a message headed 'United will go on' on the cover of the first match programme after the tragedy, 1958

If you went through the Manchester United team that won the league in 1957, you would have to look very hard to find your truly great players. Look at the whole forward line – Berry, Whelan, Taylor, Viollet, Pegg – and you will search very hard to find a truly outstanding player... But because they were playing to order and precision, with method and movement, because they were fluid and not trying to do what they could not do; because they were doing things within their limits, they were successful.
ARTHUR ROWE, former Tottenham manager, in The Encylopaedia of Association Football, *1960*

There's a hell of a lot of politics in football. I don't think Henry Kissinger would have lasted 48 hours at Old Trafford.
TOMMY DOCHERTY, former United manager, 1982

It's the only stadium in the world I've ever been in that's absolutely buzzing with atmosphere when it's empty and there isn't a soul inside. It's almost like a cathedral.
DOCHERTY in Call the Doc, *1982*

It's like being in a palace, an overwhelming and inspiring place. Even the loos have gold taps.
GARRY BIRTLES, former United striker, 1995

This team makes you suffer. I deserve a million pounds a year for doing this job.

ALEX FERGUSON after drawn FA Cup final v Crystal Palace, 1990

ICI is a world-class business. There's no way it would want to buy a second-class football team.
CITY ANALYST quoted in the Sunday Times *on rumours that ICI wanted to buy United, 1990*

Manchester United plc? It means Premier League champions, of course.
TERRY CHRISTIAN, United fan and presenter of Channel 4's The Word, *1994*

I had to get rid of this idea that Manchester United were a drinking club, rather than a football club.
FERGUSON on his problems with Paul McGrath and Norman Whiteside, in Six Years at United, *1992*

I value truth, honesty, respect for one another, compassion and understanding. I have found these qualities in Manchester United.
ERIC CANTONA in La Philosophie de Cantona, *1995*

This has been a love story... The love of the club is the most important weapon in the world. I just couldn't leave.
CANTONA on his decision to stay with United, 1995

A Manchester United player has to want the ball, have the courage to want it. He's a player with imagination, someone who sees the bigger picture.
FERGUSON, 1995

It took me an hour to get the scorch marks off the turf.
KEITH KENT, United groundsman, after a dazzling display v Bolton, 1995

Less than a month after thousands of youngsters pulled on their favourite club jersey at Christmas, the men who run the club ordered the Red Devils to trot out in blue at Southampton. Loyalty doesn't seem to be enough any more; rather it is exploited to make us pay more.
TONY BLAIR MP, Labour leader, criticising United's commercialism, 1995

I get to my feet when Chelsea fans sing: 'Stand up if you hate Man U.' But though I hate them, I have to admire them too.
KEN BATES, Chelsea chairman, 1997

We are the most loved club – and the most hated.

GARY NEVILLE, United defender, 1997

There is a terrible amount of jealousy towards this club. I don't know why.
FERGUSON, 1997

People go on about the great skill in United's side, but the most important thing is their team spirit. They give off a warmth to each other that you can almost touch.
VINNIE JONES, Premiership opponent, 1997

The Kings of Perseverance
HEADLINE in the Catalan newspaper La Vanguardia *after United's two late goals in Barcelona beat Bayern Munich in the European Cup final, 1999*

In a Cairo taxi the four words of English my driver knew were 'Thatcher', 'Blair' and 'Manchester United'.
STEPHEN BYERS MP, Labour, Trade and Industry Secretary, 1999

We would love to have a [Luis] Figo, [Zinedine] Zidane or Rivaldo at United, but we realise those sort of players are never really going to come here. Some people think it's sad, with us being the richest club in the world, but clubs have their policies and you have to respect that.
ROY KEANE, United captain, 2000

This team never lose games – they just run out of time occasionally.
STEVE McCLAREN, United coach, 2000

I'll do my utmost to bridge the gap, but United have the biggest stadium, biggest crowds and most money to buy the best players. And the manager ain't too bad, either.
DAVID O'LEARY, Leeds manager, 2000

The nation was warming to us during the build-up to last season's Champions' League final. But the warmth was only ever going to be temporary. It's the British culture of being quick to put down people at the top. We are a soft target.
FERGUSON, 2000

You have to put all the criticism down to jealousy. United have produced more people who've played for their country, more world-class players and more who've won European Footballer of the Year than any other club in the country, so we must be doing something right.
FERGUSON after United suffered a poor run, 2000

It was a disgrace to pull out of the FA Cup to take part in something that seems to be all about greed. Brazil is probably the only country in the world where United haven't a superstore, and the only thing they've got out of the trip is a couple of million quid which they hardly need, though I suppose Sir Alex Ferguson can now get a job with FIFA when he quits as manager.
TOMMY DOCHERTY, former United manager, after the club went to Brazil to play in the new World Club Cup, 2000

United have got into Europe thanks to the FA Cup. Where are they going? Brazil? I hope they get bloody diarrhoea.
BRIAN CLOUGH, former Nottingham Forest manager, on United's decision not to defend the FA Cup, 1999

Everyone knows that for us to get awarded a penalty we need a certificate from the Pope and a personal letter from the Queen.
FERGUSON after Leeds were awarded a spot kick v United, 2001

To get a penalty at Old Trafford, Jaap Stam needs to take a machine gun and riddle you full of bullets.
PAOLO DI CANIO, West Ham striker, 2001

[The club] thought merchandising was more important than the team and players. When the business is more important than the football, I don't care. I just gave up. I don't want to be treated like a pair of socks, a shirt, like shit. I'm not shit.
ERIC CANTONA, recalling why he had suddenly retired five years earlier, 2002

When I pull on a Manchester United shirt I still get a buzz that is impossible to describe.

DAVID BECKHAM, 2002

Everyone thinks he has the prettiest wife at home.
ARSENE WENGER, Arsenal manager, after Ferguson claimed United had been 'the best team in the country since Christmas' at the height of their tussle for the title, 2002

They seem to think they're entitled to everything.
TERRY VENABLES, Leeds manager, as United intensified their interest in his captain, Rio Ferdinand, 2002

You see all the faces on the wall – George Best, Denis Law, Bobby Charlton – and you just want to be part of it.
RIO FERDINAND after his £29.1m switch from Leeds, 2002

Manchester United cannot defend. We can't just play defensively. The fans, the people here, won't stand for it. It's just not United. The club has a kamikaze streak, which in a funny way I rather like.
FERGUSON, 2005

United see themselves as an international, multi-national club, not a provincial-city club. We are a globally visioned brand. We're not about England, but about the world. Nationality doesn't matter.
RICHARD KURT, deputy editor of United fanzine Red Issue, *2003*

Manchester United is a perfect vehicle for all the ambitious people in football to have a go at. If someone wants to make a name for themselves, this club provides a perfect target.
FERGUSON after the FA's chief executive, Mark Palios, backed the banning of Rio Ferdinand for missing a drug test, 2003

The FA put it to me that Rio is bang to rights. I told them they were entering a minefield taking on a club like Manchester United.
GORDON TAYLOR, chief executive of the Professional Footballers' Association, 2003

Manchester United believe they are above the law and have the right to bully refs.
JEFF WINTER, ex-Premiership referee, in Who's the Bastard in the Black, *2006*

During 90 minutes of football I want United to die.

STEVEN GERRARD, Liverpool captain, 2006

AC MILAN

When people think of Italy, after the Mafia and pizza, they think of AC Milan.
SILVIO BERLUSCONI, Milan president, 1997

MIDDLESBROUGH

Our long-term aim is to make Middlesbrough synonymous with a good team
rather than cooling towers and chemical plants. We're well on our way, even
though Ruud Gullit had never heard of us when we contacted him last summer.
STEVE GIBSON, Middlesbrough chairman, 1995

Bryan Robson has certainly brought in the big names. But it is like going into
a nightclub and getting off with a big blonde. The lads will say: 'Phwoar!' But
can you keep her?
BERNIE SLAVEN, former Boro player, as Robson made some exotic signings, 1998

My team-mates advised me to visit the city first. I went to have a look at
Middlesbrough and decided I was better off in Parma.
ANTONIO BENARRIVO, Parma player, after rejecting a move to Teesside, 2001

I didn't like the food, I hated the weather, and it's not the most beautiful city.
By the time we left, we'd developed slight Middlesbrough accents, which was
kind of cute.
*ADRIANA SKLENARIKOVA, fashion model and partner to France player Christian
Karembeu, 2002*

MILLWALL

I met a pal who'd lost track of me and asked what I was doing. I said I was
player-manager of Millwall. His wife immediately said: 'How embarrassing.'
MICK McCARTHY, 1995

We have played for some of the great clubs in Europe, but we regard this as
the pinnacle of our careers.
*SERGEI YURAN, Russian striker, on an unhappy, short-lived spell with Millwall with Vassili
Kulkov, 1996*

Personally, I thrive on a hostile environment. Maybe it's because I played for Millwall.
KASEY KELLER, United States goalkeeper, anticipating a rough reception in Costa Rica, 1997

NEWCASTLE UNITED

When I talk about our Geordie core and my hopes for a Geordie dynasty, people say: 'Does it matter? Does where somebody comes from really affect their job?' I tell them it does make a difference. I believe Geordies in key posts at this club give you a potentially vital extra one per cent that non-Geordies don't. Geordies have extra passion and understanding. We are always going to be superior.
FREDDY SHEPHERD, Newcastle chairman, 2003

A big football club with big problems.
GRAEME SOUNESS, former manager at St James's Park, as multi-millionaire Mike Ashley negotiated to buy Newcastle, 2007

Newcastle have been very unlucky with injuries this season. The players keep recovering.
LEN SHACKLETON, journalist and former Newcastle and Sunderland player, 1965

I've heard of players selling dummies, but this club keeps buying them.
SHACKLETON, 1976

Newcastle have the potential to allow me to pick up the phone and say to someone like Alex Ferguson: 'I want to buy your best.' I believe that day will come.
JIM SMITH, Newcastle manager, 1988

Tell Alex [Ferguson] we're coming to get him.
KEVIN KEEGAN, Newcastle manager, after winning promotion, 1993

We're like the Basques. We are fighting for a nation, the Geordie nation. Football is tribalism and we're the Mohicans.
SIR JOHN HALL, Newcastle chairman, 1995

It's madness – Newcastle are £40m in debt yet they are the darlings of the City.
ALAN SUGAR, Tottenham chairman, 1997

We are only flesh and blood in the end. Sometimes can't sleep. Worry about the job. Worry about the kids. Worry about growing old. Worry about interest rates going up. Worry about Newcastle going down.
TONY BLAIR MP, Prime Minister, to Labour party conference, 1999

People talk about Newcastle as a 'sleeping giant'. They last won the championship in 1927 and the FA Cup in 1955. They already make Rip Van Winkle look like a catnapper.
HUGH McILVANNEY, Sunday Times writer, 1999

We're already bigger and more financially stable than Barcelona. We can attract any player from anywhere in the world.
DOUGLAS HALL, Newcastle vice-chairman, 2001

NEWPORT COUNTY

And they were lucky to get nil.
LEN SHACKLETON on his six-goal Newcastle debut, a 13–0 win v Newport, in Clown Prince of Soccer, *1955*

NORWICH CITY

I'd love Norwich to become famous for its football club again, and not just for Delia Smith and Alan Partridge.
NIGEL WORTHINGTON, Norwich manager, 2002

The last 10 years has been one long story of learning how to cope with disappointment.
DELIA SMITH, celebrity chef, on being a Norwich City director, 2002

NOTTINGHAM FOREST

Nottingham Forest will never know how lucky they were, that day they asked me to get on with the job of rebuilding their run-down club. They didn't just need a new manager – the bloody place was so dead it needed a kiss of life.
BRIAN CLOUGH on his 18-year reign in Clough: The Autobiography, *1994*

We won two European Cups yet we never practised a free kick. 'Just give it to Robbo' [John Robertson] was the cry.
MARTIN O'NEILL, Forest player under Clough, in Clough: The Autobiography, *1994*

The only person certain of boarding the bus to Wembley for the Littlewoods Cup final is Albert Kershore, and he'll be driving it.
CLOUGH keeping his players on their toes, 1990

I've got a young team. Acne is a bigger problem than injuries.
CLOUGH, 1992

The evil slime from across the River Trent.
DAVID McVAY, journalist and former Notts County player, in his memoir Steak...Diana Ross, *2003*

NOTTS COUNTY

We're like Lady Di. She's not the Queen yet. She's not even married. But like us, she's nicely placed.
JIMMY SIRREL, Notts manager, chasing promotion as royal wedding fever spread, 1981

Most people who can remember when County were a great club are dead.
JACK DUNNETT, Notts chairman, 1983

PARTICK THISTLE

For years I thought their name was Partick Thistle Nil.
BILLY CONNOLLY, comedian, 1988

If anyone thinks the Partick Thistle team of today could hold their own in the Scottish Premier League, they have been smoking dope.
ROGER MITCHELL, SPL chief executive, as Thistle closed in on promotion, 2002

I could've put four fucking pigeons in midfield and they would have played better.
JOHN LAMBIE, Thistle manager, after a 3–0 defeat by Rangers, 2002

PORT VALE

The reason Samantha Fox is so big in Eastern Europe and the Third World is that they are neglected in terms of the range of talent prepared to visit them. So even a small star becomes big once they arrive. In football terms, she has been playing Port Vale instead of Arsenal.
MAX CLIFFORD, public relations consultant, 1992

Three years at Port Vale is enough for anybody.
LEE MILLS, Bradford City striker, after leaving the Potteries club, 1998

PORTSMOUTH

I don't even know where Portsmouth is. All I know is a lot of sailors live there.
FRANK MALONEY, boxing promoter, denying he wanted to take over Pompey, 1995

Pathetic, abysmal, gutless and disgraceful. If my players were bricklayers the house they built would fall down.
ALAN BALL, Portsmouth manager, shortly before his sacking, 1999

QUEEN OF THE SOUTH

The Queen of the South shall rise up in the judgement with the men of this generation and condemn them.

LUKE 11:31, New Testament. The Dumfries club are the only football club mentioned in the Bible

QUEEN'S PARK

Surely the greatest of all clubs! I have a great admiration, a great respect, a great esteem – nay even a great affection for the Queen's Park club. What pygmies some of our strictly modern clubs seem, how thin and poor their records, when a comparison is instituted between them and Queen's Park. What a halo of romance and glory surrounds them. What a wealth of honourable tradition is theirs!

WILLIAM McGREGOR, founder of the Football League, in Association Football and the Men Who Made It, *by William Pickford and Alfred Gibson, 1906*

QUEENS PARK RANGERS

Over the years, QPR have been a bit of a flitty, farty, we-like-a-Fancy-Dan-footballer club.

IAN HOLLOWAY, QPR manager, 2003

We were like the Dog and Duck in the first half and Real Madrid in the second.

HOLLOWAY after a draw v Hull, 2005

RANGERS

Rangers like the big, strong, powerful fellows, with a bit of strength and solidity in the tackle, rather than the frivolous, quick-moving stylists like Jimmy Johnstone, small, tiptoe-through-the-tulips type of players who excite people.

WILLIE WADDELL, Rangers manager, 1972

Playing Rangers tonight was like trying to carry a ton weight up the down escalator. You wonder how Scotland could ever lose a football match.
HOWARD WILKINSON, Leeds manager, after his team's European Cup defeat by the Scottish champions, 1992

How many Scots have they got at Ibrox now? They're rushing out buying Englishmen, Italians and Chileans when every other kid in Scotland dreams of pulling on the blue jersey.
RON DIXON, former Dundee chairman, 1998

It isn't about balance sheets. Rangers is a world brand where everything follows from what happens on the park.
DAVID MURRAY, Rangers chairman, 1998

I only ever have a drink when we win a trophy. People are starting to think I'm an alcoholic.
IAN FERGUSON, Rangers midfielder, after his 23rd medal with the club, 1999

Sometimes when you're in a hole, you stop digging.

SIR DAVID MURRAY, Rangers chief executive, referring to Paul Le Guen's ill-starred reign as manager as Walter Smith returned as manager, 2007

READING

This lot would kick the board over at Monopoly.
GRAEME MURTY, Reading captain, after a 33-game unbeaten run took them into the Premiership, 2006

REAL MADRID

To be honest I was terribly pleased I wasn't playing. I saw [Alfredo] Di Stefano and these others, and I thought: 'These people just aren't human. It's not the sort of game I've been taught.'
BOBBY CHARLTON quoted in Motson and Rowlinson's The European Cup 1955–80, on watching Real play Manchester United, 1957

They could dish out the hard stuff, too, especially [Jose] Santamaria. People gloat about them and say they never kicked anybody. Well, they certainly kicked me.
JOHN CHARLES, Juventus's Welsh centre-forward, in Motson and Rowlinson, as above

The most educated person at Real Madrid is the woman who cleans the toilets.

JOAN GASPART, Barcelona vice-president, 1997

Real Madrid, the Yankees of Soccer
HEADLINE in USA Today after Real signed David Beckham, 2003

You can never have too many stars.
JORGE VALDANO, sporting director of Real, 2003

Real have turned themselves from a football club into a circus. I've never seen a chimps' tea party like it.
ULI HOENESS, Bayern Munich director and former player, after Real made Beckham their latest galactico, 2003

If this is a five-star club that stays in five-star hotels, why would they want a two-star coach?
VICENTE DEL BOSQUE, Real coach, on rejecting a contract offer, 2003

Real's movement and touch meant it was like facing the Harlem Globetrotters at times. They were passing it about and we couldn't get near them.
GARY NEVILLE, Manchester United defender, 2003

We're like a big blockbuster movie. Like *Men in Black*, or in our case, *Men in White*. We have a great story to tell, a great production and the biggest box-office stars.
JOSE ANGEL SANCHEZ, Real's director of marketing, in John Carlin's White Angels: Beckham, Real Madrid and the New Football, 2004

The pressure [of having to win] does not oppress the great players. When we buy players, the responsibility that goes with pulling on a Real Madrid shirt is one of the most important things to consider. A great footballer sleeps equally well with or without pressure.
JORGE VALDANO, sporting director of Real, 2003

Protesting in front of the referee is a sign of weakness. Insults never achieve anything. Real Madrid never complain.
ENTRY in Real's Little Blue Book, issued by the club to players, 2004

In my time in Madrid I've had six managers, four presidents and we've signed 20 players. In a successful club you need stability, and we haven't had that.
DAVID BECKHAM shortly before leaving Spain for Los Angeles, 2007

I need a coach that respects the artistic heritage of this club.

RAMON CALDERON, Real president, on why coach Fabio Capello was ousted despite leading the club to the Spanish title, 2007

SCARBOROUGH

If only our motto 'No Battle, No Victory' wasn't taken so literally.
MARK STANIFORTH, Scarborough supporter, 1995

SHEFFIELD UNITED

Sheffield Eagles [rugby league team] play the ball on the ground more than Sheffield United.
JONATHAN FOSTER reporting on a United match in the Independent, 1990

When I was a lad and we played Wednesday, they wore blue and white stripes and we'd wear red and white stripes. Now they wear all sorts of stuff, like a fashion parade. Where have our stripes gone this season? Blades' strip looks like it was designed by Julian Clary when he had a migraine.
SEAN BEAN, actor and United fan, 1996

I remember the day when this club sold Brian Deane and Jan Aage Fjortoft. It was like when President Kennedy was shot – that's how deeply I felt.
NEIL WARNOCK, lifelong fan, on taking over as manager, 1999

SHEFFIELD WEDNESDAY

The big-city team with the small-town mentality.
HOWARD WILKINSON, Leeds and former Wednesday manager, 1991

There are Wednesday players with more money than the club, which can't be right.
GARY MEGSON, Sheffield-based West Bromwich Albion manager, on his favourite club's financial difficulties, 2002

STOKE CITY

This club is a sleeping monster.
CHRIS KAMARA, Stoke manager, 1998

Even the ball boys are 6ft 4in here. We had to stand up to it.
KEVIN BLACKWELL, Leeds manager, after a bruising win at Stoke, 2005

STONEWALL

I remember telling one of my previous team that I was starving and could murder a plate of sausage and chips. One player just looked at me and said: 'I should think you get enough sausage already, don't you?'
PAUL BARKER, captain of the gay London team Stonewall, 1995

SUNDERLAND

I might have to start persuading players that Sunderland's closer to London than it actually is.
ROY KEANE, Sunderland manager, alleging that certain transfer targets opted for the capital rather than Wearside under pressure from wives or girlfriends, 2007

I remember talking to [Sir Alex Ferguson] when we got off the bus here before a game. He said, 'Sunderland is a bloody big club.' That stuck with me.
KEANE, 2007

First, Margaret Thatcher does her best to destroy the town. Now Ben Thatcher viciously elbows our best crosser of the ball to destroy the Sunderland team at Wimbledon. Just what have they got against us?
LETTER to the Sunderland Echo, *2000*

TOTTENHAM HOTSPUR

Than the famous Spurs there is probably no more famous club in the whole of England. Did they not recover the Association Cup for the south? Did they not play pretty and effective football? Are they not scrupulously fair? Are they not perfectly managed?
WILLIAM PICKFORD and ALFRED GIBSON, authors, Association Football and the Men Who Made It, *1906*

We have no desire just to be a football club. That is not the basis for success.
PAUL BOBROFF, chairman of Tottenham Hotspur plc, 1983

INTERVIEWER: Which do you prefer, Rangers or Celtic?
ALFIE CONN: Spurs.
EXCHANGE on It's Only a Game, *TV documentary, 1986. Conn played for all three*

The cold and damp dressing room is our secret weapon for Spurs. Not forgetting their lukewarm pot of tea at half-time.
PHIL SPROSON, Port Vale defender, before the Third Division side faced Spurs in the FA Cup, 1988

Spurs were like West Ham used to be, all fancy flicks and sweet sherry.
SPROSON after scoring for Vale in their victory over Spurs, 1988

I haven't just signed a player. I've rescued a lad from hell.

BRIAN CLOUGH after buying back Steve Hodge from Spurs, 1988

When Ilie Dumitrescu asked me when Spurs last won the championship, I couldn't answer him. That shouldn't be the case for a club this big.
OSVALDO ARDILES, Spurs manager, 1995

I don't think Spurs would ever sign a superstar like [Jurgen] Klinsmann or [Dennis] Bergkamp again. Those guys are floaters. They'll go anywhere, play for anyone who pays them the most.
ALAN SUGAR, Spurs chairman, after Arsenal paid £7.25m for Bergkamp, 1995

Wimbledon with fans.
JIMMY GREAVES, former Spurs star, on Gerry Francis's team, 1996

I want a consistent team, not a flash one. When I was at Highbury, the message from White Hart Lane used to be 'let Arsenal win things with boring football, we'd rather play entertainingly and lose'. But to me that was just a psychological crutch. I want my team but to be exciting, and to win week in, week out. I'm working on it.
GEORGE GRAHAM, Spurs manager, 2000

We're good enough to survive in the Premiership and maybe have a good cup run or even earn a UEFA Cup spot if things go really well. But we are never going to win the championship.
TIM SHERWOOD, Spurs midfielder, on the 'harsh reality' of under-investment, 2002

There's only one word for Tottenham's under-achievement – mismanagement. Poor selection of, and by, the people responsible. It's not money: the managers have had that and spent it. Gerry Francis said he had a good record here, but I think he picked a batch of 20 games from his 60.
DAVID PLEAT, Spurs' acting manager, 2003

It might sound strange to say it, but Tottenham are an important club.
ROBERTO MANCINI, Lazio coach, on being linked with Spurs' managerial vacancy, 2004

I don't know about weapons of mass destruction, but it takes Tottenham Hotspur only 45 minutes to turn a 3–0 lead into a 4–3 defeat against 10 men. The thus far fruitless search for their defence continues.
LETTER to the Guardian as Manchester City won at White Hart Lane at the height of the allied invasion of Iraq, 2004

As we say in Portugal, they brought the bus and left it in front of the goal.
JOSE MOURINHO, Chelsea manager, after Spurs drew 0–0 at Stamford Bridge, 2004

WATFORD

Blimey, the ground looks a bit different to Watford. Where's the dog track?
LUTHER BLISSETT after exchanging Vicarage Road for Milan's San Siro stadium, 1983

If it was a war, it would be America against San Marino. In boxing it would be Muhammad Ali against Jimmy Krankie.
ADRIAN BOOTHROYD, Watford manager, before facing Manchester United, 2007

WEST BROMWICH ALBION

That's typical of this club. For an extra £10,000 they could have got John Snow.
JEFF ASTLE, West Bromwich Albion striker, after they bought goalkeeper Jim Cumbes, a fast bowler with Lancashire, 1969

They've made some signings, but it's like putting lipstick on a pig. It's still a pig.
RODNEY MARSH, Sky pundit and former England player, as Albion prepared for the Premiership, 2002

We haven't got his type of player at the club, someone who can pass and score goals.
GARY MEGSON, Albion manager, on signing Jason Koumas from Tranmere, 2002

WEST HAM UNITED

Even when we had Moore, Hurst and Peters, West Ham's average finish was about 17th. Which shows how crap the other eight of us were.
HARRY REDKNAPP, former player and manager at the club, 2001

It is better to play good football badly than bad football well.
PATRICK BARCLAY, journalist, in the Independent *on West Ham's adherence to 'purist' principles as Wimbledon enjoyed success with a long-ball game, 1987*

You can forget the purist stuff now. We've finished with that. When people start to compare us with West Ham, that's when we'll start to worry.
PETER TAYLOR, Brian Clough's assistant at Derby, 1973

The crowds at West Ham haven't been rewarded by results, but they keep turning up because they see good football. Other clubs will suffer from the old bugbear that results count more than anything. This has been the ruination of English soccer.
RON GREENWOOD, England and former West Ham manager, 1977

All that 'happy losers' stuff is a load of cobblers. I hate losing.

BILLY BONDS, West Ham manager, on claims that the club put style above winning, 1991

West Ham's performance was obscene in terms of the effort they put into the match.
ALEX FERGUSON, Manchester United manager, on a 1–0 defeat which damaged their championship prospects, in Six Years at United, *1992*

I understand nothing when Rio Ferdinand and Frank Lampard are talking. They speak Cocknik.
EYAL BERKOVIC, West Ham's Israeli midfielder, 1999

They can't stand foreigners.
BERKOVIC, accusing his former club of xenophobia in The Magician, *1999*

I want the West Ham fans to know that we are going to win something before I finish my career here. Otherwise I'll kill myself.
PAOLO DI CANIO, West Ham's Italian striker, 2001

We played like a bunch of drunks. I felt like crying.
YOSSI BENAYOUN, West Ham midfielder, after a 6–0 loss at Reading, 2007

WIMBLEDON

The borstal of football.
DAVE BASSETT, Wimbledon manager, 1987

The only hooligans here are the players.
BASSETT after fans invaded the pitch when the Dons won promotion to the First Division, 1986

It was just welly, welly, welly. The ball must've been screaming for mercy.
RON YEATS, Liverpool scout, after watching Wimbledon, 1988

Wimbledon are killing the dreams that made football the world's greatest game.
TERRY VENABLES, Tottenham manager, 1988

There is one London club that have got it right. Whatever you think of Wimbledon's style of play, you can't argue with their results.
BOB PAISLEY, former Liverpool manager, 1988

Wimbledon will take to Wembley. Once you've tried to get a decent bath at Hartlepool, you can handle anything.
WALLY DOWNES, ex-Wimbledon stalwart, before the FA Cup final, 1988

I've been there once before – for dog racing on my stag night.
DAVE BEASANT, Wimbledon goalkeeper, on the eve of Wembley, 1988

The Crazy Gang have beaten the Culture Club!
JOHN MOTSON, BBC TV commentator, as Liverpool were beaten, 1988

Everyone was drunk the night before [the FA Cup final]. Every single one of us was down the pub. Probably what won us the Cup. That, and taking me off after an hour because I was delirious.
ALAN CORK, former Wimbledon striker, 1991

When Wimbledon hit long balls up to a 6ft 2in black centre-forward [John Fashanu], it's destroying the game. When Arsenal hit long balls to a 6ft 4in Irishman [Niall Quinn], it's good football.
DAVE BASSETT, Wimbledon manager, 1989

We must remain the English bulldog SAS club; to sustain ourselves by sheer power and the attitude that we will kick ass. We are an academy – we find gems and turn them into finished articles.
SAM HAMMAM, chairman, 1992

Before we go down, we'll leave a stream of blood from here to Timbuktu.
HAMMAM, 1992

The best way to watch Wimbledon is on Ceefax.
GARY LINEKER, TV pundit, 1993

For us to compete in the Premiership with our finances is like going into a nuclear war with bows and arrows.
JOE KINNEAR, Wimbledon manager, 1997

It was a typical Wimbledon goal. Sad, miserable, but very effective.
BOBBY ROBSON, Newcastle manager, 2000

There are thousands of reasons why we have gone down. But there can be no excuses. When one bubble bursts you have to blow another one.
TERRY BURTON, Wimbledon manager, on relegation from the Premiership, 2000

Businessmen tried to take our club away from us so we decided to form our own. We'd like to pass them on the way up as they slip towards extinction. For the good of football, it's important they fail miserably.
KRIS STEWART, chairman of AFC Wimbledon, set up after Wimbledon pursued their intention to relocate from south London to Milton Keynes, 2002

It's the young players I feel sorry for, like Joe McAnuff. He'd be bringing the house down if there was a house to bring down.
NEIL SHIPPERLEY, Wimbledon captain, as defections to AFC Wimbledon saw crowds fall below 2,500 in the First Division, 2002

The drive [behind Wimbledon's 'Crazy Gang'] was black, urban; the music was all soul, R & B. Jonesy? He was a black man. The little rat Wisey? He was a black man.
JOHN FASHANU, former Wimbledon striker, in the TV documentary Black Flash: A Century of Black Footballers in Britain, *2003*

WOLVERHAMPTON WANDERERS

This club is an environment where, if we lose or draw, it's not good enough. It's a win-or-nothing thing. We call it Wolfism.
DAVE JONES, Wolves manager, on the expectations surrounding the club, 2003

Hail Wolves 'Champions of the World' Now
HEADLINE in the Daily Mail *after Stan Cullis's team beat Hungarian side Honved in a floodlit friendly before the launch of the European Cup, 1954*

Wolves' success does Mr [Stan] Cullis great credit, but it has also done much harm to the game in England because so many lesser managers have attempted to ape the Wolves-Cullis technique. Artistry with the ball is not all-important with Wolverhampton Wanderers.
JIMMY McILROY, Burnley midfielder, criticising Wolves' long-ball style in Right Inside Soccer, *1960*

I told my back four: 'I'm glad I didn't have you defending me when I had my court case. The judge would have put his black cap on.'
TOMMY DOCHERTY after becoming manager at struggling Wolves, 1984

We don't use a stopwatch to judge our Golden Goal competition. We use a calendar.
DOCHERTY during a goal famine at Molineux, 1985

I just opened the trophy cabinet. Two Japanese soldiers fell out.
DOCHERTY, 1985

It's a bit like joining the *Titanic* in mid-voyage.
RACHEL HEYHOE-FLINT, former England women's cricket captain, on joining the fast-declining club as PRO, 1985

I had a book of excuses for people who rang up and said: 'Where's my money?' We couldn't even pay the milk bill.
KEITH PEARSON, Wolves secretary, on the club's 1980s brush with extinction, 1993

The place was a health hazard before the stadium was rebuilt. The dressing room leaked, we were always mopping up and there were cockroaches doing backstroke in the bath.
KEITH DOWNING, Wolves midfielder, 1993

Bring back the fifties!
CHANT by Wolves' fans during protest against Graham Taylor's management, 1995

There are only four clubs I'd have considered leaving Leicester for – Manchester United, Newcastle, Rangers and Wolves. This is the last of the sleeping giants.
MARK McGHEE, Wolves manager, 1995

They are a big club that talks a good game.
McGHEE, by now with Millwall, after Wolves sacked his successor, Colin Lee, 2001

When I came here I found a lot of people living in the past, and I upset them by telling them so. Billy Wright won't win me promotion. And how is Steve Bull going to help me? Let's put all the great names in a museum, treasure the memories and move on.
DAVE JONES, Wolves manager, striving to lead the club to the Premiership, 2002

We may be a big club in history, but we're really one of the small potatoes.
ALEX RAE, Wolves midfielder, 2004

four

COUNTRIES

AMERICAN SAMOA

Their players weren't allowed to swap shirts with us at the end. I think they got theirs from a supermarket when they first arrived in Australia.
ARCHIE THOMPSON, Australia striker, after scoring 13 goals in a world-record 31–0 defeat of the Samoans, 2001

ARGENTINA

We should not have played in the 1982 World Cup. A lot of kids died in the Malvinas and as the captain, I should have done something to stop us going on the pitch.
DANIEL PASSARELLA, former Argentina captain, recalling the effect of the Falkands War shortly before their defence of the World Cup, 2001

Malvinas 2 England 1! We blasted the English pirates with Maradona and a little hand. He who robs a thief has a thousand years of pardon.
CRONICA newspaper of Buenos Aires, 1986. Malvinas is the Argentinian name for the Falkland Islands

Why the surprise over Argentina's elimination? When did a team with a large Scottish following ever qualify for the second round of the World Cup?
LETTER to the Guardian during the World Cup finals, 2002. Argentina had been in the same group as England

There haven't been so many headbands and leather necklaces on TV since the Allman Brothers played *The Old Grey Whistle Test*.
WHEN SATURDAY COMES magazine describes a 'hairy' Argentinian substitutes' bench against England, World Cup finals, 2002

AUSTRALIA

Sheilas, Wogs and Poofters

TITLE of the autobiography of former Australia captain Johnny Warren, 2003. Warren said it summed up how other sports in Australia perceived football

If we'd lost I'd already got my excuse worked out – that it took 22 of you to beat us.
FRANK FARINA, Australiu munuyer, after the Socceroos beat an England side that featured 11 substitutes, 2003

BRAZIL

We have the most important football on the planet.
LUIZ INACIO LULA DA SILVA, president of Brazil, on why his country should host the 2014 World Cup, 2007

It's an absolute myth to say we are individualists. We play a collective game, as disciplined as anybody else.
TOSTAO, member of Brazil's celebrated 1970 World Cup-winning team, 2006

Brazil played in shoes which could only be likened to Grecian slippers. We cannot laugh even about that. After all, they won the World Cup in them [in 1958].
TOM FINNEY, England winger, in Finney on Football, 1958

We have nothing to learn from these people.
ALF RAMSEY, England manager, after defeat by Brazil, World Cup finals, 1970

Our football is like our inflation: 100 per cent

HEADLINE in Jornal da Tarde after Brazil beat England, 1981

The Pope may be Polish, but God is a Brazilian.
PELE after Brazil beat Poland 4–0 in the World Cup, 1986

Brazil – You made me cry in '82, '86, '90. This time make me dance and I can die in peace
BANNER at World Cup finals, 1994

It feels like the magic has gone. It's as if we've been cursed.
RIVALDO, Brazil playmaker, after World Cup qualifying defeat by Paraguay, less than two years before he helped his country regain the trophy, 2000

There's no beautiful game any more. You are not going to see the Brazil of 1958, '62 or '70. This is 2001.
LUIZ FELIPE SCOLARI, Brazil coach, 2001

I couldn't help noticing that when our lads looked at them, it was with a touch of awe. Ronaldo, Rivaldo, Roberto Carlos: it was like we saw them as superior to us.
GARETH SOUTHGATE, England defender, in Woody and Nord: A Football Friendship, *co-written with Andy Woodman, 2003*

They are better than us, which is the difference.
SVEN-GÖRAN ERIKSSON, England manager, after Brazil beat his side in the World Cup quarter-finals, 2002

We prepare for a game much more than people think. They think we run out on the pitch, all laughter and joy and then it's goal, goal, goal.
RONALDINHO before the World Cup finals, 2006

Talent alone is not enough in football. There was no more talented side than ours, but it wasn't enough.
KAKA, Brazil midfielder, after they failed to retain the global title, 2006

It's through football that our people feel avenged. It's like a message saying: 'We may be First World in other things, but we're better at this.'
TOSTAO, member of Brazil's 1970 team, 2007

To be a winning team, you have to know how to suffer.

DUNGA, Brazil coach, after beating Uruguay on penalties en route to winning the Cop America, 2007

CAMEROON

We didn't underestimate them. They were a lot better than we thought.
BOBBY ROBSON, England manager, after a 3–2 win v Cameroon, World Cup finals, 1990

CZECH REPUBLIC

People ask what is the secret recipe of our success. Recipes are for cakes and pies.
KAREL BRUCKNER, Czech coach, 2004

DENMARK

I have told Chancellor Kohl that it is absolutely not on for the Danes to want to leave the European Community and be European champions at the same time.
BERTI VOGTS, Germany manager, after Denmark beat his team to win the European Championship, 1992

ENGLAND

The World Cup wasn't won [in 1966] on the playing fields of England. It was won on the streets.
SIR BOBBY CHARLTON, member of the class of '66, 1995

It never crossed our minds that we could lose. No, no never. It didn't come into it.
BOBBY MOORE, captain of the '66 side, in Ian Ridley, Season in the Cold, 1992

You've beaten them once. Now go out and bloody beat them again.
ALF RAMSEY to the England players before extra time, World Cup final, 1966

As we came round the corner from the 18th green, a crowd of members were at the clubhouse window, cheering and waiting to tell me that England had won the World Cup. It was the blackest day of my life.
DENIS LAW, former Scottish international, 1979

I'd have preferred it if neither team had reached the final. I'm not a great lover of the Germans – they bombed my folks' house in Clydebank during the war.
ALLY MacLEOD, former Scotland manager, on the 25th anniversary of England's World Cup victory, 1991

The English team had some outstanding players. Men like [Gordon] Banks and Bobby Moore, and Cooper and Bobby and Jack Charlton. They can play on any Brazilian team at any time, and that is no light compliment.
PELE after Brazil's defeat of England during the World Cup finals, 1970, from My Life and the Beautiful Game

England can't always win 6–0. Bobby Charlton has retired.

DAVE BASSETT, Sheffield United manager, after a 0–0 draw, 1995

DES O'CONNOR: If England win the World Cup, will you come back and sing a duet with me?
ELTON JOHN: If they win, I'll come back and sleep with you.
EXCHANGE on O'Connor's TV chat show, 1998

I can't say England are shite because they beat us in the [Euro 2000] play-offs, and that would make us even shittier.
ALLY McCOIST, former Scotland striker, 2000

Portugal play football as I like to see it played. As a neutral it was fantastic. Unfortunately I'm not a neutral.
KEVIN KEEGAN, England manager, after Portugal beat his team, Euro 2000

There is a need for honesty... The bottom line is that we were inept tactically, we were exposed against teams we could have beaten. England's failings have nothing to do with technical skill because I don't agree we're not good enough as footballers.
MARTIN KEOWN, Arsenal and England defender, after Euro 2000 exit

Tony Blair is very good-looking but unfortunately he has no bravado. Same with the England football team. They play so slow.
ADRIANA SKLENARIKOVA, Slovakian Wondrerbra model, 2000

All the European teams who have gone out have played too defensively, as if they were scared. I thought England were the worst.
GUUS HIDDINK, South Korea's Dutch coach, after his team went a stage further than England to the World Cup semi-finals, 2002

It was obvious England were overawed by Brazil, Brazil with 10 players, men against boys. You could see England's body language at the end. 'We've done OK, haven't we? Got to the quarter-finals.' England should expect to be in the semi-finals or final every time. Come on, lads, wake up!
ROY KEANE, former Republic of Ireland captain, 2002. He also claimed 'the priority' for some England players was to swap shirts with a Brazilian

I wouldn't watch a whole England game but I see the highlights.
KEANE, 2003

It would have been great to win 1–0. But 0–0 seems even better because it shows character to get such a result.
DAVID BECKHAM after England's goalless draw in Turkey, 2003

When the St George flag was burned the lads got a look at it and were fuming.

JOHN TERRY, England defender, after Macedonia fans set light to the England flag in Skopje, 2003

At Real Madrid we all kiss each other before we go out. Against Jamaica, Aaron Lennon was going to replace me and as I approached, I leaned forward to kiss him but then thought: 'Nah, better not.'
DAVID BECKHAM, 2006

We're not as good as we think we are. Me and the other players constantly claimed we could win the World Cup. It was stupid.
STEVEN GERRARD after England's failure in Germany, 2006

We went around Germany blowing our own trumpet and returned home mute with embarrassment.
GERRARD in his autobiography, 2007

'We got beat in the quarter-finals. I played like shit. Here's my book.'
JOEY BARTON, Manchester City midfielder, on what England's World Cup squad might say, 2006

Nobody in Europe likes England. England invented the sport but has never made any impact on world football.
JACK WARNER, Trinidadian vice-president of FIFA, on why England should not be awarded the 2018 World Cup, 2007

FRANCE

Half the team are foreigners who don't even know the words to the Marseillaise.
JEAN-MARIE LE PEN, leader of the far-right National Front, on the France team at the European Championship finals, 1996

Me, sing to satisfy Le Pen? I don't think so.
MARCEL DESAILLY, black France defender, 1996

A tricolour orgasm!

HEADLINE in France Soir *after France's World Cup triumph, 1998*

What would be the most logical final at Euro 2000? France A versus France B.
L'EQUIPE after Les Bleus fielded fringe players v Holland and lost only 3–2

The French team has been my life and has led me to do things I shouldn't have. It has been my mistress – a beautiful mistress.
LAURENT BLANC retiring from the national side after the triumph at Euro 2000

There's a few little things we have to change. It's clear the machine has jammed.
MARCEL DESAILLY, France captain, after the holders finished bottom of their group and without a goal, World Cup finals, 2002

Long live France – not the one he wants, but the real one! [Jean-Marie] Le Pen is not aware that there are black, blond and brown French people. He doesn't know his history.
LILIAN THURAM, France defender, on criticism of the composition of the squad by the leader of the far-right National Front, 2006

The France team all tested positive for being assholes.
LANCE ARMSTRONG, former Tour de France winner, after France lost to Italy in the World Cup final, 2006

GERMANY

Q: What do you admire most about Germany?
A: Their results.
TERRY VENABLES, England coach, after the Germans beat them on penalties, European Championship finals, 1996

The Germans are very well behaved, more like a lawyers' convention than a squad of footballers.
JEFF BURNIGE, Millwall director and German team liaison officer as Germany moved towards European Championship success, 1996

There were some strange decisions against us. Perhaps there was a secret instruction; maybe German soccer had become too successful and had to be punished.
BERTI VOGTS, Germany coach, after elimination from the World Cup finals, 1998

The reason we Germans are so good at penalties is that we have had to rebuild our country twice.
JURGEN KLINSMANN, Germany captain, in a TV documentary, On the Spot: The 12-yard Club, 1999

That was tired, junk football, which at times turned into abuse of the ball.
FRANZ BECKENBAUER, former Germany captain, on his country's dismal showing at Euro 2000

The 5–1 defeat by England was like the explosion of a nuclear bomb. The scars will last for life.
OLIVER KAHN, Germany goalkeeper on that fateful night in Munich, 2001

You have to, you know, to some degree, er, admire the Germans.
SIR BOBBY ROBSON, ITV pundit, leads the grudging praise for Germany's feat in reaching the World Cup final, 2002

Diving fucking cheats.
CHRISTIAN DAILLY, Scotland defender, after Germany's 2–1 win featured a contentious penalty, 2003

GREECE

I was delighted Greece won Euro 2004 because they played as a team, not individually. The so-called great nations – that idea makes me laugh, really – didn't produce, despite their talent. Good on the Greeks. The team with the fewest egos won, and that's always nice.
ROY KEANE, Manchester United captain, 2004

We're not just a football team, we're mates. There is a Greek saying: 'History is made by mates.'
THEO ZAGORAKIS, Greece captain, before they beat Portugal to become European champions, 2004

HUNGARY

I was in my kit, hanging around the corridor, when I saw the England inside-right Ernie Taylor, who wasn't very tall. I popped back in the dressing room and said to the others: 'We're going to be all right – they've got someone even smaller than me.'
FERENC PUSKAS on playing in Hungary's 6–3 defeat of England at Wembley 50 years earlier, 2003

The 1954 Hungarian soccer masters did not go into the record books as the champions of the world. But they went into my personal memory file, and that of millions of other football lovers, as the finest team ever to sort out successfully the intricacies of the wonderful game.
TOM FINNEY, Preston and England forward, in Finney on Football, *1958*

When I returned to the Cumberland Hotel in London, a small boy came up to me in the foyer and said: 'Please sir, take me to your country and teach me to play football.'
PUSKAS in his book Captain of Hungary, *1955*

IRAQ

It was frightening to play for Iraq because every mistake you made put you in prison. The sentence depended on the mistake: for a defensive error, two or three days; for missing a penalty, maybe three weeks.
SAITH HUSSEIN, Iraq striker, on when the national side was run by Saddam Hussein's son Uday, 2003

I'd love to go back to Baghdad and celebrate, but who's going to protect me there?
YOUNIS MAHMOUD, Iraq captain, after victory over Saudi Arabia in the Asian Cup final, 2007

ITALY

We've shown that we're not criminals but great footballers.
ALESSANDRO DEL PIERO, Italy striker, as they reached the World Cup final while his club, Juventus, were embroiled in a financial scandal, 2006

On the pitch the Italians looked no different to us. It was like playing Bournemouth on a wet Saturday.
JASON McATEER, Republic of Ireland manager, after beating Italy in the World Cup, 1994

The Italians still don't know how to lose. Mussolini was the same when he told the players not to return from France without the World Cup in 1938.
BYRON MORENO, Ecuadorian referee, after Italy complained they were cheated by him when South Korea knocked them out of the World Cup, 2002

It's ridiculous to blame problems with our boots. In Kenya they can run 100 kilometres in bare feet.
GENNARO GATTUSO, Italy midfielder, after a draw with Denmark, 2004

LIBERIA

The worst team to feature a European Footballer of the Year since George Best turned out for Dunstable Town.
ANDY LYONS, editor of When Saturday Comes magazine, on George Weah and his national team's failure at the African Nations Cup, 1996

NETHERLANDS

Mr Martinez [the referee] was slow to realise that the Dutch invented the clog.
DAVID LACEY, reporting in the Guardian *on the Italy v Netherlands match, World Cup finals, 1978*

During the European Championship finals we went out every night until two or three in the morning. The problem with Italians is that they don't like to go out after playing.
RUUD GULLIT, Dutch captain, after they became European champions, 1988

NORTHERN IRELAND

Our tactic is to equalise before the others have scored.
DANNY BLANCHFLOWER, Northern Ireland captain, World Cup finals, 1958

We're the Wycombe or Wimbledon of international football. We're ranked 124th in the world and there are countries above us who you wouldn't even know played the game.
LAWRIE SANCHEZ, ex-Wycombe manager and Wimbledon player, on becoming Northern Ireland manager, 2004

I didn't shake the hand of their manager [Sanchez] because I just wanted to get down the tunnel away from it all. I needed to get to the changing room and wash my face because I felt dirty. After watching that I had to wash it all away.
CARLOS ALBERTO, Azerbaijan manager, after a 0–0 draw with 'negative' Northern Ireland, 2004

NORWAY

The Norwegian team's eating habits surprised me, especially mixing jam with smoked fish and even bananas and mackerel.
GEORGES-MARIE DUFFARD, manager of the Norway squad's hotel, World Cup finals, 1998

We love each other, on and off the field.
ERIK MYKLAND, Norway midfielder, 2000

REPUBLIC OF IRELAND

If you have a fortnight's holiday in Dublin you qualify for an Eire cap.
MIKE ENGLAND, Wales manager, 1986

Playing for Liverpool and playing for Ireland could hardly be more different.
At Liverpool I do most of my work in the penalty area. For Ireland, when
you're not closing down defenders, you're chasing long balls over the top.
Much more of this and my legs will be worn down to stumps.
JOHN ALDRIDGE, Republic striker, 1989

The Irish force an unattractive game on the opposition. No team has managed
to escape this contagious crap.
*AHMED EL-MOKADEM, Egyptian FA official, after 0–0 draw v the Republic, World Cup
finals, 1990*

Look at the Irish. They sing their national anthem and none of them know the
words. Jack [Charlton] sings, and all he knows is 'Cushy Butterfield' and
'Blaydon Races'. But look at the pride they have in those green shirts.
*LAWRIE McMENEMY, England assistant manager, calling for Graham Taylor's team to sing
'God Save The Queen' before games, 1991*

As the first bars ring out, I notice the TV camera start to zoom in. Should I
move my lips and sing the two or three lines that I know?
*ANDY TOWNSEND, Republic captain, on an Anglo-Irishman's problems with the Irish
anthem, in* Andy's Game, *1994*

Italy turn up in Armani suits looking the dog's bollocks and we arrive in bright
green blazers and dodgy brogues.
PHIL BABB, Republic defender, at the World Cup finals, 1994

All I've got to do now is get the accent right.

*CLINTON MORRISON, London-born Crystal Palace striker, declaring his allegiance to the
Republic of Ireland, 2001*

If I opened my mouth every time there's something wrong, I'd need my own newspaper.
ROY KEANE on the Football Association of Ireland's preparations for the World Cup finals, 2002

Ireland are a team of impertinents and battlers led by Roy Keane.
CAMEROON TRIBUNE, state-run newspaper, on the eve of the country's World Cup clash with the Irish, who had sent home Keane more than a week earlier, 2002

We're the team that doesn't study the opposition, that takes supporters on the team coach, is not really bothered, that likes a pint and the craic. And yet here we are in the last 16 of the World Cup again. If that scenario were true, we must be the greatest group of guys who ever played the game.
MICK McCARTHY, Republic of Ireland manager, on the team's media image, 2002

SCOTLAND

Playing for Scotland is fantastic. You look at your dark blue shirt and the wee lion looks up at you and says: 'Get out there after those English bastards!'
BILL SHANKLY, Scotland player of the 1930s, quoted in John Keith, Shanks For the Memory, 1998

I warned it would take a great team to beat us. Let's give them their due.
ALF RAMSEY after Scotland became the first team to beat his newly crowned world champions, 1967

If patriotism is silly, then OK, we're silly. When we go on to the field for Scotland, we're ready to give blood. Of course, we'd like a lot of money, but even without it we'll play till we drop.
DAVID HAY, Scotland player, at World Cup finals, 1974

If you keep saying, 'We'll win it, we'll win it, we'll win it,' eventually they believe you.
ALLY MacLEOD, Scotland manager, before the team's ill-fated World Cup, 1978

I am proud of my team for beating the best side in Europe. I want to congratulate Scotland for the team they presented to us.
MARCUS CALDERON, Peru manager, after they beat MacLeod's Scots 3–1, World Cup finals, 1978

It riles me to think of all the great players Scotland have had over the years and yet they haven't won anything. It's criminal that there hasn't been a really successful Scotland team.
BILL SHANKLY after his country's World Cup exit, 1978

A good team with strong English character.
RUUD GULLIT, Netherlands midfielder, before match v Scotland, 1992

We've been playing for an hour and it has just occurred to me that we're drawing 0–0 with a mountain top.
IAN ARCHER, Radio Scotland summariser, during San Marino v Scotland match, 1993. The Scots won 2–0

Bagpipes, warpaint and claymores won't win us games in the European Championship or World Cup.

CRAIG BROWN, manager, 1994

Our supporters expect us to beat everybody we play. The trouble is, so do I.
BROWN after defeat by the United States, 1996

Scotsman's desire to struggle is as if sucked in almost from mother's milk.
GUNTIS INDRIKSONS, Latvian FA president, in the programme for the meeting of their countries, 1996

They'll be home before the postcards.
TOMMY DOCHERTY, former Scotland manager, before his country's first-round exit, World Cup finals, 1998

We owe the English big-time. They stole our land, our oil, perpetrated the Highland Clearances and now they've even pinched Billy Connolly.
GORDON STRACHAN, Coventry manager and former Scotland captain, before Euro 2000 play-off matches v England, 1999

Where are the Jockos to replace the likes of Jim Baxter, who played a blinder when they beat us at Wembley in 1967? The only Baxter they've got up there now is a range of soups.
JIMMY GREAVES, former England striker, in his Sun *column, 1999*

Unless we batter sides we are on a hiding. The way international football is going that won't happen very often. Yet if we don't play well and win, we're rubbish, and if we play well and don't win, we're rubbish.
CHRISTIAN DAILLY, Scotland defender, 2000

I remember when every great English club had two or three Scots in the team. Where the talent has gone, I don't know. But when I go home to Sauchie, the park I played in as a kid – jackets down, 25-a-side – is empty now.
ALAN HANSEN, former Scotland defender, after a draw with the Faroe Islands, 2002

We Scots don't mind laughing at ourselves. But it's getting to the stage where other people are laughing at us.

GORDON STRACHAN, former Scotland player, on the national team's decline, 2004

Barry Ferguson and Nigel Quashie can play in any team in the world.
BERTI VOGTS, Scotland manager, 2004

SENEGAL

Their teamwork is a good model for Christian-Muslim co-existence.
FIDES, Vatican missionary service news agency, World Cup finals, as Senegal reached the quarter-finals of the World Cup, 2002

SPAIN

REPORTER: What went wrong?
VICENTE: We're Spain. What do you expect?
PLAYER press conference after Spain's defeat by Portugal, European Championship finals, 2004

TURKEY

The Turkish people adore my team and my team adore the Turkish people.
It will be a meeting of lovers.
SENOL GUNES, Turkey coach, after taking third place in the World Cup, 2002

Their players were shouting: 'Wait till you come to Turkey.' Even their kit man
was running his fingers across his throat.
*GARETH SOUTHGATE, England defender, after a fracas between England and Turkey
players at Sunderland, 2003*

UNITED STATES OF AMERICA

The US finally came up with an exit strategy. Unfortunately it's for the
World Cup.
*JAY LENO presenting The Tonight Show on American TV three years after the US-led
invasion of Iraq, 2006*

If we lived in another country we would be asking for political asylum. Since
we're American we'll stay in New York and nobody will recognise us.
TAB RAMOS, US midfielder, after 5–1 defeat in the World Cup by Czechoslovakia, 1990

A lot of people that don't know anything about soccer, like me, are all excited
and pulling for you.
GEORGE W BUSH, American President, after the US reached the World Cup's last eight, 2002

It's easy for the US team. Everyone in their country is interested in baseball
and American football. So they're not playing under any pressure. My mother,
my grandmother and my great-grandmother could play in a team like that.
RICARDO LA VOLPE, Mexico coach, after defeat by the Americans, 2005

URUGUAY

Other countries have their history. Uruguay has its football.
ONDINA VIERA, Uruguay coach, 1966

WALES

They gave us a difficult game, for five or six minutes.
GUUS HIDDINK, Netherlands manager, after a 7–1 win v Wales, 1996

MRS MERTON: Is it your ambition to play in a World Cup final?
VINNIE JONES: I play for Wales.
EXCHANGE on TV's Mrs Merton Show, 1997

I actually want Wales to lose every game so that [manager] Bobby Gould
might be sacked. We're the Man City of international football. We rank 98th
in the world, below the Congo Republic.
NICKY WIRE of the Welsh rock group the Manic Street Preachers, 1998

The smaller the nation, like Wales, the more patriotic you seem to be.
I don't like the showy nationalism – a tattoo, wrapping yourself in the flag.
The way to show your fervour and commitment is to go and support and play
for your team.
GARY SPEED, Wales captain, 2003

five

MANAGERS

TONY ADAMS

What has shocked me is that he's in the job in the first place. When we were at Arsenal he didn't have a clue about football. You could ask him on a Thursday who we were playing on Saturday and he'd have no idea – you had to tell him.
PAUL MERSON on Adams's first week in charge of Wycombe Wanderers, 2003

I've set aside everything I learned from Arsene Wenger. It's a complete waste of time at this level [the Second Division]. They just can't take a lot of information on board.
ADAMS on his role at Wycombe, 2003

NIGEL ADKINS

Who needs Mourinho, we've got our physio.
SONG by Scunthorpe fans after Adkins was promoted from physio to manager and led the club to the League One title, 2007

DICK ADVOCAAT

I always take my notebook into the toilet with me to sketch out some match situations.
ADVOCAAT, Rangers coach, 2000

He's short, he's fat, he's going to get the sack, Advocaat.
SONG by Scotland fans after 1–0 win over the Netherlands, 2003

SAM ALLARDYCE

When I looked round Stamford Bridge last weekend with 40,000 inside, I thought back to when I was player-manager of Limerick. I remember an away game and our chairman saying: 'This is a lovely ground.' There was a metre-high concrete wall around the pitch and a row of trees trying to keep the wind out. In the corner there was a bunker they called the dressing rooms and I swear there wasn't a seat in sight. I wondered what the hell I'd let myself in for, yet my chairman thought it was great.
ALLARDYCE, Bolton manager, 2003

If my name were Alardicci people would probably think I was the best thing since sliced bread.
ALLARDYCE claiming foreign managers received more recognition than their British counterparts, 2003

Sam didn't believe in emails. If I sent one to the secretary, rather than get off my arse, walk out of my office and speak to her, I'd have been sacked. He had a computer system but hated it. The personal touch was the way forward.
PHIL BROWN, Derby manager and Allardyce's former assistant at Bolton, 2005

I can't help the way I look. I suppose some people still think of me as a big, ugly centre-half who doesn't know about the game's finer points.
ALLARDYCE on his hopes of becoming England manager, 2006

MARTIN ALLEN

Gardening can help relieve the stress of management, but it's also similar to tending a team. I took a chainsaw to clear out Brentford, got some plants in a sale and others that people thought were old and dead. Hopefully, Leicester have an excellent nursery with some impressive seedlings. We'll see what we can grow when new plants are added.
ALLEN on starting a spell as Leicester manager that would last 98 days, 2007

MALCOLM ALLISON

On the coach back from London, Allison asked where Francis Lee was. 'He's hiding in case you give him a right-hander for missing that penalty,' said Rodney Marsh. Allison was in pensive mood. 'I never tear them off a strip when they've lost. I've done it before and it's led to bad feelings that take too long to heal.' He became absorbed in his cigar. 'This game is like being in love. You've got to suffer to enjoy it.'
TONY PAWSON, author, on the aftermath of a defeat at Crystal Palace during Allison's first reign as Manchester City manager, in The Football Managers, *1973*

It's ridiculous. I've served more time than Ronnie Biggs did for the Great Train Robbery.
ALLISON, then Plymouth manager, appealing against a touchline ban, 1978

OSSIE ARDILES

I'll never compromise my ideals, whichever division I'm in. I tell the boys to try to play like Pele.
ARDILES, Swindon manager, 1990

REPORTER: Is Klinsmann Spurs' biggest-ever signing?
OSSIE ARDILES: No, I was.
EXCHANGE at press conference to unveil Tottenham's German recruit, 1995

RON ATKINSON

You're welcome to my home phone number, gentlemen. But please remember not to ring me during *The Sweeney*.
ATKINSON on taking over as manager at Manchester United, 1981

It's bloody tough being a legend.
ATKINSON at Old Trafford, 1983

As far as he's concerned, he's God. There's nobody big enough to tell him what to do.
MARGARET ATKINSON, his first wife, after news broke of Atkinson's extra-marital affair, 1984

Half an hour? You could shoot Ben Hur *in half an hour. You've got 15 seconds.*
ATKINSON to photographer who asked for 30 minutes with him, 1984

This person suffers from erotic fantasies. He thinks a lot about sex, though he is very devoted to his mother.
GRAPHOLOGIST analysing Atkinson's writing on ITV's FA Cup final coverage, 1985

I've had to swap my Merc for a BMW, I'm down to my last 37 suits and I'm drinking non-vintage champagne.
ATKINSON on life after his sacking by United, 1987

I believe there are only a select few managers who can handle the real giant clubs of this world. I happen to be one of them.
ATKINSON at Atletico Madrid, a month before his sacking, 1988

He has never slagged off United or criticised anyone here since he left, and he could have made a few bob doing so.
ALEX FERGUSON, Atkinson's successor at Old Trafford, 1991

His teams were always gifted and played some lovely football... But his legacy at Manchester United was a pool of older players. Ron always liked to buy the finished article whereas I've always preferred to watch young talent grow.
FERGUSON, 1996

Q: What was the highlight of your World Cup?
A: Bumping into Frank Sinatra.
ATKINSON at the World Cup in the US, 1994

There is this champagne-and-nightclubs image he has. But above all he loves the game. He's still a child at heart. In training this season he has been everyone from Arnold Muhren to David Ginola.
GORDON STRACHAN, Coventry player-coach, 1996

Have you seen that scene in the film *Kes*, where Brian Glover thinks he's Bobby Charlton? Ron's like that. He thinks he's the best five-a-side player in the club.
LIAM DAISH, Coventry defender, 1997

I'm still the best five-a-side player in the club. Mind you, that's probably why we're in the position we're in.
ATKINSON at 56, when his Coventry side propped up the Premiership, 1995

The last of the great character managers.
GORDON STRACHAN, before succeeding Atkinson as Coventry manager, 1996

The only relaxed boss is Big Ron. He had me drinking pink champagne –
before the match.
HARRY REDKNAPP, West Ham manager, 1995

The champagne-and-jewellery image has stuck with me, but it has been
perpetuated by people who don't know me. When I was burgled the thieves
were gutted not to find my place bulging with gold watches and trinkets.
ATKINSON on retiring as a manager at 60, 1999

I met Mick Jagger when I played for Oxford United and the Rolling Stones
did a concert there. Little did I know he'd be as famous as me one day.
ATKINSON, 2003

My favourite politician was Margaret Thatcher. She was a bugger but she
would have made the best football manager. John Major was all right. He just
had a bad team.
ATKINSON, 1999

They could have been yellow, purple with two heads so long as they could play
and they were good lads – which they were.
*ATKINSON recalling the black trio of Brendan Batson, Laurie Cunningham and Cyrille
Regis during his first spell as West Bromwich Albion manager, 2004*

[Desailly] is what is known in some schools as a fucking thick lazy nigger.
ATKINSON after a Monaco v Chelsea match when he thought the microphone was off, 2004

I must have had rocks for brains.
ATKINSON on losing his ITV contract because of the Desailly comment, 2004

What he said was unambiguous, non-negotiable and hugely offensive.

PIARA POWER, director of Kick it Out, a campaign against racism in football, 2004

I was totally out of order. I've worked longer and harder with black players than anybody.
ATKINSON, 2004

'Lazy nigger.' That's like a plantation vibe. What really gets me is that in his interviews about this he says he took off his microphone and headphones before he said it. Does that make it any better?
IAN WRIGHT, former England striker, on Atkinson's off-guard remark, 2004

Bigot Ron
HEADLINE in the Sun, 2004

You should be made to clean Rio Ferdinand's boots for 10 weeks.
DARCUS HOWE, black broadcaster, to Atkinson on the TV documentary What Ron Said, 2004

Whatever happened to forgiveness?
ATKINSON to Howe, 2004

We played at Everton in the early 1990s – when you were allowed two subs – and of the 13 players on each side, eight of ours [Aston Villa] were black and Everton didn't have one. And how many black players did Blackburn have when Jack Walker was there? Now that's what I call racism.
ATKINSON, 2004

I've known Ron since I was 16. I've been on holiday with his family. My children have been sick on him. No way is he racist.
CARLTON PALMER, former player under Atkinson, 2004

It's the language of the football field – they do swear. In that context, you wouldn't think words like 'nigger' were particularly insulting; it would be funny. Without wishing to insult any black men, it's us having fun. What about people who make jokes about my long chin?
JIMMY HILL, broadcaster and ex-player and manager, after Atkinson's sacking by ITV, 2004

ALAN BALL

Alan Ball and I didn't see eye to eye, and it had nothing to do with his being 5ft 3in and me being 6ft 4in.
DAVE BEASANT, Southampton goalkeeper, 1995

Round here we threaten young Stoke fans that Alan Ball will come back and manage the club if they don't go to bed early and eat all their vegetables.
MARTIN SMITH, editor of the Stoke City fanzine the Oatcake, *on 'the bogeyman' Ball's return as Portsmouth manager, 1999*

DAVE BASSETT

I can still see 'Harry' screaming: 'You're just a bunch of clowns and amateurs, and that's why you'll never reach the top.' Twenty minutes later, the van chugged to a halt on the M4. He had forgotten to fill it up with petrol.
WALLY DOWNES, who had been a Wimbledon player in the Fourth Division under Bassett, 1988

I know what they are all thinking – the Elephant Man is back, stand well clear. I was once called the spiv in a £400 suit. I felt right insulted. It cost at least a grand.
BASSETT on leading Sheffield United back into the top flight, 1990

I don't want my players behaving like poofters. I want them to be men.
BASSETT after Sheffield United's Tom Cowan was accused of overreacting to a push by Roy Keane, 1993

It's going to be my epitaph, isn't it? Deep in the shit, where he started.
BASSETT, facing relegation with Nottingham Forest, 1997

I ran out of petrol on the motorway on my way to the game. I phoned the police and they asked my name. When I told them 'Dave Bassett', this cop said: 'What, the Leicester manager?' I said yes and he burst out laughing.
BASSETT during Leicester's slide to relegation, 2002

One thousand games in purgatory, eh?
SIR ALEX FERGUSON presenting Bassett with an award for 1,000 matches as a manager, 2002

JOHN BECK

Beck had gone barmy before the game. The Bristol City manager, Denis Smith, had said something on the radio, a really over-the-top comment...so he [Beck] said: 'Welsh bastards!' meaning Bristol City.
COLIN BAILLIE, who had played under Beck at Cambridge United, 1992

RAFAEL BENITEZ

REPORTER: Is winning the Champions' League the greatest accomplishment in your life?
BENITEZ: In football, yes. But I have two daughters and a wife.
EXCHANGE at press conference after Liverpool lifted the European Cup, 2005

Friends ask me whether Rafa's cold attitude pisses me off, but it doesn't. My aim is still to get a 'well done' off him before I retire. But then, if he gives me a 'well done' I might need a long lie down.
STEVEN GERRARD on the Spaniard's businesslike manner, in the Liverpool captain's autobiography, 2007

When I really needed someone, he didn't just give me a hand. He gave me an arm.
JAVIER MASCHERANO, Liverpool and Argentina midfielder, on how Benitez rescued him from the West Ham bench, 2007

He's like an ideal father-in-law.
RYAN BABEL, Dutch striker, on joining Liverpool, 2007

KEVIN BLACKWELL

Unlike that cheeky sod Kevin Blackwell, Dennis Wise is not in the excuse-making business. Blackwell said Leeds United would not have been relegated last week if he'd still been in charge. He's right. We would have been down by December.
KEN BATES, Leeds chairman, after relegation to League One in May, 2007. He had fired Blackwell the previous September

JOHN BOND

Like Brian Clough, I find it impossible to keep my mouth shut.
BOND, Norwich manager, 1979

John Bond gave me my first acting lesson – how to break forward from defence and then, when you lose the ball and get stranded, how to look completely innocent as the other team close in on your goal. The lessons I learnt in the Hammers academy certainly served me well.
DAVID ESSEX, actor, singer and former West Ham apprentice, in his autobiography
A Charmed Life, *2002*

TREVOR BROOKING

The silly image of Trevor as a fence-sitter was dispelled by his two stints as caretaker-manager of West Ham. The last thing he did was sit on the fence, or even the bench. He was always jumping up and down like a raving lunatic.
GARY LINEKER, BBC and former England colleague, 2003

Go now while you're unbeaten. It won't get any better than this.
LINEKER in text message to Brooking after West Ham, fighting relegation, won his first match in temporary charge, 2004

He's the Barry Norman of football.
DAVID JAMES, West Ham goalkeeper, on Brooking's liking for video analysis, 2003

CRAIG BROWN

Kevin [Keegan] and I have 63 international caps between us. He has 63 of them.
CRAIG BROWN, Scotland manager, before the countries' Euro 2000 play-off, 1999

My job is my holiday. I travel all the time and see the world in this business. I take my holidays at home in Ayr.
BROWN on the Scotland managership, 1997

My brother Bob has three degrees from universities, my other brother Jock is an MA from Cambridge and I'm a BA from the Open University. As a player I was the one the manager would turn to last and say: 'Right, son, nothing clever from you this week.'
BROWN, 1995

You keep going because you love the game, the smell of the liniment, everything. I'm an adolescent about football. I'll quit when I grow up.
BROWN on managing Preston at 62 years old, 2004

STEVE BRUCE

The biggest mistake I made was believing that a great footballer would make a great manager.
BARRY RUBERRY, Huddersfield chairman, after the former Manchester United captain's departure, 2001

Among those who rang me was Sir Alex Ferguson, who said you couldn't damage a face like mine.
BRUCE, Birmingham manager, after his face was scarred in a scuffle with car thieves, 2004

MATT BUSBY

You would go in [to Busby's office] fighting and full of demands. And he would give you nothing at all. He might even take a tenner off your wages. And you would come out thinking: 'What a great guy.' I remember going in there once, absolutely livid. And 10 minutes later I came out, no better off, walking on air.
EAMON DUNPHY, former United reserve, in Only a Game?, *1976*

Matt was the eternal optimist. In 1968 he still hoped Glenn Miller was just missing.
PAT CRERAND, former Manchester United player under Busby, 1997

His greatest achievement was to create the illusion of beauty in a craft wretchedly deformed from the beginning.
EAMON DUNPHY, United reserve during the Busby era at Old Trafford, in A Strange Kind of Glory, *1991*

He has held his magnetism right through five decades. I remember in Rotterdam for the final of the Cup-Winners' Cup, a lot of fans were gathered at the main entrance chanting the names of players like 'Hughesy' as they went in. Suddenly Sir Matt arrived and the wild cheering turned to respectful applause. It was quite touching, just like the Pope arriving.
ALEX FERGUSON in Six Years at United, *1992*

It would have been Sir Matt Busby's 90th birthday today. All I know is that someone was doing an awful lot of kicking up there.
FERGUSON after Manchester United's last-gasp victory over Bayern Munich in the European Cup final, 1999

JACK CHARLTON

I won't die at a match. I might die being dragged down the River Tweed by a giant salmon, but a football match, no.
CHARLTON, Republic of Ireland manager, 1988

Jack makes out he is not really interested in football, and tells the world he's going fishing. But we know what he's thinking about when he's fishing. Football.
JOHAN CRUYFF, Barcelona coach, 1990

Jack is not always right, but he is never wrong.

JOHNNY GILES, former Republic of Ireland manager and ex-Leeds colleague, 1991

We like Jack. He's a crazy man but football needs characters. However, he must learn where to draw the line with his behaviour.
GUIDO TOGNONI, FIFA spokesman, announcing a touchline ban for Charlton, World Cup finals, 1994

Imagine what Ireland might have done if led and inspired by a man of vision and courage. This is not hard to do: remember Giants Stadium when, with the spur of an early goal, the players overcame miserable tactics to humble Italy.
EAMON DUNPHY, journalist and ex-Republic player, before what proved to be Charlton's final match, 1995

The honour that pleased me most of all was when the House of Commons voted me Beer Drinker of the Year.
CHARLTON, 1996

One of his cardinals introduced us, saying: 'This is Mr Charlton.' He said: 'Ah yes, the boss.'
CHARLTON after meeting the Pope with the Irish squad, World Cup finals, 1990

Charlton developed a style of play that suited his crude convictions rather than the gifts of his players.
ROY KEANE, Manchester United and former Ireland captain, alleging that Charlton had a 'primitive' approach, 2002

If Jack came in here now, he wouldn't buy you a drink. He'd be hoping somebody would buy him one.
KEANE, 2002

BRIAN CLOUGH

I wouldn't say I was the best manager in the business. But I was in the top one.
CLOUGH, 2002

He was lovable and impossible, wise and silly, attractive and appalling. He was a pickle of a man.
MICHAEL PARKINSON, journalist and broadcaster, after Clough's death, 2004

Age does not count. It's what you know about football that matters. I know I am better than the 500 or so managers who have been sacked since the war. If they had known anything about the game they wouldn't have lost their jobs.
CLOUGH on taking his first managerial post, with Hartlepools, 1965

Success? Tell me the date when my obituary is going to appear and I'll tell you whether I've been a success or not. If I get to 60 I shall have done pretty well.
CLOUGH, by now Brighton manager, 1973

He's a kind of Rolls-Royce communist.
MALCOLM ALLISON, rival manager, 1973

He's worse than the rain in Manchester. At least God stops that occasionally.
BILL SHANKLY, former managerial adversary, on Clough's pronouncements, 1979

Outside of family life there is nothing better than winning European Cups.
CLOUGH, Nottingham Forest manager, 1980

A player can never feel too sure of himself with Clough. That's his secret.
PETER TAYLOR, his assistant at Derby and Nottingham Forest, in With Clough By
Taylor, *1980*

Do you know, Sinatra once met me.
CLOUGH to colleague at Forest, 1983

It's easy enough to get to Ireland – just a walk across the Irish Sea as far as I'm
concerned.
CLOUGH confirming his application for the Republic of Ireland manager's job, 1985

I want to be manager of Scotland.
CLOUGH, 1985

I can't promise to give the team talks in Welsh, but from now I'll be taking my
holidays in Porthcawl and I've bought a complete set of Harry Secombe albums.
CLOUGH on his hopes of becoming Wales manager, 1988

Resignations are for Prime Ministers and those caught with their trousers
down, not for me.
CLOUGH after withdrawing his threat to quit Forest over Wales, 1988

I hope you were as delighted as I was last week when Nelson Mandela was
freed from a South African jail. But what I hadn't bargained for was that his
release was going to cut across the start of our Littlewoods Cup final.
CLOUGH, Nottingham Forest programme column, 1990

If the BBC ran a Crap Decision of the Month competition on *Match of the
Day*, I'd walk it.
CLOUGH as Forest headed for relegation, 1993

On a Saturday he'd waltz into the dressing room at twenty to three, put a football down and say: 'Right, this is your best friend. This is what we play with.'
DARREN WASSALL, Derby and former Forest player, 1993

He's my idol as a manager but we don't really communicate. The closest we've come is when he tried to kiss me after a testimonial match, but I smelled the aftershave and skipped past him.
NEIL WARNOCK, Notts County manager, 1991

I played under Bill Shankly and Bob Paisley, and Clough is a better manager than either of them. As a manager there's no limit to my respect for him, but as a man he's not my cup of tea. I once told him I'd never be caught standing at a bar having a drink with him. He said the feeling was mutual.
LARRY LLOYD, former Liverpool and Forest defender, 1991

My wife says 'OBE' stands for Old Big 'Ead.
CLOUGH, 1991

I'd like to retire with half of what he has achieved as a manager and a quarter of his dough.
DAVE BASSETT, Sheffield United manager, 1992

Like all the great dictators, from de Gaulle to Thatcher, he stayed on a little too long.

GAZZETTA DELLO SPORT, *Italian sports newspaper, after Clough's retirement, 1993*

He gave by far the best interview of all the candidates – confident, passionate, full of common sense and above all patriotic. If Ron Greenwood hadn't been around, he'd have clinched it.
PETER SWALES, former FA international committee chairman, on Clough's 1977 application to manage England, 1995

They didn't want an England manager who was prepared to call the Italians cheating bastards. They failed to understand that I would have curbed my language and revelled in the relief from the day-to-day grind of club management.
CLOUGH, 1995

I'm ill-tempered, rude and wondering what's for tea, same as ever.
CLOUGH on what he was like at 4.45pm on Saturdays after retirement, 1994

There was talk of a testimonial match, of a stand being named after me, but there was nothing, not even a toilet. They could have had a Brian Clough Bog.
CLOUGH alleging lack of recognition for his 17 years' service to Nottingham Forest, 1997. Two years later Forest named a stand after him

When this young man says, 'Grandad, you did not get many academic qualifications,' I get out my medals. They are my O and A levels.
CLOUGH on the Master of Arts degree bestowed on him by Nottingham University, 1999

He's the best manager of all time in my book because of what he's done and where he did it.

RON ATKINSON, one of Clough's successors at Forest, 1995

Brian Clough provided ample proof that he was one of British football's greatest managers. That he was almost certainly its rudest is perhaps another distinction he is proud to claim. He is welcome to it.
SIR ALEX FERGUSON in Managing My Life, *his autobiography, 1999*

We'd talk for 20 minutes, then decide I was right.
CLOUGH on how he dealt with discontented players, 2002

One day my grandson turned to me and said: 'You're not having a drink, Grandad, are you?' I knew something had to be done. Sometimes when I went to bed, instead of counting sheep, I'd count the drinks I'd had. If I'd had six, I'd call it five. I'd kid myself about the numbers, like all drinkers do.
CLOUGH admitting to problems with alcohol, 2003

I know most people will say that instead of walking on water I should have taken more of it with my drinks. They are absolutely right.
CLOUGH, 2003

Don't send me flowers when I'm dead. If you like me, send them while I'm alive.
CLOUGH, 2003

As someone who worked with him for 16 years and appreciated, even at 16, that I was working for a genius, it would be nice if the genius recovered.
JOHN McGOVERN, former Derby and Forest captain, after Clough had a liver transplant, 2003

To put everybody's mind at rest, I'd like to stress that they didn't give me George Best's old liver.
CLOUGH after a transplant brought him 'back from death's door', 2003

I never thought my body would reject my new liver. Reject – that's a word I've always hated. Well, ever since I was rejected for the England job.
CLOUGH, 2003

The principles he laid down stand the test of time. Honesty, hard work, don't feign or fall over when fouled and don't swear at referees.
PAUL HART, one of Clough's successors at Forest, 2003

Cloughie's philosophy on football was all about rest, which I'd never known. It was come in and do 10 minutes' training on Monday and then 'Get yourself home, big game on Saturday, don't want to see you until Friday morning.' I'm 24, enthusiasm overflowing, can't wait to train and practise. And it's three days off! Unbelievable.
TEDDY SHERINGHAM, former Forest and England striker, 2006

What I learned from Clough was never to give a rival manager an even break.
SIR BOBBY ROBSON, Newcastle manager, recalling how Clough refused to reschedule a Forest v Ipswich game, 2003

My life changed after Brian cuffed me. I was asked for my autograph; bus drivers gave me free rides; girls threw themselves at me; and my old headmaster asked me to open the school fete.
SEAN O'HARA, Forest fan hit on the head by Clough after he invaded the pitch in a 1989 match, 2004

Our loss for the second time.

MESSAGE on a Leeds shirt hung in memorial display at Forest's ground after Clough's death, 2004. Clough had been sacked as Leeds manager after 44 days

He'd be the first to say he was the greatest of all time – he was England's version of Muhammad Ali.
MARTIN O'NEILL, Celtic manager and former Clough player at Forest, 2004

John Robertson, who grew up with me at Forest, dismisses the idea that Clough ruled by fear over the whole club. He certainly scared the life out of me. Once I went in shaking with fear to ask for a pay rise. I accepted a whisky and a wage cut.
O'NEILL, 2004

Clough and [Peter] Taylor used to crack me up. They were like Morecambe and Wise. It was a real bad-cop, good-cop routine, and it worked perfectly.
KENNY BURNS, Forest defender under the late managerial duo, 2004

He gave Nottingham a name. Forget Robin Hood. Remember Brian Clough.
WAYNE STEPHENSON, Forest fan, interviewed by reporters at the City Ground after Clough's death, 2004

The fact that he was never England manager was a travesty. It was our loss – the public. We missed out because the people at FA were frightened of him.
GEOFFREY BOYCOTT, former Yorkshire and England cricketer, 2004

He was a disciplinarian and perhaps one of the sad facts was that he couldn't discipline himself.
BOYCOTT on his friend's drinking, 2004

We thought he was indestructible.
GARRY BIRTLES, former Forest striker, 2004

NIGEL CLOUGH

He's not as bright as me, despite his A levels... Everybody likes him, so there's obviously something wrong.
BRIAN CLOUGH, the Burton Albion manager's father, 2003

I'm fed up with hearing people say what a nice, fine lad he is. He doesn't get that from me. You have to be prepared to be unpopular and tell people things they don't want to hear. Would he be able to look someone in the eye and tell him he wasn't playing in a European Cup final? I had to tell Martin O'Neill and Archie Gemmill. O'Neill couldn't look at me for a week and little Archie still hasn't.
BRIAN CLOUGH, 2003

CHRIS COLEMAN

He has the look of a celebrity chef about him.
ARTICLE about the then Fulham manager in the Charlton programme, 2005

STEVE COPPELL

It's a nice feeling which I liken to when I got my O-level results or when I passed my driving test. I just felt 'I've worked hard and done well'.
COPPELL, Reading manager, on winning promotion to the Premiership, 2006

JOHAN CRUYFF

I only decided to become a manager when I was told I couldn't.
CRUYFF, former Barcelona and Ajax manager, recalls being informed by the Dutch FA that he lacked the necessary qualifications, 2004

STAN CULLIS

The night Stan Cullis got the sack
Wolverhampton wandered round in circles
Like a disallowed goal
Looking for a friendly linesman.
MARTIN HALL, poet and songwriter, on the Wolves manager of the 1950s in 'The Stan Cullis Blues', 1974

ALAN CURBISHLEY

When I was starting out at Charlton 20 years ago, Alan Curbishley had just arrived from Aston Villa. He was a senior professional, what would be termed a 'footballer' – a good passing midfielder, not much of a tackler. I recall a quiet, assured dressing-room character, but on the pitch, could he moan? So we nicknamed him Albert Tatlock.

ROB LEE, West Ham and former England midfielder, nominating Curbishley as a 'potential England manager', 2004. Tatlock was a gruff pensioner in Coronation Street

KENNY DALGLISH

I know he hates me. He walked past me on the golf course as if I were a tree. He's the moaningest minnie I've ever known.
JOHN BOND, Birmingham manager, 1987

I have no hesitation in saying he was one of the great players of all time, but I can't speak of him in the same terms as a manager. That's not a criticism, but he didn't begin the job at the grass roots, start with a Second or Third Division club or build a side from scratch. So there are some doubts.
HOWARD KENDALL, Everton manager, after Dalglish resigned at Liverpool, 1991

The pressure on match days is making my head explode. I can't go on.

DALGLISH on quitting Anfield, 1991

He's incredibly intense about football. He's the only person I've ever seen come off during a match who is still playing every ball. Normally when players are substituted, you'll see them in the dug-out, winding down. Kenny still kicks and heads everything.
ALAN HANSEN, friend and former Liverpool colleague, 1992

Kenny is such a football nut that you could mention any player in England and he'd know who you were talking about.
HANSEN, 1993

I've always felt there's a scriptwriter up on a cloud somewhere penning Kenny's life story.
GORDON STRACHAN on Dalglish's championship success with Blackburn, 1995

Is Kenny Dalglish a big girl's blouse?
JEREMY PAXMAN, presenter of BBC2's Newsnight *programme, introducing a feature about managers, 1998*

I had to be very careful around him and I still am now we are together at Celtic because he's the biggest mickey-taker imaginable. Kenny is completely different from his public image, loving a laugh in private. He is very guarded with those he doesn't know so I understand why people label him as dour.
JOHN BARNES, former Liverpool player under Dalglish, in his autobiography, 1999

BILLY DAVIES

I'm intense and the players know it. They know if they make one mistake in training I'll give them a round of 'fucks' – excuse my French.
DAVIES, Derby manager, before promotion to the Premiership via the play-offs, 2007

Me and him [Sir Alex Ferguson] both come from Govan. We both like picking up chewing gum from the street and eating it.
DAVIES on his Glasgow roots, 2007

TOMMY DOCHERTY

I talk a lot. On any subject. Which is always football.
DOCHERTY, Chelsea manager, 1967

No one will ever equal Sir Matt Busby's achievements and influence at Old Trafford, but I'd like to go down as someone who did nearly as much.
DOCHERTY after leading Manchester United to promotion, 1974

I have been punished for falling in love. What I have done has nothing at all to do with my track record as a manager.
DOCHERTY after his sacking by United because of an affair with the wife of the club physio, 1977

All this talk about Tommy Docherty not being fit to run a football club is rubbish. That's exactly what he's fit for.
CLIVE JAMES, TV critic, 1979

Preston are one of my old clubs, but then most of them are. I've had more clubs than Jack Nicklaus.
DOCHERTY, 1979

They offered me a handshake of £10,000 to settle amicably. I told them they would have to be a lot more amicable than that.
DOCHERTY on being dismissed by Preston, 1981

They sacked me as nicely as they could – one of the nicest sackings I've had.
DOCHERTY on leaving Preston, 1981

There's no excitement. Tommy's just been sacked again, that's all.

MARY BROWN, Docherty's partner, to door-stepping journalists after the Preston sacking, 1981

I've been in more courts than Bjorn Borg.
DOCHERTY, 1981

Tommy Docherty criticising Charlie Nicholas is like Bernard Manning telling Jimmy Tarbuck to clean up his act.
GORDON TAYLOR, players' union leader, after Docherty spoke of Nicholas's 'indiscipline', 1984

His interests are limited... At home he never read anything in the newspapers but the sports pages. His knowledge of what goes on outside football is so restricted that he couldn't understand why he kept getting into trouble for parking on double yellow lines. He thought they were a new form of street decoration.
CATHERINE LOCKLEY, Docherty's daughter by his first wife, 1981

He has gone 200 years too late.
ANONYMOUS MANAGER on Docherty's move to Australia, 1981

IAIN DOWIE

The relegation battle is like being on the *Titanic* with only one seat left on the lifeboat. The problem is you don't want to have to fight Iain Dowie for it.
HARRY REDKNAPP, Southampton manager, 2005. In the event, his team and Dowie's Crystal Palace both went down

My players say I look like [former Dead Or Alive singer] Pete Burns but I don't know who he is. All I know is he's obviously not blessed with good looks.
DOWIE, Crystal Palace manager, 2006

SVEN-GÖRAN ERIKSSON

I didn't take it for the money or even for the weather. I took it because it's a great challenge.
ERIKSSON, a Swede, on becoming England's first foreign manager, 2000

I'm very upset [that England have appointed a foreign manager]. The French are managed by a Frenchman, Germany by a German and the Italians have one of their own.
JACK CHARLTON, Englishman and former Republic of Ireland manager, 2000

Q: Do you know who the Leicester goalkeeper is?
A: No.
Q: Do you know who the Sunderland left-back is?
A: No. But when I come here I will know everything.
ERIKSSON on his first meeting with the English press, 2000

The nation which gave the game of football to the world has been forced to put a foreign coach in charge of its national team for the first time. What a climb-down. What a humiliation. What a terrible, pathetic, self-inflicted indictment. What an awful mess.
EDITORIAL in the Sun *on Eriksson's appointment, 2000*

England's humiliation knows no end. In their trendy eagerness to appoint a designer foreigner did the FA pause for so much as a moment to consider the depth of this insult to our national pride. We sell our birthright down the fjord to a nation of seven million skiers and hammer-throwers who spend half their year living in total darkness.
EDITORIAL in the Daily Mail, *2000*

By going to a foreign situation we've chosen to say we're not a power any more, but we, the FA, will show you how clever we are because we are designer people now, not old farts any more.
TERRY VENABLES, former England manager, 2001

It [Eriksson's appointment] is a betrayal of our heritage and coaching structure. Terry Venables isn't considered because the FA has laid down criteria which maybe even the Archbishop of Canterbury wouldn't meet.
GORDON TAYLOR, players' union leader, 2001

He's certainly different from Barry Fry.
CHRIS POWELL, Charlton defender who served Fry at Southend, before his first England appearance, 2001

I'm nervous about meeting so many new people. It's like when you go out with a woman for the first time – you're bound to wonder how it will end up.
ERIKSSON before his first game with England, v Spain, 2001

Eriksson is our superhero as five-goal Lions roar
HEADLINE in the News of the World *after England's 5–1 win in Germany, 2001*

I've read the book about all the other England managers [*The Second Most Important Job in the Country*]. They were more or less killed, all of them. Why should I be different?
ERIKSSON, 2001

If he should need any acclimatising, I'm here waiting on his call.

ULRIKA JONSSON, fellow Swede, when Eriksson became England manager – more than a year before their affair, 2001

They were actually at it, naked in the middle of the day. I don't know who got the bigger shock, them or me.
MICHELLE SMITH, Ulrika Jonsson's nanny, claiming her employer had 'sex sessions' with the England manager, 2002

Michelle told me that Sven is quite short and wears thick-soled shoes to make himself look taller.
TONY AZZOPARDI, boyfriend of Ms Jonsson's nanny, 2002

I had never known such keenness in a man.
JONSSON, 2002

My son having a romance with a weather-girl? I spoke to him this week and he talked as always about the weather, but not a weather-girl.
ULLA ERIKSSON, the England manager's mother, 2002

I don't think it [Eriksson's relationship with Ulrika Jonsson] will affect the respect he receives from the England players. If anything it could enhance it.
ARSENE WENGER, Arsenal manager, 2002

Sven is my inspiration. It is through him that I understand the power of football.
NANCY DELL'OLIO, Eriksson's partner, shortly after the 'Ulrika affair' ended, 2002

The Gulf War was a cakewalk compared with Eriksson's love life.
PAUL NEWMAN, FA head of communications and former BBC war correspondent, 2002

It's no good lying in your bed at night wondering if you have made the right choice.
ERIKSSON at height of speculation about whether he would choose Ms Dell'Olio or Ms Jonsson, 2002. The words were part of the sleeve notes to a CD of his classical-music favourites

He can't resist a bird.
ATHOLE STILL, Eriksson's agent, quoted in Joe Lovejoy's biography, 2002

We needed Winston Churchill and we got Iain Duncan Smith.

ENGLAND DEFENDER, *anonymously alleging Eriksson gave an 'uninspiring' half-time talk during England's World Cup defeat by Brazil, 2002*

When [Eriksson] speaks he makes sense but he doesn't inspire. He is easy to like but difficult to get to know.
GARETH SOUTHGATE, *England defender, 2003*

You interview Sven and he is so deadpan, so hard to get anything out of. It's part of his cleverness. He's clearly no fool.
GARY LINEKER, *BBC TV football anchorman, 2004*

When I want to tease Sven I say, 'Your language sounds like the noise made by some animals in the forest.' It's not musical. It's like speaking in the language of a telegram or text message. Very regimented, very Swedish.
NANCY DELL'OLIO, *2004*

He's got a lot of forehead.
LINEKER *when asked to describe Eriksson, 2003*

I thought as they were both Swedish and living in the UK [Eriksson and Ulrika Jonsson] they might have something in common. I was only being polite.
ALASTAIR CAMPBELL, *former press secretary to the Prime Minister, recalling how Eriksson's affair with the TV personality started with a meeting at a cocktail party, 2004*

I couldn't believe what was happening to me. He was a master in the art of love-making. He did not use a condom. There was no contraception. He was not concerned about me getting pregnant.
FARIA ALAM, *former FA secretary, on her affair with Eriksson, 2004*

The man's like a wet fish. He's got as much passion as a tadpole.
IAN WRIGHT, *former England striker and father of England's Shaun Wright-Phillips, 2005.*

Sven is a very giving man in the area of passion.
FARIA ALAM, *2006*

If you lose 2–0 to the United States, that is not exactly your decision. Whether to unzip your trousers – now that *is* your decision.
GRAHAM TAYLOR, former England manager, 2004

He just said 'Good' with a nice chuckle.
TORD GRIP, Eriksson's assistant, on his boss's reaction to the FA Board's ruling that he had no case to answer over Ms Alam, 2004

In Sweden we don't discuss our private lives. We have other things to talk about.

GRIP, 2004

If Sven had won Euro 2004, he could have slept with the guard dog and got away with it.
DAVID MELLOR, former Conservative minister and self-confessed adulterer, 2004

I know Sven has a roving eye. He is like a seagull and can wrap his wings around people.
DAVID DAVIES, executive director of the FA, during industrial tribunal at which Eriksson's former lover Faria Alam alleged unfair dismissal by the FA, 2005

Sven would have been a nice easy choice for them in terms of nothing really happens. He doesn't change anything. He sails along. Nobody falls out with him.
SIR ALEX FERGUSON on reports that Manchester United had considered Eriksson in the event of his retiring, 2003

I have great difficulties in understanding that with this England job you should be a saint, you shouldn't earn a lot of money or have a private life and should absolutely not listen to other possibilities in life.
ERIKSSON after a clandestine meeting with Chelsea became public, 2004

At the start of the second half against Portugal, I said to my grandson Stephen: 'Eriksson hasn't got the guts to substitute Beckham. He's the only candidate, he's out on his feet…' But he bottled it. Beckham's hurt feelings wouldn't have bothered me.
BRIAN CLOUGH on watching the European Championship finals on TV, 2004

If you want someone shouting, you will have to change the coach. I will never do it.
ERIKSSON, 2003

It was fantastic for John [Lennon] and Yoko [Ono] to use their popularity to promote peace and I'd be very proud to carry on. It would be fantastic for me and Sven to also do that as a couple.
NANCY DELL'OLIO, Eriksson's partner, announcing her own anti-war pressure group, Truce International, 2003

Nancy and Sven will never marry, that's for sure. Just as Nancy proposed to him, so did his first wife. Then he postponed their wedding to fit in a coaching course. How's that for romance?
ULRIKA JONSSON in her News of the World *column, 2003*

Business people have a great appetite for European gurus, and Sven strikes them as one. He has the appearance of being lucky and successful, a dream combination. He is also adept at managing highly talented people. He's an Ikea-style leader: utilitarian, down-to-earth and globally successful.
STUART CRAINER, business commentator and co-author of Leadership the Sven-Göran Eriksson Way, *2004*

INTERVIEWER: How would you like to leave the England job?
ERIKSSON: Alive.
INTERVIEW on television before the World Cup finals, 2006

If I had the same pay, I'd be ashamed of myself.
LARS LAGERBACK, Sweden manager, on his compatriot's £5m a year salary, 2006

When it comes to negative substitutions we've got the top man. I'm crapping myself for what he's going to do at half-time.
IAN WRIGHT, BBC TV pundit, 2006

I won't read Winston Churchill the day before the game or try to be like him, though I did read some of his memoirs a long time ago. There are lots of leaders you have to admire – Bill Clinton, Tony Blair, who is very good at speeches, and Nelson Mandela – but I am not one of them.
ERIKSSON the day before England went out of the World Cup to Portugal, 2006

Eriksson got his tactics wrong. To go to the World Cup with four strikers was folly. Sven devised tactics to accommodate David Beckham. That wasn't right. He got too close to Beckham.
ALAN HANSEN, BBC TV pundit, 2006

The 5–1 victory over Germany in 2001 apart, I settle down to watch every England game at 8pm. An hour and a half later my watch says 8.15.
JIMMY GREAVES, former England striker, on Eriksson's England in his autobiography, 2004

Sven has spent most of his time in this country chasing skirt. What's he done for English football? Sweet Faria Alam.
EDITORIAL in the Sun, after England's World Cup exit, 2006

Did I really do so badly with England?
ERIKSSON, by now Manchester City manager, to a reporter who suggested he had been unsuccessful in his previous job, 2007

The English people are still very nice to me. They still want my autograph.
ERIKSSON at City, 2007

ALEX FERGUSON

[Ferguson] has brought football of butterfly beauty to Old Trafford. He bought Eric Cantona, the rebel with a cause. He nurtured the Golden Generation. He discovered Ole Gunnar Solskjaer, the baby-faced assassin. He signed Wayne Rooney, the assassin-faced baby. He has brought trophies, glory, prestige and the kind of happiness, over twenty years, that United supporters once only dreamed of.
DANIEL TAYLOR, Guardian football writer, in the introduction to his book This Is the One, *2007*

You might as well talk to my [baby] daughter. You'll get more sense out of her.
KENNY DALGLISH, Liverpool player-manager, to a reporter interviewing Ferguson after a bitter Liverpool v Manchester United match, 1988

He could be great fun with his little quirks...for coming out with the strangest of things. A couple of Fergie-isms were: 'Have you ever seen a Pakistani funeral?' or 'Have you ever seen an Italian with a cold?' You would be left to ponder what he meant.

PAT STANTON, Ferguson's former assistant manager at Aberdeen, in The Quiet Man, *1989*

I don't think I ever saw Alex smile. Even when United had won 4–0 he would still have a go at someone for not defending properly or for missing a chance.

NEIL WEBB, Nottingham Forest and former United midfielder, 1993

He did at Aberdeen what he's still doing at United. He gave us a persecution complex about Celtic and Rangers, the Scottish FA and the Glasgow media; the whole West of Scotland thing. He reckoned they were all against us, and it worked a treat.

MARK McGHEE, Leicester manager and ex-Aberdeen striker, 1995

I can meet ministers and monarchs and my children are not much impressed. But when we met Alex Ferguson they realised there was some point.

TONY BLAIR MP, Labour party leader, 1995

ALEX FERGUSON: Five hours' sleep is all I need.
INTERVIEWER: Like Margaret Thatcher.
FERGUSON: Don't associate me with that woman.

EXCHANGE during a press interview, 1995

Alex always did have a hot temper. He'd have caused a fight in an empty house.

MARTIN FERGUSON, younger brother, 1995

A strange bloke, irritated by everyone.

GARY LINEKER, 1996

In the early days we named him The Hairdryer because he would come right up to your face and scream at you.

GARY PALLISTER, Manchester United defender, 1997

He's very understanding when it comes to fellow managers. Unless you beat him.
FRANK CLARK, Manchester City manager, who had got the better of Ferguson with Nottingham Forest, 1997

If there is an apology, it must be coming by horseback.
ARSENE WENGER, Arsenal manager, after Ferguson said he had apologised for the publication of off-record comments about Arsenal 'turning games into battles', 1999

When we lose, he gets very angry. I don't understand him when he is speaking normally, so when he yells it's even more difficult.
MICKAEL SILVESTRE, United's French defender, 1999

A magical manager, the greatest motivator there has ever been.

SIR BOBBY CHARLTON, United director, 1999

A knighthood? He should get a sainthood.
RICHARD WILSON, aka Victor Meldrew, after United won the European Cup, 1999

Some people said you can't be a great manager until you've won the European Cup. I don't think like that, but it was good to put that one to bed.
FERGUSON, 2005

Apparently I'm allowed to hang my washing on Glasgow Green, which is an interesting one. And if I ever get arrested in the city, I'm entitled to my own cell, which could come in handy at some point.
FERGUSON on being made a freeman of his native Glasgow, 1999

Lord Fergie, the best thing since sliced bread.
INSCRIPTION on medal offered to and rejected by Ferguson by Ken Bates, Chelsea chairman, after Charity Shield, 2000

Kevin [Keegan] spends every minute of every day with us. There's no getting away from him. That's not something I can imagine happening with Sir Alex Ferguson at United.
GARY NEVILLE, England defender, during Euro 2000

Of course they should give Fergie the England job. Give the rest of us a bloomin' chance.
JOE ROYLE, Manchester City manager, after Kevin Keegan left the England manager's job, 2000

This is the toughest, meanest and most cussed competitor I've met in the whole of my football life. To be any use to him, you have to win.
STEVE BRUCE, Ferguson's former captain, 2000

When I see Alex, I'm always civil, but there's no exchange of Christmas cards. His book should have been a celebration of his achievements, something positive, but he chose to use it as something else. He had a different agenda.
GORDON STRACHAN, another of Ferguson's former captains, on the United manager's criticism of him in his autobiography, 2000

I look upon him as a father figure, just like all the young players do who have grown up under his guidance. Maybe you're afraid of him at times but the main thing is we all have great respect for him.
DAVID BECKHAM, 2000

Sometimes I wish I'd turned 60 that night in Barcelona. That could have been the final day of my career.
FERGUSON recalling the 1999 European Cup triumph, 2001

It has got to the stage where Ferguson has even told us: 'Don't try to stay on your feet if you are in the box and get a slight kick.' He wants us to copy other sides we face in European competition and go down to win the penalty.
JAAP STAM in his autobiography Head to Head, 2001

He doesn't seem to have any problem spotting an opponent offside. He can see his watch all right when he wants to check the amount of injury time. How long before fans around the country see a foul by United and set up the chant: 'Fergie didn't see it'?
BRIAN CLOUGH, after Ferguson claimed not to have seen the foul which led to Roy Keane being sent off v Manchester City, 2001

I can't stand Alex Ferguson.

DOROTHY ELLERAY, grandmother of referee David, defending him against criticism from the United manager, 2001

I didn't see my sons grow up. Perhaps it is one of the big reasons I am leaving. I hope I can make up for lost time.
FERGUSON on announcing his intention to quit United, 2000

He has spent too much time being a father figure to players like me, which has meant he has had less time for other areas of his life. I just hope the success that his dedication and sacrifice have brought is some compensation.
RYAN GIGGS, 2001

I will certainly not be team manager. I think I've picked the right moment to retire but equally I'd love to stay on in any capacity which doesn't interfere with the football... I'm actually looking forward to watching the team play without any managerial pressures.
FERGUSON, early December, 2000

I'm definitely going. I won't be making any comebacks like singers do. I look at Bobby Robson [still managing Newcastle at 68] and think: 'Good luck to him.' But it's a decision me and my family have made. I want to enjoy a lot of other things.
FERGUSON, late December, 2000

The decision has been taken. I'm going to leave the club... I had hoped there would be another role, but that's gone now.
FERGUSON, May, 2001

The way I feel I don't think I'll change my mind about going at the end of the season. At the moment my mind is fixed on retiring. But you never know what might happen.
FERGUSON, late December, 2001

The board has entered into discussions with Sir Alex and his advisers on a new contract.
STATEMENT by United after Ferguson changed his mind, February, 2002

Maybe the timing of my announcement that I was seeking a different kind of job with United was wrong, though I don't think my motive was. I simply wanted to give the club time to find the right replacement. But it is in the past, at least for the next three seasons, and we're all united again.
FERGUSON after signing his new contract, February, 2002

I was worrying about what I was going to do at three o'clock on Saturday afternoons. I just couldn't see myself riding off into the sunset just yet.
FERGUSON after reversing his decision to retire, 2002

When I had played 15 first-team games, I knocked on the gaffer's door, went in and told him I thought I deserved a club car like the other guys were getting. He just looked at me for a moment before shouting: 'Club car? Club car? Club bike, more like.' I've never been in there since.
RYAN GIGGS, 2002

He can spot a player a mile off and motivate people well. But his tactical acumen is negligible. If you have a fantastic horse the jockey doesn't have to be great.
MARK BOSNICH, Chelsea and former United goalkeeper, 2002

His weakness is that he doesn't think he has any.

ARSENE WENGER, Arsenal manager, 2002

Sir Alex is irreplaceable. I wondered whether I could work with anyone else.
DAVID BECKHAM after Ferguson changed his mind about retiring, 2002

Alex Ferguson is a threat to my son. Sven told me it is pointless having England games in April or May because Ferguson, one way or another, makes sure his stars aren't fit.
ULLA ERIKSSON, mother of Sven-Göran, 2002

Undoubtedly, the Manchester United manager's job is the biggest club-football job in the world.
PETER KENYON, United's chief executive, 2003

He's the best sports psychologist in the world. He tests people when they are younger and weeds out the weak-minded. You can be technically and physically OK, but if you're weak-minded you can go. That's his philosophy.
GORDON STRACHAN, Southampton manager and former player under Ferguson, 2003

The manager is a very intimidating person to talk to and to confront. Until two years ago when you walked into his office, your lip started to quiver and your mouth went dry. Maybe [Ferguson] saw he didn't have that effect on me any more.
DAVID BECKHAM after leaving United for Real Madrid, 2003

This was a man I really respected. He gave me the opportunity to become the player I am by playing for United. He still hasn't spoken to me except briefly at a funeral... I just expected a bit more respect when I had been at the club for that many years.
BECKHAM, 2003

Without being unkind, we wouldn't try to sign a 61-year-old.
KEN BATES, Chelsea chairman, after reports that his club approached Ferguson, 2003

Once I left Rangers, that was it. I don't look at Aberdeen's results either. The only team I look out for now is Benburb, my local junior team.
FERGUSON on how he shook off his boyhood allegiance after Rangers sold him, 2003

It's squeaky-bum time.
FERGUSON as the title race intensified between Manchester United and Arsenal, 2003

Football is an emotional game. Sometimes people making comments at the end of a game become mental.
JOSE MOURINHO, Porto coach, after Ferguson defended Roy Keane following his dismissal for stamping on goalkeeper Vitor Baia, 2004

He used to think he could speak the lingo when we went abroad just by adding an 'o' at the end of certain words. The fish was superbo, the meat was magnifico.
NEALE COOPER, Hartlepool manager and former Aberdeen player under Ferguson, 2003

Alex is football itself. No, that's wrong. He is more than football.
CARLOS QUEIROZ, assistant to Ferguson, on joining Real Madrid as head coach, 2003

I have never seen anyone work so hard. I never remember arriving at the training ground before Sir Alex, and he was last to leave every day.
QUEIROZ after the United manager suffered a minor heart problem, 2003

If I tried it a million times I couldn't do it again. If I could, I'd still be playing.
FERGUSON denying he kicked a boot deliberately into David Beckham's face in the dressing room after a match v Arsenal, 2003

What happened in United's dressing room has happened to me 50 times. I've kicked bottles of water, bags and shoes, but I've never hit a player. It's a question of technique, and the Scots must be superior.
MARCELLO LIPPI, Juventus coach, on the 'boot' incident, 2003

Alex Ferguson loves the game and will die on the United bench, I am sure of that.
ERIC CANTONA, 2003

He's a work alcoholic.
GERARD HOULLIER, Liverpool manager, 2003

Mr Wenger has lost his voice, unlike Mr Ferguson, who has lost his head.
PAUL BURRELL, Arsenal public-address announcer, after another stormy encounter, 2003

He does what he wants. I will never answer questions any more about this man.
ARSENE WENGER, Arsenal manager, on his differences with Ferguson, 2004

What were you like when you were 19? I was trying to start a workers' revolution in Glasgow. My mother thought I was a communist.
FERGUSON after Wayne Rooney was substituted in a volatile display for England v Spain, 2004

For all his horses, knighthood and championships, he hasn't got two of what I've got. And I don't mean balls.
BRIAN CLOUGH on his two European Cups with Nottingham Forest, 2004

A great manager, but not, in my opinion, a great man.

TOMMY DOCHERTY, former United manager, 2005

Fergie is driven by anger. It's like petrol to him.
GORDON STRACHAN, 2005

I don't think I'll work for a better manager... He's like my missus – telepathic
Just like her, he always knew which buttons to press.
ANDY COLE, Manchester City and former United striker, 2005

I know people don't like upsetting Sir Alex.
NEIL WARNOCK, Sheffield United manager, after referee Rob Styles refused his team a
'blatant' penalty at Old Trafford, 2007

As long as his brain is still active, he'll probably still be staggering out of the
dug-out in 2020.
STEVE COPPELL, Reading manager and ex-United player, 2007

My pension can wait. There's nothing doing here for a couple of years.
FERGUSON after United recaptured the Premiership title, 2007

DARREN FERGUSON

I can't change my name, can I?
DARREN FERGUSON on the pressures of being Alex Ferguson's son after becoming player-
manager of Peterborough, 2007

GERRY FRANCIS

The transfer market's completely dead out there. I've even been phoning
myself up and disguising my voice just for a little bit of interest.
FRANCIS, Queens Park Rangers manager, 2000

TREVOR FRANCIS

Francis could not spot a great footballer if the bloke's name had four letters,
started with 'P' and ended in 'E'.
ALAN HUDSON, former England midfielder, on the new Birmingham manager, 1997

a thin dividing line between winning and not quite winning. I suppose
early been a success.

NCIS in charge at Crystal Palace, 2003

BARRY FRY

His management style seems to be based on the chaos theory.
MARK McGHEE, Wolves manager, as Fry managed nearby Birmingham, 1996

Q: If you won the National Lottery, what would you buy?
A: 27 new strikers.
FRY, Birmingham manager, in programme Q & A, 1996

Kirstine's out shopping as usual. I'm down the Job Centre looking for
employment. Funny old game, innit?
FRY'S answerphone message after Birmingham sacked him, 1996

Someone said you could write Barry's knowledge of tactics on a stamp.
You'd need to fold the stamp in half.
STEVE CLARIDGE, Birmingham striker, 1997

These days I no longer run down the touchline when we score. I just waddle
a bit.
FRY, by now Peterborough manager, 2000. He had suffered two heart attacks

If I got as many points for football as I do for driving offences, I'd be in the
Premiership by now.
FRY, Jaguar driver, 2001

PAUL GASCOIGNE

I broke my neck and haven't looked back since.
GASCOIGNE on starting what proved a brief spell as manager of non-league Kettering, 2005

OK, I had a double brandy before the game, but it used to be four bottles
of whisky.
GASCOIGNE after drinking was cited as a reason for his sacking by Kettering, 2005

One minute I was manager of a football club. The next I was banged up in a police cell with just a bed and a potty.
GASCOIGNE on the day he lost his job, 2006

BOBBY GOULD

He'd make a great double-glazing salesman. We had a meeting and by the end we thought: 'When's he going to sell us a new car?'
NEVILLE SOUTHALL, Wales goalkeeper, after Gould became national manager, 1995

I resigned as Coventry manager in the gents' toilet at QPR. This time I sorted out the terms of my departure in the dope-test room in Bologna.
BOBBY GOULD, quitting as Wales manager after 4–0 defeat v Italy, 1999

GEORGE GRAHAM

I remember George. He was a bit of a poseur at first, a bit lazy when he played up front, the last one you could imagine going into management. Different now. He has poseurs for breakfast.
FRANK McLINTOCK, captain of the 1971 Arsenal 'Double' side, on Graham's methods as manager at Highbury, 1992

If ever there was a player I felt definitely would not have what it took to be a manager it was George Graham. Running a nightclub? Yes. A football club? Absolutely not.
DON HOWE, Arsenal coach during Graham's 1970s playing days, 1999

I admit I'm single-minded. I think all of the great football managers have been single-minded.
GRAHAM on the Arsenal players' nicknames for him – 'Ayatollah' and 'Gadaffi', 1991

Mr Graham did not act in the best interests of the club.

STATEMENT by Arsenal announcing their manager's dismissal, 1995. The Premier League found him guilty of accepting a 'bung' from an agent

The meeting with [agent Rune Hauge] was all very normal but the money came as a shock. I thought: 'Jesus, what a Christmas present. Fantastic...' The ridiculous thing is it wouldn't have changed my life. I was on a good salary, but greed got the better of me. I'm as weak as the next man when it comes to temptation.
GRAHAM after being sacked by Arsenal, 1995

He loved a 1–0 win, he really did.
STEVE BOULD, Arsenal defender, 1997

I will always have Arsenal-red blood running through my veins.
GRAHAM, then manager at Highbury, in his autobiography, 1996

In six months he said just two words to me: 'You're fired.'

TOMAS BROLIN, Leeds's Swedish international, 1997

I came back last season with blond hair, and I think that did his head in.
LEE SHARPE, Leeds midfielder, 1999

We are good friends but I wouldn't like to play for him again. I've told him that, but I think he reckons I'm joking.
TONY ADAMS, Graham's former captain at Arsenal, 1999

People say he is ruthlessly professional. I would say he's professionally ruthless.
JOHN LUKIC, Graham's former goalkeeper at Highbury, 1999

At least all the aggravation will keep me slim.
GRAHAM on encountering fan hostility at Tottenham because of his Arsenal background, 1999

He's a gutless coward who will not stand up and admit he has made mistakes. Like Spurs fans, I got mugged into believing that this Adonis of the football world was the be-all and end-all in management skill and tactics.
ALAN SUGAR, former Tottenham chairman, on the last manager he appointed, 2001

In my time at Tottenham I made lots of mistakes. The biggest was possibly employing him.
SUGAR, 2001

With George, everything was predicated on winning. If they weren't winning anything there was absolutely nothing to watch.
NICK HORNBY, writer and Arsenal fan, in Jasper Rees's book Wenger: The Making of a Manager, *2003*

RON GREENWOOD

There's only one thing better than getting an interview with Ron Greenwood. That's not getting one.
TONY FRANCIS, ITN reporter, on the England manager, 1981

JOHN GREGORY

He handled the pressure brilliantly during our poor spell, except when he smashed the physio's bag across Goodison Park.
GARETH SOUTHGATE, Aston Villa captain, 2000

I'm a much better manager than when I started, but not half as good as I will be.
GREGORY in his autobiography The Boss, *2000*

RUUD GULLIT

I was just as disappointed as Mandela.
GULLIT after a meeting with South African president Nelson Mandela had to be cancelled, 1997

Ruud said very craftily today that he had asked for £2m. That's true and I immediately said: 'Gross?' And he said: 'No, netto. I always talk netto.'
COLIN HUTCHINSON, Chelsea managing director, 1998

If you're a playboy and you're not there, you can't win the FA Cup and be second in the Premier League. That's impossible.
GULLIT answering Chelsea's reasons for sacking him, 1998

You don't need to be Sherlock Holmes to realise Ruud was pushing his luck.
DAVID MELLOR, former Tory MP, broadcaster and Chelsea fan, 1998

I always found him relaxed and easy to get on with, a good winner and a
good loser.
ALEX FERGUSON on Gullit's demise, 1998

It has become one big laugh between us, because she has told me, in all
seriousness: 'I thought you were a poof!' Can you imagine it – Rudi, a poof!
GULLIT, on his partner Estelle Cruyff, in My Autobiography, *1998*

Gullit told me within his first week that I was a bad player and he didn't want
me here. When he went I had a little party.
ALESSANDRO PISTONE, Newcastle defender, 1999

And I want to thank all the restaurants where I have been for their marvellous
food and hospitality.
GULLIT in his resignation statement, 1999

He's certainly big in the trouser department.
LISA JENSEN, Tyneside pizza-house waitress, claiming affair with Gullit, 1999

Ruud loved conflict. He enjoyed being at loggerheads with certain players.
And he was just so arrogant. His ego was as big as Amsterdam and he didn't
even try to disguise it.
ROB LEE, Newcastle midfielder, 2000

On meeting Gullit, I could understand the accusations of arrogance. He was
always amazingly friendly for about 20 seconds, then seemed completely to
lose interest.
DAVID BADDIEL, comedian and Chelsea fan, 2000

I once spent ages in a bar talking to a chap I thought was the pop singer Seal.
I later found out he was someone called Ruud Gullit.
LAURENCE LLEWELYN-BOWEN, interior designer and TV personality, 2000

After the Sunderland defeat, Ruud apologised to me and said he'd completely
lost the players. Because of that he said he didn't want a penny in
compensation, which is very unusual for a manager and makes him an
honourable man.
FREDDY SHEPHERD, Newcastle chairman, 2003

RAY HARFORD

I'm going to be as natural as I can; by that I mean a right miserable bastard.
HARFORD on taking over as West Bromwich Albion manager, 1997

GLENN HODDLE

He's got a very, very tough persona, despite the fact that they used to call him Glenda.
PETER SHREEVES, Hoddle's assistant at Chelsea and his former manager at Tottenham, 1996

You won't be surprised to know that I have some faith in astrologers and particularly what the stars predict for Scorpios.
HODDLE, by now England manager, 1998

You and I have been given two hands, two legs and a half-decent brain. Some people have not been born like that for a reason.
HODDLE, arguing in The Times interview which brought him down that people born disabled were being punished for sins in a previous life, 1999

Hoddle's attitude betrays a disabled mind. It seems he has no compassion, no allowance for weakness.
IAN DURY, handicapped singer and actor, 1999

Had he stuck to football rather than theology he would have been playing on a better pitch.
RAY STIRLING, Hoddle's former father-in-law, 1999

At the end of the Argentina game I found myself asking the same question again and again: 'Why am I here?'
HODDLE, England manager, World Cup finals, 1998

My biggest mistake of the World Cup was not taking Eileen Drewery.
HODDLE, as the controversy over his faith healer continued after England's exit from the World Cup, 1998

If promotion with Swindon and keeping Chelsea in 11th place qualifies a man to lead England in a campaign against the Germans and the Argentinians and the French, a bloke who can make a paper aeroplane is qualified to pilot a jumbo jet.
BRIAN CLOUGH in Cloughie: Walking On Water, *2002*

We didn't get on. I couldn't warm to the man. He was very egotistical and incredibly arrogant. I think it annoyed him that people compared me to him. He probably thought I was deeply inferior.
MATT LE TISSIER, former England player, on Hoddle's time as Southampton manager, 2002

Glenn made many mistakes [at Tottenham], but when anybody challenged him he never agreed with them. He was always right; he always got his own way.
STEFFEN FREUND, former Tottenham midfielder, after Hoddle's sacking, 2003

Because of his pride, he wanted to be the best player in training every day – at 46 years of age. I don't think you can see the whole picture when you're out there training with the guys. Can you imagine Arsene Wenger playing with Thierry Henry and the rest?
DAVID PLEAT, acting Tottenham manager, on his predecessor, 2003

ROY HODGSON

My lasting memory of him is that he always had a runny nose.
DAVE MOGG, Bath City goalkeeper, after Hodgson, once his manager at Bristol City, took charge of Inter Milan, 1995

IAN HOLLOWAY

Before, I believed I was a kind, considerate person who believed in free speech. The anger-management expert showed me I was a jumped-up, obnoxious little git who wouldn't listen at home because of what had happened at work.
HOLLOWAY after taking part in the BBC TV series The Stress Test, *2004*

I'm so unlucky that if I fell in a wheelbarrow of boobs I'd come out sucking my thumb.
HOLLOWAY, Queens Park Rangers manager, after a defeat, 2004

I'm going to enjoy this win, take my brain out and stick it in an ice bucket.

HOLLOWAY after a QPR victory, 2004

There was a spell in the second half when I took my heart off my sleeve and put it in my mouth.
HOLLOWAY after QPR won at Coventry, 2004

We threw everything at them – the kitchen sink, the golf clubs, emptied the garage. It wasn't enough but at least my garage is tidy now.
HOLLOWAY, now manager of Plymouth, after FA Cup defeat by Watford, 2007

BRIAN HORTON

It doesn't take a scientist to work out that when a team has lost 5–0, it's a bit strange if the centre-forward takes the bulk of the criticism.
NIALL QUINN on life under Horton at Manchester City, 1995

GERARD HOULLIER

You don't need to have been a horse to be a good jockey.
HOULLIER, Liverpool manager, on his lack of top-class playing pedigree, 1999

I have never spoken to him and never will. I could have killed him from hate, not for what he did to me but because he made the people I love cry.
DAVID GINOLA, recalling how Houllier called him 'a criminal' for a mistake which cost France a place in the 1994 World Cup finals, 1998

They are two-faced and treat people like dirt.
PAUL INCE, former England captain, on Houllier and his No. 2, Phil Thompson, after leaving Liverpool for Middlesbrough, 1999

He comes from France and I can't believe he has managed a team because he certainly doesn't know how to. It's OK coming out with all this technical stuff about the game, but when it comes to managing players off the field, as people, he hasn't got a clue.
INCE, 1999

Sometimes in the morning before training, I wouldn't know whether to tell the missus to go and iron my old school uniform or get my tracksuit. Every day the Liverpool players were treated like kids.
INCE, 1999

I wasn't disappointed with his comments because I know the man.

HOULLIER responding to Ince, 1999

They call Houllier the French professor. Well, if he really is going to fork out millions on [Emile] Heskey, I can only say I'm glad he wasn't the professor who operated on me when I was rattling the Pearly Gates.
ALAN HUDSON, former England midfielder, 2000

I have been described as a French revolutionary with a guillotine, but I prefer to convince people rather than dictate to them.
HOULLIER after leading Liverpool to a Cup Treble, 2001

There are those who say maybe I should forget about football. Maybe I should forget about breathing. As Arnold Schwarzenegger said: 'I'll be back.'
HOULLIER during his recovery from heart surgery, 2002

I've changed my routine since the heart surgery. I get in to work at 8.30am instead of 8.00.
HOULLIER on resuming his duties, 2002

He's a very intelligent, rounded person, capable of dealing with different nationalities, finance and sports medicine. He fits exactly the profile of a top modern manager. He's also very modest. It's like Mrs Thatcher said: 'To be powerful is like being a lady; if you have to tell people you are, then you aren't.'
ANDY ROXBURGH, UEFA coaching official and ex-Scotland manager, 2002

Some people said I should forget football. I replied that I may as well stop breathing.
HOULLIER on recovering from heart surgery, 2002

My surgeon said I should take short holidays during the international breaks. For the last one, in Dubai, I picked a hotel where there were no football managers and turned off my mobile.
HOULLIER, 2003

We're in year six of a five-year plan.
STEVE MORGAN, Merseyside businessman and would-be investor in Liverpool, criticising Houllier, 2004

[Houllier] ended up as a chequebook manager of the worst sort.
ROBBIE FOWLER, striker sold by the Frenchman, in his autobiography, 2005

DON HOWE

If we came in smelling of booze, Don would train us until we spewed.
PETER MARINELLO, Arsenal player of the 1970s, on the club's coach in his time at Highbury, 2005

It was like finding Miss World was free and asking for a date.
BOBBY GOULD, Bristol Rovers manager, after Howe agreed to coach his side, 1986

You get great coaches and great managers, and they're not always the same. I mean, Don bloody Howe... What a man. He was a really great coach, but [as a manager] he sometimes had me playing left full-back for West Brom. Come to think of it, I was the original wing-back.
WILLIE JOHNSTON, former West Brom and Scotland winger, 2003

MARK HUGHES

Is it true you used to play for Barcelona? That's not Barcelona football.
CESC FABREGAS, Arsenal and Spain midfielder, to Hughes after Blackburn's defensive display in a 0–0 draw at the Emirates Stadium, 2007

PAUL JEWELL

REPORTER: When do you stop thinking about relegation and start thinking about Europe?
JEWELL: After about 10 pints.
JEWELL, Wigan manager, in an interview with Sky Sports as Wigan hit the Premiership's top six, 2005

REPORTER: Do you have a Churchillian speech up your sleeve for games like this?
JEWELL: I'll just say what I usually say: 'Get out there and win the fucking game, you cunts!'
JEWELL to a journalist before the game which decided whether Wigan or Sheffield United would stay up, 2007

MARTIN JOL

Can you imagine how the players would react if I turned up one day and said: 'I'd like you to meet Cock and Dick'?
JOL, Tottenham's Dutch manager, on why he does not employ his brothers, 2005

I was nervous towards the end. My heart rate was 189. Almost a heart attack.
JOL after Tottenham's victory over Chelsea, 2006

DAVE JONES

People in football and outside have been fantastic. I don't have to decorate my kitchen because it is covered in cards.
JONES on returning to management with Wolves after clearing his name of sex crimes in court, 2001

ROY KEANE

Barring a personality transplant, his only job at Old Trafford will be as a player.
GEORGE BEST when asked about Keane's managerial potential, 2003

INTERVIEWER: Do you think Roy Keane will make a good manager one day?
NIALL QUINN: No, I don't think so.
EXCHANGE on television, 2005. Quinn, who had sided with Mick McCarthy against Keane, was the Sunderland chairman who appointed Keane as manager

REPORTER: Great players don't always make great managers.
KEANE: That's all right because I was never a great player.
EXCHANGE at a Sunderland press conference, 2006

You still see the mad eyes come out when he gives the ball away in training. They were never going to go.
ROBBIE ELLIOTT, Sunderland defender, 2006

I don't see Sunderland as a stepping stone to something bigger. That would be an insult to this club. I don't sit at home every night thinking that one day I'd like to manage Manchester United.
KEANE after leading Sunderland to promotion to the Premiership, 2007

If you're going to give everything and push it to the limit, Roy Keane's the manager for you. The players love him, and I just wish I had worked with him when I was playing. I wish I had bought into his way of thinking earlier.
NIALL QUINN on the eve of Sunderland's return to the Premiership, 2007

I was definitely born to play for Manchester United and I feel I was born to manage Sunderland. Sometimes I believe the man upstairs has great plans for me.
KEANE before going back to United with Sunderland, 2007

KEVIN KEEGAN

I tell you honestly, I would love it if we beat them. Love it!
KEEGAN, Newcastle manager, in an emotional tirade after Alex Ferguson said teams tried harder against Manchester United than title rivals Newcastle, 1997

God on the Tyne

HEADLINE in FHM *magazine on Keegan interview, 1993*

If Kevin Keegan fell into the Tyne, he'd come up with a salmon in his mouth.
JACK CHARLTON, one of Keegan's Newcastle predecessors, 1995

For the first time since I became leader, my children were impressed by something I did. 'Did you really meet Kevin Keegan, Dad?' 'Did you really do 27 consecutive headers?'
TONY BLAIR MP, Labour leader, after sharing a photo opportunity with the Newcastle manager, 1995

People are saying that Kevin leaving is like the Queen dying, but it's worse than that.
JOHN REGAN, secretary of Newcastle Independent Supporters' Association, after Keegan's resignation, 1997

He wasn't tactically aware. He just had a charisma and used it to hide the deficiencies.
MALCOLM MACDONALD, former Newcastle striker, after Keegan left, 1997

When Kevin broke into the squad he used to sit on my knee when we travelled away. I would pretend to be a ventriloquist and he would let me bounce him up and down on my knee.
TOM TAYLOR, journalist and father of ex-England manager Graham, on when Keegan started his career at Scunthorpe, 1999

I'm glad it is not Ukraine because I'm not your man for a 0–0 in Kiev.
KEEGAN after England drew Scotland in the play-offs for Euro 2000, 1999

I don't sit down with boards and start painting pictures all over the place, it is not my style and I think the FA knew that when they appointed me. They saw a different style of management where we get people to play by getting into their minds and improve them that way.
KEEGAN after England qualified for Euro 2000 despite a home defeat by Scotland in the play-offs, 1999

He is feeding on rocket fuel. He's perfect to work with.
WATT NICOL, Scottish 'guru of self-motivation', after Keegan asked him to help inspire the England squad, 1999

A lot of my time is taken up with thinking adventurously.
KEEGAN before Euro 2000

Kevin has a lot of strengths but standing up to failure isn't one of them.

NOEL WHITE, FA international committee chairman, responding to Keegan's claim that he would resign if England did not win Euro 2000 [they did not]

I've told the players that that's me finished. I just feel I fall a little short of what is required in this job. I sat there in the first half and could see things weren't right but I couldn't find it in myself to solve the problem. In my heart of hearts, I'm not up to the job.
KEEGAN on resigning as England coach after defeat by Germany at Wembley, 2000

The last thing I want is to be known as the man who lost the last game at Wembley.
KEEGAN after Germany beat England, 2000

Some parts of the job I did very well, but not the key part of getting players to win football matches.
KEEGAN, 2000

If Kevin is anything like I was, his first difficulty, the first problem to overcome, will be coming out of the house and facing people.
GRAHAM TAYLOR, one of Keegan's predecessors with England, 2000

He walked away from the Newcastle job, he walked away from the Fulham job and he walked away from the England job. We'll have to wait and see if he'll walk away from the Manchester City job.
RODNEY MARSH, former City player and TV pundit, 2001

We defended really well. That's very unlike my team. I must do something about that.
KEEGAN after City's 1–0 win over Chelsea, 2004

HOWARD KENDALL

30,000 stay-at-home fans can't be wrong. Bring back attractive, winning football. Kendall out!
SLOGAN on Everton Action Group banner, December 1985. In May, Kendall's team won the FA Cup; the following season they were champions

JOE KINNEAR

I'm out at the moment, but should you be the chairman of Barcelona, AC Milan or Real Madrid, I'll get straight back to you. The rest can wait.
KINNEAR'S answerphone message, 1995

Me and Joe are so close that we will carry on living in the same underpants.
SAM HAMMAM, Wimbledon chairman, after Kinnear's departure, 1999

BERTIE MEE

Bertie would be perfect in today's game. All this stuff about foreign coaching is nonsense. What the majority of managers do now is hire a coach, discuss tactics and let them get on with it. That is what he did 30 years ago.
GEORGE GRAHAM, Arsenal player in Mee's Double-winning side and later manager at Highbury, in David Tossell's Seventy-One Guns, *2002*

GARY MEGSON

No disrespect to Gary, but anyone who knows him knows he is the biggest moaner in the world.
NEIL WARNOCK, Sheffield United manager, after his West Brom counterpart alleged Warnock withdrew two players due to injury after having three sent off, causing their match to be abandoned, 2002

I hear Gary is writing a book. That's good news for insomniacs everywhere.
WARNOCK, 2004

JOE MERCER

Look, son, imagine this huge pot of money. Franny [Lee] has had a bit, Colin [Bell] has dipped in and of course Malcolm [Allison] has had a dollop. In fact, all the lads have had a bit. So there's none left for you.
JOE MERCER, Manchester City manager of the 1960s, to a player seeking a pay rise, quoted in Fred Eyre's Another Breath of Fred Eyre, 1982

PAUL MERSON

After what I've gone through – life-threatening problems – managing a football club feels like an absolute pleasure.
MERSON on taking the reins at Walsall, 2004

SUPPORTER: What is your favourite pie filling?
MERSON: I'm a Londoner and we don't have pies.
EXCHANGE at a Walsall fans' forum, 2004

JOSE MOURINHO

I am not out of a bottle. I am a special one.
MOURINHO at his introductory press conference at Chelsea, 2004

I'm the Special One. He's not taking that away from me.
PAUL GASCOIGNE, 2005

Welcome to Porto… From here each practice, each game, each minute of your social life must centre on the aim of being champions. First-teamer will be a meaningless term. I need all of you. You need each other. We are a team.
MOURINHO in a letter to Porto's players on taking over, 2002

Motivation + Ambition + Team + Spirit = Success
MOURINHO'S 'winning formula' at Porto, 2002

I understand why he [Sir Alex Ferguson] was a bit emotional. You would be sad if your team got clearly dominated by one built on 10 per cent of your budget.
MOURINHO after Porto's 2–1 win over Manchester United in the Champions' League, 2004

I had never been a first-class player who could feel, for example, what [Luis] Figo felt on returning to Barcelona [with Real Madrid]. So I had no idea what it would be like to have 80,000 people whistling and jeering at me. Upon hearing the whistles and jeers I felt like the most important person in the world.
MOURINHO on taking Porto to his former club Benfica, in Mourinho: Anatomy of a Winner, *by Patrick Barclay, 2005*

If I want a quiet, easy job, I would stay with Porto. There is a beautiful blue chair, we were league champions, won the UEFA Cup and Champions' League. There was God, and after God, me.
MOURINHO in his first week in charge of Chelsea, 2004

We have top players and – sorry if I am arrogant – we have a top manager.

MOURINHO on why he expected success at Stamford Bridge, 2004

I like the look of Mourinho. There's a bit of the young Clough about him. For a start, he's good-looking, and like me he doesn't believe in the star system. He's consumed with team spirit and discipline.
BRIAN CLOUGH shortly before his death, 2004

When he talked his mind, [Brian] Clough was funny. Mourinho, for all his colourful opinions, is never funny. And we all know how hard it is to like a man who seems to lack a sense of humour.
ALAN HANSEN, TV pundit and ex-Liverpool captain, 2004

People think the reason I went to Chelsea was financial. I'm not a hypocrite – I don't say that the money isn't important for my family. But the reason I went there was to work under pressure.
MOURINHO, 2005

His swagger, his sense of melodrama, his polyglot sophistication.
EDITORIAL in left-wing journal New Statesman *on why he was its Man of the Year, 2005*

He makes minimalism work in the everyday, and by doing so makes it modern.
EDITORIAL in the style magazine GQ on naming Mourinho Britain's second best-dressed man, 2005

That coat's from Matalan.
SONG by Manchester City fans as Mourinho patrolled the technical area in an overcoat, 2005

People like Mourinho are the enemy of football.

VOLKER ROTH, chairman of UEFA referees' committee, after Swedish referee Anders Frisk quit the game following accusations by Mourinho and threats against him, 2005

Sometimes, if you give success to stupid people, it makes them more stupid, not more intelligent
ARSENE WENGER, Arsenal manager, after Mourinho accused him of a 'voyeur'-like interest in Chelsea, 2005

REPORTER: Do you believe in God?
MOURINHO. I think more important is love. Love is what matters.
EXCHANGE during interview, 2005

The worst thing about playing Chelsea is having to listen to Mourinho afterwards.
EDMILSON, Barcelona defender, 2006

He's like a Yorkshireman with a Portuguese accent.
NEIL WARNOCK, Sheffield United manager, 2006

When I take my kids to the zoo in Los Angeles, they always look longest at the creature that moves least, especially in the reptile house. I asked myself: 'Who are the people that are pretty cool but also very still and monotone in their expression?' And I thought of Jose Mourinho.
JULIAN SANDS, actor, on the inspiration for the Russian villain he played in the television drama 24, 2006

Maybe I'm not such a good manager. And maybe the players are not such good players.
MOURINHO after Chelsea's home draw v Fulham, 2006

The Paris Hilton of Premiership managers: spoilt, petulant, vain and lapdog-owning.
SIMON MILLS, style journalist, 2006

If I don't go to the semi-final then I will go to the wrestling at Earls Court with my kids.
MOURINHO after Chelsea drew at home with Valencia in the Champions' League quarter-finals, 2007

Mourinho's the funniest thing to come out of London since Del Boy and Rodney.
JAMIE CARRAGHER, Liverpool defender, on the Chelsea manager's sniping at Liverpool before the clubs' Champions' League semi-final, 2007

He embarrasses himself. He's just like a big baby. A great manager but I don't think you can say he's a great man.
CARRAGHER, 2006

It was a beautiful and rich period of my career. I want to thank all Chelsea supporters for what I believe is a never-ending love story.
MOURINHO after suddenly leaving Stamford Bridge by mutual consent, 2007

DAVID MOYES

Davey, Davey Moyes – he's got red hair but we don't care.
SONG by Everton fans, 2006

When he realised I was getting so much of the limelight, I felt he resented it.
WAYNE ROONEY on his former Everton manager in My Story So Far, *2006*

I'd have gone almost anywhere just to get away from David Moyes. He appeared overbearing.
ROONEY, as above

MICK McCARTHY

The ref gave Arsenal a goal and as I turned around I saw this big furry microphone so I laid into it. I kicked it and it spun away like a boomerang before landing 20 yards away. Then the Sky touchline reporter came up to me and said: 'So, Mick, you must be disappointed.'
McCARTHY, Millwall manager, 1995

You were a crap player, you're a crap manager. The only reason I have any dealings with you is that somehow you are manager of my country and you're not even Irish, you English cunt. You can stick it up your bollocks.
ROY KEANE, Republic of Ireland captain, to McCarthy during a team meeting which led to Keane being sent home from Japan on the eve of the World Cup finals, 2002

My reaction when I was offered this job? Yee-hah!
McCARTHY on becoming Sunderland manager, 2003

The other lads will be asking Jason McAteer: 'What's he like? Is he all right? Has he got a sense of humour? What's his training and coaching like? Is he a big-nosed miserable sod?'
McCARTHY at Sunderland, 2003

It wasn't just a monkey on my back, it was *Planet of the Apes*.
McCARTHY after Sunderland gained their first Premiership victory in nearly three years, 2005

Mick is very South Yorkshire. He's slow to get his round in, but I'm enjoying working with him.
BOB MURRAY, Sunderland chairman, 2005

STEVE McCLAREN

Steve's first game as United coach was an 8–1 win at Nottingham Forest. I told him afterwards: 'We're looking for some improvement.'
SIR ALEX FERGUSON on the new England coach's spell with Manchester United, 2006

Steve's lucky. He's the luckiest guy I've ever worked with. Some have it, others don't, but he has it all right.
JIM SMITH, Oxford manager, on his former assistant at Derby, 2006

Every defeat hurts. You might think it doesn't, but you ask the family. You ask the dog.
McCLAREN, Middlesbrough manager, 2006

I wouldn't say I'm a counter-attacking coach. I'm a find-a-way-to-win coach.
McCLAREN before his first game in charge of England, 2006

Only in England could a man with such limited abilities be made into the national coach. The ever-smiling McClaren is without doubt the most two-faced, false person I've had the misfortune to meet in football.
MASSIMO MACCARONE, former McClaren player at Middlesbrough, 2007

They'll have to drag me kicking and screaming out of Soho Square.
McCLAREN on calls for his head after poor early results as England manager, 2007

MARK McGHEE

He's fat, he's round, he's taken Leicester down.
SONG by Reading fans aimed at their former manager, 1995

I am fat. It's difficult not to get that way with my lifestyle, but the important thing is that it doesn't affect my golf swing.
McGHEE responding to the taunts, 1995

He's covering his backside in a way that takes the biscuit.
GRAHAM TAYLOR after being criticised by McGhee, his successor at Wolves, 1997

ALEX McLEISH

Master of Paris
HEADLINE in the Scottish Sun after McLeish's Scotland side won in France, 2007

The decision was a doddle because the Tartan Army would've strung me up if I'd left.
McLEISH on staying as Scotland manager after spurning an interested English club, 2007

ALLY MacLEOD

Q: What will you do if you win the World Cup?
A: Retain it.
EXCHANGE between reporter and Scotland manager MacLeod before the ill-fated World Cup campaign in Argentina, 1978

I think Ally believes tactics are a new kind of peppermint.
SCOTLAND DEFENDER, World Cup finals, 1978

With a bit of luck in the World Cup I might have been knighted. Now it looks as though I might be beheaded.
MacLEOD, 1978

When you talk as much as he does none of it can mean very much.
RON GREENWOOD, England manager, 1978

TERRY NEILL

I read in the papers that Terry Neill says he's going to put the joy back in Spurs' football. What's he going to do – give them bloody banjos?
EDDIE BAILY, Bill Nicholson's former assistant manager, 1974

MIKE NEWELL

Some can't work out whether I'm brave or stupid. But I'm not stupid.
NEWELL, Luton manager, alleging a 'bung' culture in English football, 2006

BILL NICHOLSON

I did not enjoy dancing around, waving trophies in the air. I'm sure he [Nicholson] didn't like it either. His comments regarding success were always cold... I was embarrassed by the boasting around us but I escaped it with humour. He gruffed his way out of it. Our satisfaction was in doing the job.
DANNY BLANCHFLOWER, Nicholson's Double-winning captain at Tottenham, 1961

DAVID O'LEARY

David O'Leary was one of those players we all looked up to. We'd go to him for advice as a senior pro and he was always willing to help. I must admit, though, when Frank McLintock said George Graham was the last player he expected to go into management, I thought the same about O'Leary.
IAN WRIGHT, former Arsenal team-mate, 1999

The fans might have said, 'Clear off back to London with your mate,' but the reception was brilliant so I thought, 'Right, I'll stay if they pick me.'
O'LEARY on why he changed his mind about not wanting to succeed George Graham as Leeds manager, 1998

He used to think I was a boring old sod.
O'LEARY, recalling how he lectured his former Arsenal colleague Tony Adams on the dangers of drink, 1998

He almost wanted to attack me and he was extremely lucky he stopped short of that. I had four or five people with me and he would have faced a very humbling experience.
SAM HAMMAM, Cardiff chairman, after a confrontation with O'Leary after the clubs' FA Cup tie, 2002. Hammam's bodyguard was a convicted hooligan

He was the kind of guy who would call you 'Top man', then put the phone down and probably hammer you. If there was someone more important in the room he would almost certainly make a beeline for them. The sort of man who will buy the chairman's wife a bunch of flowers at Christmas.
TONY CASCARINO, former Republic of Ireland colleague, 2002

Friends said: 'But you don't need football.' They meant financially and in a sense they were right. But I do need it. Not for the money, but for me. I need it because it's what I want to do with my life. My wife, Joy, thought the year away from the game was great – so many normal family weekends – but she knows that kind of normal life is not for me.
O'LEARY, by now Aston Villa manager, on his 'sabbatical' after being sacked by Leeds, 2004

I was a bit of an arsehole during my last year at Leeds. I became too opinionated about things that had no relevance to myself. I started playing a media game, spinning and counter-spinning. Too bleedin' quote-happy.
O'LEARY reflecting on his final season at Elland Road, 2004

EGIL OLSEN

He doesn't look like an international manager, but what does an international manager look like anyway? A wee baldy man with bad knees, like me?
CRAIG BROWN, Scotland manager, on the Norway and future Wimbledon manager, 1998

The Norwegian FA's highest honour is their gold award, which has only gone to three or four people. In nine years he took Norway from a land of Eskimos to the No. 2 team in the world. Normally the award goes to ex-presidents who are 176 years old.
LARS TJERNAAS, Wimbledon coach, on his manager's absence for a few days during their unsuccessful struggle against relegation, 2000

A brain surgeon shouldn't have to work with peasants.
STALE SOLBAKKEN, Norwegian ex-Wimbledon player, on the club's sacking of Olsen, 2000

MARTIN O'NEILL

Anyone who can do anything in Leicester but make a jumper has got to be a genius.
BRIAN CLOUGH, O'Neill's former manager at Nottingham Forest, 2001

His obsession with Grantham Town was total, even when we were going to places like Bridgnorth to play before three men and a dog. What summed him up was that he once phoned me at one o'clock in the morning after we'd lost at Spalding to ask whether I thought their third goal was offside. When I told him the time he said: 'Gerraway.' He was always saying that.
PAT NIXON, secretary of the Southern League club where O'Neill cut his managerial teeth, 2000

I looked upon O'Neill as a bit of a smart-arse.
BRIAN CLOUGH in Clough: The Autobiography, 1994

Martin runs up and down the touchline quicker and more often than his No.2, John Robertson, used to during his playing days at Nottingham Forest.
RON ATKINSON, television pundit and former manager, 2000

I'm not even liked in my own household, so I'll be fine.
O'NEILL on the prospect of abuse from Rangers' fans after becoming Celtic manager, 2000

It takes one to know one. It seems to me that Martin O'Neill is losing his 'Mr Clean' image.
KEN BATES, Chelsea chairman, responding to the Celtic manager's suggestion that he was a 'footballing cretin', 2000

Managing the football team is hard enough without going on to the board and deciding whether to sack myself or not.
O'NEILL on declining to become a Celtic director, 2001

I will calm down when I retire or die.

O'NEILL on his manic touchline style, 2002

Martin gets very wound up on that touchline and I'd say he's a racing certainty for a heart attack.
KENNY BURNS, former Nottingham Forest team-mate, 2003

If there was one player I clashed with more than any other during my time in management, it was Martin O'Neill. Management gave him the platform on which he can display his intelligence. He had an opinion on almost anything and was never slow to express it.
BRIAN CLOUGH, O'Neill's manager at Forest, in Clough: The Autobiography, *1994*

My ban might be good news for the players. The last thing they want to see is a nervous wreck of a manager who's speaking nonsense.
O'NEILL on being banned from the touchline for Celtic's UEFA Cup match v VfB Stuttgart, 2003

If the players are looking for a sign from me, I'm sorry but I'll be in the toilet somewhere.
O'NEILL before Celtic faced Porto in the UEFA Cup final, 2003

It's not my job to keep everyone happy. I'm not a social worker.
O'NEILL, 2003

You don't live in a democracy when he's in charge – it's more of a Martocracy. You do it his way or not at all. He can scare some players.
KASEY KELLER, goalkeeper under O'Neill at Leicester, advocating him for the Tottenham vacancy, 2004

I'd dearly love to have played lead guitar with Jethro Tull. That would have done me. I saw Tull playing Birmingham Odeon in 1974 and they had a fellow called Jeffrey Hammond-Hammond who made Pete Townshend look 90.
O'NEILL, 2004

If Brian Clough, who had an ego the size of 15 houses, had the humility to go for an interview for the job, the rest of us mortals should be able to subject ourselves to that.
O'NEILL on his unsuccessful bid to become England manager, 2006

During 90 minutes I can show my passion for 10, but with Martin it is 90. He shouts at everything and complains about everything.
JOSE MOURINHO, Chelsea manager, after drawing v O'Neill's Aston Villa, 2006

WILLIE ORMOND

Willie never gave us talks about foreign teams because he couldn't pronounce their names. But once in Scandinavia he stopped us as we went out and said: 'Watch out for the big blond boy at set pieces.' When we got out and looked across at them, there were about six big blonds. Well, we were playing Sweden.
SCOTLAND DEFENDER, who preferred to remain anonymous, 1974

BOB PAISLEY

His great strength was that he knew something about everything... He could watch a game, even on television, and forecast that a player was going to have an injury, and invariably he would be right.
KENNY DALGLISH, former Liverpool player under Paisley, in Manager of the Millennium, *by John Keith, 1998*

His smile was as wide as Stockton High Street. He had the nicest face in football.
BRIAN CLOUGH, former managerial adversary, on Paisley's death, 1996

He has broken this silly myth that nice guys don't win anything. He's one of the nicest you could meet in any industry or walk of life.
CLOUGH, 1978

Sponsors! They'll be wanting to pick the team next.
PAISLEY at Liverpool, 1981

CARLTON PALMER

Who's to say I won't be England manager in 10 years' time?
PALMER, Stockport manager, before their 11th successive defeat, 2002

STUART PEARCE

When people ask if I find certain places intimidating I say, 'Behave yourself.' The more intimidation, the more it means to win. I remember going to Derby with Forest and they were spitting on me and chucking coins when I took throw-ins. And that was just the old ladies. I loved it.
PEARCE, Manchester City manager, before the derby at Old Trafford, 2005

My daughter told me Beenie the horse wanted to sit next to me by the drinks holder on the touchline. It's difficult to tell a seven-year-old: 'This is the Premiership, I'm known as Psycho and I'm a hard man.'
PEARCE with a cuddly toy on the touchline after City beat West Ham, 2006

Beenie went to my daughter's first netball game and even they got beat.
PEARCE on the mascot's fall from grace, 2007

My lucky charm was my wife, though I never laid her on the touchline.
GRAHAM TAYLOR, former England manager, watching Pearce's antics as a radio summariser, 2006

I was probably the first of the footballing night-watchmen. I got sent in to bat through the night until some money was available.
PEARCE, England Under-21 coach, after being succeeded at Manchester City by Sven-Göran Eriksson, 2007

DAVID PLATT

The Nottingham Playhouse hosted a David Platt in Conversation evening on 13 September. I kid you not. Forest could make a fortune flogging the tape to insomniacs.
LETTER to the Daily Express about the then Forest manager, 2000

DAVID PLEAT

As the last man in Britain still sporting a quiff, David is used to things falling a bit flat after a promising start.
JIMMY GREAVES, former playing contemporary, as Pleat's Sheffield Wednesday dropped down the Premiership, 1995

ALF RAMSEY

He's the most patriotic man I've ever met.
GEOFF HURST, Ramsey's World Cup-winning centre-forward, 1966

I feel like jumping over the moon.
RAMSEY, Ipswich manager, in an early example of moon-jumping, after his team clinched the championship, 1962

I am not one to jump over the moon or off a cliff.
RAMSEY, by now England manager, 1967

I suppose I'll have to get used to being addressed as 'Sir', but if a player gets formal on the field I will clobber him.
RAMSEY on being knighted, 1967

REPORTER: Welcome to Scotland.
ALF RAMSEY: You must be fucking joking.
EXCHANGE at Prestwick Airport when Ramsey arrived with England, 1968

He is more careful of his aspirates than his answers.

ARTHUR HOPCRAFT, author, The Football Men, *1968. Ramsey had received elocution lessons*

Alf was never one for small talk when he was with England parties [as a player]; football was his one subject of conversation. He was always a pepper-and-salt man, working out moves and formations with the cruets on the table.
JACKIE MILBURN, former England team-mate, 1968

We've all followed Ramsey. The winger was dead once you played four defenders. Alf saw that in '66 and it just took the rest of us a little longer to understand.
DAVE BOWEN, Wales manager, in Tony Pawson's The Football Managers, *1973*

Ramsey recognised that the real strengths and values of English football were embodied not by Trevor Brooking, but by Nobby Stiles. Ramsey was right.
EAMON DUNPHY, media pundit and former Republic of Ireland player, 1981

On the one hand, Alf had Geoff Hurst and Roger Hunt who could be relied upon to sweat cobs. On the other he had Jimmy Greaves, a fantastic finisher but a moderate team player. Alf did what he thought was best for the team. Mind you, if we'd lost, he would have been condemned for the rest of his days.
BOBBY CHARLTON looking back to England's World Cup triumph, 1991

We talked Alf into letting us have a bit of sun [by the hotel pool]. He blew a whistle and we all lay down. Ten minutes later he blew it again and we all turned over.

JACK CHARLTON, former England defender, on the 1970 World Cup finals in Mexico, in Jeff Dawson, Back Home, *2001*

CLAUDIO RANIERI

I am a lovely man as long as everyone does what I say.

RANIERI on becoming Chelsea manager, 2000

Driving a car in England is still a problem. If I am alone on the road I begin to ask whether I am driving on the right side. And when I go back to Italy I have started to wonder the same thing. It is confusing.

RANIERI, 2001

My team showed good stamina and good vitamins.

RANIERI after Chelsea beat Arsenal in the Champions' League quarter-finals, 2004

I was like Pavarotti out there, trying to stimulate my players.

RANIERI on his shouting from the touchline, 2004

My team is like an orchestra. To play the symphony correctly I need some of the boom-boom but also some of the tweet-tweet. Sometimes the boom and the tweet go well together.

RANIERI, 2004

The team is my baby. When it is ready to get out of the pram, I will lead it by the hand.

RANIERI at Chelsea, 2003

I am happy when our fans are happy, when our players are happy and our chairman is on the moon.

RANIERI, 2004

Ranieri is an Italian Kevin Keegan, always smiling and making jokes. But when he's serious, he's deadly serious.

JOE COLE, Chelsea midfielder, 2004

This is my culture. I am Italian. In Italy, you win one match, draw the second and are sacked by the third.
RANIERI as speculation grew about his imminent sacking, 2004

I saw the 'Save Ranieri' campaign in the *Evening Standard* with a little picture of me. It was very flattering except for one thing: if I'm to fight like a gladiator, they can't run a picture of me wearing my glasses. Gladiators don't wear glasses in the Colosseum.
RANIERI shortly before leaving Stamford Bridge, 2004

I find it strange that when he beat Arsenal [in the Champions' League quarter-finals] he was acclaimed one of the best managers in the world. We lose to Monaco and suddenly he has to go.
KEN BATES, former Chelsea chairman, 2004

What can I say? The maniacs have wielded the knife and cut down their best asset.
RENATTA RANIERI after her son was sacked by Chelsea, 2004

I could say: 'What has he ever won?' But I won't.
JOSE MOURINHO, Ranieri's successor, 2004

The Manchester City challenge reminds me of my experience at Chelsea, where we built a good team without spending £1. I created the Chelsea miracle from nothing and my achievement convinced [Roman] Abramovich to buy the club.
RANIERI on the offer to manage City before leaving Parma to coach Juventus, 2007

HARRY REDKNAPP

I told my chairman that David O'Leary spent £18m to buy Rio Ferdinand from us and Leeds have given [O'Leary] £5.5m in share options, whereas I bring in £18m and all I get is a bacon sandwich.
REDKNAPP, West Ham manager, 2000

I can't even work my video, so it's no good to me.
REDKNAPP on the launch of a system to take football transfers on to the internet, 2000

The Del Boy comparisons piss me off. I'm not like him at all. I've been married 35 years and this is my third football club in 20-odd years. I'm not a ducker and diver. I may be a Cockney, but that doesn't mean I fit some silly stereotype.
REDKNAPP, Portsmouth manager, 2003

I'll be mightily relieved when this transfer window closes. Morning, noon and night over the past few weeks it has been non-stop phone calls. I took the missus out for a meal. I was outside the restaurant for a good hour and a half negotiating with three other parties.
REDKNAPP, 2004

I don't get involved in transfers in any way, shape or form.
REDKNAPP after Portsmouth owner Milan Mandaric called him 'a wheeler dealer', 2004

Wheeler dealer. Coo, ain't you got a lucky face, guv. That whole thing has been going on too long.
REDKNAPP replying to Mandaric, 2003

Harry, put your coat on. Come up to the stand. It's freezing. You'll catch pneumonia. We're 3–0 up. The game's over now.
MANDARIC phoning his manager during a match, 2006

OTTO REHHAGEL

I am the only man in Athens who is allowed to drive in the bus lane.
REHHAGEL, Greece's German coach, after their European Championship triumph, 2004

PETER REID

He's a Cloughie for the millennium.
BOB MURRAY, Sunderland chairman, 1999

If I lose two games on the trot here they are calling for my head. If I did that with England I wouldn't be able to go out of the house.
REID, Sunderland manager, ruling himself out after Kevin Keegan's departure, 2000

You must be an idiot if you want to manage Leeds United.
REID on succeeding Terry Venables at financially stricken Leeds, 2003

DON REVIE

An utterly brilliant manager, but knotted with fear.
GARY SPRAKE, former Leeds goalkeeper, 1980

If he had one chink in his armour it was that he probably paid teams more respect than they deserved. He should have just told us certain points and then told us to go out and beat them. Just left it to us.
NORMAN HUNTER, ex-Leeds defender, in An Alternative History of Leeds United, *1991*

It makes me angry to hear criticism of a man who is working himself into the ground and trying all he knows to get things right for the England team.
DICK WRAGG, chairman of the FA international committee, defending Revie days before he jumped ship to Dubai, 1977

Don Revie's appointment as England manager was a classic example of poacher turning gamekeeper.
ALAN HARDAKER, former Football League secretary, in Hardaker of the League, *1977*

As soon as it dawned on me that we were short of players who combined skill and commitment, I should have forgotten all about trying to play more controlled, attractive football and settled for a real bastard of a team.
REVIE after resigning as England manager, 1977

I just don't like him. I don't like the way he goes about football.
BRIAN CLOUGH, then Derby manager, criticising Revie in a TV interview with David Frost, 1970s

He was called greedy and deceitful but anyone who knows him knows he was just the opposite.
DUNCAN REVIE on his father, 1987

He has been out of football 10 years but he still stops the traffic.
DUNCAN REVIE, 1987

Don Revie was the cleverest of all of us [England managers]. He walked out before they threw him out.
SVEN-GÖRAN ERIKSSON, 2003

BOBBY ROBSON

I'm fed up with him pointing to his grey hair and saying the England job has aged him 10 years. If he doesn't like it, why doesn't he go back to his orchard in Suffolk.
BRIAN CLOUGH, 1983

If the pressure had frightened me, I'd have kept my quality of life at Ipswich. I'd have kept driving my Jag six miles to work every day and got drunk with the chairman every Saturday night.
ROBSON on calls for his resignation after England's failure at the European Championship finals, 1988

Eighteen years as a professional player in Framham and West Bromwitch Albion...a manager for Ibswich...and England's managing job after the World Cup finals in Spain when Mr Wood Green retired.
EGYPTIAN GAZETTE profile, 1989

The Spencer Tracy of football.
CORRIERE DELLO SPORT, Italian newspaper, 1999

We advise people of pensionable age to have fun and do whatever they want. If they want to manage a football team, that sounds great.
HELP THE AGED spokesman on the 66-year-old Robson's appointment by Newcastle, 1999

On my way here I followed a car with the number plate SOS1. Perhaps someone was trying to tell me something.
ROBSON on his first day in the Newcastle job, 1999

I intend to be at St James's Park as long as my brain, heart and legs all work...simultaneously.
ROBSON, 1999

I bleed black and white.
ROBSON, 1999

This is my love, my life, my drug, my motivation. Some managers have had enough at my age, but not me.
ROBSON before his 67th birthday, 2000

SUPPORTER: Which would you choose, Viana or Viagra?
ROBSON: That's easy. Saturday afternoon Viana. Saturday night Viagra.
EXCHANGE at Newcastle fans' forum, 2003. Hugo Viana was a Portuguese midfielder with the club

Football is my life, my obsession, my hobby, my theatre.
ROBSON, 2003

Don't you think people are actually saying: 'Oh, he's a silly old goat.' I am concerned what people think of me at 70, still working and acting like a raving lunatic.
ROBSON, 2003

BRYAN ROBSON

He's the only man I've ever known who could drink 16 pints and still play the next day.
PAUL GASCOIGNE on his admiration for Robson, who later became his manager at Middlesbrough, 1997

ANDY ROXBURGH

Can you believe my luck? Scotland are in the World Cup finals and the guy who's in charge wears a wig and has a nose that could cut a wedding cake.
CRAIG BROWN, Scotland assistant manager, teasing his boss, 1990

Roxburgh's a ned. Good on preparation, crap on football.
TERRY BUTCHER, Rangers and England defender, in Pete Davies, All Played Out: The Full Story of Italia 90, *1990*

JOE ROYLE

I may be a Scouser but I'm not stupid.
JOE ROYLE, Manchester City manager, 1999

I might have been the captain when we went down, but not when we hit the iceberg.
ROYLE on City's relegation to the Second Division, 1999

JOHN RUDGE

Every game I go to, he's there with his 'bonnet' on. That's dedication. Port Vale should go down on their knees and thank the Lord for having him.
ALEX FERGUSON on the long-serving Vale manager, 1995

I've been at Port Vale 16 years. Even the Great Train Robbers didn't get that long a sentence. Here you're manager, coach, chief scout, chief cook and bottle-washer. But I've loved every minute.
RUDGE, 1996

RON SAUNDERS

RON SAUNDERS: Giving the boys the usual old rubbish, Ron?
RON ATKINSON: Yes, Ron. I was just telling them what a good manager you are.
EXCHANGE during Atkinson press conference after a match between their teams, 1982

LUIZ FELIPE SCOLARI

If someone talks about my private life, I'll give them a good punching. I'm not interested in suing. I like to sort things out my way.
SCOLARI, then coach to Brazilian club Palmeiras, 1999

General Pinochet tortured a lot of people, but there is no illiteracy in Chile.
SCOLARI in an interview with Argentinian magazine El Graphico, *2001*

I wouldn't accept 50 trucks full of cash if they didn't let me appoint my own coaching staff.
SCOLARI, coach to Cruzeiro of Brazil, on his conditions for joining Barcelona before he eventually took charge of Brazil, 2001

I will go down as the Brazil coach that lost to Honduras. It's horrible.
SCOLARI after Brazil's defeat in Copa America, 2001. The following year he led Brazil to World Cup triumph

I'm going home to give my wife a big hug, because I doubt if I can manage anything else.
SCOLARI, Portugal coach, after a 'draining' victory over Spain, European Championship finals, 2004

BILL SHANKLY

Shankly – He Made The People Happy
INSCRIPTION on a bronze statue of Shankly at Anfield, 1990s

Football's not a matter of life or death. It's much more important than that.
SHANKLY, Liverpool manager, 1964

He's got a heart the size of a caraway seed.
SHANKLY on a player he transferred, 1968

I'm a people's man, a player's man. You could call me a humanist.
SHANKLY, 1970

I don't drop players, I make changes.
SHANKLY, 1973

A million wouldn't buy him. And I'm one of them.
SHANKLY, 1971

First is first, second is nothing.
SHANKLY, 1971

If a player isn't interfering with play or seeking to gain an advantage, what the hell is he doing on the pitch?
SHANKLY on the offside rule, 1967

I've been so wedded to Liverpool that I've taken Nessie [his wife] out only twice in 40 years. It's time she saw more of my old ugly mug.
SHANKLY on his retirement, 1974

Last thing every night Bill takes the dog out for a walk on the Everton training pitch. The poor animal is not allowed back in until he's done his business.
NESSIE SHANKLY, 1983

I'm glad he's not here now. He would have been devastated.
NESSIE, now a widow, as Liverpool struggled, 1993

I believe Shankly died of a broken heart after he stopped managing Liverpool and saw them go on to even greater success without him. Giving your whole life to a football club is a sad mistake.
JOHNNY GILES, former Republic of Ireland manager, 1984

A great man, great manager and great psychologist. He made you feel any mountain could be climbed.
KEVIN KEEGAN, a Shankly signing for Liverpool, 1998

I was managed by the best sports psychologist the world has ever seen. Bill Shankly made us feel we were super human.
RAY CLEMENCE, former Liverpool goalkeeper, 2002

PETER SHILTON

Peter Shilton would not know a footballer if he saw one. All he has ever been interested in is getting enough players back to protect his selfish hide.
ALAN HUDSON, ex-Stoke and England midfielder, on his former club mate's managerial ambitions, 1991

WALTER SMITH

Smith admits he is rarely at home of an evening and that his wife and family see him mainly in transit. His idea of relaxation is to pop in to watch Dumbarton Reserves.
BRIAN MEEK, Glasgow Herald *columnist, 1991*

It always gets back to the same question for me. Could a former electrician from Carmyle win the European Cup?
SMITH as Rangers failed honourably, 1993

I didn't know Walter personally. But I knew he must be Scottish because I used to see him carrying big discount cases of lager back from the supermarket.
PAUL GASCOIGNE on his first acquaintance with his future Rangers manager in Florida, 1995

GRAEME SOUNESS

He has gone behind my back right in front of my face.
CRAIG BELLAMY, Newcastle striker, on his feud with Souness, 2004

What impressed me most was his attitude – he wanted to bring the best out of people... In the heat of the moment the gaffer has knocked containers of orange squash flying, brought a TV set crashing to the floor and damaged several dressing-room doors.
TERRY BUTCHER, Rangers defender, in Both Sides of the Border, *1987*

Anyone who plays for me should be a bad loser.
SOUNESS on becoming Liverpool manager, 1991

He came in raging about a tackle by Dennis Wise on Nigel Clough. I had to tell him: 'Calm down, you've just had a triple heart by-pass.'
KEITH HACKETT, Premiership referee, 1994

Souness labelled me negative but if I strung defenders across the park, his job was to beat me, not moan about my team.
TOMMY McLEAN, Dundee United manager, 1997

At Rangers it was a case of 'my way is right'. Now I'm more prepared to listen to players' opinions though that's not to say I'm not still aggressive. I know that has upset people in the past, but I can't help that. It was in the gene pool when I got mine.
SOUNESS after becoming Blackburn manager, 2000

My health is not a problem, although who knows what's going on inside. But if you want a fight we can go out on to the car park.
SOUNESS, who had undergone major heart surgery, on taking over at Blackburn, 2000

I was so excited that I wasn't sure whether my pills were working properly.
SOUNESS after Blackburn drew with Manchester United, 2001

If I get a hostile reception from the Celtic support, I'll take that as a great compliment. If I had gone to Rangers and not done well, there would be no big deal about going back. In my five years at Rangers we won the championship four times. If I get lots of stick, I'll be chuffed to bits.
SOUNESS before taking Blackburn to Celtic for a UEFA Cup tie, 2002

I had to remind my players that I've had open-heart surgery and there's no way I can have that every week.
SOUNESS after a 4–3 win for his new team, Newcastle, over Manchester City, 2005

STEVE STAUNTON

If you keep picking the same players, who aren't performing, that's insanity. There's a fine line between loyalty and stupidity.
ROY KEANE, Sunderland manager, on Staunton's selection policy as manager of the Republic of Ireland, 2007

JOCK STEIN

John, you're immortal.
BILL SHANKLY, Liverpool manager, to Stein in the Celtic dressing room after the European Cup final triumph over Inter Milan, 1967

The greatest manager in the history of the game. You tell me a manager anywhere in the world who did something comparable, winning the European Cup with a Glasgow district XI.
HIGH McILVANNEY, journalist, in his TV documentary Busby, Stein and Shankly: The Football Men, *1997*

Jock had everything. He had the knowledge; he had that nasty bit that managers must have; and he could communicate. On top of it all, he was six feet tall, and sometimes he seemed to get bigger when he was talking to you. He was the best.
GRAEME SOUNESS, former Scotland captain, in Jock Stein: The Authorised Biography, *1988*

GORDON STRACHAN

He was good at tennis but very aggressive. Every ball he tries to get back, so it was nice entertainment for me. I beat him once and next day he told everyone: 'Never play tennis with George because he cheats. Every time he hits a winner he thanks the Lord, so it's always two against one.'
GEORGE BOATENG, Coventry midfielder under Strachan's management, 1999

We're used to our manager signing players we've never heard of. But now he is signing them from countries we've never heard of.
COVENTRY FAN on local radio phone-in after Jairo Martinez arrived from Honduras, 2001

I know how people see me, but all my life I've been a victim of self-doubt. There have been many times when I have felt despondent, when I think I'm useless. I felt it many times as a player and I've often experienced it as a manager.
STRACHAN shortly before leaving Coventry, 2001

REPORTER: Welcome to Southampton. Do you think you're the right man to turn things around?
STRACHAN: No. I was asked whether I thought I was the right man and I said: 'No, I think they should have got George Graham because I'm useless.'
EXCHANGE at a press conference on Strachan's arrival at St Mary's Stadium, 2001

There's more important things to think about than what [Augustin] Delgado is saying in the papers. I've got a yoghurt in the fridge to finish. The expiry date is today.
STRACHAN after criticism by Southampton's Ecuadorian Delgado, 2002

REPORTER: Bang goes your unbeaten run. Can you take it?
STRACHAN: No, I'm just going to crumble like a wreck. I'll go home, become an alcoholic and maybe jump off a bridge.
EXCHANGE at a press conference, 2002

REPORTER: Gordon, you must be delighted with that result.
STRACHAN: Spot on. You can read me like a book.
EXCHANGE after a Southampton victory, 2002

REPORTER: What was your impression of Leeds?
STRACHAN: I don't do impressions.
EXCHANGE after a draw at his old club, 2003

REPORTER: What areas did you think Middlesbrough were superior in?
STRACHAN: That big grassy one out there for a start.
EXCHANGE after a Southampton defeat, 2003

If you came in last in the training runs you were in the North Sea by 6.45am. It was freezing cold and I thought my head was going to explode. I certainly wasn't thinking about the FA Cup final back then. I was thinking: 'I wish he'd clear off.'
CHRIS MARSDEN, Southampton midfielder, recalling pre-season training in Scotland when the club reached the FA Cup final, 2003

Sometimes I have to turn the telly over when I'm watching Gordon going berserk on the touchline. I'm worried that he might have an aneurysm and burst a blood vessel.
MARK McGHEE, Brighton manager and friend of Strachan's, 2003

I'm not trying to 'find myself'. I know exactly who I am. Dinnae worry about that.

STRACHAN on taking trips abroad and to the Edinburgh fringe festival during a break from management, 2004

People don't understand a manager wanting to spend more time with his wife and family. Do I wait until people are screaming at me, my wife is going off her head and I'm a nervous wreck? I love football, but it's not an obsession.
STRACHAN still 'between jobs', 2004

When I'm dead, it will be inscribed on my headstone: 'This isn't as bad as that night in Bratislava.'
STRACHAN, by now manager of Celtic, after a 5–0 Champions' League defeat by Slovakian side Artmedia Bratislava in his first game, 2005

I've never taken drugs but I wonder if it's a bit like this.
STRACHAN on winning at Kilmarnock to clinch the Scottish title with Celtic, 2007

GRAHAM TAYLOR

Graham was never a good player. He was always trying to hit the long ball.
RON GRAY, Taylor's former manager at Lincoln, 1992

As a vision of the future it ranks right up there alongside the SDP and the Sinclair C5.
JOE LOVEJOY, football correspondent of the Independent, *on Taylor's intention to get England playing a more direct style, 1992*

It was nearly my finest hour, but life is made up of so-nearlies.
TAYLOR after his England side surrendered a 2–0 lead to draw with the Netherlands, 1993

Napoleon wanted his generals to be lucky. I don't think he would have wanted me.
TAYLOR after England failed to reach the World Cup finals, 1993

I can live with a newspaper putting a turnip on my head, except that it encourages people to treat me like shit.

TAYLOR, former England manager, on why he no longer attended England matches at Wembley, 1998

If a journalist wrote that about me, he'd have to go into hiding.

JACK CHARLTON on the Suns' *'turnip' jibe, 1993*

I used to quite like turnips. Now my wife refuses to serve them.

TAYLOR, between jobs, 1995

You can call me a turnip, but don't ever call me Gordon.

TAYLOR after being incorrectly addressed before Turkey v England match, 2003

PETER TAYLOR

I'm not equipped to manage successfully without him. I'm the shop front, he is the goods at the back.

BRIAN CLOUGH, Derby manager, when he and Taylor still worked together, 1973

We pass each other on the A52 going to work on most days of the week. But if his car broke down and I saw him thumbing a lift, I wouldn't pick him up. I'd run him over.

BRIAN CLOUGH, by now managing Nottingham Forest while Taylor was in charge at Derby, after their falling-out, 1983

PETER TAYLOR

He's very experienced. He's done his time. He's managed Dover Athletic.

JOHN GREGORY, Aston Villa manager, on Taylor's appointment as caretaker-manager of England, 2000

I was sitting there during the game thinking to myself: 'I can't believe this – I am manager of England.'

TAYLOR, Leicester manager and England caretaker manager v Italy, 2000

In a few months I went from being a football genius to a hopeless prat.
TAYLOR, by now Hull City manager, on his 'fall', 2004

STAN TERNENT

I ran up, smacked him in the face and nutted him for good measure...
If you're going to get into a fight, you don't wait for them to strike first.
TERNENT, Burnley manager, on a half-time fight with Kevin Blackwell, Sheffield United coach, in Stan the Man, *with Tony Livesey, 2003*

PHIL THOMPSON

All Tommo does is shout his mouth off, he doesn't coach. A few years ago
Tommo was slagging off the lads at Liverpool as a TV pundit. He should
realise that coaching is not about swearing at players, and that's all he does.
I'd love to hear something constructive from him, but all you get is effing this,
effing that.
PAUL INCE, England midfielder, after leaving Liverpool soon after Thompson's appointment as Gerard Houllier's assistant, 1999

JOHN TOSHACK

REPORTER: Did you realise it's Wales's worst home defeat in 98 years?
TOSHACK: I didn't, but I've broken records all my life, so that's another one.
EXCHANGE after Wales' 5–1 defeat by Slovakia, 2006

LOUIS VAN GAAL

Van Gaal deserved what happened to him at Barcelona. He had many bad
things to say about me, and for that nonsense, God punished him.
RONALDO, Real Madrid and former Barca striker, 2003

TERRY VENABLES

Terry made everybody, including the players, feel better about themselves.
DAVID DAVIES on leaving the post of executive director of the Football Association, 2006

When I arrived in the summer, one of my predecessors told the Spanish press that Meester Terry would be gone by Christmas, but he forgot to say which year.
TERRY VENABLES, Barcelona coach, 1984

The main thing I miss about London? The sausages.
VENABLES on life in Catalonia, 1984

A lot of people seem to think I'm just a slippery Cockney boy with a few jokes. It's taken one of the biggest clubs in the world to acknowledge what I can really do: coach.
VENABLES on his initial success with Barcelona, 1985

I can still go out as long as it's after midnight, I'm wearing dark glasses and it's a dimly lit restaurant.
VENABLES as Barca suffered the bad run that led to his sacking, 1987

Tottenham without Terry is like Westminster without Big Ben.
PAUL GASCOIGNE reacting to Venables's sacking by Alan Sugar, 1993

I must be the only person who actually gets less publicity by becoming manager of England.
VENABLES, newly appointed England manager, on controversy over his business dealings, 1994

When we're away on holiday he obviously still thinks about what he's going to do because he doodles attack plans on napkins. All our newspapers are covered in crosses and arrows.
YVETTE VENABLES, the England manager's wife, 1995

He's a great tactician, which is something I admire because I don't do tactics.

BARRY FRY, Birmingham manager, 1995

I do not accept his evidence as totally reliable, to put it at its most charitable.
MR RECORDER WILLIAMS, giving judgement against Venables over an unpaid bill from his nightclub, Scribes West, 1995

His conduct in relation to the four companies has been such as to make him unfit to be connected in any way with the management of a company.
ELIZABETH GLOSTER QC, representing the Department of Trade & Industry, after Venables was banned from company directorships, 1998

I was going to ask him what he thought of my idea for an El Tel theme nightclub called Wormwood Scribes, but I chickened out.
FRANK SKINNER, comedian, on meeting Venables, 1996

People say I should concentrate on being a football person, but what does that mean? Get home in the afternoon and go to the betting shop, the pub and the snooker hall? All I've done is try to learn how to use a typewriter. Sorry about that!
VENABLES, 1998

Terry gave us an extra dimension in [Euro] 96. We had always had good technique – I'll argue that endlessly because I've played with enough top players to recognise it. We've just been a little bit slow up top. We were all heart and no brains but Terry started putting that right.
TONY ADAMS, Arsenal and England defender, 1999

Terry saw me coming, but who can blame him? He took advantage of a young, inexperienced man with an enthusiasm for football. I was naïve. I didn't have my business head on.
MARK GOLDBERG, Crystal Palace chairman, claming he had paid Venables £1.3m a year plus loans and a house, 2003

If there's a better coach than Terry Venables out there, believe me, he must be bloody good.
TONY CURRIE, former QPR midfielder under Venables, after his ex-manager took charge at Leeds, 2002

Never winning the league rankles with me, and this is certainly an opportunity. Just look at the players I've got.
TERRY VENABLES, on taking over at Leeds, 2002. Within 10 months he was fired amid player sales and a relegation battle

He might think he's God in England but in the world he's nothing.
OLIVIER DACOURT, Roma midfielder, accusing Venables of trying to 'kill my career' at Leeds, 2004

I wouldn't let Venables handle my pension, but in the end it's just a sport.
TONY BANKS MP, Labour, former Minister for Sport, quoted in Tom Bower's book Broken Dreams, *2003*

Purely in terms of trophies, what has Terry Venables won? His profile on the official website of the League Managers' Association begins: 'Terry Venables is a name synonymous with success in English football.' Go on, then, show us your medals, Tel.
BILL BORROWS, journalist, in the Observer Sports Magazine, *2004*

JO VENGLOS

Jo was always the favourite in the back of my mind.
DOUG ELLIS, Aston Villa chairman, after appointing the Slovak as manager, 1990

GIANLUCA VIALLI

You wouldn't trust a learner driver with a Formula One car.
FABIO CAPELLO, coach with various Italian clubs, on Vialli's promotion to succeed Ruud Gullit at Chelsea, 1998

He'll do well because he's a perfectionist. He's so fussy. If you went to his house you'd see everything laid out neatly: cushions, books, magazines. When you room with him, he'll open his case and he's got his little shirts and socks all tidy.
DENNIS WISE, Chelsea player, 1998

I am addicted to pressure. When there isn't any, I don't give my best.
VIALLI, Chelsea manager, after three successive defeats, 1999

BERTI VOGTS

If people saw me walking on water you can be sure someone would say: 'Look at that Berti Vogts, he can't even swim.'
VOGTS, Germany coach, on mounting criticism of his style, 1996

One thing I can bring to the job is that I have never been beaten by England as a manager.
VOGTS, newly appointed Scotland manager, 2002

I can't see what Berti is attempting to do. Where are the tactics? Where is the discipline?
GUNTER NETZER, former Germany team-mate, after Scotland scraped a draw with the Faroe Islands in their sixth match without a win under Vogts, 2002

I thought he knew more about football than I did but I was wrong. It takes a special skill to put a team of players on the park who look as though they have never met each other.
WILLIE MILLER, former Scotland defender, 2004

I'd like to be going to Manchester United v Arsenal to watch players for my Scotland team. The reality is that I'm more likely to be at Wigan v Bristol City.
VOGTS, 2003

What's his name? Vorti Begts? I don't like Germans. They shot my dad.
BRIAN CLOUGH, 2003

Get stuck into the fucking Germans.
VOGTS to the Scotland team before a World Cup qualifier between the countries, 2003

VOGTS: I want to get back to the days of Denis Law – that's my dream.
REPORTER: Looking at your midfield, I bet you'd kill for a Graeme Souness.
VOGTS: Yes, but we must stop all the time looking back to the past.
EXCHANGE at a Scotland press conference, 2003

He's as well up there. I don't understand him at the best of times when he's
on the touchline.
*BARRY FERGUSON, Scotland captain, after Vogts was banished to the stand for verbally
abusing a referee, 2004*

The subtleties of our language were maybe a little beyond him.
JOHN McBETH, Scottish FA president, after the 'mutual' parting with Vogts, 2004

RUDI VOLLER

You wouldn't believe what I'd give to play in this game, if I were a few kilos
lighter.
VOLLER, Germany manager, before a match v Scotland, 2003

JOCK WALLACE

This city needed something to believe in, so I gave it me.
WALLACE, Leicester manager, 1980

NEIL WARNOCK

When I'm doing an in-growing toenail operation, I find my patient talking to
me and I'm not listening. At the end I say: 'I'm very sorry, Mrs Kirk, I was
away – I was just picking the side for Saturday.'
WARNOCK, Scarborough manager and chiropodist, 1987

I'd love to manage Wednesday. I'd buy so many tosspots – their current squad would do – and fuck 'em up so badly. Then I'd retire to Cornwall and spend the rest of my life laughing my fucking head off.
WARNOCK, Sheffield United manager, 2002. He later claimed he had been taken 'out of context' and denied including the current squad in his remarks

For me to get the Manager of the Month award, I'd have to win nine games out of eight.
WARNOCK, 2003

Being a loudmouth, I don't get many managers wanting to have a drink with me. There are a few, but I keep their identities quiet in case it damages their reputations.
WARNOCK, 2003

I'm disappointed now if opposing fans don't call me a wanker.
WARNOCK, 2006. Internet sites called him by the anagram 'Colin Wanker'

A penalty, an offside not given. I'm starting to sound like Neil Warnock.
PAUL JEWELL, Wigan manager, after a draw at Aston Villa, 2007

ARSENE WENGER

When Bruce Rioch was sacked, one of the papers had three or four names. It was Venables, Cruyff and then at the end, Arsene Wenger. I remember thinking as a fan: 'I bet it's fucking Arsene Wenger... Trust Arsenal to appoint the one you haven't heard of.'
NICK HORNBY, author, journalist and Arsenal fan, in Jasper Rees's Wenger: The Making of a Legend, *2003*

He arrived unnoticed at the training ground. A meeting was called, the players filed in and in front of us stood this tall, slightly built man who gave no impression whatsoever of being a football manager.
LEE DIXON, Arsenal and England defender, on Wenger's first day, in Rees's book, 2003

I've got to play for a Frenchman? You have to be joking.
TONY ADAMS, Arsenal captain, recalling his reaction to Wenger's arrival, 1997

At first I thought: 'What does this Frenchman know about football? He wears glasses and looks more like a schoolteacher. He's not going to be as good as George [Graham]. Does he even speak English properly?' Weeks later, I was still insisting: 'He hasn't a clue.'
ADAMS, 1998

He has put me on grilled fish, grilled broccoli, grilled everything. Yuk!
IAN WRIGHT, Arsenal striker, on Wenger's dietary regime, 1997

He can explode, especially at half-time, if we've been playing badly and making mistakes. But he is more like a father getting angry with his sons.
EMMANUEL PETIT, Arsenal's French midfielder, 1998

The Sigmund Freud of football managers.

LAURENCE MARKS, TV sitcom scriptwriter and Arsenal devotee, in A Man For All Seasons, *1999*

He is a diplomat, a linguist and listening to him is like attending a university lecture. Yet he is obsessed with football. He knows so much. When he bought Patrick Vieira, all the people around me at Highbury were saying: 'What a bloody idiot, he should have bought Jason McAteer.' Now, when Wenger buys a player, the fans don't criticise. They know he must be right.
MARKS, 1999

Mr Wenger's a very clever man, but I have to say that what he said is crap.
PETER REID, Sunderland manager, after his Arsenal counterpart claimed an opponent had helped get Patrick Vieira sent off, 2000

Those people who complain about the fixture schedule should clear off to a country where they play fewer games.
DAVID O'LEARY, Leeds manager and ex-Arsenal defender, after Wenger bemoaned fixture congestion, 2000

Arsene Wenger disappoints me when he is reluctant to give credit to Manchester United for what we have achieved. And I don't think his carping has made a good impression on other managers in the Premiership.
SIR ALEX FERGUSON, 2000

Arsene Wenger is somebody I'd like to get to know better. People who do know him tell me he is a good man but I don't suppose I'll ever find out for myself. He seems to pull down the shutters when you meet him and he never has a drink with you after the game.
FERGUSON quoted in Jasper Rees's Wenger: The Making of a Legend, *2003*

Wenger has an English mind but also a German mind, which is very disciplined.

GLENN HODDLE, a Monaco player under Wenger, in Myles Palmer's book The Professor, *2001*

REPORTER: What are the differences between George Graham and Arsene Wenger?
TONY ADAMS: How long have you got?
EXCHANGE at an Arsenal press conference, 2002

I call him the miracle worker. He makes an average player into a good player, a good player into a very good player and a very good player into a world-class player.
DAVID DEIN, Arsenal vice-chairman, after the Double was won, 2002

The Arsene brand of football is based on five things: power, pace, skill, technique and, in capital letters, YOUTH. He looks for perfection in those areas... In his time at Arsenal, only one player has achieved his ideal – Thierry Henry, although Dennis Bergkamp, Patrick Vieira, Robert Pires and Sol Campbell have come close.
BOB WILSON, former Arsenal goalkeeper and coach, 2004

For Arsene, I'm convinced it's all about intelligence on and off the field. He told me once: 'You can lose the head with your players only three times in a season. They listen the first time but after that, they're not interested.'
WILSON, 2004

Arsene is a great manager, but first of all he is a human being. Other managers forget how important that is.
THIERRY HENRY, 2003

You'll never figure him out.
MARK HATELEY, former England striker who played under Wenger at Monaco, 2003

During my rehabilitation on the Cote d'Azur, he'd phone to check on my progress. He was at the World Cup in the Far East and would ring at three in the morning, what with the time difference. But he's Le Boss, so you don't complain.
ROBERT PIRES, Arsenal midfielder, 2003

The biggest bollocking I got in six years of playing for Arsene was when we lost a game and he came in and said: 'I cannot stand for this. This is not acceptable.'
TONY ADAMS, former Arsenal captain, 2003

To not apologise to another manager for the behaviour of the players is unthinkable. It's a disgrace. But I don't expect him to ever apologise.
SIR ALEX FERGUSON on his feud with Wenger, 2004

I can't comment on the sending-off without sounding like Arsene Wenger. It was an extremely hot day and the sun was in my eyes.
MICKY ADAMS, Leicester manager, after Dion Dublin's dismissal on his debut, 2004

It takes talent to manage talent. I spoke to a group of elite coaches recently and projected those words on to a screen with Arsene's picture above them.
ANDY ROXBURGH, UEFA technical director, 2004

I like to read a book or talk to my wife or daughter, for an hour or so. But to have a whole day without thinking about football – that is impossible.
WENGER, 2003

You live in a marginal world as a manager. I know three places in London: my house, Highbury and the training ground [in Hertfordshire].
WENGER, 2003

There are some guys who, when they're at home, have this big telescope to see what happens in other families. He must be one of them. Being a voyeur is a sickness.
JOSE MOURINHO, Chelsea manager, alleging Wenger was obsessed with his club, 2005

RAY WILKINS

Ray has been at clubs like Milan where you have to wear a suit in bed, so he's very strict about the dress code.
DANIELE DICHIO, Queens Park Rangers striker, 1995

HOWARD WILKINSON

When Wilkinson said last year that Wednesday were just two players away from being a championship side, I didn't realise he meant Maradona and Gullit.
LETTER to Sheffield's Green 'Un, 1989. Wilkinson had recently joined Leeds

There are bigger heads than mine in this division – Howard Wilkinson springs to mind.
BRIAN CLOUGH, 1991. He later apologised for the remark

He disliked personalities who had a rapport with the fans.
ERIC CANTONA in Cantona: My Story, *1994*

If ever I am reincarnated, I'd like to return as a personality.

WILKINSON, Leeds manager, 1995

I know it sounds nuts but for some reason I thought I was signing for Howard Kendall. He was the only Howard I had really heard of.
VINNIE JONES in Vinnie: The Autobiography, *1998*

At the end of Wilkinson's team talks we'd be thinking: 'Eh?'
DAVID BATTY, England midfielder, on Leeds's former manager, 1999

I'm healthy, I've got a house, I eat well. How can I be unhappy? There's thousands out there with none of those things.
WILKINSON, during a poor run at Leeds, 1993

I've worked for the last three England managers and seen what it did to them. I saw Ron Greenwood break out in sores, Bobby Robson go grey and poor Graham Taylor double up in anguish and stick his head so far between his legs that it nearly disappeared up his backside. If I was single, with no kids, it'd be no problem. But I've a wife and three children and I've seen how this job can affect your family. It won't happen to mine.
HOWARD WILKINSON, Leeds manager, after Graham Taylor's exit, 1994. Wilkinson later took on the job as 'caretaker' on two occasions

WALTER WINTERBOTTOM

Just because I play for England, he thinks I understand peripheral vision and positive running.
JIMMY GREAVES, Chelsea striker, on the then England manager, 1960

I'm as bad a judge of strikers as Walter Winterbottom – he gave me only two caps.
BRIAN CLOUGH, Nottingham Forest manager, 1988

DENNIS WISE

Not a nice man to work for... A bully who couldn't handle any conflict or someone with an opinion.
KEVIN NICHOLLS, Preston midfielder, on falling out with Wise at Leeds after being appointed captain by him, 2007

TERRY YORATH

Terry, you're a lovely man but please do the best thing for Sheffield Wednesday and resign.
FEMALE SUPPORTER to Yorath after tapping him on the shoulder during a match at Hillsborough, 2001. He quit the next morning

six

MANAGING

With your club it is a love story that you have to expect will last for ever and
also accept that you could leave tomorrow.
ARSENE WENGER, Arsenal manager, 2006

We jump up and down like fucking lunatics for 90 minutes, but it doesn't have
any effect.
PAUL JEWELL, Wigan manager, 2007

If you don't know what's going on, start waving your arms about as if you do.

*GORDON STRACHAN, Southampton manager, on how to be seen as a bona fide
manager, 2003*

Ranting and raving gets you nowhere in football. If you want to be heard,
speak quietly.
BOB PAISLEY, Liverpool manager, 1982

I don't think I'm big-mouthed enough to be a manager.
ROBERT PIRES, Arsenal and France midfielder, 2004

I love football and all the build-up to a game, but I absolutely hate match
days. I wake with a knot in my stomach and it never goes away until the final
whistle.
SAM ALLARDYCE, Bolton manager, 2002

If it weren't for Saturdays, managing would be the best job in the world. You
get that horrible feeling in your guts and your head is going round.
RONNIE MOORE, Oldham manager, 2006

I work in the most intense job where my day starts at 6am and finishes very
late. The advantages are that I'm well paid and love what I do. But your highs
are never as high as your lows are low. After a defeat or bad performance I feel
physically ill.
GARY MEGSON, West Bromwich Albion manager, 2004

Ninety minutes before a match, there's not much a manager can do. You can't talk to players, so you sit drinking tea.
SVEN-GÖRAN ERIKSSON, England manager, 2006

In my line of work, if you win, you continue. If you don't, you're out. I must build something special this year. If I don't, I'm a dead man walking.
CLAUDIO RANIERI, Chelsea manager, 2003

Football managers are like a parachutist. At times it doesn't open and you splatter on the ground. Here, it is an umbrella. You understand, Mary Poppins?
RANIERI under growing pressure at Chelsea, 2004

A manager can't give players what they haven't got. The job is to make them find what they need inside themselves.
DAVID BECKHAM in his book My Side, 2003

A lot of players think they'll go into management and stay friends with everybody, but you have to make unpleasant decisions that will hurt people. If you don't like that, don't go into football management.
GEORGE GRAHAM, former manager, 2002

I have mates who did become teachers and I know that I couldn't have done it. It's ridiculously hard – far harder than what I do.
STEVE COPPELL, Reading manager, 2006

Sometimes I'm still at work at three in the afternoon.
PAUL MERSON on being caretaker player-manager at Walsall, 2004

People say you have to take your coaching badges to be a manager. I don't agree. When I went to Newcastle my only qualification was 1,000 rounds of golf in Spain, but it didn't do me any harm.
KEVIN KEEGAN, 2007

I never wanted to be a manager; I wanted to be a coach. But to have the power of coaching you've got to be the manager because the manager tells you how to coach. So the only reason I'm a manager is to be a coach.
GORDON STRACHAN at Southampton, 2003

The glory moment is when you sign the contract. From then on the situation deteriorates.
CARLOS QUEIROZ on becoming coach to Real Madrid, 2003

My brother always said you would have to be mad to be a manager. What other job is there where your livelihood depends on 11 daft lads?
FRANCIS LEE, Manchester City chairman, 1996

In my office I often regret the fact that players do not sit in chairs fitted with a lie-detector and an ejector seat.
GORDON STRACHAN, Southampton manager, 2002

I left out a couple of my foreigners the other week and they started talking in 'foreign'. I knew they were saying: 'Blah, blah, blah, le bastard manager, fucking useless bastard.'
HARRY REDKNAPP, Portsmouth manager, 2004

Some managers in England are fat and drink beer. How can players respect that, and not drink and stay fit?
ERIC CANTONA, 2003

Management is the only job in the world where everyone knows better.
I would never tell a plumber, a lawyer or a journalist how to do his job but they all know better than me every Saturday.
JOE ROYLE, Manchester City manager, 2001

Who wants to be out of management? Nobody. We all want to be there, winning and losing, reading in the papers that we don't know anything about football.
SVEN-GÖRAN ERIKSSON, England manager, 2001

Having one year without football [after the England job] has been the most stressful time, far worse than sitting on any bench. After one month off it is awful to wake up in the morning not knowing what to do.
ERIKSSON on returning to management at Manchester City, 2007

The face of the manager is a mirror to the health of the team.
ARSENE WENGER, Arsenal manager, 2002

Football management these days is like nuclear war. No winners, just survivors.

TOMMY DOCHERTY, 1992

We all end up yesterday's men in this business. You're very quickly forgotten.
JOCK STEIN, former Celtic manager, in Archie Macpherson, The Great Derbies: Blue and Green, *1989*

As a manager it's a case of have suitcase, will travel. And I certainly don't want to travel with my trousers down.
IAN HOLLOWAY, Plymouth manager, 2006

One minute you're God, the next you're something the dog left behind.
KIM HOLLOWAY, wife of Ian, on the insecurity of management, 2004

When you're a football manager you don't have fitted carpets.
JOHN BARNWELL, Walsall manager, shortly before his sacking, 1990

There aren't many managers who truly believe they can stay at one club long enough to qualify for a gold watch.
GORDON STRACHAN shortly before quitting as Southampton manager, 2003

I wouldn't go to a club that changes manager every six months. I'm not a fan of upheaval in football. Big clubs tend to win trophies only when they have stability. Spending money is one thing; building a team is another.
ARSENE WENGER as Arsenal closed in on the Premiership title, 2004

My son is a surgeon and makes life-and-death decisions every day. Yet I think of my job as the most important imaginable.
DAVID PLEAT, Sheffield Wednesday manager, 1997

Managing is a seven-day-a-week, almost 24-hour-a-day job. There's no rest or escape but I'm hooked on it.
BARRY FRY, Peterborough manager, 1999

I'm not a politician, a social worker or clergyman. I'm a provider of distraction, and fans want to go home happy to whatever bores the arse off them during the week.
HOWARD WILKINSON, Leeds manager, 1994

You have to have a bit of everything these days: coach, social worker, the lot. If Claire Rayner knew soccer, she'd be a great manager.
MICK McCARTHY, Millwall manager, 1995

Every dressing room should have a poster that says: 'There is more to life than just football and football management.'
GERRY FRANCIS, Bristol Rovers manager, 1988

There are too many silly, unrealistic demands on a manager, and they can take the pleasure out of this job. He's a very influential person so he can expect a certain amount of criticism and blame. But you can't expect one man to be responsible for everything.
GRAHAM TAYLOR, Watford manager, 1999

Being a manager means responsibility. It's an awful, thankless task most of the time. The only thing you get is that adrenalin rush you had as a player.
GARY LINEKER when his ex-Everton team-mate and fellow TV presenter Andy Gray was reputedly offered the Everton job, 1997

[Managers] have a great deal of influence in a club. But when the chips are down on match day, it's not up to them to kick the ball. They are one step removed from the action. That may be extremely frustrating, particularly if the manager thinks he could do better.
PROFESSOR ANDREW STEPTOE of University College, London, 2003

I still miss playing. Management offers only second-hand thrills.

JOE ROYLE, Everton manager, 1997

My guts are eating my insides again and I haven't felt that since I was a player.
STEVE WIGLEY, acting manager of Southampton after Gordon Strachan's departure, 2004

Playing was great. Managing was unrewarding and stupid.
GEOFF HURST, former England World Cup player and ex-Chelsea manager, 1991

You think you're working hard when you're a player but you really just have to look after yourself, physically and mentally. As a manager you can multiply all that by 14, which tells you how much tougher it is.
CRAIG LEVEIN, Cowdenbeath manager and former Scotland defender, 1999

In the public's mind, players win games and managers lose them.

BRYAN ROBSON, Middlesbrough player-manager, 1995

A manager is responsible for 10 per cent of wins and 90 per cent of defeats. That's how it works.
DIDIER DESCHAMPS, Monaco manager, after Chelsea's Champions' League defeat by his team was blamed on Claudio Ranieri, 2004

Many people think a coach accounts for around 80 per cent of a team's results, but I'd say it's more like 15 per cent.
SERGIO CRAGNOTTI, Lazio president, after Sven Göran Eriksson's departure, 2000

Did I put something of myself into the team? When we were playing well, yes. When we were playing shite, no.
FRANK BURROWS, caretaker-manager of West Bromwich Albion, 2004

Managers get too much credit when things go well and too much blame when they go badly.
GRAHAM TAYLOR, England manager, 1994

The nice aspect of football captaincy is that the manager gets the blame if things go wrong.
GARY LINEKER, former Leicestershire schools cricket captain, on being named England football captain, 1990

As a coach you have a squad of 24. You can only pick 11, so you have 13 enemies straight away. And you can multiply that by four – they all have wives, parents, kids.
JOHN TOSHACK, Wales manager, 2007

A manager's aggravation is self-made. All he has to do is keep 11 players happy – the 11 in the reserves. The first team are happy because they're in the first team.
RODNEY MARSH, Manchester City striker, 1972

As a manager you've got 30 or 40 players and staff to look after, and every one of the players' problems is your own because you're relying on them. I'd know if my centre-back's little boy had a problem, but my own wife and kids I knew nothing about. Your own life and family end up 50th best.
CHRIS NICHOLL, former Southampton and Walsall manager, 2003

I had a pile of books by my bed and I turned to my wife one night and said: 'I could die tomorrow and not know any of these, but I could tell you the name of every centre-forward in the bottom two divisions.' You think it's the most important thing, but in the whole scheme of life it isn't.
FRANK BARLOW, caretaker-manager of Nottingham Forest, 2006

It takes an enormous amount of energy to manage or coach properly. It's not only a matter of technique and tactics, but you have to move deep into the soul of your squad.
MARCO VAN BASTEN, former Netherlands striker and soon-to-be manager, 2003

I hate to work with a big squad. It's like a big box of oranges and one goes rotten. A month later, you have to throw the lot in the bin.
JOSE MOURINHO, Chelsea manager, 2004

There isn't another industry in the world where the employees still call the manager 'Boss' or 'Gaffer'. It's a throwback to the days of the Victorian mill-owners.
JON HOLMES, players' agent, in Colin Malam, Gary Lineker: Strikingly Different, 1992

If footballers think they are above the manager's control, there is only one word to say: 'Goodbye.'

ALEX FERGUSON, 1999

In this business you've got to be a dictator or you haven't a chance.

BRIAN CLOUGH *at Hartlepools, 1965*

The real key to management is to inject character into a club, not just the players. Jock Stein, Bill Shankly, Brian Clough – they dominated the whole place.
GEORGE GRAHAM, *former Arsenal, Leeds and Tottenham manager, 2002*

Football is in my blood, but do I want to put myself in a world where I rely on players, get sacked after six games and not see my two children grow up?
GARETH SOUTHGATE, *Middlesbrough captain, 2003. Southgate became Boro manager in 2006*

When you're building a team, you're looking for good players, not blokes to marry your daughters.
DAVE BASSETT, *Sheffield United manager, after buying Vinnie Jones, 1990*

My youngest daughter gets married on Saturday, which is more important to me than either job.
GRAHAM TAYLOR, *Aston Villa and soon-to-be England manager, 1990*

One thing I have learned about management is that you don't fall in love with players.
TAYLOR, *by now England manager, 1992*

To me there's no point in having confrontation for the sake of it. Look at Ruud Gullit. Can you tell me that he was a shrewd manager in what he did to Rob Lee, who was captain of Newcastle and Alan Shearer's best mate? Why make problems for yourself.
HARRY REDKNAPP, *West Ham manager, 2000*

I've told my players never to believe what I say about them in the papers.
GRAHAM TAYLOR, *Aston Villa manager, 1988*

I'm like a dad to my players, mixing small tellings-off with a lot of love.
GORDON STRACHAN, *Coventry manager, 1999*

Q: Who is your closest friend at the club?
A: I am the manager. I have no friends.
STRACHAN in a Coventry programme Q&A, 1999

Q: Best mates at the club?
A: Managers have very few.
JOHN RUDGE, Port Vale manager, in a programme Q & A, 1993

I love football, but management is the loneliest job in the world. You sometimes think it is you against the world.
DICK ADVOCAAT, Netherlands manager, 2004

As a manager you're like a prostitute – you depend on other people for your living.
STEVE COPPELL, Crystal Palace manager, after a controversial refereeing decision in his club's FA Cup defeat by Hartlepool, 1993

Being a football manager is a thankless, hopeless task. It's a dreadful job and most of them can be seen on the brink of madness or deep depression.
GARY LINEKER on why he went into the media rather than management, 1999

My wife says: 'If you're going to get ill, get wet pyjamas in the night, then pack it in.'
DAVID PLEAT, Sheffield Wednesday manager, 1997

There are grounds where you know you'll get covered in spittle and you wear your old clothes.
DAVE BASSETT, Sheffield United manager, after Wolves' Graham Taylor was abused at Bramall Lane, 1995

Losing is like experiencing a death in the family. For a while there is no comfort in anything.
JOHN GREGORY, Aston Villa manager, 1999

I always enjoy the summer. You can't lose any matches.

ROY EVANS, Liverpool manager, 1997

It's like being in the middle of an oven.
BOB PEARSON, Millwall manager, after stepping from the post of chief scout into a long run of defeats, 1990

It was like being in the dentist's chair for six hours.
HOWARD WILKINSON, Leeds manager, after a tense match v Leicester, 1990

I feel raped.
RAY GRAYDON, Walsall manager, after a 4–1 defeat by Crewe, 1999

No one, unless they manage a team, can know how I feel. No one, not an assistant manager, a player, anyone. They haven't a clue.
GORDON STRACHAN, Coventry manager, after a home defeat v Middlesbrough, 2000

If you're obsessed with winning and you don't do it, you end up a lunatic.
STRACHAN at Coventry, 1998

When you win you feel 25 years old. When you lose you feel more like 105.
GORDON LEE, Leicester manager, after a 5–2 defeat v Swindon, 1991

The world looks a totally different place after you've won. I can even enjoy watching *Blind Date*.
GORDON STRACHAN, Coventry manager, 1996

You wait a lifetime for a feeling like tonight.
ALEX FERGUSON after Manchester United's first title success in 26 years, 1993

It's the best day since I got married.
FERGUSON after winning at Sheffield United, 1992

I think my team are trying to kill me.
JOE ROYLE, Oldham manager, after a successful fight to stay in the Premiership, 1993

If it meant getting three points on Saturday I would shoot my grandmother. Not nastily. I would just hurt her.
BRIAN CLOUGH at the foot of the Premier League with Nottingham Forest, 1992

If I became a manager the first thing I'd do is buy a bottle of Grecian 2000.
CHRIS WADDLE, former England player, 1997

Welcome to the Grey Hair Club.
KEVIN KEEGAN in a message to John Aldridge when he became player-manager of Tranmere, 1996

The plan is to get out of management while I've still got all my marbles and all my hair.

JOE ROYLE, Manchester City manager, 2000

We really go through it on the bench. Last night when we were 2–1 up and Cambridge got a couple of late corners, the others were all laughing at me because I was curled up in a ball in the corner of the dug-out saying: 'I hate this job.'
BRIAN LITTLE, Leicester manager, 1993

I love football but I positively hate being a manager.
LOU MACARI, West Ham manager, 1989

If you don't get uptight, you're either a saint or you don't care. And there aren't many who don't care.
DON HOWE, England coach, before suffering a heart attack, 1988

I loved everything about the job – even the chants of 'Sit down Pinocchio'.
PHIL THOMPSON, former assistant manager to Gerard Houllier at Liverpool, 2004

How can anybody call this work? People in the game don't realise how lucky they are. You drive to the ground, play a few five-a-sides, then have lunch. It's wonderful, enjoyable fun.
RON ATKINSON, Aston Villa manager, 1993

No crowd, no money – sometimes I ask myself why I do the job.
JOE KINNEAR, Wimbledon manager, 1997

It's getting to the point where I'm ready to swear.
RAY GRAYDON, Walsall manager, after defeat at Charlton, 1999

I'm convinced a big-name manager will actually top himself soon.
PROFESSOR TOM CANNON, stress expert, 1997

I was there the night Jock [Stein] died in Cardiff, and I know where Bobby [Robson] is coming from, but I want to go when I'm in bed with my beautiful young wife.
GRAEME SOUNESS, Blackburn manager, after Robson talked of the possibility of a manager dying from stress, 2001

It doesn't matter whether you're successful, moderate and hopeless, whether it's Peterborough United and Manchester United, the pressure follows you around like a monkey on your back.
BARRY FRY, Peterborough manager, 1999

You are under pressure in war zones, not in football.
ARTHUR COX, Derby manager, 1993

The biggest pressure is to have no pressure.
ARSENE WENGER, Arsenal manager, 2006

Stress is when you have no money and are living on the street, or lying in hospital fighting for your life. Stress is being bottom of the league. This is pure joy.
RUUD GULLIT on life as Chelsea player-manager, 1997

Pressure to me is being homeless or unemployed. This isn't pressure, it's pleasure.
ANDY ROXBURGH, Scotland coach, after losing 17 players from his squad to face Germany, 1993

Pressure goes with the job, whether you're spending £3m or £30,000.
PHIL NEAL, Bolton manager and former Liverpool team-mate of Kenny Dalglish's, 1991

Five grand a week? That's my kind of pressure.
LOU MACARI, Birmingham manager, after Dalglish's shock departure from Liverpool, 1991

I happen to like the aggravation that goes with football management. It seems to suit my needs.
GRAEME SOUNESS on succeeding Dalglish at Anfield, 1991

My cardiologist tells me that for some people, what I do would represent pressure. For others, pressure is going home and sitting in front of *Coronation Street* with your slippers on. I would find that very stressful.
SOUNESS, by now Blackburn manager, 2001

I've learned how to relieve managerial stress. When the ball gets into your last third, avert your eyes. Turn to your physio, ask for chewing gum, have a few words about the match. Anything. It stops the tension building up. You might miss a goal, but someone will always tell you how it happened.
BILLY BINGHAM, Northern Ireland manager, 1992

I close my eyes every time the ball comes near our penalty area.

JOHN TOSHACK, Real Madrid coach, on his erratic goalkeeper Albano Bizarri, 1999

You want to try sitting in the dug-out when it's your arse in the bacon-slicer.
MICK McCARTHY, Republic of Ireland manager, on being told by a reporter that he 'looked tense' during a World Cup game v Saudi Arabia, 2002

Some do it by smoking hash, others by making love or racing a rally car. We managers experience extremes all the time. You can find yourself at the highest point or the lowest ebb in the same week.
ARSENE WENGER, Arsenal manager, 2002

I can feel when I'm ready to lose it. Then I get my things and go home. I read a book for an hour or watch TV and come back a different man. It's what I call experience.
WENGER, 2002

I always thought managers were more involved. But when it comes down to it, I just sit there and watch like everyone else.
KEVIN KEEGAN in his early days at Newcastle, 1993

We've lost seven games 1–0 and drawn another seven 0–0. If we'd drawn the 1–0 games we lost, we'd have another seven points. If the seven draws had been 1–0 to us, we'd have 28 points more and we'd be third in the Premiership instead of going down.

ALAN SMITH, Crystal Palace manager, sliding towards relegation, 1995

As I mulled it over on the bus, reliving every kick, I could hear the players laughing and playing cards. They soon forget, but it's a seven-day punishment for managers.

ANDY KING, Mansfield manager, 1994

As manager, it's your head on the block. You have to make cold-blooded decisions and if you can't, you shouldn't be in the job. To be honest, I found it difficult to be a bastard.

TERRY BUTCHER, former Coventry and Sunderland manager, 1994

I've heard it said that you can't be a football manager and tell the truth. Well, I'm going to have a go at it.

LIAM BRADY, newly appointed Celtic manager, 1991

When I was appointed manager of Stoke, the first phone call I received was from Joe Mercer, then with Aston Villa, offering congratulations. He told me: 'My advice is never to trust anyone in the game, and when I put down the phone don't trust me either.'

TONY WADDINGTON, former Stoke manager, 1990

Lots of times managers have to be cheats and conmen. We are the biggest hypocrites. We cheat. The only way to survive is by cheating.

TOMMY DOCHERTY, manager of numerous clubs, 1979

There are two types of people who succeed in coaching: the conman and confidence trickster, or the intelligent man who builds your confidence and belief. I'm the conman.

MALCOLM ALLISON on becoming chief coach to Bristol Rovers aged 65, 1992

You hope and you pretend that you know what you're doing.

KEVIN KEEGAN, newly appointed Newcastle manager, 1992

The buying and selling of players sounds rather like a slave market. Moreover, the payment of large transfer fees can be the refuge of the incompetent manager.
SIR NORMAN CHESTER, chairman of committee examining English football's problems, 1968

The power managers, like Brian Clough, Alex Ferguson and, up to a point, myself are beginning to drift out of the game. Alex can take negotiations about 85 per cent of the way, but there are very few like him. Things have changed.
GEORGE GRAHAM, Tottenham manager, 2000

There are no bungs in football. With my so-called reputation, I would be the one they approached. I deal with most managers, most clubs and I've never been asked for or offered a bung. Fact.
ERIC HALL, players' agent, 1995

When Leeds sacked me, all my worries about pensions and bringing up three kids were gone, and I became a better manager.
BRIAN CLOUGH on his £90,000 'golden handshake' from Leeds 16 years earlier, 1990

When [the sack] arrives, I won't cry. I will enjoy my family, then the next week, or month, I'll get another club. Remember, the richest managers are those that are sacked the most.
JOSE MOURINHO, Chelsea manager, 2004

You've never really been a manager until you've been sacked.

BRIAN HORTON on replacing Peter Reid as manager of Manchester City, 1993

There are only two certainties in this life. People die and football managers get the sack.
EOIN HAND, Limerick and Republic of Ireland manager, 1980

There's only two types of manager. Those who have been sacked and those who will be sacked in the future.
HOWARD WILKINSON, Leeds manager, 1995

Every manager gets sacked, but it's better to be sacked by Real Madrid than any other club.
JOHN TOSHACK, on becoming Real's coach for a second (short-lived) spell, 1999

Ninety-nine per cent of managers that lose their jobs deserve it.
MARK McGHEE, Wolves manager, 1996

I told the chairman that if he ever wants to sack me, all he has to do is take me into town, buy me a meal, a few pints and a cigar, and I'll piss off.
MICK McCARTHY, Millwall manager, 1995

The manager picks the team but invariably it's the punters who pick the manager.
ALAN BALL alleging a 'get-rid-of-the-manager' syndrome after leaving Manchester City, 1996

Managers are like fish. After a while, they start to smell.

GIOVANNI TRAPATTONI, Fiorentina coach, confirming his departure, 2000

A manager can smell the end of his time. The whole club reeks of an imminent sacking. Not that they actually say: 'You're bloody fired!' It's all innuendo and muttering – 'Things aren't going well, are they?' But you know they're after your blood, and if truth were told you've already had your bag packed for weeks.
ROY SPROSON, former Port Vale manager, 1988

I stood up and was counted.
ROGER HYND on being sacked as Motherwell manager, 1978

How ironic that I should have been sacked on the anniversary of the Coventry blitz. When the chairman phoned me, I felt like my house had been bombed.
JOHN SILLETT on his dismissal by Coventry, 1991

King Louis XVI had his head cut off in the French Revolution. It's the same for managers.
JEAN TIGANA, Fulham manager, pondering possible dismissal during a long run without a win, 2002

You just have to wait for someone to suffer the same misfortune as you. It's the only job where you can study the vacancies on Teletext as they happen.
GRAHAM TURNER, Hereford United manager, 1995

When the TV people asked whether I'd play a football manager in a play, I asked how long it would take. They told me 'about 10 days', and I said: 'That's about par for the course.'
TOMMY DOCHERTY, 1989

It's me in the electric chair now.
BOBBY COLLINS on succeeding Norman Hunter as Barnsley manager, 1984

I had to go. Towards the end I felt like a turkey waiting for Christmas.
FRANK CLARK, after leaving the Nottingham Forest manager's job, 1996

Remember that film *A Bridge Too Far*? Well, I probably came a game too far.
GERRY FRANCIS leaving the QPR manager's job after a 5–0 defeat by Wimbledon, 2001

Football is about now, it's about your contract... We're in the age of instant solutions and the job of being manager is set in that context. You could argue, given the demands today, that you don't want to be at a club more than three years.
HOWARD WILKINSON, former Leeds manager, 1999

You have to be a masochist to be an international manager.
ARSENE WENGER, 1998

The England job should be the best in the world but it's become a horrible job. To think of my children getting hammered in the school playground because their dad is England manager. Perhaps we should be looking for a guy who's divorced with no kids.
GLENN HODDLE, then Chelsea player-manager, 1994. Within two years he was in charge of England

I wouldn't take the England job for a big gold clock.

STEVE COPPELL, former Crystal Palace manager, 1993

The only way I'd be interested in the England job is as player-manager.

RON ATKINSON, *Aston Villa manager, 1993*

As England manager you know that you're probably the most hated man in the country, apart from the Chancellor [of the Exchequer].
OSSIE ARDILES, *Tottenham manager, ruling himself out of the running, 1993*

Even the Pope would think twice about taking the England job.
ROY HODGSON, *Switzerland manager, 1993*

The England manager has to fight the system and fight the press from day one.
HOWARD WILKINSON, *Leeds manager, 1993*

There's no difference between coaching England and coaching Newbury Town. The reason is that they're all blokes. There are England blokes, Manchester United blokes, Arsenal blokes and Newbury blokes. You are coaching men, human beings.
DON HOWE, *who worked with both the England squad and his local Isthmian League part-timers, 1994*

I'm the man for the job. I can revive our World Cup hopes. I couldn't do a worse job, could I?
SCREAMING LORD SUTCH, *leader of the Monster Raving Loony Party, on why he should succeed Graham Taylor as England manager, 1994*

Football managers are treated like the proverbial football. Unfortunately, instead of being passed around, they get a real good kicking.
GRAHAM TAYLOR *on leaving Watford (of his own volition), 2001*

Managers are treated as public property, as if we do not have feelings or families. People feel we can cope and are impervious to hurt.
MARK McGHEE, *Wolves manager, 1997*

After a few years, managing in England is like working for the weather forecast office. You know when a storm is coming.
ARSENE WENGER, Arsenal manager, 1999

One person who thinks it is ridiculous that I earn so much money from football is my grandmother. She never understood you get so much from kicking a ball. So every time I go to see her she gives me £5 or £10.
SVEN-GÖRAN ERIKSSON, England manager, 2002

Just because a coach comes from overseas, it doesn't mean he's a tactical genius.

TONY ADAMS, former England captain, cautioning against expecting too much from Eriksson, World Cup finals, 2002

We get carried away with coaching and coaches. I have my coaching badges but they came out of a cornflakes packet.
HARRY REDKNAPP, West Ham manager, 2001

Coaching is for kids. If a player can't pass and trap the ball by the time he's in the team, he shouldn't be there in the first place. At Derby I told Roy McFarland to go out and get his bloody hair cut. Now that's coaching at the top level.
BRIAN CLOUGH after retiring as Nottingham Forest manager, 1994

Fulham Football Club seek a Manager/Genius.
NEWSPAPER advert, 1991

Charisma comes from results, and not vice versa.
CRAIG BROWN, Scotland manager, 1996

It would've taken a brave man not to wear brown pants after comparing our team-sheet with theirs.
NEIL WARNOCK, Notts County manager, after playing Arsenal, 1991

I always say I'll get over it when I grow up, but there are no signs of it happening yet. I still find it impossible to drive past any sort of match. I've got to stop and watch it.
CRAIG BROWN, Scotland Under-21 manager, 1988

The greatest thing about being a manager is when you're out on the training pitch with your players. No phones, agents, media or directors, just you and a group of players committed to improving themselves.
GRAHAM TAYLOR, Watford manager, 1999

Great teams don't need managers. Brazil won the World Cup in 1970 playing exhilarating football, with a manager they'd had for three weeks. What influence can a man have who has only been with them that length of time? What about Real Madrid at their greatest? You can't even remember who the manager was.
DANNY BLANCHFLOWER, former Tottenham captain, in his Sunday Express column, 1972

The Monday after we won at West Brom in the FA Cup I received 193 calls from assorted media and well-wishers. I even got a call from my first wife's parents, which surprised me seeing as they hadn't bothered to ring in the 15 years since our divorce.
GEOFF CHAPPLE, manager of non-league Woking, 1992

It may sound selfish but I want to dedicate this triumph to my dog, who died two years ago.
CARLOS BIANCHI, Boca Juniors coach, after his team won the Treble in Argentina, 2001

You could have Mickey Mouse in charge of the team on Saturday. You could stick a bucket out there with a mop in it or a snowman with a carrot for a nose. It wouldn't matter because no one needs motivating for a match like this.
IAN ATKINS, Carlisle manager, before the Third Division club's FA Cup tie v Arsenal, 2001

I've come from caviar to fish 'n' chips. At Spurs you can buy daft. At Leicester I have to buy sensibly.
DAVID PLEAT, Leicester manager, 1987

I haven't seen the lad but he comes highly recommended by my greengrocer.
BRIAN CLOUGH on signing Nigel Jemson from Preston, 1988

The easiest team for a manager to pick is the Hindsight XI.
CRAIG BROWN, Scotland manager, 1998

The last manager who led this club to the FA Cup semi-finals [Archie Macauley in 1959] ended up as a traffic warden in Brighton.
DAVE STRINGER, Norwich manager, on reaching the last four, 1989

I'm going to go out and get lambasted on wine.
MARTIN O'NEILL, Leicester manager, after his team won the Coca-Cola Cup, 1997

We will worry about the final later. Now is the time for wine and cigarettes!
KLAUS TOPPMOLLER, Bayer Leverkusen coach, after his team reached the Champions' League final at Manchester United's expense, 2002

Funny how other managers always want to swap one of their reserves for your best player.
MURDO MacLEOD, Partick Thistle manager, on exchange deals, 1996

seven

THE GAME

What would we do without football, for God's sake?
SIR BOBBY CHARLTON, 2006

There is absolutely no question that the world turns around a spinning ball.
EDUARDO GALEANO, Uruguayan poet, journalist and football fan, 1995

Football's a difficult business and aren't the players prima donnas? They fall down and roll around.
QUEEN ELIZABETH II while knighting Premier League chairman David Richards, 2006

Football is the most important of the unimportant things in life.
ARRIGO SACCHI, Milan coach, 1992

Football is nothing compared to life. For me, pressure is bird flu.
JOSE MOURINHO, Chelsea manager, 2006

Football is like the world. It's a bit crazy.
MOURINHO, 2007

Football is important, but life is important too.
MAXIME BOSSIS, France player, after defeat by West Germany, World Cup semi-final, 1986

Football at a professional level is an interval between real life and real life.

TONY AGANA, Sheffield United striker, 1990

Football is like a beast. It can overtake your whole life so you forget who you are and who your family are.
IAN HOLLOWAY, Plymouth Argyle manager, 2007

Football has a habit of destroying your confidence in human beings.
KEVIN BLACKWELL, Luton manager, reflecting on his sacking by Leeds, 2007

Football is the one international language.
NANCY DELL'OLIO, Sven-Göran Eriksson's partner, 2003

Football is a game – the language it don't matter as long as you run your bollocks off.
DANNY BERGARA, Stockport's Uruguayan-born, Spanish-speaking manager, 1991

Football is a bitch goddess.
BILL KENWRIGHT, Everton chairman, 2005

Football. Bloody hell.
ALEX FERGUSON to TV interviewer moments after Manchester United had won the European Cup with two last-gasp goals v Bayern Munich, 1999

Football is about what happens in the two penalty areas. Everything else is propaganda.
GORDON STRACHAN, Southampton manager, 2003

Football is an excuse to feel good about something.
JORGE VALDANO, sporting director of Real Madrid, 2003

Football is a great healer.
RIO FERDINAND, England defender, after a strike by England players was averted and they drew with Turkey to qualify for the European Championship finals, 2003

Football is loved by everyone, everywhere, because it has no definitive truth
MICHEL PLATINI, former France captain and manager, 1998

Football is a battle, a small war. You can't expect 22 players to behave like Sunday-school boys. You have to remember they are human.
SVEN-GÖRAN ERIKSSON, England manager, 2002

Football became popular because it was considered an art, but now too many pitches are becoming battlefields.
SOCRATES, Brazil captain, 1981

Football's like war. When the chips are down, you need fighters.
IAN BRANFOOT, Southampton manager, 1991

Football doesn't matter a damn. It used to be a game, now it's a war.
ANTHONY BEAUMONT-DARK MP, Conservative, 1991

Football is war without bloodshed.
SHIMON PERES, Prime Minister of Israel, 2005

Football is not just a simple game. It is also a weapon of the revolution.
CHE GUEVARA, Argentinian revolutionary, 1960s

Football is the biggest thing that's happened in creation, bigger than any 'ism' you can name.
ALAN BROWN, Sunderland manager, 1968

Football turns stupid people into thugs and bright people into bores.
CHARLES SPENCER, Daily Telegraph *theatre critic, 2003*

Football is a damn sight more important than arty-farty people pushing themselves around the Royal Opera House.
TERRY DICKS MP, Conservative, 1990

Football is the opera of the people.
STAFFORD HEGINBOTHAM, Bradford City chairman, 1985

Football as popular culture is a space of intertextuality.
RICHARD HAYNES, author, The Football Imagination: The Rise of Fanzine Culture, *1996*

Football is not family entertainment.
CILLA BLACK, TV presenter, after ITV replaced her Blind Date *show with* The Premiership, *2001*

Football is a game and people have to be cunning.
RIVALDO, Brazil midfielder, after admitting he feigned injury to get an opponent sent off in a World Cup match v Turkey, 2002

Football's a rat race and the rats are winning.
TOMMY DOCHERTY, 1982

Football is a much more cynical game all round than cricket.
PHIL NEALE, Lincoln defender and Worcestershire cricketer, 1982

Football is self-expression within an organised framework.
ROGER LEMERRE, France coach, 1999

Football is a fertility festival. Eleven sperm trying to get into the egg. I feel sorry for the goalkeeper.
BJÖRK, Icelandic singer, 1995

Football is a permanent orgasm.
CLAUDE LE ROY, Cameroon coach, 1998

Football is a pantomime of pain and disappointment.
NICK HANCOCK, Stoke City supporter and TV celebrity, 1999

Football and cookery are the two most important subjects in the country.
DELIA SMITH, television chef, after becoming a Norwich City director, 1997

Football has become the religion of the 20th century... Its fervour, enthusiasm, battle cries, violence and flags have replaced the wars of yesteryear.
EDITORIAL in the French newspaper Le Figaro *– by its literary critic, 1998*

Football is like a flower. When you attack, the flower is open and in bloom. Defend and the flower closes.
TOMMY SODERBERG, Sweden coach, 2000

Football's like dope. You try to take a few months away, but it keeps pulling you back.
LEO BEENHAKKER, Dutch coach of Trinidad & Tobago, 2006

Football is a state of mind and when the mind is healthy, the performances follow.
RONALDINHO, Brazil and Barcelona striker, 2004

Football is a simple game made complicated by people who should know better.
BILL SHANKLY, Liverpool manager, 1968

Football is a simple game. The hard part is making it look simple.
RON GREENWOOD, England manager, 1978

Football is a beautiful box of surprises, and the reason is that the ball is round. The day they make the ball square, the Germans or Japanese will dominate everything because they're good at maths.
TONINHO CEREZO, former Brazil player, 2004

Football is not mathematics. In this game two plus two almost never makes four. Sometimes it's three, other times five.
LEO BEENHAKKER, Dutch coach of Trinidad and Tobago, 2006

Footballers are the modern-day gladiators.
GIORGIO ARMANI on being named official couturier to the England team, 2003

It's the entertainment industry, for heaven's sake, not life or death.
MATT LE TISSIER after retiring as a Southampton player, on the 'strain' of playing for 'heavy-handed' managers, 2002

The beauty of football is that win, lose or draw, you can't relax.
ROY KEANE, Sunderland manager, 2007

Football has gone global. If you'd told me 30 years ago that Brazilians would be playing in Moscow, I'd have said you were crazy. Now it's the reality.
FRANZ BECKENBAUER, former West Germany captain and coach, 2007

Football is fashionable. Political parties jockey to enlist football men to their cause; celebrities and glamorous women speak openly about their love for football; and literary critics pepper their erudition with references to 'the beautiful game'.
JOHN WILLIAMS, lecturer at the Sir Norman Chester Institute for Football Research, Leicester University, 1998

The story of rugby and football is the story of two nations – not of rich and poor, or privileged or unprivileged, but of two approaches to life. Rugby represents much of what is best about our society, football much of what is worst.
EDITORIAL in the Daily Mail *after England won rugby union's World Cup, 2003*

We invented the game and let everybody play it and we haven't seen a penny in royalties. It makes you sick.
JOHN CLEESE, comic actor and former member of Monty Python, *2006*

Football is bankrupt without the TV deals. If the banks ever withdrew, you would see a bigger collapse than Black Monday.
SIR JOHN HALL, Newcastle chairman, 1995

Premier League football is a multi-million-pound industry with the aroma of a blocked toilet and the principles of a knocking shop.
MICHAEL PARKINSON, Daily Telegraph column, 2003

The reason the transfer market exists is to provide a means of shifting dodgy money around a bent game.
PARKINSON, 2003

The great fallacy is that the game is first and foremost about winning. It's nothing of the kind. The game is about glory. It's about doing things in style, with a flourish, about going out and beating the other lot, not waiting for them to die of boredom.
DANNY BLANCHFLOWER, former Tottenham captain, in Hunter Davies's book The Glory Game, *1972*

See the boy Rudyard Kipling, who said it wasn't whether you won or lost but how you played the game that mattered, well, he obviously never played football. Winning is the only thing that matters.
ANDY GORAM, Rangers and Scotland goalkeeper, 1996

The fair play gave me goose pimples. Everyone respected each other. It was beautiful.
SEPP BLATTER, FIFA general secretary, after West Germany v England, World Cup semi-final, 1990

Everything is beautiful in English football. The stadiums are beautiful, the atmosphere beautiful, the cops on horseback beautiful. And the crowds respect you.
ERIC CANTONA on making an early impact at Leeds, 1992

The most beautiful game is winning matches.

GLENN HODDLE, Chelsea manager, 1995

I would rather play ugly football and win than play beautifully and lose.
MARIO ZAGALLO, Brazil coach, 1997

I told them I'd like them to win ugly and they certainly won ugly today. That was the ugliest thing I've seen since the ugly sisters fell out of the ugly tree.
TERRY BUTCHER, Motherwell manager, 2005

Thank you for letting me play in your beautiful football.
ERIC CANTONA accepting the PFA Player of the Year award, 1994

It was beautifully done. It was wrong but it was necessary.
JACK CHARLTON, former England defender, commenting as a TV pundit on a 'professional foul' in a Barcelona v Dusseldorf game, 1979

When you're winning, you want to be playing every day. When you've had bad results, you start to feel tired.
GRAEME SOUNESS, Blackburn manager, 2002

The one thing you can guarantee in football is disappointment. If you expect it, it's not so hard to take when it comes along.
SOUNESS, 2004.

You feel so good, so comfortable, so powerful when you win. If you don't win, it's terrible.
MARCEL DESAILLY, Chelsea and France defender, 2000

It's the greatest game in the world. It is also the most frustrating, exasperating, infuriating, desolating game. But there is nothing else.
KEN BATES, Chelsea chairman, 1995

In football you can be close to being in hell then rise to heaven just like that.
JENS LEHMANN, Arsenal goalkeeper, after his penalty save at Villarreal put his team in the Champions' League final, 2006

There is a God up there. I love Margaret Thatcher, Ken Livingstone and everybody. It's not Rwanda, it's not Bosnia and it's not Ethiopia. It's crazy, it's wonderful. It's football.
MICHAEL KNIGHTON, Carlisle chairman, after his club again avoided relegation from the league on the season's final day, 2000

Great players are always the same. If you ring them and ask them to play a
game with friends, will they say yes? If they love the game, they'll play, even if
they're on holiday.
ARSENE WENGER, 2003

What the fuck is art? A picture of a bottle of sour milk lying next to a smelly
old jumper? What the fuck is that all about? And look at opera. To me it's a
load of shit. But people love it. I'd say football is art. When I watched France v
Holland at Euro 2000, I was orgasmic.
JOHN GREGORY, Aston Villa manager, in Loaded *interview, 2000*

We've all heard that Einstein is a genius but few of us are in a position to
judge. Football is one of the few areas of life where, even if you're untutored,
you can go to a ground, see George Best beat three men and you can realise:
'I have seen a genius.'
SIMON KUPER, writer on world football, 1999

No player, manager, director or fan who understands football, either through
his intellect or his nerve-ends, ever repeats that piece of nonsense: 'After all,
it's only a game.' It has not been a game for 80 years; not since the working-
classes saw in it an escape route out of drudgery and claimed it as their own.
ARTHUR HOPCRAFT, author, The Football Man, *1968*

Even if George Orwell's Big Brother is ruling us in 1984, people will still be
talking about football.
NEIL FRANKLIN, Stoke and England defender, in Soccer At Home and Abroad, *1956*

Football in Britain could not be in a sorrier state. Sport is dying. The future
lies in culture, spirituality and religion.
ROBERT MAXWELL, millionaire publisher and chairman of various clubs, 1990

People are always kicking, old or young. Even an unborn child is kicking.
SEPP BLATTER, general secretary of football's world-governing body, FIFA, 1990

*Twenty-two grown men chasing
a piece of leather round a field.*
BERNARD LEVIN, English journalist, describing English football in the New York Times
after the Hillsborough disaster, 1989

I jolly well hoped that they would keep hold of me so I would never have to hear about the blasted game again.
TERRY WAITE, former hostage in Lebanon, on his dislike of football, 1999

The culture of the 1990s can be summed up by *Neighbours* and football.
SPIKE MILLIGAN, comedian, 1999

Sport is an unfailing cause of ill will, and if the visit of Moscow Dynamo had any effect at all on Anglo-Soviet relations, it could only be to make them worse.
GEORGE ORWELL, in the socialist Tribune *newspaper, 1945*

If this is what soccer is to become, let it die.
EDITORIAL in L'Equipe, *French sports paper, after 39 spectators died following trouble at the European Cup final, 1985*

If somebody is celebrating it means we still have much to learn.
GIORGIO CARDETTI, Mayor of Turin, after Juventus beat Liverpool in the European Cup final, 1985

All that I know most surely about morality and the obligations of man, I owe to football.
ALBERT CAMUS, French philosopher, novelist and goalkeeper for Oran of Algeria, 1957

I believe that sport is on the highest possible plane...as something above real life.
DAVE SEXTON, Manchester United manager, 1980

There were plenty of fellas [in the 1950s] who would kick your bollocks off. The difference between then and now is that they would shake your hand at the end and help you look for them.
NAT LOFTHOUSE, former Bolton and England centre-forward, 1986

I'm so old I can even remember the days when tackling was allowed in this sport.
PETER REID, Leeds manager, 2003

I would kick my own brother if necessary. That's what being a professional is all about.
STEVE McMAHON, Liverpool and England midfielder, 1988

It's the first time that we've had to replace divots in the players.
RON ATKINSON, Manchester United manager, after a European match against a rugged Valencia side, 1982

Nobody ever won a tackle with a smile on his face.
BRUCE RIOCH, Bolton manager, 1994

Men like me were never a danger anyway. It wasn't that we were desperately late, just a little slower in getting there.
CHRIS KAMARA, Sun columnist and former midfield hard man, 1999

In open play I don't think I would use gamesmanship, but if someone went through with just the goalkeeper to beat and I could catch him by bringing him down, I would bring him down. If I didn't, I'd feel I'd let my team-mates and my fans down.
BRYAN ROBSON, Manchester United and England captain, in David Hemery, The Pursuit of Sporting Excellence, 1986

Football is made for cunning people. It's not true that you are disloyal to the sport if you feign injury or tug a shirt or do something else to win the game, which is the purpose of football. Cheating the referee is not a sin if it helps your team to win. I play against cheating forwards every week.
PAOLO MONTERO, Juventus and Uruguay defender, 2003

Sometimes you feel that someone is tugging your shirt and you take a quick look at where the linesman is and then you hit the opponent on the hands or in the stomach. Sometimes you get in front of the defender and pull his shorts. If you get hold of 'the package', you pull a bit harder.
HENRIK LARSSON, Celtic and Sweden striker, 2004

I've played my last match, scored my last goal and elbowed my last opponent.
MARTIN DAHLIN, Swedish international striker, announcing his retirement, 1999

When I called my midfield the 'Dogs of War', it was done half-jokingly. But the game has changed: the playmaker who stands on the ball and sprays it everywhere after five pints and a cigar in the pub simply doesn't exist any more.
JOE ROYLE, Everton manager, 1995

Brazil don't expect Zico to tackle back. It might be worth England taking a chance on a midfield player whose principal asset is not his lungs.
PETER SHREEVES, Tottenham coach, in defence of Glenn Hoddle, 1982

Tackling is better than sex.
PAUL INCE, England midfielder, 1998

The only thing I miss about football is that feeling you get in the 10 seconds after you've scored, when you completely lose your head. I wouldn't say it's better than sex, but it's a close call.
LEE CHAPMAN, former striker with 10 clubs, 1999

For me, the ball is a diamond. If you have something that precious you don't get rid of it, you offer it.
GLENN HODDLE on signing for Monaco, 1988

People keep on about stars and flair. As far as I'm concerned you find stars in the sky and flair at the bottom of your trousers.
GORDON LEE, Everton manager, 1974

His problem was that they kept passing the ball to his wrong feet.

LEN SHACKLETON, former England player, recalling an unidentified team-mate, 1955

It took me 16 years to realise that football is a passing game and not a dribbling game.
JIMMY HILL, television presenter and ex-Fulham forward, 1974

[Sven-Göran] Eriksson goes on about pace but nothing and nobody can run faster than the ball.
LUIZ FELIPE SCOLARI, Brazil coach, after his team beat England, World Cup finals, 2002

Our game is being crippled by the lawmakers. Those out-of-touch people who think players should not be allowed to tackle or talk for the period of 90 minutes.
IAN WRIGHT, former England striker, after a weekend of 15 red cards in the English league, 1999

I start from the principle that the more you shout at each other [during a match], the better you play.
FABIEN BARTHEZ, Monaco and France goalkeeper, 2000

Attack and be damned.
DAVID PLEAT, Luton manager, 1982

All-out attack mixed with caution.
JIM McLAUGHLIN, Shamrock Rovers manager, on his tactics for a European Cup game, 1985

There's no rule to say a game can't finish 9–9.
GRAHAM TAYLOR, Watford manager, after 7–3 defeat at Nottingham Forest, 1982

It only takes a second to score a goal.
BRIAN CLOUGH, Nottingham Forest manager, 1984

If ye dinnae score, ye dinnae win.
JIMMY SIRREL, Notts County manager, 1983

The best team always wins. The rest is only gossip.
SIRREL, 1985

Strikers are very much like postmen. They have to get in and get out as quick as they can before the dog starts to have a go.
IAN HOLLOWAY, Queens Park Rangers manager, 2005

Strikers win you games, but defenders win you championships.
JOHN GREGORY, Aston Villa manager, 1998

The secret of winning championships? Good players working hard.

GEORGE GRAHAM after managing Arsenal to the title, 1991

If you don't start belting that ball out of our penalty area, I'll get some big ignorant lad who can do the job better.
BRIAN CLOUGH to defenders Colin Todd, Roy McFarland and David Nish after Birmingham v Derby game, 1973

No footballer of talent should play in the back four.
MALCOLM ALLISON, manager with various clubs, 1975

It's a lot easier to rip the picture up than to paint it. I've spent my career ripping the picture up. I can kick the ball high into the stand and people say: 'Oh, great defending.'
RICHARD GOUGH, Everton captain, 1999

A goalkeeper is a goalkeeper because he can't play football.
RUUD GULLIT, 1997

I'm looking for a goalkeeper with three legs.

BOBBY ROBSON after Newcastle goalkeeper Shay Given was twice nutmegged by Marcus Bent of Ipswich, 2002

I'd be the ruination of the game if I got my way. All I want to see is goalies keeping clean sheets. And that's not what the fans want, is it?
ALAN HODGKINSON, former England keeper and Scotland goalkeeping coach, 1996

The goalkeeper is the jewel in the crown and getting at him should be almost impossible. The biggest sin in football is to make him do any work.
GEORGE GRAHAM, Leeds manager, 1997

The penalty is the one thing goalkeepers don't fear, because they can't lose. If it is scored, no one blames him. If he saves it, he's a hero.
DAVE SEXTON, Queens Park Rangers manager, on the Wim Wenders film The Goalkeeper's Fear of the Penalty, *1975*

A penalty is a cowardly way to score.
PELE, whose 1,000th goal came from the penalty spot, 1966

I know only one way to take penalties: to score them.
ERIC CANTONA in La Philosophie de Cantona, *1995*

I asked the players who wanted to take a penalty and there was an awful smell coming from some of them.
MICK McCARTHY, Millwall manager, after victory in a shoot-out, 1995

It is not possible to play football with your pants full.
ERNST DOKUPIL, Rapid Vienna coach, after defeat by Manchester United, 1996

Any player not inspired by that atmosphere should go off and play golf with his grandmother.
CLEMENS WESTERHOF, Nigeria coach, in Boston during the World Cup finals, 1994

Angels don't win you anything except a place in heaven. Football teams need one or two vagabonds.
BILLY McNEILL, Manchester City manager, 1983

If you threaten certain spiv players, you must carry it out and not let them get away with it. A football team only has 11 players. It just needs one bad 'un to affect the rest. In ICI, with thousands and thousands of people, you can afford to carry scoundrels. Not in a football team.
BRIAN CLOUGH, Brighton manager, 1973

It would be great if we could put a load of kennels alongside the training pitch to put the players in afterwards. Luxury kennels, take them out, feed them at 9am, train them at 10, get them back out after lunch and then back in the kennels and keep them there.
DAVID O'LEARY, Aston Villa manager, pondering ways to control errant players, 2004

Players today look after themselves far more than I ever did. I used to do what all young men do when they've got the hormones raging. It was a mental thing. If you can get your head strong, you can achieve anything.
GRAEME SOUNESS, Blackburn manager, 2002

Players are a strange breed. If everything is going smoothly they are happy to take the plaudits and rewards which come with success. But once results start going wrong they look for an excuse or someone to blame.
RON ATKINSON, TV summariser and former manager, 1999

They're squeezing the entertainment out of football now. Footballers with no character and referees behaving like Nazis. Fucking basketball on grass now, innit?
VINNIE JONES, by now a film actor, 1999

You ought to get a bunch of clowns if you just want entertainment.
ALAN DURBAN, Stoke City manager, answering critics of his team's negative display at Arsenal, 1980

Over the past 10 years a myth has grown up that football should in some way strive to be entertaining. Sport is not entertainment. It's an activity for the benefit of the participants. If you run away from that fact, you risk having the wrong pipers calling the tune.
HOWARD WILKINSON, Leeds manager, 1990

The game almost broke the health of a highly intelligent man like Joe Mercer. It cut George Best off at adolescence. It has the power to destroy because it releases unnatural forces. It creates an unreal atmosphere of excitement and it deals in elation and despair and it bestows these emotions at least once a week.
MALCOLM ALLISON, manager, in Colours Of My Life, *1975*

When the Queen came to the Bahamas, I told her – and football is not her favourite pastime: 'Ma'am, you must realise that people live for this game.'
SIR JACK HAYWARD, Bahamas-based owner of Wolves, 1994

Acting is the easiest thing in the world. You just do it and do it until you get it right. It's not like being a footballer, where you ruin everyone's week if you get it wrong.
GARY LINEKER, 1999

I'm sure Sunday-morning players get more pleasure than professionals.
JIMMY PEARCE, Tottenham winger, in Hunter Davies's The Glory Game, *1972*

I love football but I do not like the professional version.
GARETH SOUTHGATE, Middlesbrough and England defender, in Woody and Nord: A Football Friendship, *co-written with Andy Woodman, 2003*

I never say I'm going to play football. It's work.
MIKE ENGLAND, Tottenham and Wales player, in The Glory Game, *1972*

We looked bright all week in training, but the problem with football is that Saturday always comes along.
KEITH BURKINSHAW, Tottenham manager, 1983

I asked the manager for a ball to train with. He couldn't have been more horrified if I'd asked for a transfer. He told me they never used a ball at Barnsley. The theory was that if we didn't see it all week, we'd be hungry for it on Saturday. I told him that come Saturday, I probably wouldn't recognise it.
DANNY BLANCHFLOWER, former Tottenham captain, recalling his first English club, 1961

I am grateful to my father for all the coaching he did not give me.

FERENC PUSKAS, Hungary captain, 1961

Everywhere I go there are coaches. Schoolmasters telling young boys not to do this and that and generally scaring the life out of the poor little devils. Junior clubs playing with sweepers and one and a half men up front, no wingers, four across the middle. They are frightened to death of losing, even at their tender age, and it makes me cry.
ALEC STOCK, former manager with several clubs, in A Little Thing Called Pride, *1982*

I'm uncoachable, it's true. That's because I know more than the stupid coaches.
GIORGIO CHINAGLIA, New York Cosmos striker, 1979

I don't think the average English fan knows much about coaching. I don't believe we are a coaching nation.
DARIO GRADI, Crewe Alexandra manager, 1999

You have to coach the players' minds…get them to understand the need for sacrifice.
ALEX FERGUSON, Manchester United manager, 1999

You just cannot tell star players how they must play and what they must do when they are on the field in an international match. You must let them play their natural game… I have noticed that in recent years these pre-match instructions have become more and more long winded while the ability of the players has dwindled.
STANLEY MATTHEWS in The Stanley Matthews Story, *1960*

I've given him carte blanche, as Ron Greenwood used to say, though I didn't use that phrase in the dressing room. Told him to go where he likes.
GEOFF HURST, Telford player-manager and former England striker, in Brian James's Journey to Wembley, *1977*

If the tacticians ever reached perfection, the result would be a 0–0 draw, and there would be no one there to see it.
PAT CRERAND, Manchester United and Scotland midfielder, 1970

Some of the jargon is frightening. They talk of 'getting round the back' and sound like burglars. They say 'You must make more positive runs' or 'You're too negative', which sounds as if you're filling the team with electricians.
BOB PAISLEY, Liverpool manager, 1980

Another feature of England training is 'mime practice'. As you jog round you go through all the motions without the ball that you do when you have the ball. You trap, pass, volley, head for goal, head clear and weight imaginary passes. All that is missing is the ball.
PHIL NEAL, Liverpool and England defender, in Attack From the Back, *1981*

I'm very keen on a maxim by the American football coach Vince Lombardi: the only place where winning comes before work is in the dictionary.
HOWARD WILKINSON, FA technical director, 2000

My football philosophy is never to overplay it. The best advice I ever heard was from [former Chelsea captain] Ray Wilkins: simplicity is genius.
JOHN TERRY, Chelsea and England defender, 2006

The world's best 11 players wouldn't make a team. You must have blend.
LEN SHACKLETON, former England player, in Clown Prince of Soccer, *1955*

You can't have stars in winning teams – only great players.
LUIZ FELIPE SCOLARI, Portugal and former Brazil coach, 2004

Players don't win trophies. Teams win trophies.
JOSE MOURINHO, Chelsea manager, 2005

Everybody likes each other. It's not like we're all friends, but it's a good team. You can have 11 enemies in a team and still win.
SANDER WESTERVELD, Netherlands goalkeeper, at Euro 2000

Team spirit is an illusion that you glimpse only when you win.
STEVE ARCHIBALD, Barcelona and Scotland striker, 1985

It's amazing what can be achieved when no one minds who gets the credit.
HOWARD WILKINSON, Sheffield Wednesday manager, on the value of teamwork, 1982

Team individualism is what you want. It might sound daft, but there's a lot of sense in it.
DAVID JAMES, England goalkeeper and student of sports psychology, 2004

If I had wanted to be an individual I would have taken up tennis.
RUUD GULLIT after the Netherlands' European Championship triumph, 1988

But you cannot have enjoyed it. There were so many mistakes, so much unprofessional play.
SIR ALF RAMSEY, England manager, to a journalist enthusing over a five-goal match between Stoke and Liverpool, quoted in The Football Managers, *1973*

The pitch was playable. I've been in football over 25 years and it has become a game for poofters.

JOHN BURRIDGE, veteran Manchester City goalkeeper, after his match was postponed, 1995

Could I point out that the gay Stonewall FC's third XI played a West End League fixture on a Somme-like afternoon in Regent's Park on Sunday, thereby challenging [Burridge's] theory that sexual orientation has any connection with getting muddy knees.
LETTER to the Independent, *1995*

I always thought golf was a poof's game. Now I prefer it to football.
JULIAN DICKS, West Ham defender, 1998

It's hard to be passionate twice a week.
GEORGE GRAHAM, Arsenal manager, on the physical demands of the English game, 1992

Hump it, bump it, whack. That may be a recipe for a good sex life, but it won't win us the World Cup.
KEN BATES, Chelsea chairman, after England's failure to qualify for the World Cup under Graham Taylor, 1993

Make it simple, make it accurate, make it quick.
ARTHUR ROWE, manager of Tottenham's push-and-run side of the 1950s, on his football philosophy, 1975

Since I've been in football there has been a basic question to face. Are you pretty or are you efficient? It's as if you have to choose. It makes me happy this season that we've won games but people have enjoyed watching us. It's dangerous for football when people become convinced you must play boringly to win.
ARSENE WENGER as Arsenal moved towards a complete unbeaten Premiership season, 2004

Speed has become everything, not just the physical speed of players, but the speed of moving the ball and speed of thought. This is absolutely what Arsenal are about. The counter-attack has become the key factor.
ANDY ROXBURGH, UEFA technical director and ex-Scotland manager, 2004

What I look for in a young player is game intelligence, speed (not purely physical speed but speed of reaction and speed with the ball) and technique. But even if they just have attitude and technique, you can build on that. What makes you saddest of all is to see talent but no desire to achieve something.
WENGER, 2003

Left-wing football is about creativity, attack and pleasure, and about out-scoring the opposition. Right-wing football is negative, cautious and result-oriented.
CESAR LUIS MENOTTI, left-wing former coach of Argentina, 1985

What counts, winning or putting on a show? Success remains in the record books. Having fun passes with time.
FABIO CAPELLO, Juventus coach, 2006

As a kid I thought the top of the game would be packed with unbelievable quality. Now I work with international players who have poor technique and a lack of focus.
GARETH SOUTHGATE, Middlesbrough and England defender, in Woody and Nord: A Football Friendship, *co-written with Andy Woodman, 2003*

The good player keeps playing even without the ball. All the time he is placing himself so that when the ball comes to him he is able to make good use of it. We improved the English saying of 'Kick and run' to 'Pass accurately and move into a good position'.
FERENC PUSKAS, Hungary player, on his country's 6–3 win v England at Wembley, 1953

People who talk of short passes and on-the-ground moves as the essence of good football do not help the progress of football in Britain.
STAN CULLIS, Wolves manager, defending his 'scientific kick-and-rush football' in All For the Wolves, *1960*

Our failure has not been because we have played the British way, but because we haven't. Football should be open, honest, clean, passionate. Part of a nation's culture, its heritage. And the English way is with passion, commitment.
GRAHAM TAYLOR, manager of 'long-ball' exponents Watford , after England's World Cup exit, 1982

Possession and patience are myths. It's anathema to people in the game to say this, but goals come from mistakes, not from possession.
TAYLOR as Watford established themselves in the top division, 1982

I can't watch the long-ball teams like Wimbledon, Watford and Sheffield Wednesday. Football wasn't meant to be run by two linesmen and air-traffic control.
TOMMY DOCHERTY, 1988

People who talk about sophisticated football don't know what they're talking about. To me, the more shots you can get, the more times you threaten the opposition keeper, the better chance you have of winning. Is that any different at international level than on a Sunday park? I happen to believe that it's not.
GRAHAM TAYLOR, by now England manager, 1991

Because I'm a British centre-forward they expect me to be heading the ball all the time.
IAN RUSH, Welsh striker, during his season with Juventus, 1987

A pass rising a yard above the ground should be a foul. A player receiving a pass has two feet and only one head.
WILLIE READ, St Mirren manager, 1959

Balloon ball. The percentage game. Route one. It has crept into the First Division. We get asked to loan youngsters to these teams. We don't do it. They come back with bad habits, big legs and good eyesight.
RON ATKINSON, Manchester United manager, on the long-ball game, 1984

If God had meant football to be played in the air, he'd have put grass in the sky.
BRIAN CLOUGH, Nottingham Forest manager, 1992

If current trends continue, it'll be a game of 6ft 10in defenders heading the ball back and forth with 6ft 11in forwards.
JOHN CARTWRIGHT, former director of the FA National School, on his fears over the prevalence of the long-ball game, 1992

When I had him at Derby, Stefano Eranio could stop the ball dead with his toe. One game, at half-time, he said to our big, ugly centre-half Spencer Prior: 'Spencer, why you always put ball in stand? No players in stand.'
JIM SMITH, Oxford manager, 2006

My philosophy is to play in their half of the pitch. Get the ball in behind them. Get the buggers turning, turning. When you've done that enough times, holes will open up, and one of our fellas, whoever's nearest, gets to the ball first. And then all the rest pile in.
JACK CHARLTON, Republic of Ireland manager, 1988

We don't favour a passing game [at Crewe] because of any moral principles, but because it's the best way to play. If bashing the ball were the best way, we'd do it.
DARIO GRADI, Crewe Alexandra manager, 1999

The first time I came to England, I said to myself: 'Without a doubt, football was created here!'
ARSENE WENGER, Arsenal's French manager, 2002

Sometimes now, when I watch the continental matches on TV, I'm a bit bored. I'm thinking: 'Where's the intensity?'
WENGER, 1998

I've never seen so much violence on the pitch as in England. Before certain matches, I'm scared an opponent might harm me.
FRANK LEBOEUF, Chelsea's French defender, 1999

I spent five years playing non-league football for Wealdstone. If Frank [Leboeuf] thinks the Premiership is hard, he should see what goes on there. Referees had to protect me from the wingers I was marking.
STUART PEARCE, England defender, 1999

It's rubbish to suggest that fair play in England is dead. I'm not siding with or against Leboeuf. But some people might question what he is about as a player.
PETER WILLIS, former president of the Referees' Association, 1999

I have watched football all over the world and can assure you that there is more free play and fewer stoppages in the Premiership than anywhere else.
GERARD HOULLIER, Liverpool's French manager, disagreeing with Leboeuf, 1999

It's a bit of a nancy game now. And if Leboeuf isn't too happy, he should go home. Anyway, spitting is the vilest thing in the world, and the Vieira lad and some other foreigners have brought that with them.
TOMMY SMITH, former Liverpool defender, 1999

Why is it that so many foreign players are queuing up to come here if our football has so many faults? I don't hear Gianfranco Zola complaining about the English game.
GORDON TAYLOR, players' union leader, responding to Leboeuf, 2000

I'm committing wicked fouls that would have horrified me six months ago. That's how you have to play in England... Going for a high ball I use my elbow or I'm dead.
THIERRY HENRY, Arsenal and France striker, 2000

This is a man's game – unless the FA want us to walk out carrying handbags and wearing lipstick. 'Chopper' Harris and Tommy Smith wouldn't have lasted two minutes the way the game is run today.
PAUL INCE, Middlesbrough midfielder, 2001

Guys like 'Chopper' Harris, Nobby Stiles, Tommy Smith, Jack Charlton and Norman Hunter would be sent off every week these days. It would be a doddle for me playing today.
GEORGE BEST on his 50th birthday, 1996

I once described English football as the working man's ballet. It's more like a clog dance now.
TONY WADDINGTON, former Stoke manager, 1991

English football's just like rugby. All the balls go flying through the air or you're kicked into the stand.
RICHARD WITSCHGE, Dutch midfielder, recalling a loan spell with Blackburn, 1996

I think of myself as one of the old guard. When I started playing you could kick owt that moved.
DAVID BATTY, Leeds midfielder, 2000

English football is all about running, fighting war for 90 minutes non-stop.
TONY YEBOAH, former Leeds striker, happy to be back in German football, 1999

English football is hard work. You have to run all the time.
NWANKWO KANU, Arsenal's Nigerian striker, 1999

A great pianist doesn't run around the piano or do push-ups with his fingertips. To be great, he plays the piano. To be a great footballer is not about running, doing press-ups or physical work. The best way to become a great player is to play football.
JOSE MOURINHO, Chelsea manager, 2005

I love the speed of the game here [in England]. Playing from goal to goal, keeping the momentum going at all times. There's beauty in the game here. The spontaneity is beautiful.
ERIC CANTONA, from La Philosophie de Cantona, *1995*

In the English league you can't play at less than 100 per cent. I've had to change my mentality since joining Arsenal to become more aggressive. The English game makes that inevitable.
ROBERT PIRES, Arsenal and France midfielder, 2002

The average Englishman is a very limited player.

GLENN HODDLE, England midfielder, on moving from Tottenham to Monaco, 1987

The English prejudice against educated footballers has not only led to yobbery off the pitch but to a certain mental weakness on the pitch. The England players had plenty of heart. What they lacked was the ability to think; they were out-thought by their opponents.
EDITORIAL headlined 'Why can't we pass?' in the Spectator, *after Euro 2000*

The attitude in England is that tricks are OK if they work. If they don't you're a wanker. It doesn't seem to have sunk in that if you never try you'll never succeed.
DUNCAN McKENZIE, maverick striker, 1976

The English are plagued by industrial football, yet the potential remains enormous.
MILJAN MILJANIC, Real Madrid manager, on the congested schedule of England's top clubs, 1976

Football is like a car. You've got five gears, but the trouble with English teams is that they drive in fourth and fifth all the time... When they crash in Europe they say it's bad luck. It isn't – it's bad driving.
RUUD GULLIT on joining Chelsea after playing in Italy and the Netherlands, 1995

When English clubs play in Europe, their opponents know what is coming: the long ball into the penalty area, which gets nowhere; the next ball, which the opposition win; and the counter-attack, which the English cannot deal with.
ANTONIO PACHECO, Portugal player, 1995

England will never win World Cups. We simply don't have enough people who believe in playing football.
ALEX FERGUSON, Manchester United manager, 1995

I love watching English football but I used to love playing against English teams. They always gave you the ball back if you lost it. Still do.
JOHAN CRUYFF, former Ajax, Barcelona and Netherlands captain, 1998

I don't want people in Spain to regard me as an English footballer in the traditional sense, an idiot with lots of money who boots long balls upfield.
STEVE McMANAMAN, Real Madrid midfielder, 2001

I love English football, even though it strikes me sometimes as a crazy game. Where are the best playmakers? Not in England.
MICHEL PLATINI, former France captain and vice-president of the French FA, 2002

English football is based on physicality. To be honest, I don't like it much. It's certainly different. It's interesting. Like a rollercoaster.
FRANCESCO TOTTI, Roma and Italy player, 2007

You must take care of your own football culture. English football is world-famous, but the result of all the foreigners in the Premiership is that the national team is second-class.
JOHAN CRUYFF, former Barcelona coach, after England's failure at Euro 2000

I love English football, but the tactics haven't changed in the past 20 years – 4-4-2 and a flat back four pushing up as far as possible makes it easier for strikers to shine than in Europe.
MICHEL PLATINI, former France captain, 2002

Dennis Bergkamp told me the Dutch always thought of the English as strong but stupid.
TONY ADAMS, Arsenal and England defender, 1997

The most important space on the pitch is between the ears.
ADRIAN BOOTHROYD, Watford manager, 2006

I admire the English mentality because they are so strong, so hard-working. But we have talent.
SVEN-GÖRAN ERIKSSON, then coach of Portugal's Benfica, after his side knocked Arsenal out of the European Cup, 1991

English and British players still kick the ball while continental players prefer to pass it. And while British players want to crack the ball at goal, today's really top players want to pass it into the net.
CRAIG BROWN, Scotland manager, after watching Euro 2000

I've been infected by the English football virus. I'd miss that anywhere I went.

ARSENE WENGER, Arsenal manager, on signing a new contract, 2004

The reason we haven't signed any English players is that there aren't enough good ones about, as the European Championship showed.
KEN BATES, Chelsea chairman, 2000

The British don't like fancy dans or fanny merchants, as they used to call them, but different players give 100 per cent in different ways.
JOHN BARNES, former England midfielder, 2000

Passion is the most overworked word and excuse in English football. Control is the key to winning. Fire in the bellies is all very well but you need ice in the head too.
BILL BESWICK, sports psychologist, 1999

There are too many hammer-throwers in the Scottish League. I sign a world-class player and have him put out of action after a game and a bit. This league is too tough.
GRAEME SOUNESS, Rangers manager, after injury to Oleg Kuznetsov, 1990

I got a shock when I first saw a Scottish League match on TV. The keeper was basically elbowed off the ball at a corner-kick, but the goal was given. It was a wake-up call.
FABIEN BARTHEZ, Manchester United's French keeper, 2000

In Scotland the mentality is not to pass the ball in midfield. It goes directly to the attack, which makes it difficult for midfielders like me.
JUNINHO, Brazilian midfielder, shortly before leaving Celtic, 2005

I would hate to play that kind of football. The pleasure of playing that would be zero. As a player you want to enjoy the game. I don't think the players enjoy it there. It's no fun playing with 10 men behind the ball. I wouldn't pay to watch Liverpool, but I would to watch Arsenal or Manchester United.
FRANK DE BOER, Barcelona player, on Liverpool's 0–0 draw in the Nou Camp in 2001 before the sides were again goalless there in the Champions' League, 2002

The leagues I like are Spain, England and Holland, where most teams try to play football. Italy is horrible. If you put a camera above an Italian stadium you just see this line of activity across midfield. Incredible! It's just fighting in the midfield and expecting to score goals from free kicks. It's in the culture – the Italians have always played for results.
FRANK DE BOER, 2002

We are all footballers and as such we should be able to perform competently in all positions.

ALFREDO DI STEFANO, Real Madrid striker, anticipating 'total football', 1961

In Europe you have more time to use the ball, to turn around. In England they are on top of you as soon as you get the ball. That pressure, that obsession with contact, makes life hard for me. But it's the downfall of English teams in Europe because they leave space that European players know how to use.

LUIS GARCIA, Liverpool and Spain striker, 2007

In Spain, all 22 players make the sign of the cross as they enter the pitch. If it worked, it would always be a draw.

JOHAN CRUYFF, former Barcelona player, 2006

A 0–0 draw in Italy is crap. A 0–0 draw in England can be really interesting.

IAN WRIGHT, Arsenal and England striker, 1995

When a game goes to 2–0 in Italy you tend to think the losing side will accept it won't happen for them. That never happens in England. We don't have that way of thinking.

SIR ALEX FERGUSON, 2006

Italian League football was rubbish – totally defensive. Games were either no score or 1–0... When we had lost a couple of matches, we began to feel the attitude of the directors. It was as though we had lost a war. With a reaction like that, players don't want to be adventurous.

DENIS LAW, Scottish international, on his spell with Torino, An Autobiography, 1979

The Premiership took a page out of American football and now have Saturday Showdowns and Super Sundays... This is high-calibre marketing, taking an inferior product and improving it through packaging.

ALEXI LALAS, president of the Major League Soccer club Los Angeles Galaxy, 2007

In England our league is considered second class, but I honestly believe if you took a helicopter, grabbed a bunch of MLS players and took them to the perceived best league in the world, they wouldn't miss a beat and the fans wouldn't notice any drop in quality.
LALAS, 2007

Goodbye soccer, hello football!

SLOGAN aimed at Mexicans to games at Los Angeles-based Major League Soccer club CD Chivas, 2006

In England, soccer is a grey game played by grey people on grey days.
RODNEY MARSH, former England player, to a Florida TV audience at the peak of the North American Soccer League's popularity, 1979

America is the land of opportunity for soccer.
RON NEWMAN, English coach of NASL club Fort Lauderdale Strikers, 1978

America is an elephants' graveyard.
GIANNI RIVERA, Italian international forward, rejecting an offer from an NASL club, 1978

If the US becomes enthralled by soccer it will be when every back street and stretch of urban waste ground has its teams of kids playing their makeshift matches, the players claiming the temporary identity of the world's stars... Environments like that produce those stars. Football is an inner compulsion. It cannot be settled on a people like instant coffee.
ARTHUR HOPCRAFT, author, The Football Man, *1968*

To say that American soccer is the football of the future is ludicrous. You've got to see football in the black townships of South Africa or in Rio de Janeiro before you can talk about the future of football. Who can name five top American players?
JACK TAYLOR, English World Cup referee, 1978

Soccer is a game in which everyone does a lot of running around... Mostly, 21 guys stand around and one guy does a tap dance with the ball. It's about as exciting as *Tristan and Isolde.*
JIM MURRAY, sportswriter, Louisville Courier Journal, *1967*

Those Stoker guys are so cocky. They make me mad saying our game
[baseball] is dull. Boy, if ours is dull, theirs is even duller. Those nuts. Running
around in shorts, chasing a big ball like a bunch of schoolboys.
JOE AZCUE, Cleveland Indians baseball coach, 1967. Cleveland Stokers were Stoke City,
guesting in the US city for the summer

In this bloody country, Americans think that any guy who runs around in
shorts kicking a ball instead of catching it has to be a Commie or a fairy.
CLIVE TOYE, English general manager of New York Cosmos, 1970

With such refinements as a 35-yard offside law, synthetic pitches which are not
conducive to tackling and shoot-outs to eliminate drawn games, the country
which gave the world Disneyland has provided a Mickey Mouse football industry.
JACK ROLLIN, editor, Rothmans Football Yearbook, *1979*

Biathlon. Luge. Soccer.
Three of a kind.
THE PLAINS DEALER *newspaper, Ohio, on the prospect of the US staging the World Cup*
finals, 1990

They're going to bring this thing to the US in 1994 and charge people money
to watch it? Listen, if this thing were a Broadway show it would have closed
after one night.
FRANK DEPFORD, editor-columnist of the US-based the National, *on the World Cup*
final, 1990

Soccer is cruel, fate is relentless and the most coveted championship in the
world hinged on the caprice of a leather boot striking a leather ball on a chalk
spot 12 yards from goal.
REPORT in Los Angeles Times *after goalless World Cup final was settled on penalties, 1994*

If I could live for a thousand years I'd now set aside a decade for soccer.
Before this World Cup, I'd have given it the same time slot in eternity as auto
racing: maybe a week.
THOMAS BOSWELL, sportswriter and baseball aficionado, Washington Post, *1994*

Soccer will never take over from baseball. Baseball is the only chance we blacks get to wave a bat at a white man without starting a riot.
EDDIE MURPHY, actor, during the US World Cup, 1994

For us Americans the bottom line is to win a championship. So we invent baseball and call ourselves world champions. We invent [gridiron] football and do the same. But they're not world champions, just the best team in the US in that professional sport. Only soccer has a true world championship. Our challenge is magnified thousands of times. Our situation is so much more difficult and complicated. This is the real one.
BRUCE ARENA, US coach, World Cup finals, 2002

The FA Cup final is better than the Oscars because it's honest.
VINNIE JONES, footballer turned actor, at the Hollywood awards ceremony, 2000

Our football comes from the heart, theirs comes from the mind.

PELE on the difference between South American and European football, 1970

These are players – men who play with their heads and their hearts.
FERENC PUSKAS, Real Madrid player, 1961

Lots of footballers don't have a high IQ to start with, so it would be difficult to gauge the effects of heading the ball too much.
JOHN COLQUHOUN, former Scotland striker, on research which claimed that heading led to brain damage, 1995

What is the world coming to when you get a red card and fined two weeks' wages for calling a grown man a wanker? It's an adults' game, so what's wrong with a bit of industrial language in the workplace?
PAUL GASCOIGNE after being sent off for Middlesbrough v Chelsea, 2000

Everyone knows I am looking for a striker but I hope that makes the players say: 'I'll show that bastard that I can do it.'
EBBE SKOVDAHL, Aberdeen manager, 2001

These days you spend £2m before you realise the player can't even trap a ball.
GRAHAM TAYLOR, back as Watford manager, 2000

When I was at Bournemouth I kicked a tray of cups up in the air. One hit
Luther Blissett on the head. He flicked it on and it went all over my suit
hanging behind him. Another time, at West Ham, I threw a plate of
sandwiches at Don Hutchison. He sat there, still arguing with me, with cheese
and tomato running down his face. You can't do that any more, especially with
all the foreigners. They'd go home.
HARRY REDKNAPP, West Ham manager, 1999

Let us not forget that the place of truth for an athlete is, and always will be,
the stadium.
ERIC CANTONA, from La Philosophie de Cantona, 1995

The hardest part is what you find to replace football, because there isn't
anything.
KEVIN KEEGAN, 'chief operating officer' at Fulham, 1998

Sometimes, driving home from a game, you do wonder if you're getting a bit
old. But I always remember what Kenny Dalglish once told me: 'Never forget
that football made you feel knackered when you were 17.'
GORDON STRACHAN, Leeds and Scotland midfielder, in An Autobiography, 1992

I'm frightened to stop because there can be no life as enjoyable as this.
STRACHAN on a footballer's life at 35, 1992

I've still got what every old footballer misses – the banter of the dressing
room. It's vicious. If you're a sensitive peach in this business, you're buggered.
ALAN BIRCHENALL, former player, on his PR role with Leicester City, 2004

Let nobody tell you that life begins at 40. Death begins at 40. You get fat,
your hair falls out and you get arthritis… Now I'm just trying to grow old as
gracefully as I'm able to.
MIKE CHANNON, racehorse trainer and former England striker, 2004

They shoot horses, don't they? A lot of players would prefer to be shot once
their career was over.
JIMMY GREAVES, former England striker, 2003

eight

THE
LIFESTYLE

When I first told her I was a footballer, she said: 'Yes, but what do you do for a living?'
CHRISTIAN KAREMBEU, former France midfielder, on his wife Adriana Sklenarikova, the former Wonderbra model, 2005

I read this piece by the car man, Jeremy Clarkson, saying a footballer goes out in the morning, gets in his Aston Martin, forgets to take a drugs test, takes coke, has a drink, then shags a bird. And that was 'a day in the life of a footballer'. But a lot of players are decent fellas.
FRANK LAMPARD, Chelsea and England midfielder, 2003

Footballers like to think they are boss drinkers, boss gamblers and boss shaggers.
MICK QUINN, former striker with several English clubs, in his autobiography Who Ate All The Pies, *2003*

If you retire at 35 you can live wherever you bloody well like: London, Monaco, whatever. Any half-decent footballer will be a multi-millionaire.
ROY KEANE, Sunderland manager, claiming some transfer targets snubbed Wearside in favour of cities with better shopping for their wives, 2007

Do the players think they're in the shop window? You only have to see the look on their faces when they hear Roman Abramovich is in the stadium.
ALAN CURBISHLEY, Charlton manager, at the European Championship finals, 2004

People say I'm cocky because I have two cars and a diamond watch. But that means 90 per cent of footballers are cocky. We're in a fortunate position and we can afford these things.
KIERON DYER, Newcastle and England midfielder, 2004

Footballers are the new pop stars. Who cares about a pop singer drinking lots and taking drugs. People want to read about footballers now.
MICKEY THOMAS, former Wales midfielder, 2003

Hero worship has gone through the roof and footballers have replaced rock stars in popularity. But footballers can't start behaving like rock stars. Many musicians die at a young age because of their lifestyle. Football is going the same way.
TERRY VENABLES, former England manager, 2003

I advise players to surround themselves with people who don't idolise them. If we commit traffic offences we should pay the fines. And at the restaurant we should wait our turn like others.
JOSE MOURINHO, Chelsea manager, 2006

The perception of footballers has changed a lot since I played. There used to be celebrity, showbiz and football. Now it's all one thing.
KEVIN KEEGAN, England manager, 2000

There will never, ever be a better time to be a footballer than now.
ALAN SHEARER, England captain, 1999

I detest politicians saying that footballers should be role models. If anyone should be, it's the politicians.
GRAHAM TAYLOR, Aston Villa manager, 2003

If you become a big star today, the mass media is marking you, man to man, 24 hours a day. Boys of 18 or 19 could get away with taking a wrong step 20 years ago. Now it's on the front page of the *Sun* or *Bild*. We don't want front pages, we want back pages.
SVEN-GÖRAN ERIKSSON, England manager, 2005

There's a word you don't hear around footballers' dressing rooms any more – mortgage.
NIALL QUINN, former Sunderland striker, on the handsome salaries of top players, 2002

When you're chatting in the dressing room, the last thing you talk about is football.
HERNAN CRESPO, Chelsea and Argentina striker, 2004

I've become cynical about my profession. Players abuse their position, signing long contracts and then not bothering to play, happy sitting in the reserves. Clubs employ staff for years and then sack them. Football has become a business rather than a sport and a passion.
GARETH SOUTHGATE, Middlesbrough and England defender, 2003

There are lots of players who will kiss your club's badge one week and the badge of another club the next.
ALAN CURBISHLEY, Charlton manager, on reluctantly selling Scott Parker to Chelsea, 2003

Sir – I was delighted to read that 50 per cent of GPs now earn an annual salary which is less than Rio Ferdinand's weekly wage. I am sure society has its values right.
LETTER to the Daily Telegraph, *2005*

I don't think the salaries can ever be good for the game. You think to yourself: 'How has it come to this?'

SIR ALEX FERGUSON, Ferdinand's manager at Manchester United, 2004

I worry about the ones who have got a lot of money and are expected to stay at the top and how much you can keep the hunger in them. It's an unconscious thing. I signed a new contract and the first thing I thought after I'd put my name on that line was: 'I'm comfortable now.'
FERGUSON, 2003

Players' attitudes have changed because of money. Getting vast amounts takes away the hunger, that little edge. Players of today say, 'I go out and play with the same desire,' but it can't be that way when the comfort zone comes so quickly and easily.
ALAN BALL, former England World Cup-winner, 2006

[The big salaries] distort the way you look at life. When someone would value going out for a meal, perhaps buying a car, you've bought your car at 19. It's very dangerous. There's no discipline.
TONY FINNIGAN, players' agent and ex-player, 2003

They're on £20,000 to £30,000 a week, and they're not earning it. It makes you resentful. I've reached the stage where I don't like footballers.
DAVID SULLIVAN, co-owner of Birmingham City, 2006

It's crazy. If you want to win, you have to pay up to £100,000 a week to a player who can hardly read or write.
MOHAMED AL FAYED, Fulham chairman, 2007

Semi-educated, foul-mouthed players on £100,000 a week hold clubs to ransom until they get, say, £120,000.
SEPP BLATTER, president of football's world governing body, FIFA, 2005

I find it bizarre that the head of an organisation which has built its wealth on the backs of players is having a go at these players.
GORDON TAYLOR, chief executive of the players' union, the PFA, replying to Blatter, 2005

I don't feel any guilt about anything I earn. It's life. Businessmen earn 100,000 times more than us.
MARCEL DESAILLY, Chelsea and France defender, 2003

I never think about the money. I have never, ever gone on the pitch thinking: 'I have to win to get the bonus.' I don't care about the bonus, just about the game.
THIERRY HENRY, Arsenal and France striker, 2003

Money is important. Why shouldn't players make as much as they can?

LUIS FIGO, Internazionale and Portugal midfielder, 2005

What's a £1,500 fine for a Premiership footballer? Nothing.
BRIGITTE CHAUDHRY of the road-safety campaign Roadpeace, after Leeds's Seth Johnson was fined £1,500 for driving at 135mph with two-and-a-half times the permitted amount of alcohol in his blood, 2003

I have a little girl and I hope she never comes home with a professional footballer. Even the car insurance for footballers is expensive because the companies know they drive under the influence of alcohol.
GEORGE BOATENG, Middlesbrough's Dutch midfielder, 2003

I understand Lazio are in a difficult position financially, but I cannot go to the supermarket and buy groceries for my family with shares.
JAAP STAM, Dutch defender, on his club's 'laughable' request for him to take a pay cut from £45,000 a week to £21,000 plus shares, 2003

The game's full of young, rich, spoilt thugs. A lot of footballers haven't the moral fortitude to say: 'Stick your money, I'd rather be myself.'
MARK BOSNICH, former cocaine addict and ex-Premiership goalkeeper, 2005

I get paid on the last Thursday of the month and from there my mam looks after it… I don't go round flashing the cash. That's not me. I came here for ridiculous money. It's not my fault, it's the job I'm in. I didn't ask for the game to be like this. I play because I love the game. That, and the fact that it's the only thing I'm good at.
DAMIEN DUFF, £17m Chelsea winger, 2003

Between the ages of 14 and 20 I knew I was getting paid the same as the guy next to me. At 18, we all signed the same contract until we were 22. That breeds a spirit of 'We're all in this together.' Imagine if you're on £1,000 a week at 16 – it would breed a feeling of 'I want to play for the first team but don't need to.' I didn't want that kind of money before I'd played in the first team.
GARY NEVILLE, Manchester United and England defender, 2003

I don't hold with those who say they would play for England for nothing. I'd play for Northern Ireland for nothing if they let everybody in for nothing. If they are collecting a £50,000 gate, playing for hope and glory has nothing to do with the facts.
DANNY BLANCHFLOWER, Tottenham captain, in The Encyclopaedia of Football, *1960*

Johnny Haynes is a top entertainer and will be paid as one from now on. I will give him £100 a week to play for Fulham.
TOMMY TRINDER, Fulham chairman and comedian, making Haynes the English game's first £100-a-week player, 1961

Italian players wonder how on earth players like Haynes live on such a salary! If anyone suggested that the Italians should play a whole season and bank only £5,000, plus another £90 or so in expenses, there would be a nationwide strike.
JOHN CHARLES, Juventus and Wales player, in The Gentle Giant, *1962*

You always want hungry players, but the country is getting richer and that's already been bad for boxing. I can also see it harming football.
BILL SHANKLY, Liverpool manager, 1968

The permissive society has given us young footballers totally concerned with what they can get rather than what they ought to be giving.
BERTIE MEE, Arsenal manager, 1974

People say the wages are too high, but it's a short career.

SIR STANLEY MATTHEWS, whose own playing career lasted 40 years, 1987

You can't blame the players for taking advantage. If you can get £40,000 a week, you'll take it. That's human nature.
ALAN HANSEN, TV pundit and former Liverpool captain, 1999

My first contract was bigger than my father, an electrician, had ever earned in his life. So I realise how it is. Then again it would be crazy to say: 'No, I don't want it.' It's just how it is in football. Everybody makes money. Why shouldn't we? A lot of people are there to watch.
DENNIS BERGKAMP, Arsenal striker, 1999

Society finds it hard to accept men from the lower classes, where most footballers are recruited, being paid salaries that would normally be out of bounds to them.
LETTER to The Times amid criticism of the top Premiership players' wages, 2002

A successful football career used to be about winning things. Now it's about how much money you end up with.
GRAEME SOUNESS, Liverpool manager, 1993

Too many players these days judge themselves by how good their car is and by the size of their house, rather than by the medals they've won. I see players who are rich after five years in the game but have never got close to winning anything. I can see people retiring at 25 in the future.
PAUL MERSON, Aston Villa and England midfielder, 2000

I wince at players who cheat and foul, who abuse referees and who think only about winning and the money it will bring.
TONY BLAIR MP, Labour, on the modern game, 1995

Some of the players think: 'I've got a million in the bank. Why work harder?'
RAY HARFORD, Blackburn manager, on the champions' poor start to the season, 1995

They are just guys who get paid ridiculous amounts of money for not doing very much.
JADE JOHNSON, international long-jumper, on modern footballers, 2002

It's weird, isn't it? I remember when a hundred quid seemed like loads of money.
JONATHAN WOODGATE, Leeds defender, after his club paid £18m for Rio Ferdinand, 2000

It will be a story about how young men can earn £20,000 a week and virtually own whole cities, yet somehow think that they're bullet-proof.
ALLEN JEWHURST, Granada TV producer, planning a drama-documentary on the case that led to the trial of Leeds's Lee Bowyer and Jonathan Woodgate, 2002

Rolex watches, garages full of flashy cars and mansions, set up for life, forgot about the game, lost the hunger that got you the watches, cars and mansions.
ROY KEANE, Manchester United captain, reacting to their Champions' League semi-final defeat by Bayer Leverkusen, 2002

Some players are cocky gits. You see them out and about, giving it large but they haven't done anything in the game to justify it.
KEANE, 2000

If you're a top player, you have a fucking great big ego that follows you round everywhere. Sometimes it gets in the way, though you must have it.
GRAEME SOUNESS, Blackburn manager, 2004

There's a great American saying: 'Why bother to get out of bed when you're wearing silk pyjamas?' I think it applies to some young players. A lot earn huge amounts before they're the finished article and undoubtedly find it hard to motivate themselves.
STEVE COPPELL, Crystal Palace manager and former players' union chairman, 1999

Some players would still be world-class if you paid them £20 a week. But for others it's now all about how much you can earn. I don't begrudge them the big salaries, but how can you say that someone on £30,000 a week does a better job than a nurse or a policeman, who have to risk their lives for £14,000 a year?
NEVILLE SOUTHALL, former Everton and Wales goalkeeper, 1999

Whenever we take our young players away they have to dress in shirt and tie. They have to learn how to eat properly in restaurants and how to make speeches of thanks to the opposition. We don't produce greedy, money-grabbing bastards.
KIT CARSONS, director of Peterborough United's youth academy, 1999

Money brings bad habits. The players live too easily.
JAVIER CLEMENTE, Marseilles coach, 2001

Being a footballer has its advantages. Earning £40,000 to £80,000 a month deserves some sacrifice. Guys in the street work hard for eight hours a day. Players put in only one hour a day and two on Saturday.
BERNARD TAPIE on returning to Marseilles as director of sport, 2001

Money is not a criterion for some people. There are multi-millionaires who still get up at 6am to get going about their business. They are winners. For players it doesn't matter what bonus they are on, playing is the meat and drink and winning is the bonus. It's the winning that gives them the kicks.
ALEX FERGUSON, Manchester United manager, 1995

What makes big players is their love of the game. Money should not control the game. It alienates fans. If tomorrow there was no money in football, I would still love it.
ARSENE WENGER, Arsenal manager, on losing Nicolas Anelka to Real Madrid for 'non-footballing reasons', 1999

I wouldn't give up football even if I won the £18m jackpot on the National Lottery. I love this job and I would even pay to play.
DEAN HOLDSWORTH, Bolton striker, 1995

People will say I've got a screw loose, but perhaps I'm in the 0.1 per cent of footballers who don't give a toss about unlimited money.
MATTHEW LE TISSIER on why he had stayed loyal to Southampton, 1995

I took a pay cut to come here. As long as the fridge is full, I'm happy.
GORDON STRACHAN on joining Coventry as player-coach from Leeds, 1995

The money I make, I give it all to my mother. I don't even know where it goes.
CHRISTIAN VIERI, Inter Milan striker, after Vatican criticism of players' wages, 1999

You go into a shop and it's just Armani this and that, and you buy it. Clothes you don't even need. I spent a grand once. Bit of a waste.
GARY KELLY, Leeds and Republic of Ireland defender, 1995

I earn more than all you wankers put together.

CARLTON PALMER, Leeds midfielder, to police after he was arrested during a night out in the city, 1997

I was nearly a soccer brat, but the more I earned the louder my conscience became.
NIALL QUINN, Sunderland striker, on giving the proceeds of his testimonial match to charity, 2002

They are rich, they've got everything, but there must be something else. Something you cannot buy: honour, morals and inner desire.
GUNTER NETZER, former Germany midfielder, after his country's exit from Euro 2000

You can make a player fitter by giving him a pay rise. It may sound daft, but he works harder and he's happier at home.
LOU MACARI, Swindon manager, 1986

I cannot feed my child on glory.
PAOLO ROSSI, Italy striker, during pay dispute with Juventus, 1982

Two months ago [after he helped Italy win the World Cup] Rossi was over the moon. Now he is asking for it.
JUVENTUS OFFICIAL, 1982

It's almost theft taking money after a performance like that. I'll be using the winter break to make the players' lives as miserable as possible.
CRAIG LEVEIN, Hearts manager, after defeat at Aberdeen, 2001

We are meant to be these hard-headed, money-obsessed professionals but we are still little boys at heart. Just ask our wives.
ROB LEE, Newcastle midfielder, before playing in the FA Cup final, 1998

Three cheers for FIFA [football transfers to be scrapped, 1 September]. At last the likes of Keane and Beckham will be able to receive the rewards they deserve, rather than struggling on today's paltry sums.
LETTER to the Guardian, 2000

Footballers are well paid and have a fantastic lifestyle. They get up every morning and go to training grounds and work a couple of hours a day. Any player who moans should have to work a month down the pits in a real job.
RON ATKINSON, TV summariser, former player and manager, on BBC TV's Room 101, 2003

When a manager rests players because they've played two games in six days, I laugh my cock off.
RICKY HATTON, IBF world welterweight boxing champion and Manchester City fan, 2005

Every day is Christmas for a footballer, doing a job they love for huge amounts of money in most cases. A quiet Christmas, preparing for the next match, is a small price to pay for the privilege of playing for a living.
GORDON STRACHAN, Southampton manager, on the 'small sacrifices' players make over the festive season, 2003

Footballers, particularly those like me who are lucky enough to play for one of the more glamorous clubs, have a great life. You feel that nothing can touch you. You feel somehow totally protected. Then something happens to let you know that you are just as vulnerable as everyone else.
DENNIS WISE, then a Chelsea player, in his autobiography, 2000

The image of the footballer as a glamorous, show-business type, surrounded by pretty girls and flash cars, is firmly implanted in most people's minds. I know him more accurately as the deeply insecure family man or the tearful, failed apprentice.
EAMON DUNPHY, Republic of Ireland player, 1973

Footballers are the most vulnerable people. They exude confidence but inside they are so lacking in it. They know they can lose form or be injured. The profession is so insecure you wouldn't believe it.
GORDON TAYLOR, chief executive of the players' union, the PFA, 2003

Of course it would help [the public perception of footballers] if they were choirboys and gave all their money to charity. Life doesn't work like that.
GORDON TAYLOR, 2003

Take away *Match of the Day* and all the hangers-on and it's all very empty and lonely being a footballer.
RODNEY MARSH, England striker, 1971

Footballers are only interested in drinking, clothes and the size of their willies.

KARREN BRADY, Birmingham City managing director, 1994

Today you have prima donnas and they are highly paid. Their intelligence, across the board, is a lot higher than in my day. *Comic Cuts* was the typical newspaper of the dressing room then whereas now it's the serious papers. We actually got complaints that there was only one public phone in the changing rooms because they wanted to ring their stockbrokers after training.
DOUG ELLIS, Aston Villa chairman, 2000

[Footballers are] scum. Total scum. They don't know what honesty or loyalty are. All they're interested in is themselves.
SIR ALAN SUGAR, former Tottenham owner, 2005

I like a bit of rough – footballers, roofers, blokes who get banged up.
DANNIELLA WESTBROOK, EastEnders actress, 1996

I hope that 2003 brings me a fantastic, intelligent and kind man. Not a footballer.
VANESSA KELLY, Australian model, dismissing reports of romance with the Italy striker Christian Vieri, 2003

I prefer footballers not to be too good or clever at other things. It means they concentrate on football.
BILL NICHOLSON, Tottenham manager, 1973

I wouldn't quote Kipling to the lads. They'd probably think I was talking about cakes.
ROB KELLY, Leicester manager, 2006

Politics is my specialist subject. Let me tell you, not all footballers are thick, no matter what the press would have you believe.
PAT CRERAND, former Manchester United midfielder, 2004

When you're away with a team, everyone has their way of filling in the time. Mine is a book, a movie or replying to my mail. But you still get bored. In 2002 I stayed in hotels for 260 days. It was the most horrible thing. For me, travel creates the most stress of anything I do in my job. By comparison, the playing is relaxation.
JENS LEHMANN, Arsenal's German goalkeeper, 2004

The glut of football books is a sorry reflection of our current cultural life. The status of footballers and the money they earn is appalling. They may not even be writing these books. Most are ghosted. They are simply selling their names and lifestyle.
FAY WELDON, novelist, 2005

Further to your recent letter I am sorry that we cannot help you with your search for academic footballers. In fact, two of the back four cannot read.
JOE ROYLE, Oldham manager, replying to a journalist researching a feature on footballers with degrees, 1987

Without being rude, footballers are not the best talkers in the world.
JIMMY HILL, former player, chairman and TV pundit, 1998

What they say about soccer players being ignorant is rubbish. I spoke to a couple yesterday and they were quite intelligent.
RACQUEL WELCH, American actress, after a visit to Chelsea match, 1973

We're paid to play football, not to think.
PAUL BASTOCK, Boston United goalkeeper, when asked whether he thought an FA inquiry into the running of the club had affected their start in league football, 2002

Excuse me, but there are footballers who think.
SOL CAMPBELL, Arsenal and England defender, rebutting the stereotype of the 'thick' footballer during a press interview, 2002

There are only two things you can be certain of with footballers. One, they'll let you down. Two, you don't know when they'll let you down. They are flawed characters.
SECRETARY *of a Premiership club, quoted anonymously in the press, 2000*

I never wanted to be a coach because I have a low opinion of players. Footballers are the most obnoxious, ignorant and selfish people.
EDWIN STEIN, *Birmingham coach, 1993*

Professionalism in rugby union implies a soccer-style mentality; training in the morning and reading comics in the afternoon.
ED GRIFFITHS, *chief executive of the South African Rugby Union, 1995*

Footballers couldn't run a fish-and-chip shop.

BOB LORD, *Burnley chairman, 1961*

I would not hang a dog on the word of an ex-professional footballer.
ALAN HADAKER, *Football League secretary, 1961*

I can remember the day when, as a goalkeeper playing for Reading against Millwall at The Den in 1951, I collected ninepence in old pennies which had bounced off my skull. We needed the money in those days.
LETTER *to the* Daily Telegraph *after coin-throwing incidents at matches, 2002*

My role, when I wasn't working the lathe, was that of general dogsbody and butt of jokes. Once I was told to go and fetch a bucket of steam. Another time it was a left-handed screwdriver. Being young and naïve I actually went looking for them.
NORMAN HUNTER, *former Leeds and England defender, recalling his first job in an engineering works, in his autobiography* Biting Talk, *2004*

I walked to work when I was captain of West Brom [before the abolition of the maximum wage in 1961]. I didn't have a car and at that stage I never looked like getting one either.
SIR BOBBY ROBSON, *Newcastle and former England manager, 2004*

If Mr Football Fan went to many a car park when the players are rolling up for training he would probably be unable to restrain himself from a muttered 'Cor blimey'. For he'd see a fair number of the 'slaves' turning up for their daily stint in nice, shiny cars. At my own club, for instance, many of the lads have cars. I have myself, I'll admit.
RONNIE CLAYTON, Blackburn and England player, in A Slave to Soccer, *1960*

Some folks tell me we professional players are soccer slaves. Well, if this is slavery, give me a life sentence.
BOBBY CHARLTON a year before the lifting of the maximum wage, 1960

None of the players can change a tyre. One asked Albert the kit man to look at his car as he thought he had a nail stuck in a tyre. Albert asked where the key was to loosen the locking wheel nuts. He was confronted by a bemused-looking footballer who told him: 'If it's a problem I'll just phone the garage and get them to swap the car for a new one.'
BRIAN McCLAIR, Manchester United youth coach and former player, 2004

These stories about Manchester United players with six cars worry me. I fear some young players are losing touch with reality. Because there is so much money in the game, it's only right that we get our proper share, but I'd like to see young players on big, five-year contracts being paid that money over a 10- or even 15-year period, so they didn't have so much in their pocket.
NIALL QUINN, Sunderland and Republic of Ireland striker, 2000

Motivating players isn't easy when their first signing-on fee pays off the mortgage. There is great consolation in not playing and going home in a Porsche. In my day the car park was all Vivas and Cortinas.
JOE ROYLE, Manchester City manager, 2001

Dwight [Yorke] is getting £100,000 for this book but it couldn't be further down his priorities. His Ferrari cost twice as much, so why bother?
HUNTER DAVIES, journalist, on collaborating on Yorke's autobiography, 2000

We're going to burn your Ferraris.

CHANT by Real Madrid fans after their 5–1 defeat by Zaragoza, 1999

The Bosman ruling has ensured that players have much more power. Look at the car park: it used to be the directors who drove fancy motors, now it's the players.
GEORGE GRAHAM, Tottenham manager, 2000

Q: What car do you drive?
A: Two Mercs and a Porsche.

ADE AKINBIYI, Crystal Palace striker, in a programme questionnaire, 2002

Maybe it's difficult to motivate players if they earn 40 grand a week, have three Mercs and mistresses everywhere.
JOE KINNEAR, Wimbledon manager, 1997

Players are a club's best assets, so they must be dealt with grandly. We are not looking for a bargain but for a great player, and he deserves everything his rank and industry can get.
DON RAIMUNDO SAPORTA, vice-president of Real Madrid, 1961

It's not the likes of me who have pushed transfer fees and wages sky high but the clubs competing for our services.
TREVOR FRANCIS, England striker, before his move into Italian football, 1982

As a player you're nothing more than a piece of meat. We're nothing more than cattle. I had a conversation with Roy Keane about it and he agreed. He said: 'They sold you like a cow.' The fact is he [Alex Ferguson] sold me behind my back. I don't know anything about it. He fired me because he had problems about his own reputation.
JAAP STAM on his surprising transfer from Manchester United to Lazio, 2001

As a footballer you can be happily playing away, your children can be doing well at school and your wife settled. But if the manager wants rid of you he can make life very difficult until you agree to go.
MARK McGHEE, Wolves manager, 1995

A lot of players think they need them agents but that's not the case. They need good advice from a solicitor or an accountant, not people taking hundreds of thousands off them.
GARY NEVILLE, Manchester United captain, 2007

I sometimes say to footballers' agents: 'The difference between you and me is that if there were no more money in football tomorrow, I'd still be here, but not you.'
ARSENE WENGER, Arsenal manager, 2003

A footballer's ability is in his feet and his head. They are not used to doing deals. Agents do that on their behalf and you would expect them to be remunerated. Anyone who does not see that is not in the real world.
DAVID GILL, chief executive of Manchester United, after 2003 figures revealed the club paid £5m to agents, 2004

No football-club owner in his right mind would willingly invite an average agent into his academy, any more than a brothel owner would let a syphilitic nutter into his brothel.
SIMON JORDAN, Crystal Palace chairman, 2005

Agents are nasty scum. They are evil and divisive and pointless. They survive only because the rest of the sport is so corrupt and because leading football people employ their sons in the job.
JORDAN on the 'bullshit world' of football, 2004

Take away corruptible managers and officials, and you take away the problem [of 'bungs']. And that's far easier a concept to get your head around than the proposed alternative – FIFA weeding through every agent worldwide, choosing the churchgoing ones and culling the rest.
JORDAN, 2006

I can't argue with people seeing us as the scum of the earth.

COLIN GORDON, Steve McClaren's agent, 2006

Greed and blackmail drive the game now. Players and agents run football, not managers and chairmen. Half the time I'm not dealing with players but with millionaires.
DAVE BASSETT, Nottingham Forest manager, 1998

The fees some of them take for spending a few hours on the phone! Don't forget that money goes out of football and doesn't come back.
JOE ROYLE, Ipswich manager, 2003

The money coming into the game is incredible. But it's just the prune-juice effect – it comes in and goes out straight away. Agents run the sport.
ALAN SUGAR, Tottenham chairman, 1997

It used to be the wives who affected players, now it's agents.
BOBBY GOULD, Wimbledon manager, 1988

Agents do nothing for the good of football. I'd like to see them lined up against a wall and machine-gunned... Some accountants and solicitors with them.
GRAHAM TAYLOR, Watford manager, 1983

I wouldn't cross the road to talk to an agent, let alone go to Manchester.
GRAHAM KELLY, FA chief executive, declining an invitation to a meeting attended by agents, 1992

We have to deal with these people [agents], but Bill Shankly wouldn't have done.
BRIAN CLOUGH, 1991

What do I think of agents? Dogs, worms, vermin.

JOE KINNEAR, Wimbledon manager, 1995

There's always a tendency for players to under-price themselves. No one likes to say: 'I'm worth this or that.' It's better if someone else does the talking for you and leaves you to do the playing.
RAY WILKINS, former England captain, 1993

Manchester United were bad payers in the 1970s. They had the mentality that people would play for them for nothing. People moan about agents but I wish they had been around in my day.
STUART PEARSON, former United and England striker, 1995

Agents are disliked by managers and directors but this is because they give players power – through the simple device of letting them know the going rate. No one I know, in any job anywhere, wants to earn less than the going rate. Footballers are no different.
ROB LEE, Newcastle and England midfielder, 1998

I am trained in economics, I have the ability to run a company and I don't see why I shouldn't put these gifts at the service of my brother. But the football scene is crawling with sharks and profiteers, and my diplomas did not prepare me for facing them.
DIDIER ANELKA, Nicolas's brother, on acting as his agent, 1999

It is turning into a spivs' market place.
JIM SMITH, Derby manager, 2000

Most agents wouldn't know a ball from a banana.
JOHN LAMBIE, Partick Thistle manager, 2002

Q: Who's your favourite player?
A: I can't say. I don't know anything about football.
ERIC HALL, self-styled 'monster' agent, interviewed in Total Football *magazine, 1995*

Don't know much about the game, don't even like it much. What's that got to do with it? My business is selling people. Makes no difference what they do.
HALL, 1990

I now believe in Father Christmas, I really do. I owe him [Jean-Marc Bosman] a monster Christmas present.
HALL after the European Union's highest court ruled the game's transfer system illegal, 1995

I have no morals when it comes to dealing with my clients. I would deal with the Devil to get the best deal for them.
HALL, 1989

If there was a really star name who was represented by the Devil, there would still be a queue of clubs wishing to negotiate with him.
ATHOL STILL, players' agent, 1999

When people ask my wife what I do, she tells them I'm a Kwik-Fit fitter rather than admit I'm an agent.
JON HOLMES, players' agent, 1996

You think I want to get together with other agents? I wouldn't have most of them in my garden.
HOLMES, 2006

I realised how sinister it had become when I was manager of Peterborough and I tried to sign a lad who had played one league game. He told me to talk to his agent. There are 2,000 professionals in England, but only 20 need an agent.
MARK LAWRENSON on his stint as an 'alternative agent', backed by the players' union, 1991

Every player needs an agent because whatever their status, they are in no position to negotiate contracts. As for signing up young players I see nothing wrong in that. I also handle showbiz people and often take on groups before they have made a record.
ERIC HALL responding to Lawrenson, 1991

I don't want my players playing for England because when they come back, all they want is big wages, sponsored cars, a big house, Page Three birds, ecstasy and cocaine. I'm happy they don't know about all that lark.
DAVE BASSETT, Sheffield United manager, 1990

What can footballers do? They can't drink, can't smoke, can't take drugs. They have to have something to do. Some people can have a bet and walk away and then there are others, like me, who have to keep on chasing, chasing and chasing.
PAUL MERSON, gambling addict and former England player, 2003

If players are earning £50,000 a week, they're not going to bet in fivers.

JAMIE REDKNAPP, former England midfielder, on reports of a gambling epidemic among top players, 2006

When you're a millionaire, winning a few quid on a horse means nothing.
HARRY REDKNAPP, Portsmouth manager, on his players' lack of interest in racing, 2004

I've won and lost tens of thousands. It's like a drug. You start on cigarettes and end up on heroin. I started on £10 or £20 a race, finished up on many thousands. You can't go back.
STEVE CLARIDGE, widely travelled striker and gambling addict, 2003

With me, the gambling was a serious problem. With him, if you're talking £40,000 over two years with the wages he's earning, it's pocket money. He has probably got more cash in his ashtray than that.
CLARIDGE after reports of Michael Owen's gambling, 2003

I had an understanding with the bookies where they added a nought to whatever I put on. My missus thought I was phoning up with £250 bets when it was really £2,500. People laugh, but it's an illness.
JOHN HARTSON, West Brom striker, 2006

They [gambling addicts] lose their self-respect and before they know it they are nicking money out of their kids' savings to have a bet.
TONY ADAMS, former England captain and recovering alcoholic, 2003

It's nobody's business how much I've lost because it's my money. I've earned it and can do whatever I want with it. Doctors, lawyers and newspaper publishers go to casinos, so what's the problem?
JIMMY FLOYD HASSELBAINK, Chelsea striker, on reports that he had lost £1.1m on gambling, 2003

From the first time I kicked a ball as a pro 19 years ago, I began to learn what the game was all about. It's about the drunken parties that go on for days. The orgies, the birds and the fabulous money. Football is just a distraction: you're so fit that you can carry on all the high living in secret and still play at the highest level.
PETER STOREY, former Arsenal and England player, 'telling all' in a tabloid, 1980

Everywhere you go in football, you're offered booze.
BRIAN CLOUGH on the roots of his problems with alcohol, 2003

They were on a lager diet.
RON ATKINSON describing the European Cup-winning sides of Nottingham Forest and Liverpool 25 years earlier, 2003

The team that drinks together wins together.
RICHARD GOUGH, Rangers captain, on how a group 'binge' helped with bonding, 1995

I used to go to the Alva Supporters' Club function every year. I'd go after a Saturday game, stay all day Sunday and get home at some point on the Monday. We called it the equestrian because it was a three-day event.
ANDY GORAM, former Rangers goalkeeper under Gough's captaincy, 2005

It just goes to show that cricketers can be as stupid as footballers.
GRAHAM TAYLOR, former England manager, after England all-rounder Andrew Flintoff was drunk on a pedalo at the cricket World Cup, 2007

When I first went out for a night with some English players, they couldn't believe I didn't drink. Coke? They said it like they had never heard of such a thing. 'Go on. Go on,' they said. 'Have a drink. What's wrong with you?'
MARIO MELCHIOT, Chelsea's Dutch defender, 2004

There's only one drug at Bayern and that's beer... After a night of cards and lager I used to spread the empties around the hotel corridor so it wouldn't give the impression there was an alcoholic in my room.
STEFFEN EFFENBERG, former Germany midfielder, in his memoir I've Shown Everything, *2003*

Even after a skinful, I don't have a hangover and can still be up with the others [in training].
BRYAN ROBSON, former England captain, on reports that he was a heavy drinker, 1990

The legendary drinkers at a club are usually the best trainers. They go out and get into an unathletic state, but come the next training day, they put in more effort than the non-drinkers because they feel they have to.
JOHN COLQUHOUN, Hearts striker, 1996

Quite a few of them [footballers] can knock back a pint or two, but none are alcoholics.

JIMMY HILL, then a Fulham player, in his book Striking for Soccer, *1961*

Of course I'm against Sunday soccer. It'll spoil my Saturday nights.

JOHN RITCHIE, *Stoke City player, as his club prepared to play in one of the first-ever Sunday matches, 1974*

It was a totally different culture [in the 1960s and 70s]; big lapels, kipper ties. You had a good time until Wednesday, Friday lunchtime you were back to being reasonable and Saturday night you were out. But Saturday afternoon you really wanted to be on that team-sheet.
MIKE CHANNON, *racehorse trainer and former England striker, 2004*

The young players of today drink a lot more than in my teenage-to-early-twenties period. We used to be pint sinkers but now the orders are more likely to be Bacardi and Cokes or gin and tonics. I have seen them pay out for a single round what I used to earn in a week at Chelsea.
JIMMY GREAVES, *recovering alcoholic and former England striker, in* This One's On Me, *1979*

When I was a young player, if I ever went into a pub or restaurant and my manager came in, I'd sneak out the back door. Nowadays a player would probably come up and ask me if I wanted a drink.
PAUL JEWELL, *Bradford City manager, on the modern player's lack of fear of their manager, 2000*

All the great players I've ever known have enjoyed a good drink.
JIM BAXTER, *former Scotland midfielder, 1993*

The players can get out of their brains every night as long as they're man of the match on Saturday.
JOHN GREGORY, *Aston Villa manager, 1999*

There are one or two players around who'd like it renamed the Vodka and Coca-Cola Cup.
RON ATKINSON, *Aston Villa manager, 1994*

When he first arrived all he could say was 'yes', 'no' and 'morning'. A week later he'd added, 'thank you' and 'a Budweiser, please'.
JIM DUFFY, Dundee manager, on Czech defender Dusan Vrto, 2003

Now it's a gallon or two of cold lager, a day to recover and back to the building site at 7 o'clock on Monday morning.
CHRIS BRINDLEY, part-timer with non-league Kidderminster, after an FA Cup win at Birmingham, 1994

Some of the younger players think lager makes you invisible.
CRAIG BROWN, Scotland manager, 1999

I have always been against players drinking and I'm always thinking of ways of getting a team that doesn't drink.
ALEX FERGUSON, Manchester United manager, 1997

I won't stand for booze. One player who joined the club said: 'I may as well tell you, I like a drink.' I found out he was taking others along… Instead of one lager they had three. Three becomes four and it escalates. I had to get rid of him.
LOU MACARI, Swindon manager, 1986

One drink was too many and after that, a thousand wasn't enough. If I was happy, I'd be down the pub. If I was sad, I'd be down the pub.
CLARKE CARLISLE, Queens Park Rangers defender and recovering alcoholic, 2003

Football is an industry where you don't want to show any weakness. Only the strongest survive. Even if you're not feeling good, you put on a front so that people think you are.
CARLISLE, 2003

If I had my time again, I wouldn't do anything different. Except that knowing what I do now, I'd never open a pub.
GERD MULLER, former West Germany striker, on his alcoholism, 1991

Alcohol controls me. It's a disease and has nothing to do with me personally. I never go a day without thinking about drinking.
GEORGE BEST, 1990

If I go into a bar and have a lager shandy, word goes back that I'm knocking back bottles of champagne. By the time it gets to the papers or my manager at Arsenal, it's me lying in the gutter.
CHARLIE NICHOLAS, Arsenal and Scotland striker, 1984

Scottish players booze, smoke and eat whatever comes to hand.

JEAN LUC WETZEL, French agent, 2000

One reason [why Portuguese clubs are doing better than English teams in Europe] is that they don't bloody drink. There are no 12-pints-a-night men here. They go straight home to their families and behave like responsible adults.
BOBBY ROBSON, Porto coach, 1995

Alcohol isn't part of the lifestyle for Italian players. They work on the principle that your body's a machine. When you drain that machine, the one thing you don't fill it with is alcohol.
GRAEME SOUNESS, Liverpool manager and ex-Sampdoria player, 1991

In France if you say the players can have a drink, they have two. Here they have double figures.
GERARD HOULLIER, Liverpool manager and former French FA technical director, 1999

I compare top players to racing cars. Drinking alcohol is as silly as putting diesel in a racing car.
HOULLIER, 2000

If left to their own devices the players would have two weeks in Tenerife, another two in Cyprus and two more in the pub.
DAVID SULLIVAN, joint owner of Birmingham City, on allegations that the club's pre-season training was too gruelling, 1995

The Italians smoke, yet they're world-class. They even nip into the toilets at half-time for a crafty fag.
PAUL GASCOIGNE, 1998

Drink lots of beer and smoke loads of fags.

GERRY TAGGART, *Leicester and Northern Ireland player, when asked for his advice to aspiring players, 2001*

The beers are for laughing and the fags for opening up the lungs.
STEVE DAVEY, *postman and striker with Harrogate Railway Athletic, detailing his habits during the club's FA Cup run, 2003*

Liverpool won the FA Cup a few years ago with a team of 11 foreigners, including Scots, Welsh and Irish. Now we have Spanish, French and Italians. They speak better English, are more civilised and know how to use a knife and fork.
KEN BATES, *Chelsea chairman, on the influx of players from abroad, 2000*

They've got to stop going in betting shops, going out boozing and eating McDonald's and start living how a young professional should. If not, they're going to get their P45.
DAVE ALLEN, *Sheffield Wednesday director, on the club's young players, 2002*

In the 1960s and 70s football gave you an education in life. We were the postwar generation. Nobody came out of a centrally heated house. In my first season I went to the Royal in Southampton for our pre-match meal and the waitress asked how I'd like my steak cooked. I hadn't a clue – my mum cooked for me.
MIKE CHANNON, *racehorse trainer and former England striker, 2004*

We were encouraged to open ourselves to the Japanese cuisine on offer, but having been away from home so long I could have died for a McDonald's.
DANNY MILLS, *England defender, at the end of the team's World Cup run, 2002*

We eat a lot of McDonald's, where you have Ronald McDonald. So we chose the name Ronald.
RONALDO, *Brazil striker, on his new-born son, 2000*

The odd hamburger doesn't do you any harm but you can't live on them.
MATTHEW LE TISSIER *on losing weight after his actress girlfriend, Emily Symons, encouraged him to eat more healthily, 2000*

I have never known a group of people like footballers for eating. A huge evening meal is digested and forgotten by 9.30pm. Then they still want endless rounds of sandwiches.
ALEC STOCK, former manager, in A Little Thing Called Pride, *1982*

'A bit crude when eating' states the report of an Arsenal scout, referring to a well-known international in whom Arsenal were interested... Personal background sometimes damns a player who has the necessary football qualifications.
BERNARD JOY, journalist and ex-Arsenal player, in Forward, Arsenal, *1952*

Once I saw John Charles shift two steak pies, a heaped plate of potatoes and vegetables, two helpings of apple tart and literally gallons of tea.
ROY PAUL, Manchester City and Wales player, in A Red Dragon of Wales, *1956*

Chelsea were a sausage, egg and chips club before the foreign players arrived. That's what we had to eat before training. Andy Townsend, Vinnie Jones, Tony Cascarino and me went to the cafe for a slosh-up before training. I have even had it before games.
DENNIS WISE, Chelsea midfielder, 2000

The diet in Britain is really dreadful. The whole day you drink tea and coffee with milk and cakes. If you had a fantasy world of what you shouldn't eat in sport, it's what you eat here.
ARSENE WENGER, Arsenal manager, 1997

The players go on to the training pitch clutching cups of coffee. Apparently they are given bacon sandwiches with all kinds of colourful sauces. That would be unthinkable in France.
MICKAEL SILVESTRE, Manchester United defender, 1999

My only problem seems to be with Italian breakfasts. No matter how much money you've got, you can't seem to get any Rice Krispies.
LUTHER BLISSETT after transfer from Watford to Milan, 1983

My team-mates at Chelsea have very funny ways of celebrating. In France, when it's your birthday, they buy you champagne and cake. Here they just shove your face in the mud. Very strange.
FRANK LEBOEUF, Chelsea defender, 1999

They go and eat free scampi after a game while I go home with indigestion from watching them play like that and I'm up all night because I can't sleep.
ULI HOENESS, Bayern Munich commercial manager and ex-player, after defeat by lowly St Pauli, 2000

Q: Are you romantic?
A: I'm great at romantic meals. I can only make beans on toast and Pot Noodles, so I buy a takeaway, pile up some dirty pans and serve it up so it looks like I've cooked it.
MATT JANSEN, Blackburn striker, in a newspaper questionnaire, 2001

If you're a footballer in England, girls come to you. If you're an ordinary person, you have to go to girls. That's the difference. It's so easy for the players, and the girls just say: 'Let's go, we'll have sex, no problem.' There was no chat, which was strange.
LARS LEESE, ex-Barnsley goalkeeper from Germany, 2004

Women will come to you and start leaving the signs, talking dirty and everything. So obviously a young footballer would just go with the flow... If a girl comes up to you and says 'I want to do this to you', if you turned it down there must be something wrong with you.
NIGEL REO-COKER, Wimbledon midfielder, on the sex life of wealthy young players, 2003

I'm like 90 per cent of footballers. When we meet a woman, we're thinking: 'Are they just after me for the money?'

SOL CAMPBELL, England defender, 2003

Players are no worse now than they were 30 years ago. It's getting to a stage where players will have to carry a contract in their pockets for girls to sign, saying that they consent to sex and won't go running to the papers.
PETER LORIMER, Leeds player in the 1970s, recalling how he and seven Scotland team-mates had sex with a woman during the World Cup finals, 2005

I told the players these opportunities may never come again, so they should get out there and do it for their wives, girlfriends – or both for that matter.
PAUL JEWELL, Wigan manager, after beating Arsenal in the Carling Cup semi-final, 2006

How does your girlfriend or wife feel about your travelling away from home with all these beautiful American women about?
AMERICAN JOURNALIST to Manchester United players at press conference on their US tour, 2003

I'm just a normal boy of 19. I like going out with my mates and having a meal and a few drinks. Of course I get propositioned sometimes, and it's nice. My mates love it – they get all the cast-offs.
MARK BURCHILL, Celtic striker, 1999

Maybe my players have a rampant sex life when they stay at home on Friday nights.
TERRY BURTON, Wimbledon manager, on his team's poor home form, 2001

Of course a player can have sexual intercourse before a match and play a blinder. But if he did for six months he'd be a decrepit old man. It takes the strength from the body.
BILL SHANKLY, Liverpool manager, 1971

Sex before a match? The boys can do as they please. But it's not possible at half-time.
BERTI VOGTS, Germany coach, World Cup finals, 1998

After having sex the night before a match I lose all feelings in my feet. I'm totally empty. I can't control the ball. Instead I watch erotic movies the night before. That doesn't affect my power.
FREDRIK LJUNGBERG, Sweden and Arsenal midfielder, 2000

It's not the sex that tires out young players. It's staying up all night looking for it.
CLEMENS WESTERHOF, Dutch coach to Nigeria, 1994

We don't want them to be monks. We want them to be football players because monks don't play football at this level.
BOBBY ROBSON, Newcastle manager, after some of his players visited nightclubs until the early hours, 2002

FOWLER: I know someone who had a wank two hours before a game and went out and scored a hat-trick.

McMANAMAN: I know him. He captains his country. But I think the no-sex thing is a load of shite really.

INTERVIEW with Robbie Fowler and Steve McManaman in Loaded *magazine, 1995*

This is supposed to make us world champions. Of what? Masturbation?

LUIS PEREIRA, Brazil player, on his country's policy of no women in their camp, World Cup finals, 1974

I don't think sex could ever be as rewarding as winning the World Cup. It's not that sex isn't great, just that this tournament comes around only every four years and sex is a lot more regular than that.

RONALDO, Brazil striker, immediately after his goals won the World Cup for Brazil, 2002

Q: What's more satisfying, scoring a hat-trick or having great sex?
A: The missus might be reading this, so I'd better say the sex.

KEVIN PHILLIPS, Sunderland striker, in Loaded *magazine interview, 1999*

If it was a straight choice between having sex and scoring a goal, I'd go for the goal every time. I've got all my life to have sex.

ANDY GRAY, Sky TV summariser and ex-Scotland striker, 1995

Gazza said that scoring was better than an orgasm. Lee Chapman reckoned it wasn't as good. I'll go with Pele – he thought it was about the same.

RYAN GIGGS, Manchester United winger, 1994

Footballers come pretty high up the list now in terms of shagability. Rock stars must still be first, but then it's footballers, then actors, firemen, insurance brokers, then TV quiz show hosts.

ANGUS DEAYTON, host of the TV quiz Have I Got News For You, *1997*

Dwight [Yorke] and Fabien [Barthez] could definitely do with some extra coaching from Angus [Deayton].
CAROLINE MARTIN, kiss-and-sell 'vice girl', claiming sexual liaisons with the TV personality as well as with the two Manchester United players, 2002

Let the players show their athletic torsos. We can't understand how the voluntary showing of a gorgeous male chest can be objectionable.
MOTION to the German parliament by two female Green MPs after Cristiano Ronaldo was booked in Euro 2004 for removing his shirt when celebrating a goal, 2004

The average English footballer could not tell the difference between an attractive woman and a corner flag.
WALTER ZENGA, Italy goalkeeper, responding to Wimbledon manager Bobby Gould's quip that his players wanted the phone numbers of the Italian players' wives while the Azzurri were away at the World Cup, 1990

There have been a lot of rumours about players sleeping with each other's wives. But it's not true. We're all pulling together.
FABIEN WILNIS, Ipswich defender, 2001

When I was with Norwich my wife Dawn had a baby and we called her Darby. A month later I joined Derby. The Norwich lads told me they were all trying for babies and were going to name them Lazio or Barcelona.
ASHLEY WARD, Derby striker, 1996

With the luck we've been having, one of our players must be bonking a witch.
KEN BROWN, Norwich manager, 1987

The young lads [at Leeds] mock me because if you phone me I'm always at home at night. If you want a long career you've got to learn to like a quiet life.
NIGEL MARTYN, Leeds and England goalkeeper, 2000

I tend to buy family men. With a married player you generally know he is at home of an evening, watching *Coronation Street*.
BRUCE RIOCH, Arsenal manager, 1995

Q: Girl groupies?
A: Last year I got more Valentine's cards off blokes than girls. They write love poems. It's scary.
MATT JANSEN, Blackburn striker, in newspaper questionnaire, 2001

I'd say that more than 25 per cent of football is gay. It's got to be higher than average. It's a very physical, closed world, a man's world, and you form deep bonds with people you hardly know.
JUSTIN FASHANU, *homosexual striker then with Torquay, 1992*

Football's Coming Homo

SLOGAN *of the International Gay & Lesbian Football Association to publicise the 2008 Gay World Cup, 2007*

When we qualified for the World Cup, me and Marcus [Hahnemann] sang some Slipknot together. The other guys were like: 'You've got to be kidding.'
KASEY KELLER, *United States goalkeeper, on his liking for metal and prog-rock music, 2006*

When the England team was travelling you always knew which hotel room Dave Watson was in because he took with him a radio-cassette player with big speakers, and you could hear the music all the way down the corridor. His favourite group was Status Quo.
TREVOR BROOKING *on the former England centre-half in* 100 Great British Footballers, *1988*

People say footballers have terrible taste in music but I would dispute that. In my car at the moment I've got The Corrs, Cher, Phil Collins, Shania Twain and Rod Stewart.
ANDY GRAY, *Sky TV presenter and former Scotland player, 2000*

I hate golf and like architecture. I don't say much but I do think a lot. Which seems to surprise people who think all footballers are thick.
BRIAN DEANE, *former England striker, 1996*

I'd definitely prefer Brooklyn to be a golfer. It's a better profession than football.
VICTORIA BECKHAM, 2000

My golf handicap is 16. I'm the only black man who can beat them. They don't want to be beaten by me.
RUUD GULLIT *on playing golf with his Chelsea colleagues, 1996*

I've learned [English] from watching cartoons. Now I've progressed to films.
GILLES GRIMANDI, *Arsenal's French defender, 2000*

Q: What films do you like?
A: Quentin Tarantino and stuff like that. There's nothing better than a good bit of violence.
MARK DRAPER, Aston Villa midfielder, in a Big Shot *magazine questionnaire, 1995*

One of the first things Arsene Wenger did at Arsenal was to make sure players couldn't get pay-per-view in hotels. If players are exciting themselves quite a few times then it's going to affect their physical condition.
TONY ADAMS, former Arsenal captain, 2006

I room with Robbie Keane on away trips. If we're staying in a hotel on a Friday before a game we'll watch *Trigger Happy TV* then *So Graham Norton*. After that we cuddle up together and fall asleep. There's always the temptation of pay-per-view channels in hotels, but that would be embarrassing on your room bill.
RIO FERDINAND, Leeds defender and 'EastEnders fanatic', 2001

Q: Do you watch football when you're not playing?
A: I watch highlights, but not whole games – they take too long.
DJIBRIL CISSE, Liverpool and France striker, in magazine interview, 2004

Three or four of the Villa lads buy the quality papers. At Palace it was always eight *Sun*s, four *Mirror*s.
GARETH SOUTHGATE, Aston Villa and England defender, 1996

I've always been right of centre [politically]. Most footballers are. When you are told to go out and tear your opponents apart, it tends to make you right wing.
JIMMY GREAVES, TV personality and former England striker, 2003

Labour. Definitely. Aren't all the players Labour?
STEVE PERRYMAN, Tottenham player, in Hunter Davies's The Glory Game, *1972. Only two of the players turned out to support Labour; nine were Conservatives*

I've never voted anything but Labour in my life. And never will.
KEVIN KEEGAN, England player, 1980

Football and politics are much the same. They're both full of people who are jealous of success.
TONY BANKS MP, Labour, former Minister of Sport, 1999

At Burnley, no moustaches, no sideburns, long hair discouraged. But when I was with Chelsea I could go through the menu, wine and all, phone home for hours, entertain friends, all on the club. If I run up a 2p call with Burnley, I get the bill. Keeps your feet on the ground, I'm telling you.
COLIN WALDRON, Burnley defender, 1975

Dyed hair, long hair and weird hairstyles are all strictly prohibited. All players must cut their hair short. Before becoming a soccer star you must learn to behave as a true man.
FENG JIANMING, director of youth coaching with the Chinese FA, to his country's Under-17 squad, 2004

Q: *Have you ever used public transport?*
A: *Yes, I've been in a taxi.*

GEORGE WEAH, former Chelsea striker, in newspaper questionnaire, 2001

A crazy perception persists that a footballer must have suffered a deprived childhood, not knowing where his next meal or pair of boots was coming from, to acquire the desire to turn football into a career. That is nonsense. My passion to succeed matches anybody's. My commitment to football may be even stronger because alternative career paths would have opened up for me.
JOHN BARNES, in his autobiography, 1999

The hardcore stereotypes are still there, but there are individuals in the game… I'm still eyed with suspicion for being different.
GRAEME LE SAUX, Blackburn defender, shortly before his on-the-pitch fight with team-mate David Batty over a remark made by the latter, 1995

Footballers are pampered by fans, massaged by management, stroked by the media. They are so cosseted that any criticism becomes an insult to their manhood.
MICHAEL PARKINSON, columnist, Daily Telegraph, 2001

Professional sport is a jungle and the higher you go, the worse it gets. They should stop talking about love of the shirt and being faithful. All that no longer exists, apart from in national teams.
NICOLAS ANELKA on quitting Arsenal for Real Madrid, 1999

They [footballers] are just like film stars. They want to withdraw inside their shells and live in a closed world. If I were boss of Paris Saint-Germain I would have put it in [Nicolas] Anelka's contract that he had to be filmed at home, eating his lunch and talking to his girlfriend. Show it on TV and watch it get a two per cent rating. Then no one would care any more and he'd be left in peace.
JEAN-LUC GODARD, French film-maker, 2002

The worst pressure I'm under is my baby crying at night.
ALAN SHEARER, Blackburn striker, playing down the 'pressure' of his £3.3m price tag, 1992

Football takes all my pressures away. The police have my passport and I'm not allowed to train with the other players, but nothing bothers me out on the pitch.
MICKEY THOMAS, Wrexham captain, as his team's FA Cup run coincided with his release on bail on charges of counterfeiting currency, 1992

Nothing scares me in football. I'm the same at home – the bills come in left, right and centre, but I never look at them until the red ones arrive.
STEVE STONE, Nottingham Forest and England midfielder, 1995

As a player it's like living in a box. Someone takes you out of the box for training and games, and makes all the decisions for you. I have seen players – famous internationals – all stand up in an airport lounge and follow one bloke to the lav. Six of them, maybe, standing there not wanting to piss themselves but following the bloke who does. Like sheep, never asking why, because that's the way they've been trained.
GEOFF HURST, former England striker, in Brian James's Journey to Wembley, *1977*

In every squad of 20 players there's going to be the one who hates blacks, foreigners. He don't know why. He just hates 'em.
VINNIE JONES on racism in football, 1991

In France, if I go to a boutique and staff don't recognise me I see them looking at each other as if to say: 'Watch out, what's he doing in a classy place like this?' In Italy it's worse. I'd be the only black person in a nice restaurant, the only black person with a nice car. You absolutely have to be a footballer to get to the higher echelons.
MARCEL DESAILLY, Chelsea and France captain, praising the 'tolerance' he found in England, 2004

The players themselves are very liberal now. They've grown up in a multi-racial country. Some might do this macho thing about 'women should only be in the kitchen', but they don't mean it. You can see players with their new babies and it's often them that's doing the cleaning and changing nappies.
RACHEL ANDERSON, players' agent, 1999

Someone asked me last week whether I missed the Villa. I said: 'No. I live in one.'
DAVID PLATT, former Aston Villa striker, on life with Bari in Italy, 1991

When you come to a place like Barcelona, you think: 'Bloody hell, I wish I was back in England.'
TERRY BUTCHER, Ipswich and England defender, 1979

On my debut for Besiktas they sacrificed a lamb on the pitch. Its blood was daubed on my forehead for good luck. They never did that at QPR.
LES FERDINAND, England striker, recalling his spell in Turkey, 1995

Q: England's best supermarket?
A: Tesco and Harrods.
SLAVISA JOKANOVIC, Chelsea midfielder, in a programme questionnaire, 2001

Q: Last tin you opened?
A: Not tin. Bottle of wine.
MARCEL DESAILLY, Chelsea defender, in a programme questionnaire, 2001

Just when I thought it was safe to go to parties again and say I was a footballer.
GARRY NELSON, striker with numerous clubs, on Eric Cantona's leap into the crowd at Selhurst Park, in Left Foot Forward: Diary of a Journeyman Footballer, *1995*

I'm the last old-fashioned centre-half. They're all fancy dans now, too many good-looking bastards like Rio Ferdinand who all go out with pop stars.
NEIL RUDDOCK, in interview with Loaded *magazine, 2000*

I don't speak much after a defeat. Footballers can be murder to live with. Every one I know is grumpy.

CHRIS SUTTON, Blackburn striker, 1994

You start hiding in your house because you feel ashamed of yourself.
MAGNUS HEDMAN, Coventry goalkeeper, after a run of poor results, 2000

Q: What's the worst thing anyone has ever said to you?
A: You're not playing.
MARK STEIN, Chelsea striker, in a newspaper questionnaire, 1995

Football has given me riches, popularity and privileges, but I want even more. I live for indescribable emotions and football can give me those.
GIANLUCA VIALLI on leaving Juventus for Chelsea, 1996

It's like turtles in the South Seas. Thousands are hatched on the beaches, but few of them reach the water
STEVE COPPELL, players' union official and England player, on career prospects for young players, 1983

Take it from me, as a failed footballer, there is no better way to earn a living, to be paid for what is a hobby and a passion.
HOWARD WILKINSON, Leeds manager, to graduates from the FA National School, 1992

I remember knocking on the manager's door at Sheffield Wednesday. I said: 'Could I have a little of your time? I don't know whether I'm coming or going.' 'Wilkinson,' he said, 'you're definitely going.'
HOWARD WILKINSON, Leeds manager, on under-achieving as a player, 1992

You can't accuse footballers of failing society. They are very kind, going to hospitals and seeing kids, but in the main, the press don't seem to want to write a good word about them.
ALEX FERGUSON, Manchester United manager, 2000

Footballers are funny old buggers. As long as they've got their wage packet and car, they'll distance themselves.
STUART PEARCE, Nottingham Forest acting manager, on his team-mates' reaction to a boardroom takeover at the club, 1997

If I wasn't playing, I'd be putting slates on roofs back in Ireland. Playing has got to be better than that.
PAUL McGRATH, Aston Villa defender, 1993

EDITOR: What would you be if you weren't a footballer?
MARK FLATTS: On the dole.
ARSENAL programme Q & A with the reserve forward, 1993

Q: What would you have done if you hadn't been a footballer?
A: A funeral director. I like looking at dead bodies.
CHRIS SUTTON, Chelsea striker, in the club magazine Onside, 1999

Q: If you weren't a footballer, what do you think you would be?
A: SAM ALLARDYCE (then a Bolton defender): A chef.
STAN BOWLES (QPR midfielder): A bookmaker.
DAVID O'LEARY (Arsenal defender): No idea.
CHARLIE GEORGE (Arsenal forward): I've never thought about it.
PETER TAYLOR (Crystal Palace winger): Miserable.
PETER REID (Bolton midfielder): A fat factory worker.
OSSIE ARDILES (Tottenham midfielder): A solicitor or professor of law.
ANSWERS to a regular questionnaire in Shoot! magazine, 1970s–80s

nine

PHILOSOPHERS

To put it in gentlemen's terms: if you've been out for a night and you're looking for a young lady and you pull one, some weeks they're good-looking and some weeks they're not the best. Our performance today would have been not the best-looking bird, but at least we got her in the taxi. She weren't the best-looking lady we've ended up taking home, but she was very pleasant, so thanks very much and let's have a coffee.
IAN HOLLOWAY, Queens Park Rangers manager, on a 3–0 win over Chesterfield, 2003

When you're dealing with someone who has only a pair of underpants on and you take them off, he has nothing left. He's naked. You're better off trying to find him a pair of trousers, to complement him rather than change him.
ARSENE WENGER on the need to encourage flair, 2007

It is necessary to wear the sandals of humility and not let this win go to our heads.

ANTONIO LOPES, Vasco da Gama coach, after beating Manchester United, 2000

If it is just the case that you need a first XI and three or four more players, then why did Christopher Columbus sail to India to discover America?
CLAUDIO RANIERI, Chelsea manager, 2004

When the seagulls follow the trawler it is because they think sardines will be thrown into the sea.
ERIC CANTONA addressing the media after escaping jail for his 'kung fu' attack on an abusive fan during Manchester United's visit to Crystal Palace, 1995

If a Frenchman goes on about seagulls, trawlers and sardines, he's called a philosopher. I'd just be called a short Scottish bum talking crap.
GORDON STRACHAN, former Leeds team-mate of Cantona's, 1995

The moral of the story is not to listen to those who tell you not to play the violin but to stick to the tambourine.
JOSE MOURINHO, Chelsea manager, 2005

Young players are like melons. Only when you open and taste the fruit are you 100 per cent sure that it's good. Sometimes you have beautiful melons but they don't taste good. Other times they're ugly but the taste is fantastic.
MOURINHO, 2007

Playing against a footballer with no attacking intent is like making love to a tree.
JORGE VALDANO, sporting director of Real Madrid, 2006

People worship God when they worship footballers because football is His creation.
DELIA SMITH, Norwich director, 2006

'If' is the biggest word in football, son.
SIR BOBBY ROBSON, Newcastle manager, to a conjecturing reporter, 2004

In football, things happen now and again.
SVEN-GÖRAN ERIKSSON after a Sol Campbell 'winner' for England was disallowed v Portugal, European Championship finals, 2004

Sometime in the season we will have unluck, as you say.
ERIKSSON after his Manchester City side's fortuitous derby win over United, 2007

We need a point as soon as possible, the tooter the sweeter.
ROBSON at Newcastle, 2002

We showed great bouncebackability.

IAIN DOWIE, Crystal Palace manager, 2004

We can do better footballistically.
ARSENE WENGER, 2004

The decisions decided a lot of things, but I'll leave other people to decide.
DAVID O'LEARY, Aston Villa manager, bemoaning the referee's role in a 3–0 defeat at Doncaster in the Carling Cup, 2005

The proof of the pudding is in the rankings.
KENNY DALGLISH, former Scotland player, on his country reaching a highest-ever placing of 14th in FIFA's world rankings, 2007

It's all about putting square pegs in square holes.
STEVE McCLAREN, England manager, 2006

Extra time probably came at the wrong time for us.
MARK HUGHES, Blackburn manager, after defeat by Chelsea in the FA Cup, 2007

At 2–0 down I'd have given my right arm for a draw, but I'm glad I didn't as I wouldn't have been able to clap the fans at the end.
GARY PETERS, Shrewsbury manager, 2006

We weren't beaten today, we lost.
HOWARD WILKINSON, Sunderland manager, after his side scored three own goals v Charlton, 2003

I can't tell you what's going to happen tomorrow – only today. And I can't even tell you what's going to happen today.
DAVID PLEAT, Tottenham caretaker-manager, 2004

The door is always open until it is closed.
HOPE POWELL, England women's coach, on selection for the World Cup, 2007

At the time it happened, I regretted it in hindsight.
JOEY BARTON, Manchester City midfielder, 2006

Rightly or wrongly, we've been wronged.
CHRIS COLEMAN, Fulham manager, 2007

Hard work is never easy.
JOHN TOSHACK, Wales manager, 2006

I definitely want Brooklyn to be christened, though I don't know into which religion.
DAVID BECKHAM after the birth of his and Victoria's first child, 2000

I'd rather be a footballer than an existentialist.
ROBERT SMITH, singer-writer with the rock group The Cure, 1991

Like the Tibetans I have learned to understand myself, even if you never fully can.

EMMANUEL PETIT, 1999

One minute you can be riding the crest of a wave and the next minute you can be down. It's a funny old game. It's a great leveller, and you can't get too cock-a-hoop about things. It's an old cliché but you've got to take each game as it comes and keep working at it. In playing or management, you're only as good as your last game.
BILLY BONDS, West Ham manager, 1990

In terms of a 15-round boxing match, we're not getting past round one. Teams will pinch your dinner from under your noses. If you don't heed the warnings, you get nailed to the cross.
GORDON MILNE, Leicester manager, 1983

My ankle injury has been a real pain in the arse.
DAVID PRUTTON, Southampton midfielder, 2007

The Achilles heel that has bitten us in the backside all year has stood out like a sore thumb.
ANDY KING, Swindon manager, 2005

We were done by our Achilles heel, which has been stabbing us in the back all season.
DAVID O'LEARY, Aston Villa manager, after Manchester City equalised in stoppage time, 2006

Steve McClaren will have a pair of sharp, canny shoulders to listen to.
DAVID PLATT, former England player, 2006

We've got to roll up our sleeves and get our knees dirty.
HOWARD WILKINSON, Sunderland manager, 2002

The big monster called relegation is there, ready to bite us on the arse.
STEVE COPPELL, Crystal Palace manager, 2000

Keith Curle has an ankle injury but we'll have to take it on the chin.
ALAN BALL, Manchester City manager, 1995

I've got irons in the fire and things up my sleeve.
STEVE McMAHON, Swindon manager, 1997

I have other irons in the fire, but I'm keeping them close to my chest.
JOHN BOND on leaving the Manchester City manager's job, 1983

John Spencer's hamstring is making alarm bells ring in his head.
CRAIG BROWN, Scotland manager, 1996

If someone in the crowd spits at you, you've just got to swallow it.
GARY LINEKER quoting the advice of ex-Leicester manager Gordon Milne, 1995

I felt a lump in my throat as the ball went in.

TERRY VENABLES, England coach, 1996

We can only come out of this game with egg on our faces, so it's a real banana skin.
RAY STEWART, Stirling Albion manager, on facing non-league opposition in the Scottish Cup, 2001

If we think they'll be easy meat, we'll end up with egg on our faces.
TERRY DOLAN, Bradford City manager, 1989

Obviously for Scunthorpe it would be a nice scalp to put Wimbledon on their bottoms.
DAVE BASSETT, Wimbledon manager, 1984

I've sewn a few seeds and thrown a few hand-grenades. Now I'm waiting for the dust to settle so I can see how the jigsaw pieces together.
GARY JOHNSON, Yeovil manager, 2004

Although we're playing Russian roulette, we're obviously playing catch-22 at the moment.
PAUL STURROCK, Plymouth Argyle manager, 2003

I had a contract offer on the table but it was swept from under the rug.
CHRIS PERRY, West Bromwich defender, after Iain Dowie's arrival as manager hastened his exit at Charlton, 2006

If we can bring some silverware to the club that would be a nice little rainbow at the end of a dark tunnel.
TERRY McDERMOTT, Newcastle coach, 2005

It's a vicious circle. Once the bandwagon starts rolling it's a snowball effect. Obviously you've got to take it with a pinch of salt.

MICHAEL OWEN at an England media briefing after press criticism of David James, 2004

You can't switch the lights on every time and we didn't smell that one coming. The car was in neutral and we couldn't put it in drive.
GLENN HODDLE, Tottenham manager, after a home defeat, 2003

No one wants to commit hara-kari and sell themselves down the river.
GARY LINEKER, England striker and captain, explaining the dearth of goals at the European Championship finals, 1992

We climbed three mountains and then proceeded to throw ourselves off them.
BILLY McNEILL, Celtic manager, after beating Partizan Belgrade 5–4 but losing on aggregate, 1989

If you can't stand the heat in the dressing room, get out of the kitchen.

TERRY VENABLES, England coach, 1995

The cat's among the pigeons and meanwhile we're stuck in limbo.
BERNIE SLAVEN, Middlesbrough striker, after Colin Todd's demise as manager, 1991

The tide is very much in our court now.
KEVIN KEEGAN, Manchester City manager, 2004

We miss Maine Road but we don't really miss it.
KEEGAN after City moved to a new stadium, 2003

Goalkeepers aren't born today until they're in their 30s.
KEEGAN, 2003

Argentina are the second best team in the world and there's no higher praise than that.
KEEGAN, then England manager, 2000

Argentina won't be at Euro 2000 because they're from South America.
KEEGAN, 2000

At this level, if five or six players don't turn up, you'll get beat.
KEEGAN after some Manchester City players 'went missing' at Villa Park, 2002

England have the best fans in the world, and Scotland's are second to none.
KEEGAN, 1999

Young Gareth Barry, you know, he's young.
KEEGAN, 2000

Our squad looks good on paper, but paper teams win paper cups.
HOWARD WILKINSON, Sunderland manager, 2002

A lucky goal or the run of the ball can be triggers, but they can only be triggers if you have gunpowder.
WILKINSON at Sunderland, 2002

We had a very constructive discussion at half-time, then decided to give it the full bollocks.
RON ATKINSON, Aston Villa manager, 1993

Their goal unsettled us, and no matter what you say at half-time, there's always that little bit of toothache in their minds.
STEVE COPPELL, Reading manager, 2004

If you take liberties with the opposition they'll pull your trousers down.
BILLY BONDS, West Ham manager, 1991

If you don't believe you can win, there's no point in getting out of bed at the end of the day.

NEVILLE SOUTHALL, Everton and Wales goalkeeper, 1990

At the end of the day it's all about what we do on the night.
BRYAN HAMILTON, Northern Ireland manager, before game v Germany, 1996

At the end of the day it's not the end of the world.
JIM McLEAN, Dundee United manager, after UEFA Cup final defeat v Gothenberg, 1987

There is a rat in the camp trying to throw a spanner in the works.
CHRIS CATTLIN, Brighton manager, 1983

We want to go upwards, not stand still and go backwards.
CHRIS ROBINSON, Hearts chief executive, 2004

It doesn't matter what happened – we got the three points and that's all that counts.
WAYNE BRIDGE, Chelsea defender, after victory v Arsenal – in the Carling Cup final, 2007

Our back four was at sixes and sevens.

RON ATKINSON, Aston Villa manager, 1992

There are 0–0 draws and 0–0 draws, and this was a 0–0 draw.
JOHN SILLETT, Coventry manager, 1989

It's 60–40 against him being fit but he's got half a chance.
GLENN HODDLE, Wolves manager, 2006

Five per cent of me is disappointed while the other 50 per cent is just happy we've qualified.
MICHAEL OWEN after England finished second in their group, European Championship finals, 2004

We must have had 99 per cent of the match. It was the other three per cent that cost us.
RUUD GULLIT after Chelsea lost to Coventry, 1997

We're not here just to make up the numbers. We're here to just stay in the league.
PAUL JEWELL, Wigan manager, preparing for Premiership life, 2005

We're a second-half side. The problem is the second halves aren't long enough.
DELIA SMITH, Norwich director, 2004

It was a game of two halves, and we were rubbish in both of them.
BRIAN HORTON, Oxford United manager, 1990

In cup competitions, Jack will always have a chance of beating Goliath.
TERRY BUTCHER, Sunderland manager, in his programme column, 1993

The FA Cup touches so many people. It's a fair bet that, by the end of today, players you have never heard of will be household names – like that fellow who scored for Sutton United against Coventry City last season.
BOBBY CAMPBELL, Chelsea manager, in his programme column, 1990

The first goal was a foul, the second was offside, and they would never have scored the third if they hadn't got the other two.
STEVE COPPELL, Crystal Palace manager, explaining defeat by Liverpool, 1991

If corner-kicks hadn't been invented, this would have been a very close game.
NEIL WARNOCK, Sheffield United manager, after a 4–1 defeat at Newcastle, 2000

We were in an awkward position against Yugoslavia in that in order to win we needed to score more goals than they did.
JOSE ANTONIO CAMACHO, Spain coach, 2000

I just wonder what would have happened if the shirt had been on the other foot.
MIKE WALKER, Norwich manager, claiming refereeing decisions went against his side v Manchester United, 1994

My players ran their socks into the ground for Manchester United.
ALEX FERGUSON, 1997

If we played like that every week, we wouldn't be so inconsistent.
BRYAN ROBSON, Manchester United captain, 1990

If I was still at Ipswich, I wouldn't be where I am today.

DALIAN ATKINSON, Aston Villa striker, 1992

Germany are a very difficult team to beat. They had 11 internationals out there today.
STEVE LOMAS, Northern Ireland captain, 1999

If I played for Scotland, my grandma would be the proudest woman in the country if she wasn't dead.
MARK CROSSLEY, English-born goalkeeper (who later represented Wales), 1995

The World Cup is every four years so this is going to be a perennial problem.
GARY LINEKER, TV football presenter, 1998

You never know what could happen in a couple of one-off games like these.
GRAEME SHARP, former Scotland striker, before the play-off fixtures v England, 1999

Even when you're dead, you shouldn't lie down and let yourself be buried.
GORDON LEE, Everton manager, 1981

Football matches are like days of the week. It can't be Sunday every day.
There are also Mondays and Tuesdays.
GEORGE WEAH, Milan and Liberia striker, 1995

We had enough chances to win the game. In fact we did win it.
ALEX SMITH, Aberdeen manager, 1991

It was a draw, so in the end we didn't win.
DAVID BECKHAM to a TV interviewer after Manchester United drew with Croatia Zagreb, 1999

When their second goal went in, I knew our pig was dead.
DANNY WILLIAMS, Swindon manager, after they lost an FA Cup tie to West Ham, 1975

Having players you've sold come back and score against you is what football's all about.
ALEX FERGUSON, Manchester United manager, 1992

The missing of chances is one of the mysteries of life.
SIR ALF RAMSEY, England manager, 1972

Being given chances and not taking them, that's what life is all about.
RON GREENWOOD, England manager, 1982

Always remember that the goal is at the end of the field and not in the middle.
SVEN-GÖRAN ERIKSSON to his England squad, 2002

Too many players were trying to score or create a goal.
GERARD HOULLIER, Liverpool manager, after home defeat by Watford, 1999

It was a Limpalong Leslie sort of match.
PETER SHREEVES, Tottenham manager, after win v Coventry, 1985

It was a bad day at Black Rock.
SHREEVES after Spurs' 5–1 defeat v Watford a fortnight later, 1985

What's the bottom line in adjectives?
SHREEVES after home loss to Coventry, 1985

We threw caution to the wind and came back from the dead. Well, it is Easter Monday.

GLENN HODDLE, Swindon player-manager, after they came from 4–1 down to win 6-4 at Birmingham, 1993

He was flapping about like a kipper.
JOHN BARNWELL, Notts County manager, on Nicky Law's costly handling offences v Tottenham, 1989

We held them for 89 minutes and then they kippered us.
DOGON ARIF, Fisher Athletic manager, after defeat by Telford, 1989

You get it [the ball] in the bollocks, in the nose, in the gob, and I don't care if it knocks out their ruddy crowns. I've got lads more than prepared to get in the kipper. But you do not turn your back and let it hit you up the arse and spin up into the top corner.
MICK McCARTHY, Wolves manager, after a member of his defensive wall broke ranks and deflected a Watford free-kick into the net, 2007

You must kill the bull or you haven't done nowt.
DANNY BERGARA, Stockport's Uruguayan manager, 1992

It was a mistake as big as a house.
RENE HIGUITA, Colombia goalkeeper, after his error let in Cameroon's Roger Milla for a goal, World Cup finals, 1990

This for me is without exception possibly my last World Cup.

RAY WILKINS, *England midfielder, en route to Mexico, 1986*

The unthinkable is not something we're really thinking about at the moment.
PETER KENYON, *chief executive of Manchester United, on the possibility of being eliminated from the European Cup, 2000*

The new manager has given us unbelievable belief.
PAUL MERSON, *Arsenal midfielder, on Arsene Wenger's impact at Highbury, 1996*

I'm not a believer in luck, but I do believe you need it.
ALAN BALL, *Manchester City manager, 1996*

Sometimes we are predictable, but out of that predictability we are unpredictable.
JOHN BECK, *Cambridge United manager, 1991*

He's such an honest person it's untrue.
BRIAN LITTLE, *Aston Villa manager, on midfielder Ian Taylor, 1996*

That's understandable and I understand that.
TERRY VENABLES, *England coach, 1996*

That is in the past, and the past has no future.
DAVID PLEAT *on losing the Sheffield Wednesday manager's job, 1997*

The road to ruin is paved with excuses.
BOBBY GOULD, *Coventry manager, after defeat by Leeds, 1993*

I'm told we need a big name. Engelbert Humperdinck is a big name but it doesn't mean he can play football.
RAY HARFORD, *Blackburn manager, 1996*

We're a First Division club in every sense of the word.
NAT LOFTHOUSE, *Bolton president, when the club languished in the Third, 1992*

My team won't freeze in the white hot atmosphere of Anfield.
RON SAUNDERS, Aston Villa manager, 1980

We're halfway round the Grand National course with many hurdles to clear.
So let's make sure we all keep our feet firmly on the ground.
MIKE BAILEY, Charlton manager, as his team chased promotion, 1981

REPORTER: What are your impressions of Africa?
GORDON LEE: Africa? We're not in bloody Africa, are we?
EXCHANGE between journalist and the Everton manager in Morocco, 1978

Professional and amateur football have as much in common as a strawberry
milkshake and a skyscraper.
HARALD SCHUMACHER, West Germany goalkeeper, in Blowing the Whistle, *1987*

You can't compare English and German football. They're like omelette and
muesli.
ERIK MEIJER, Dutch striker, leaving Liverpool for Hamburg, 2000

There's no question of us playing for the draw. As we say in Germany: 'We will
be going for the sausages.'
JURGEN ROBER, Hertha Berlin coach, before a game v Chelsea, 1999

The wall we had before Bochum scored from that free-kick looked as if it was
built by Andy Warhol.
ULI HOENESS, Bayern Munich general manager, 2001

The plastic pitch is a red herring.
GRAHAM TAYLOR, Aston Villa manager, after losing FA Cup tie at Oldham, 1990

The players still had Christmas cake in their feet.
SERGIO CRAGNOTTI, Lazio president, after defeat by Napoli, 2001

I can see the carrot at the end of the tunnel.
STUART PEARCE, England defender, on recovering from injury, 1992

No one hands you cups on a plate.
TERRY McDERMOTT, Newcastle assistant manager, 1995

Statistics are just like mini-skirts – they give you good ideas but hide the most important things.
EBBE SKOVDAHL, Aberdeen manager, 2001

We're now arithmetically, not mathematically, safe from relegation. There's neither algebra nor geometry involved in the calculations.
TOM HENDRIE, St Mirren manager, 1999

Never in the history of the FAI Cup had a team wearing hooped jerseys lost a final in a year ending in 5.
HOME FARM (Dublin) programme notes, 1985

Which Spanish side did John Toshack take over after leaving Sporting Lesbian?
QUIZ QUESTION in a Leek Town programme, 1999

The transfer market has changed because of the Bosnian ruling.
JOE KINNEAR, Wimbledon manager, 1998

I expect the Croats to come out... Oh dear, I better not say fighting, had I?
PETER SHREEVES, Tottenham manager, before a match v Hajduk Split from war-torn Croatia, 1991

If players won't die for this club, then I don't want them.
ALEX MILLER, Hibernian manager, 1990

Our guys are getting murdered twice a week.

ANDY ROXBURGH, Scotland coach, on the hectic schedule in British football, 1991

I'd shoot myself if I had the bottle.
VINNIE JONES after being sent off for the 10th time, 1995

I'd hang myself but the club can't afford the rope.
IAIN MUNRO, Hamilton Academical manager, 1995

The shoot-out is like shooting wee ducks at a fairground to try to win a prize.
ALEX SMITH, Aberdeen manager, after winning the Scottish Cup on penalties, 1990

Being top won't change much. It'll probably rain tomorrow and the traffic lights will still be red.
HOWARD WILKINSON, Leeds manager, on leading the league for the first time in his career, 1991

I feel like Korky the Cat, who has been run over by a steamroller, got up and had someone punch him in the stomach.
WILKINSON after Leeds's FA Cup defeat by Arsenal, 1993

When one door opens, another smashes you in the face.

TOMMY DOCHERTY on his dismissal as manager of Preston, 1981

You are always one defeat away from a crisis. On that basis, we're in deep shit.
JOHN GREGORY, Aston Villa manager, during a losing sequence, 1999

I never heard a minute's silence like that.
GLENN HODDLE, England manager, at Wembley after Princess Diana's death, 1997

If we beat Real [Madrid] it will be a nationwide orgasm.
JESUS GIL, Atletico Madrid president, before the derby, 1995

Dani is so good-looking that Villa didn't know whether to mark him or bonk him.
HARRY REDKNAPP, West Ham manager, on his Portuguese signing, 1996

We let the convict out of jail, and we know what they are like when they get free.
HOWARD WILKINSON, Leeds manager, after 3–0 defeat by VfB Stuttgart, 1992

Rotherham reminds me of Bermuda. It's small so you bump into the same people two or three times a day.
SHAUN GOATER, Rotherham and Bermuda striker, 1993

I never realised Lincoln was a seaside town.
BRIAN LAWS, Scunthorpe manager, after losing on a liberally sanded 'beach' of a pitch, 2003

Q: Which TV programme would you most like to appear in?
A: *Thunderbirds*. I'd like to fly in *Thunderbird II*.
KEVIN KEEN, West Ham midfielder, interviewed in club programme, 1992

Claim to fame outside soccer: I once put together an MFI wardrobe in less than four days.
TERRY GIBSON, Coventry striker, 1985

There is nothing going on in the world at the moment that I find distressing or have a view on.
MICHAEL OWEN, 1999

The trouble with you, son, is that your brains are all in your head.
BILL SHANKLY to unnamed Liverpool player, 1967

I don't like being on my own because you think a lot and I don't like to think a lot.

PAUL GASCOIGNE on the TV documentary Gazza's Coming Home, *1996*

I'm only 33 but my hair is 83.
ANDY RITCHIE, balding Oldham striker, 1994

I know more about football than about politics.
HAROLD WILSON MP, Labour, Prime Minister, 1974

I thought the No. 10, Whymark, played exceptionally well.
MARGARET THATCHER MP, Conservative, after the FA Cup final, 1978. Trevor Whymark was listed in the programme but did not play

It's like going to a different country.
IAN RUSH on life in Italy with Juventus, 1988

What you call football is like cricket to us.
ANDY WILLIAMS, American pop singer, 2002

How can you tell your wife you are just popping out to play a match and then not come back for five days?

RAFAEL BENITEZ, Liverpool manager, on Test cricket, 2005

In programme notes there is a great deal of clap trap where subconsciously people tend to become excuse worthy. I have often said to the players that there is talking and doing. Today will be a day of doing. At least we know the macabre has a habit of flourishing in different settings.

COLIN MURPHY, Lincoln manager, from his programme column 'Murph's Message', 1989

I happen to believe no one can work miracles and it strikes me that applies even to people like Holmes and Watson, the Marx Brothers, Bilko, Inspector Clouseau or Winston Churchill. All these had immeasurable qualities but I don't know whether any of them had the attributes to be able to win promotion for Lincoln City FC with all the injuries and suspensions we have had.

MURPHY from 'Murph's Message', 1988

We are now into a new season and I have no doubt that George and Mildred are delighted to be selling their cheese rolls in the Fourth Division... If we all remember that the fires of war should have some good feelings then we shall not be far short at the finish.

MURPHY after Lincoln won promotion back to the Football League, 1988

Music soothes the savage breast. The cobra has been tamed. Losing. A losing sequence, namely three games, always appears to put doubts in people's minds irrespective of the club's predicament and the doubting Thomases doubt no more and the judges become experts. The cobra has an excellent habit of wriggling free and indeed Gordon Hobson wriggled three at Burnley.

MURPHY, 1988

People get mad over football, people enthuse over it, people exultate, and people sadly even have started fighting and destructing over it.
MURPHY, 1988

REPORTER: It was a funny game, Jim.
JIMMY SIRREL: Human beings are funny people.
EXCHANGE between journalist and the Notts County manager after a match at Arsenal, 1982

Footballers are no different from human beings.
GRAHAM TAYLOR, England manager, 1992

I don't make predictions and I never will.
PAUL GASCOIGNE, 1997

There's not a word to describe how I feel, but I'm just ecstatic.
MARY PHILIP, Arsenal women's player, after the team won the UEFA Cup, 2007

ten

FANS

Places like this are the soul of English football. The crowd is magnificent, singing: 'Fuck off, Mourinho.'
JOSE MOURINHO, Chelsea manager, at Sheffield United, 2006

Those who don't get behind the team should shut the hell up or they can come round to my house and I will fight them.
IAN HOLLOWAY, Queens Park Rangers manager, 2004

The people chanting 'Taylor out!' were the same ones singing 'Give us a wave' when we were two up on Everton.
GRAHAM TAYLOR, Aston Villa manager, 2002

I have a bank manager, a solicitor, an agent, and I would never dream that I could do their job better than them. Football is probably the only job where totally unqualified people think they know everything.
PETER TAYLOR, Hull manager, on fan pressure at his previous clubs, 2003

Every club has three types – fans, parasites and people who work their bollocks off, even ladies.
KEN BATES, Leeds United chairman, 2006

There are two sorts of fans – those that understand what we have been doing at this club and those who do not.
GERARD HOULLIER, Liverpool manager, after hostile graffiti was sprayed on the training-ground walls, 2004

Football isn't a game to hate the opposition. It's a game we all love.
HARRY REDKNAPP, Portsmouth manager, after his team's fans applauded Arsenal's players warmly during a 5–1 defeat, 2004

I expected abuse, but I also got a hamburger and about £4.50 in change.
GARY NEVILLE, Manchester United captain,. on objects thrown at him at Liverpool, 2006

I got an email from a British soldier in Afghanistan. He tells me he wears a Pompey shirt under his uniform, and that he's just read we lost 5–0 to West Brom and the players didn't try. He says: 'When I go out on a mission, I don't know if I'm coming back. But I'm committed to my mission. Are you committed to yours, Mr Chairman?' I almost cry.
MILAN MANDARIC, Portsmouth chairman, 2003

Men have two passions. One is in bed and the other is watching their football team.
DAVE WHELAN, Wigan chairman, 2005

A man can change wives, political parties or religions, but he cannot change his favourite football team.
EDUARDO GALEANO, Uruguayan poet, journalist and football fan, 1995

The only loyalty in football is between the supporter and his club. That will never die.

STEVE COPPELL after leaving the Crystal Palace managership, 2000

Football is the only subject that can induce a bloke to swank about his fidelity.
HARRY PEARSON, author and Middlesbrough fan, in The Far Corner: A Mazy Dribble Through North-East Football, *1994*

I have measured out my life in Arsenal fixtures, and any event of any significance has a footballing shadow. When did my first real love affair end? The day after a disappointing 2–2 draw at home to Coventry.
NICK HORNBY, author, in Fever Pitch, *1992*

There's often talk about supporters winning representation on the board of their clubs. What's anyone doing on the board who isn't a fan in the first place?
MATTHEW HARDING, Chelsea vice-chairman, 1996

Every thousandth person created, God unhinges their heads, scoops out their brains and issues them to football clubs as supporters.
MIKE BATESON, Torquay chairman, 1996

There's a fine line between loyalty and madness, and I'm not sure which side he's on. I think it's madness.
GARY ROWELL, former Sunderland player, on a fan who changed his name to Gary Sunderland AFC Lamb (and cited Rowell as his favourite-ever player), 2002

I heard this bloke in the stand shouting 'McGraw [Alan, manager], we're fucking sick of what you're doing to Morton, buying bastards like Gahagan.' Two minutes later I scored the winner and as I ran back I heard the same guy shouting: 'Yesssss, Johnny boy, gies another one!'
JOHN GAHAGAN, Morton player, 1990

Things worth knowing: That Association Football is becoming notorious for disgraceful exhibitions of ruffianism. That the rabble will soon make it impossible for law-abiding citizens to attend matches.
SCOTTISH ATHLETIC JOURNAL, *1887*

A northern horde of uncouth garb and strange oaths.

PALL MALL GAZETTE *describing Blackburn Rovers' fans in London for the FA Cup final, 1884*

There is no real local interest to excuse the frenzy of the mob, since the players come from all over the kingdom and may change their clubs each season.
C.B. FRY'S MAGAZINE *on crowd trouble, 1906*

Miserable specimens...learning to be hysterical as they groan or cheer in panic unison with their neighbours, the worst sound of all being the hysterical scream of laughter that greets any trip or fall by a player.
LORD BADEN POWELL, founder of the Boy Scouts, describing football spectators in Scouting for Boys, *1908*

If they knew more about football than we do, there would be 50,000 players and 22 spectators.
BILL McCRACKEN, Newcastle and Northern Ireland player, on being barracked, 1911

Generally he is short of stature, anaemic-looking, with a head too big to suggest it contains only brains, a high shrieking voice, reminiscent of a rusty saw in quick staccato action. He is blind to every move initiated by the Swansea Town players, but his attention to a faulty clearance or badly placed pass is microscopic.
CYGNET, columnist in Swansea's Sporting News, *on barracking at the Vetch Field, 1921*

Why not covered accommodation for spectators, dry ground to stand on and a reduced admission if possible? Many a wreath has been purchased by standing on wet ground on Saturday afternoons.
LETTER to the Birmingham Mail, *1905*

A policeman called me at home. Friday night again. He'd caught a dozen courting couples in the stand and asked me what to do with them. I told him to fix the bloody fence and board 'em in. Best gate of the season it would've been.
FRED WESTGARTH, Hartlepools manager, 1957

Q: What will you do when Christ comes to lead us again?
A: Move St John to inside-right.
CHURCH SIGN and answering graffiti on Merseyside, 1965

Football crowds are never going to sound like the hat parade on the club lawns of Cheltenham racecourse. They are always going to have more vinegar than Chanel.
ARTHUR HOPCRAFT, author, The Football Man, *1968*

They tend to start off with things like 'Dear Stupid' or 'Dear Big Head'. One man wrote to me, beginning: 'Dear Alfie Boy'.
SIR ALF RAMSEY on his postbag, in Arthur Hopcraft's The Football Man, *1968*

My favourite [letter received] is one which said: 'You, Smith, Jones and Heighway had better keep looking over your shoulder. You are all going to get your dews.'
EMLYN HUGHES, Liverpool captain, 1977

The only point worth remembering about Port Vale's match with Hereford on Monday was the fact that the attendance figure, 2,744, was a perfect cube, 14 x 14 x 14.
LETTER from 'Disillusioned Supporter' to Stoke-on-Trent's Sentinel *newspaper, 1979*

Girls have sent me suggestive pictures and said what they would like to do to me. I'm absolutely shocked by their suggestions. Then I get Sarah [Whatmore, his girlfriend] to act them out.
JAMES BEATTIE, Southampton and England striker, 2003

I got some girl's knickers through the post the other day but I didn't like them. To be honest, they didn't fit.
JAMIE REDKNAPP, Liverpool midfielder, 1995

Funny stalkers, scary stalkers, every kind of stalker. One woman turned up at my place every day for two weeks and just left different pairs of underpants for me in the mail-box. Luckily, they were always brand new.
DAVID BECKHAM on life as a Madrid galactico, 2004

I got the ball in the middle of the field and a voice in the centre stand shouted out: 'Give it to Taylor.' So I gave it to Taylor. Five minutes later, I got the ball again and the same voice shouted: 'Give it to Matthews.' So I gave it to Matthews. A couple of minutes later, I got the ball again, but this time there were three Arsenal players around me. So I looked up at the stand and the voice came back: 'Use your own discretion.'
STAN MORTENSEN, former Blackpool and England player, in Robin Daniels's Blackpool Football, *1972*

It's gone now, mainly because of hooliganism. I wouldn't dare walk about now, in my old outfit, in another town. They'd be after me, wouldn't they? Around 1963, I could feel some spectators were getting out of hand.
SYD BEVERS, leader of the 'Atomic Boys', a group of Blackpool fans who attended games in fancy dress, 1972

Five Newport County supporters were arrested after they turned up at a Kidderminster Harriers match in drag. About 150 visiting fans arrived in the town but 40 went to the Oxfam shop and bought women's clothes. 'I don't know whether this is a new style, or what it is,' said Superintendent Peter Picken.
REPORT in the Worcester Evening News, *1989*

There was this male MP who was found dead in stockings and suspenders. He was also wearing a Manchester City scarf but the police kept that bit quiet so as not to embarrass the relatives.
BERNARD MANNING, comedian and City supporter, 2000

The Spurs fans, marching and shouting their way back to the station, banged on the windows of the team coach as it threaded its way through the crowds. 'Go on, smash the town up,' said Cyril [Knowles], encouraging them.
HUNTER DAVIES, The Glory Game, 1972

The club call us hooligans, but who'd cheer them if we didn't come? You have to stand there and take it when Spurs are losing and the others are jeering at you. It's not easy. We support them everywhere and get no thanks.
TOTTENHAM FAN quoted in The Glory Game, *1972*

I'd like to kill all the Arsenal players and then burn the stand down.

TOTTENHAM FAN, as above

The only answer is for decent supporters, and they are in the majority, to become terrace vigilantes. A few thumps on the nose would soon stop these silly youngsters.
ALEC STOCK, Fulham manager, 1975

No one likes us, we don't care.
SONG by Millwall fans to the tune of 'Sailing', 1980s

Apparently they couldn't find one decent Millwall supporter.
DENIS HOWELL MP, Labour, Minister for Sport, complaining about an 'unbalanced' investigation into hooliganism by BBC TV's Panorama, *1977*

Really good Millwall supporters, right, they can't stand their club being slagged down, you know, and it all wells up, you know, and you just feel like hitting someone.
MILLWALL FAN quoted in Roger Ingham et al, Football Hooliganism: The Wider Context, *1978*

At 6.45 the Millwall supporters were taken under escort towards the stadium. As they passed a public house, a group of 30 to 40 males came out, and bottles and glasses were thrown and pub windows smashed. After a while it became apparent that both groups were from Millwall and each thought the other were Bristol City supporters.
REPORT from the National Criminal Intelligence Unit after a match at Ashton Gate, 2001

What you don't want to do is replace the image of Millwall, which is one of hostility, pride and belligerence. Frankly, your fellow supporters don't give a flying fuck for anyone else in the league or any sort of political correctness.
ROD LIDDLE, broadcaster, journalist and Millwall fan, arguing against trying to turn the club into a 'family' club like Charlton, 2006

We don't normally have any police at our matches, unless one happens to wander up on his bike.
SALISBURY TOWN OFFICIAL after the non-league club drew Millwall in the FA Cup, 1979

He told me I was a dead man and that I wouldn't get out of The Den alive. Then he said I was fat. I said: 'Have you looked at yourself lately?'
KEVIN PRESSMAN, Sheffield Wednesday goalkeeper, on being confronted by a pitch invader at Millwall, 1995

If Cantona had jumped into our crowd he'd never have come out alive.

ALEX RAE, Millwall midfielder, after the Frenchman's Selhurst Park fracas, 1995

The Millwall football cheer exists for the same reason as 'Louie Louie'. It's the soundtrack of our lives.
KIM FOWLEY, 'wild man' American rock singer and record producer, 2003

I must have done all right for them to gob all over me.
STEVE JONES, Bournemouth striker, after running a gauntlet of Birmingham fans, 1994

The most violent offenders should be flogged in front of the main stand before home games. I feel so strongly on this that I'd volunteer to do the whipping myself.
ALLAN CLARKE, Leeds manager, 1980

I know it sounds drastic but the only way to deal with hooligans is to shoot them. That'll stop them.
BOBBY ROBERTS, Colchester manager, 1980

There are more hooligans in the House of Commons than at a football match.
BRIAN CLOUGH, Nottingham Forest manager, 1980

I met these football fans smoking in a non-smoker on the railway, so I said:
'Put it out...put it out.' And they did. I think they're far less dangerous
than dogs.
BARBARA WOODHOUSE, dog trainer and TV personality, 1980

What comes next – water cannon, guards, tanks and consultant undertakers to
ferry away the dead?
SIMON TURNEY, Greater London Council official, on Chelsea's proposed electric fence, 1985

You can't turn a fire extinguisher on fans. It'll only inflame the situation.
*JOHN BALL, West Ham safety officer, after their followers were doused at French club Metz,
1999*

There have always been hooligans. In Germany they were in the Gestapo and
in Russia they were in the KGB.
*HOWARD WILKINSON, Leeds manager, after violence by his club's fans at Bournemouth,
1990*

What's the first word to come into your head when I say 'British soccer fan'?
It was 'subhuman', wasn't it? I rest my case.
*PHILADELPHIA INQUIRER, doubting the wisdom of the United States staging the World
Cup, 1990*

There were three countries in the world whose presence would have created
logistical and security problems, so we're very pleased they won't be coming:
Iraq, Iran and England.
ALAN ROTHENBERG, chairman of the US World Cup committee, 1994

Every British male, at some time or other, goes to his last football match.
It may very well be his first football match.
MARTIN AMIS, novelist, reviewing a book on 'football' hooliganism, 1991

The fans all had the complexion and body scent of a cheese and onion crisp,
and the eyes of pit-bulls.
AMIS on his experience of watching Queens Park Rangers, 1991

English fans are brilliant. In England, when you ask someone which club he supports, it means something. The guy supports a club for his whole life, whatever the ups and downs. In France, there's no loyalty. If you're not top of the league, the fans go to another club.
ERIC CANTONA, newly signed to Leeds, on hearing England fans had rioted in Sweden, 1992

I hope [England] are on the first plane back from Deutschland. They've got the players to do well, but they're not my team. I'm from the People's Republic of Mancunia. I'll have to leave if they win it. The country will be full of Cockneys going on about it for years.
MANI, Primal Scream and former Stone Roses bass guitarist, before the World Cup finals, 2006

They eat sausages and eggs for breakfast, drive on the left, play baseball with an oar, set times for drinking and think they are the best.
ARTICLE in the Portuguese newspaper 24 Horas on the 'ridiculous' England fans before Portugal v England, European Championship quarter-final, 2004

Football matches are now the substitute for the old medieval tournaments. They are aggressive and confrontational by their nature. It's perfectly natural for some of the fans to be obstreperous.
ALAN CLARK MP, Conservative, defending rioting England fans, World Cup finals, 1998

Now that we don't have war, what's wrong with a good punch-up? We're a nation of yobs. Without that characteristic, how did we colonise the world? With so many milksops, left-wing liberals and wetties around, I rejoice that some people keep up our historic spirit.
DOWAGER MARCHIONESS OF READING, aged 79, after hooliganism by England fans, World Cup finals, 1998

The people kicking up a fuss in Marseilles are true fans. They feel passionate enough about the England team to go out and fight for them.
ELLIS CASHMORE, sociology professor, 1998

The disrespect shown by the English fans to our national anthem was wrong. It shows that the countries who are said to be advanced culturally are actually behind.
SENOL GUNES, Turkey coach, after whistling and booing during his country's anthem at Sunderland, 2003

It's not surprising some fans behave badly when you realise how little consideration they receive from the clubs.
COLIN SMITH, Chief Constable, Thames Valley Police, 1990

Football violence is like smoking. If you try it once and hate it, you don't do it again. But if you try it once and like it, it's bloody hard to give up.
DOUGIE and EDDY BRIMSON, self-confessed Watford hooligans, in their book Everywhere We Go, *1996*

The terraces are the very last bastion of our once male-dominated culture, where boys can grow up and act like men...scream, shout, abuse, swear, even cry if we like without feeling like some effeminate twat.
DOUGIE BRIMSON, Watford fan and author of A Geezer's Guide to Football: A Lifetime of Lads and Lager, *1998*

I think going to football and fighting is an illness. I don't think you can just stop.
DANNY WALFORD, 21-year-old Chelsea 'hooligan', in the Donal McIntyre TV programme Under Cover, *1999*

Like other infections, new strains of football hooliganism are developing that are clever, resilient and increasingly resistant.
BRYAN DREW, National Criminal Intelligence Service spokesman, 2001

Football is not about people setting out to watch a match and never returning home.
PETER RIDSDALE, Leeds chairman, after two of the club's fans were stabbed to death in Istanbul, 2000

Even the hooligans had a good time and enjoyed the party. Maybe the cannabis relaxed them.
JOHAN BEELAN, Dutch police chief, on the behaviour of England fans in Eindhoven, 2000

We don't welcome yobs in any form, but that isn't to say we're against tribal loyalty. And our tribe aren't half fearsome when they want something.
KARREN BRADY, Birmingham City managing director, 2002

The English stick their psychos in Broadmoor, while the Welsh put theirs in Ninian Park.

FULHAM FANZINE There's Only One F in Fulham, *awarding Cardiff supporters 0 out of 10 in their Best Fans poll, 1995*

I went over to take a kick where the Chelsea fans were and they started chucking sticks of celery and sweetcorn. It made me laugh to think of them popping into greengrocers' shops on the way to Wembley.
RYAN GIGGS after the FA Cup final, Manchester United v Chelsea, 1994

I made a two-finger gesture towards the fans to show that I'd scored twice, and that must have been misinterpreted.
PAUL PESCHISOLIDO, West Bromwich Albion striker, after confrontation with Port Vale supporters, 1997

Helping fuel soccer riots for 40 years
SLOGAN advertising Strongbow cider in the United States, 2003

The Scotland fans' ability to smuggle drink into matches makes Papillon look like a learner.
SCOTTISH POLICE FEDERATION spokesman, 1981

Communism v Alcoholism
SCOTTISH BANNER at Soviet Union v Scotland, World Cup finals, 1982

Let all France have whisky on its breath.
LYRIC from the Scotland World Cup song 'Don't Come Home Too Soon', by Del Amitri, 1998

Drinking alcohol can be dangerous as it leads to drunkenness.
UEFA HANDBOOK offering advice to fans at the European Championship finals, 2004

The kind of commitment Scots invest in football means there's less left for the more important concerns.
WILLIAM McILVANNEY, novelist and journalist, in a feature on Scottish independence, reprinted in Surviving the Shipwreck, *1992*

When Patrick Kluivert scored, it was the same feeling as when Mel Gibson got hung, drawn and quartered at the end of *Braveheart.*
DOMINIK DIAMOND, broadcaster and Scotland fan, after a late Dutch goal v England eliminated Scotland from the European Championship finals, 1996

We'd never support a Great Britain football team, even if there were 11 Scots in it.
HAMISH HUSBAND, Association of Tartan Army Clubs spokesperson, after talk of entering a GB side in the 2012 Olympic Games, 2005

We dream of beating the English, not playing in the same team as them.
GORDON McQUEEN, former Scotland defender, 2005

Get intae them! Get intae them!
CHANT by Scotland fans as Scotland kicked against no opposition after Estonia refused to agree to switch the kick-off time, 1996

One team in Tallinn, there's only one team in Tallinn.
SONG by Scotland fans when Estonia failed to turn up for a match v Scotland, 1996

Most Scotland supporters have woken up to the fact that wearing the kilt is probably the easiest way in the world of attracting the opposite sex.
HAGGIS SUPPER, Scotland fanzine, 1999

Who are the people?
We arra people!
RANGERS FANS call-response chant, 1960s

The Glaswegian definition of an atheist: a bloke who goes to Rangers–Celtic match to watch the football.
SANDY STRANG, Rangers supporter, in Stephen Walsh, Voices of the Old Firm, *1995*

In football a day is a decade and the game before is another history. But it's different in Old Firm matches – the fans love you if you play shite in other matches but great against Celtic.
MIKEL ARTETA, Spanish midfielder with Rangers, 2004

After I joined Celtic I was walking down a street in Glasgow when someone shouted: 'Fenian bastard.' I had to look it up. Fenian, that is.
MICK McCARTHY, Yorkshire-born Republic of Ireland manager, 1996

I'm a small, balding, ex-Communist, Celtic-supporting Catholic and Unionist. Therefore everyone seems to hate me.
DR JOHN REID MP, Labour, Secretary of State for Northern Ireland, 2001

I would rather watch Celtic than be a bishop.

RODERICK WRIGHT after relinquishing his post as Bishop of Argyll, 1996

I'm not a violent man but when you see the first flash of green or a Republic of Ireland jersey, something inside of you snaps.
RANGERS SUPPORTER, interviewed on Channel 4 documentary Football, Faith and Flutes, *1995*

They call themselves Protestants. But they say that just because they want to be different from Catholics. Most of them are atheists.
CELTIC SUPPORTER on Football, Faith and Flutes, *1995*

In Glasgow half the football fans hate you and the other half think they own you.
TOMMY BURNS, Celtic midfielder, 1987

For a while I did unite Rangers and Celtic fans. There were people in both camps who hated me.
MAURICE JOHNSTON on his spells on either side of Glasgow's great divide, 1994

I hear that couples sometimes arrive at the Mersey derby together but wearing opposing colours. If you did that in Glasgow you'd get lynched.
JOHN COLLINS, Everton and former Celtic midfielder, 1998

It angers me to see Rangers or Celtic fanatics getting all steamed up in the name of religion when most of them have never been near a church or a chapel in years.
DEREK JOHNSTONE, Rangers player, in Rangers: My Team, *1979*

Do you want your share of the gate money, Jock, or shall we just return the empties?
BILL SHANKLY to opposing manager Jock Stein after visiting Scots threw bottles when Liverpool beat Celtic in the European Cup-Winners' Cup, 1966

After the match against Inverness Caley [Celtic lost 3-2] I felt I was caught up in the Kosovo war, not a damaging football result. Some so-called fans covered my car in spit and shouted obscenities at me... It was Stone Age stuff from reptiles.
IAN WRIGHT, Celtic and former Arsenal striker, 2000

We were thrown to a veritable wild horde. It was a meeting of warriors where neither weakness nor nonchalance had a place. It was a test in the pure British tradition.
FABIEN BARTHEZ, Monaco goalkeeper, on the atmosphere at Rangers, 2000

Sigmund Freud once described humour as being as incongruous as a buckled wheel, but he never played the old Glasgow Empire on a wet Monday night after both Rangers and Celtic had lost on the Saturday.
KEN DODD, comedian, 2002

Sinatra would kill to sing here.

BILL SHANKLY, Liverpool manager, hails The Kop, 1964

Roman's got his roubles, Glazer's got his dollars. All we want from Rafa [Benitez] is five Euros.
BANNER as Liverpool won their fifth European Cup, 2005

The missus thinks I'm working
And I've lied to the gaffer
Coz I'm here in Istanbul
With Stevie G and Rafa
BANNER by Liverpool supporters in Istanbul, Champions' League final, 2005

Joey ate the Frogs' legs
Made the Swiss roll
Now he's Munching Gladbach
BANNER in praise of Liverpool defender Joey Jones, European Cup final, 1977

For those watching in blue and white, this is what the European Cup looks like
BANNER at the Liverpool v Chelsea Champions' League semi-final, 2007

Our Reason, Our Inspiration, Our Pride: 96
BANNER by Liverpool fans commemorating the 96 who died in 1989 at Hillsborough,
Champions' League final in Athens, 2007

We'll be in Seville. You'll be watching *The Bill*
BANNER by Celtic fans, aimed at Rangers' supporters during build-up to the UEFA Cup
final, 2003

We dream of playing in the shirt. Today God chose you. Play like we dream
BANNER by Manchester City fans, 2004.

Victoria! Betray him with me!
BANNER by Switzerland fans against Beckham's England, European Championship finals,
2004. Other Swiss supporters held up placards saying 'And me'

You can stick the league title up your arse
BANNER by AC Milan fans at the celebration of their Champions' League triumph, 2007.
The slogan, mocking Inter Milan's Serie A title, was unwittingly unfurled by vice-captain
Massimo Ambrosini

Mum, get the pasta on!
BANNER by Italy fans as Sweden and Denmark fought out the 2–2 draw which would
eliminate the Italians, European Championship finals, 2004

We've come to get our bicycles back
BANNER by Netherlands supporters at the match against West Germany, 1988. The Nazis had
confiscated the Dutch people's bikes during the Second World War

Jesus is a Wiganer
BANNER by Wigan fans after Jesus Seba was signed from Zaragoza, 1996

Brazil would pick Le Tiss
BANNER by Southampton fans protesting against his omission from the England squad v Brazil, 1995

Paul McGrath limps on water
BANNER by Derby fans in praise of the injury-blighted defender, 1997

We don't need Viagra to stay up
BANNER by Charlton fans, a month before their team were relegated, 1999

Our husbands think we're shopping in Dublin
BANNER by Republic of Ireland fans in Portugal, 1995

Sex and Drugs and Oranje Goals
BANNER at Dutch matches, Euro 2000

Forget Ulrika – There's only one Good Johnsen
BANNER by Chelsea fans in honour of Eidur Gudjohnsen, 2002

The Silence of the Rams
SLOGAN on anti-Derby T-shirt sold outside Nottingham Forest ground, 1993

Sex. Beer. Football. Have I forgotten something?
SLOGAN on Denmark supporters' T-shirts, European Championship finals, 2004

I don't really think it's much fun when 50,000 spectators are singing 'Posh Spice takes it up the a***' every weekend.
VICTORIA BECKHAM on the TV documentary Victoria's Secrets, *2000*

I thought I had seen it all when it comes to the fickleness of football folk. Then I heard the Spurs fans singing: 'There's only one Alan Sugar.'
MICK McCARTHY, Millwall manager, 1994

We seem to be lumbered with the 'Inger-lund, Inger-lund, Inger-lund' chant. That may be boring but at least everyone knows the words.
HELEN JOSLIN, Football Supporters' Association official, as England reached the semi-finals of the European Championship, 1996

I wish there were 10,000 more in the ground chanting for my blood.
LEN WALKER, Aldershot manager, after demonstration against him by 50 fans, 1983

Are you Tamworth in disguise?
SONG by Burton Albion fans as Manchester United were held 0–0 in the FA Cup against the non-league side, 2006

We all live in an Orange submarine.

SONG by Netherlands fans, European Championship finals, 2004

Who let the Frogs out?
SONG by Leicester fans to Arsenal's French-dominated side, 2003

Deep-fry yer pizzas, we're gonna deep-fry yer pizzas.
SONG by Scotland supporters in Italy, 2007

Live round the corner, you only live round the corner.
SONG by Chelsea supporters to Manchester United's supposedly London-based following, 2004

Crying on the telly, we saw you crying on the telly.
SONG by Manchester United fans to Chelsea supporters soon after the London club's exit from the Champions' League, 2004

What's it like to stink of fish?
SONG by Millwall fans on the visit of Grimsby, 2003

Cedric, Cedric, show us Uras.
SONG by Falkirk fans to the club's French defender Cedric Uras, 2007

He's fat, he's round, he's given us a ground, John Prescott, John Prescott.
SONG by Brighton fans after the Deputy Prime Minister approved the plan for a new stadium at Falmer, 2005

Peter Shilton, Peter Shilton, does your missus know you're here?
SONG by Arsenal North Bank to the Nottingham Forest keeper after a tabloid revealed he had been caught in a compromising position in a car late at night, 1980

We hate Jimmy Hill, he's a poof, he's a poof.
SONG by Scotland fans, 1990s. As a TV summariser, Hill had described David Narey's goal for Scotland v Brazil in the 1982 World Cup as a 'toe-poke'

We all agree, *Emmerdale*'s better than *Brookside*.
SONG by Halifax fans during FA Cup tie v Marine on Merseyside, 1992

We all agree, Asda is better than Harrods.
SONG by Charlton fans at Mohamed Al Fayed-owned Fulham, 1999

You must've come on a skateboard.
SONG by Nottingham Forest fans to Yeading's 60 followers, FA Cup tie, 2006

Our average away support is eight. We're the only football club where the players know all the fans by name.
BILL PERRIMAN, Yeading's commercial director, after the Ryman League side were drawn against Newcastle in the FA Cup, 2004

You fill up my senses
Like a gallon of Magnet
Like a packet of Woodbines
Like a good pinch of snuff
Like a night out in Sheffield
Like a greasy chip buttie
Come Sheffield United, come fill me again.
SONG by Sheffield United supporters to the tune of John Denver's 'Annie's Song', 1990s

There's this staunch Stoke City fan who's getting some earache from his missus. 'You'd rather go and watch Stoke than take me out,' she complains. 'Correction,' he replies. 'I'd rather go and watch Port Vale than take you out.'
PETE CONWAY, Potteries comedian and father of singer Robbie Williams, 1991

You dirty Northern bastards.

CHANT by Plymouth fans to Watford supporters, FA Cup quarter-final, 2007

Come and have a go if you think you're hard enough.
CHANT by Manchester City supporters when boxer Ricky Hatton, a City fan, took his seat at a match for the first time since winning the IBF world welterweight title, 2007

UNITED FANS: We want 10! We want 10!
IPSWICH FANS: We want one! We want one!
CHANT and response during the closing stages of Manchester United's 9–0 win, 1995

It wasn't so much the death threats or the vandalism, but when you sit with your family in the directors' box and hear a couple of thousand people chanting 'Gilbert Blades is a wanker', then you feel it's time to go.
GILBERT BLADES, on resigning as Lincoln chairman, in Anton Rippon's book Soccer: The Road to Crisis, *1982*

I always answer letters from supporters. It's the death threats I object to.

REG BURR, Millwall chairman, 1990

I understand and sympathise with their strong feelings, but I cannot accept their conservatism or parochialism.
ROBERT MAXWELL, Oxford chairman, on opposition from Oxford and Reading fans to his proposed merger of the clubs as Thames Valley Royals, 1983

You can't force people to sit down, even if they have a seat. They want to sing, and unless you're Val Doonican you can't do that sitting down.
KEVIN KEEGAN, Newcastle manager, speaking against all-seated stadia, 1992

In 10 years' time they will be sitting in the stand, watching the match, and their children will say: 'Daddy, did you really stand over there, in the wind and the rain? And did the man behind you urinate in your back pocket? And did you have a pie from that awful shop and a pint of beer thrust in your hand on a cold day?' The kids just will not understand.
SIR JOHN HALL, Newcastle chairman, 1995

The World Cup in America was a throwback to the 1950s, in the way that 'rival' supporters enjoyed mixing with each other. The only trouble I saw was at a concert in the Dodgers Stadium.
RON ATKINSON, ITV pundit and Aston Villa manager, 1994

The atmosphere in the USA isn't right. The American public look at a game as a day out to eat hot-dogs and popcorn. In Europe the fans can't eat because their stomachs are tight with tension.
ANTONIO MATERRESE, Italian FA president, 1994

The tension felt by football fans during penalty shoot-outs can trigger heart attacks and strokes in male spectators. The day Holland lost to France in Euro 96, deaths from heart attacks and strokes rose by 50 per cent.
DR MIRIAM STOPPARD, 2002

It may have been an awful night, but the meat and potato pies were brill.
'AWAY TRAVELLER', columnist in Crewe Alexandra supporters' newsletter after a visit to Halifax, 1983

It's bad enough having to go and watch Bristol City without having things stolen.
JUDGE DESMOND VOWDEN QC, sentencing a man who stole from a City fan's car, 1984

It is the right of every Englishman to fall asleep if he wants – particularly if he is watching Arsenal.
JUDGE MICHAEL TAYLOR quashing a fan's conviction for drunkenness after he dozed off during a match, 2004

I knew my days were numbered when I was warming up behind the goal at Parkhead and one of our fans shouted: 'Kinnaird, we like the Poll Tax more than we like you.'
PAUL KINNAIRD, Partick Thistle player, on his time with St Mirren, 1992

Football fanzines are a case of successful cultural contestation in and through sport.
JOHN HORNE, Staffordshire Polytechnic lecturer and co-author of a paper on fanzines in Sociology Review, 1991

The worse the team, the better the fanzine.

JOHN HORNE, sociology lecturer, 1991

Look Back in Amber
HULL CITY fanzine title, 1990s

Dial M for Merthyr
MERTHYR TYDFIL fanzine title, 1990s

Hyde! Hyde! What's the Score?
PRESTON fanzine title, 1990s. The name refers to North End's 26–0 win v Hyde in 1887

And Smith Must Score!
BRIGHTON fanzine title, named after the TV commentary to Gordon Smith's last-minute miss in 1983 FA Cup final, 1988

Sing When We're Fishing
GRIMSBY fanzine title, 1988

City Till I Cry
MANCHESTER CITY fanzine title, 1999

The only time I turn my pager off is when I'm watching Burnley.

ALASTAIR CAMPBELL, press secretary to Prime Minister Tony Blair, 1999

They're not happy in Burnley unless they're moaning. You could win 5–0 and they still wouldn't be happy. They're good folk, but they'll moan about owt.
STAN TERNENT, Burnley manager, 2003

He has very broad musical taste, anything from Elgar and Bach to Genesis and Supertramp. He also supports Arsenal, but then nobody's perfect.
BRIAN PEARSON, secretary to the Archbishop of Canterbury, Dr George Carey, 1990

I will die a Catholic. I will die an Arsenal fan. And I will die a Tory.
CHRIS PATTEN, former chairman of the Conservative party, 2000

When we won the league in '89 it was the most cosmic thing that had ever happened. Better than any orgasm ever.
EMMA YOUNG, Arsenal fan, quoted in Tom Watt, The End: 90 Years of Life on Arsenal's North Bank, *1993*

Fans are interested in their team being successful. If they wanted to see entertaining football rather than get results week in, week out, why don't all the Arsenal supporters follow Spurs or Chelsea?
DAVE BASSETT, Sheffield United manager, 1995

To celebrate Arsenal's defeat in Europe, 10 per cent off everything.
ADVERT by the food retailer World of Kosher in the Jewish Chronicle, *2004*

I do hate Arsenal. With a passion. No money in the world would ever tempt me to play for them.
TEDDY SHERINGHAM, Tottenham player and fan, 1996

Q: Which TV programme would you switch off?
A: Soaps and Luton on *Match of the Day*.
VINNIE JONES, childhood Watford fan, in Chelsea programme questionnaire, 1991

Q: If you could go back in time, where would you go?
A: Wembley 1967, QPR's finest hour.
PETE DOHERTY, Babyshambles singer, in Guardian Weekend *magazine questionnaire, 2007*

If your woman sleeps with your best mate, it's over. If the Rs' manager Ian Holloway slept with my best mate, QPR would still be my team.
DOHERTY, 2005

Football feeds the soul. [Manchester] United have fed mine a damn sight more than acting ever will. Acting has never been my dream. I'd give it up tomorrow to play just once for United.
JAMES NESBITT, Irish actor, 2003

I support West Bromwich Albion. I hate people who support teams like Chelsea. You have to support a proper club and follow them through everything.
GORAN IVANISEVIC, Croatian tennis player, 2007

When I was a boy kicking a ball in the streets of Belfast my favourite team were Wolves. It was around the time of their great games against the continentals and me and my friends used to play Wolves v Spurs.
GEORGE BEST in John Roberts's book Fall of a Superstar, *1973*

I am a human being. I support Aston Villa, but I am still a human being.
JOHN TAYLOR, prospective Conservative candidate for Cheltenham, on being labelled a
'bloody nigger' by fellow Tories, 1990

I still support the Villa but I don't like football as much as I did because the
game has been tailored to the wine-bar fraternity. The culture has gradually
been eradicated.
NIGEL KENNEDY, classical violinist, 1997

Villa have actually stopped scattering people's ashes on the pitch because some
players were put off the idea of doing sliding tackles, but they've made an
exception for me. It would be hilarious to be cremated wearing a Villa kit,
even if I was 80.
NIGEL KENNEDY, 2004

I like Aston Villa because the name is just so sweet. It sounds like a lovely spa.
TOM HANKS, American film star, 2003

You lose some, you draw some.
JASPER CARROTT, comedian/actor, on being a Birmingham City fan, 1979

Q: *What's the worst thing anyone's ever said to you? A: Do you support Sheffield Wednesday?*

SEAN BEAN, actor and Sheffield United director, in Guardian Weekend *magazine
questionnaire, 2007*

Any man who is paid to serve his country should never try to gain financially.
That may seem an old-fashioned idea, but I am very patriotic at every level.
I adore my county cricket team, Somerset, and my football team, because
I support the greatest team in England, Bristol Rovers.
JEFFREY ARCHER, author and Tory politician, during the Spycatcher *case, 1987*

It says on my birth certificate that I was born in the borough of West Bromwich, in the district of West Bromwich. I said all right, all right, I'll support the bloody Albion – no need to twist my arm.
FRANK SKINNER, comedian, 1995

My great heroes are Sir Stanley Matthews and Dave Beasant.

JUNE WHITFIELD, comedy actress and Wimbledon supporter, 1988

Q: What was the first gig you ever went to?
A: Wolves 2 Moscow Dynamo 1 on 9 November 1955.
ROBERT PLANT, Led Zeppelin singer, interviewed in Q magazine, 1993

As much as I love women and music, my first love will always be football.
ROD STEWART, pop singer, former Brentford trialist and Scotland fan, 1995

John Lennon has a feeling for words and storytelling and is in a pathetic state of near-literacy. He seems to have picked up bits of Tennyson, Browning and Robert Louis Stevenson while listening with one ear to the football results on the wireless.
CHARLES CURRAN MP, Conservative, in the House of Commons, 1964

Famous Carlisle United fans: Melvyn Bragg (unless he's in London, then he's an Arsenal supporter) and Hunter Davies (unless he's in London, then he's a Spurs fan).
TOTAL FOOTBALL magazine, 1995

You folks may be rightly proud of your title 'Football's Fairest Crowd', but for my part I would like to see a lot more partisanship in favour of Chelsea. All too many people come to Stamford Bridge to see a football match – instead of to cheer Chelsea.
TED DRAKE, Chelsea manager, in his programme column, 1952

I collected Chelsea programmes for years, took them to New York with me when I moved there. But when I arrived and unpacked, I discovered they had all been stolen. It was very sad.
VIDAL SASSOON, hairdresser, 1988

[Fidel] Castro called the victory by the Cuban volleyball team over the US a 'sporting, psychological, patriotic and revolutionary triumph'. At Chelsea we're quite happy to settle for three points.
SEBASTIAN COE, former athlete and Chelsea fan, 1990

When I called Coventry supporters a bunch of wankers, it was the best 15 grand I ever spent.
IAN WRIGHT, Arsenal striker, recalling one of the fines he incurred, 1999

Adrian attends Bromley Comprehensive and is a keen goalkeeper. In his spare time he likes listening to music and playing computer games. His favourite players have left the club.
CRYSTAL PALACE programme on the mascot for a game v Leicester, 1999

Fulham's support is an enigma. I asked one woman how she'd feel if we signed a £2m player. She said: 'We don't want £2m players here.'
KEVIN KEEGAN, 'chief operating officer' at Craven Cottage, 1998

Fans travelling to Elland Road should ridicule their abhorrent adversaries.

ADVICE on the official Manchester United website, 2003

Do they hate us? You go to take a corner at Elland Road and you've got 15,000 horrible skinheads in their end yelling murder at you.
RYAN GIGGS on Leeds fans, 1994

After Rio Ferdinand's transfer I saw a T-shirt at Leeds that said 'Traitors' and had my name and Joe's [Jordan], then Eric Cantona and Rio. And that's 25 years after I left. Some of the people wearing it weren't even born when I left.
GORDON McQUEEN, a centre-back who also left Elland Road for Old Trafford, 2003

I got soured against Alex Ferguson and to a lesser degree Arsene Wenger. I was behaving like a Leeds fan.
DAVID O'LEARY, Aston Villa and former Leeds manager, 2003

We'll take our fair share of support down there [to Gillingham]. We'll take support whether it's Kent or the Arctic circle.
KEVIN BLACKWELL, Leeds manager, on his club's first away match after relegation from the Premiership, 2004

Mr Stanley Heathman, married with five children, said they had never been in any doubt that they would be liberated. It was just a matter of how and when. He astonished one soldier by asking: 'Can you tell me – have Leeds been relegated?'
POOLED DESPATCH by journalists covering the Falklands War, 1982

It's often said that no club have a divine right to be in the First Division. Well, we bloody have.
THE HANGING SHEEP, Leeds fanzine, 1988. Leeds had been in the Second for six years

The accused claimed he was the reincarnated brother of Conan the Barbarian, that he was turning into an elk and had played for Leeds United. A defence psychiatrist said he was mad.
COURT REPORT, Daily Telegraph, 1988

Man offers marriage proposal to any woman with ticket for Leeds v Sheffield United game. Must send photograph (of ticket).
ADVERT in Yorkshire Evening Post as Second Division title race came to the boil, 1990

I was in the Leeds fans' end, chanting and going mad, and the fans were saying: 'Hang on, what's he doing here?'
NOEL WHELAN, Leeds-born Coventry striker, on continuing to follow his previous club when off duty, 1996

I even judge people's characters according to whether they support Manchester United.

ARDAL O'HANLON, Leeds-supporting comedian, 2001. His father, Irish politician Dr Rory O'Hanlon, is a Manchester United fan

I don't expect people to change the team they support easily. I've supported Leeds United all my life and always will.
NASSER HUSSAIN, England and Essex cricket captain, on suggestions that British-based Asians should support England, 2001

I told my lads that if they signed for Man United they would have to keep their shirts in their garage.
MARCUS WALMSLEY, Leeds fan, whose eight-year-old twins turned down United for Leeds, 1999

I'd like to have been born Bob Latchford and then become Nye Bevan when I was too old to play football.
DEREK HATTON, Everton fan and former Labour councillor in Liverpool, 1988

You always knew when it was derby week [on Merseyside]. The postman would say: 'We'll be ready for you.' Then the milkman would come round: 'You're in for it Saturday.' Then it would be the taxi driver. You never got away from it.
GORDON LEE, former Everton manager, in Brian Barwick and Gerald Sinstadt, The Great Derbies: Everton v Liverpool, *1988*

My father and mother had a mixed marriage: Liverpool and Everton. There were always rucks. I can't believe they're still together.
PETER REID, Leeds manager, 2003

If I found out a candidate was a closet Man United supporter I would have to think very hard about voting for them.
ADRIAN HENRI, poet, painter and Liverpool fan, during the General Election, 1992

What other set of fans steal tickets from their fellow supporters or out of the hands of children?

WILLIAM GAILLARD, UEFA director of communications, labelling Liverpool fans 'the worst in Europe' after ticketing problems in Athens, Champions' League final, 2007

The fans keep waiting for something to go wrong. I call it City-itis. It's a rare disease whose symptoms are relegation twice every three years.
JOE ROYLE, Manchester City manager, as the club chased promotion, 2000

I inherited two fatal flaws from my father: premature baldness and Manchester City, neither of which I can change.
HOWARD DAVIES, former deputy governor of the Bank of England, 1996

I was in a bar in Manchester after watching City and these people wanted me to sign their programmes. One wanted me to put: 'You can bank on City for promotion.'
NICK LEESON, City fan and the trader who brought down Barings Bank, 1999

I didn't watch the 1968 European Cup final. I never watch any match I think United might win.
MANCHESTER CITY fan on the TV programme Manchester United Ruined My Life, *1998*

Our new guitarist and bassist have to have nice taste in shoes and a good haircut, and not be a Man United fan. If they can do that, they're sorted.
LIAM GALLAGHER, City-supporting singer with Oasis, 1999

I'm too involved in show business to get involved as a City director. If I did spend money on football, I'd buy Old Trafford and put houses on it.
BERNARD MANNING, comedian and City follower of 65 years, 1999

The Stone Roses will reform the day Man City win the European Cup.
MANI, United-supporting bass guitarist with Primal Scream, 2005

If we win I'll jump off the stand roof with a parachute. If I lose I won't bother with the parachute.
MIKE SUMMERBEE, City fan and ex-player, before the derby against United, 2006

United, Kids, Wife – In That Order
BANNER displayed by Manchester United fans, 2007

'Not for Sale' seems a curiously outdated slogan, given that United have measured their lives in price tags for as long as anyone can remember.
PAUL HAYWARD, Daily Telegraph sports writer, on the fans' protests against the take-over by American billionaire Malcolm Glazer, 2005

United fans have no gratitude. They are a bunch of miserable, hypocritical, whingeing bastards. These are the people who are too stupid to acknowledge the part [former chairman] Martin Edwards played in making United the biggest club in the world.

TONY WILSON, TV presenter and United fan, dissenting from hostility towards new owner Malcolm Glazer and his family, 2005

United fans might support France, Argentina, China... We've got a Scottish manager, we're historically a Catholic club and England are deemed to be Protestant, Queen and country, and all that bollocks. I reckon 80 per cent of United fans don't support England. You wouldn't take a St George flag to Old Trafford. You might even be confronted.

RICHARD KURT, editor of United fanzine Red Issue, 2003

When we go away, there are all the supporters' coaches from places like Dover and Falmouth. I had never even heard of Falmouth. I like that passion. It seeps into you.

ALEX FERGUSON on Manchester United's nationwide following, 1995

Q: How many Man United fans does it take to change a lightbulb?
A: Three. One to change the bulb, one to buy the 2007 lightbulb-changing commemorative DVD and one to drive the other two back to Devon.

'QUICK QUIZ' in the Sun, 2007

Fans can get very snooty about football. So a couple of ponces from Hampstead support Man United? Good luck to them.

PAUL WHITEHOUSE, comedian, actor and Welsh-born Tottenham fan, 1999

The further you go from home, the more of the sad bastards there are. Kent is full of them. Half the kids who go to my lad's school take their dinner in a Stretford Sam lunch box, tucked away in a Fred the Red rucksack.

MANCHESTER CITY fanzine, King of the Kippax, on United fans, 1999

I love Newcastle, I love that raw passion. I remember being there once and hearing newspaper vendors shouting: 'Sensation! Andy Cole Toe Injury!' Most people use the word 'sensation' for 'Major Resigns' or 'Aids Spreading Over Country'. It's unbelievable. Glasgow's like that.

ALEX FERGUSON, 1995

With all those replica strips in the stands, coming to Newcastle is like playing in front of 40,000 baying zebras.
DAVID PLEAT, Sheffield Wednesday manager, 1997

During the kerfuffle over Michael Heseltine's pit closures, Brian Clough led a march past my surgery, which is a short walk from the City Ground. Forest were heading for relegation at the time and I threatened to lead a counter-march past the ground.
KENNETH CLARKE MP, Conservative, Nottingham Forest fan, in Football and the Commons People, 1995

I've got this tattoo on my arm that says '100 per cent Blade'. When we were filming the steamy scenes in *Lady Chatterley's Lover*, Ken Russell used to hide it with a strategically placed fern.
SEAN BEAN, actor and Sheffield United supporter, 1996

I did my grieving when I was kicked out of the band. Frankly, I'm more concerned about how Port Vale get on in the FA Cup tonight.
ROBBIE WILLIAMS as Take That broke up hours before Vale beat Everton, the Cup holders, 1996

Do you want me to buy a left-back or help to save children's lives? Are people dying as a result of Port Vale's troubles? No.
WILLIAMS on why he donated money to a children's hospice rather than invest in Vale, 2003

Supporting a second team in the Premier League is like Yasser Arafat saying he has a soft spot for Judaism.

NICK HANCOCK, TV presenter and Stoke City fan, 1997

Can anything be done about entertaining us after the kick-off?
STOKE SUPPORTER during discussion of pre-match entertainment during the club's AGM, 1999

What a nightmare. I'm a Tottenham fan and I get cuffed to you.
TONY ADAMS, Arsenal captain, on what was said by the prisoner handcuffed to him following his arrest for drink-driving, 1998

When socialists fall out, the Tories rejoice. When Sheffield Wednesday supporters fall out, the gods weep.

ROY HATTERSLEY, Wednesdayite and ex-deputy leader of the Labour party, 2000

All that Sheffield has talked about for months is football. If there is a pit closure, or a factory goes down the pan, the MP has to get involved, so why shouldn't we use our influence to try to save this club?
JOE ASHTON MP, Labour, Wednesday fan and former director, responding to accusations of interfering in the club's affairs by arguing that Danny Wilson should be relieved of the manager's job, 2000

I genuinely do struggle to understand why some people seem to have suffered a mini emotional collapse following our relegation. Bitter disappointment and hurt I can understand, but the fathers and grandfathers of some of our complainants were able to show far greater resilience under far worse conditions [in World War II].
TERENCE BROWN, West Ham chairman, 2003

Anyone who has had to support the Labour party these past five years knows what it's like to be a West Ham fan. There is a great similarity in the 'Oh, fucking hell', head-in-hands response you have to what they do, the own goals and ridiculous defeats.
BILLY BRAGG, singer-songwriter and socialist, 1991

You need players with big balls at West Ham. The one thing I ask before signing is can you handle 35,000 crowds because they're gonna give you stick. 'Oi mate, you're fat, you've got big ears, a fat arse, a big hooter. You're ugly. I'll do your bird a favour when I see her down the pub.'
ALAN PARDEW, West Ham manager, 2004

Will the owner of a horse attached to a rag-and-bone cart in the visitors' car park return to his vehicle immediately.
ANNOUNCEMENT at Cardiff City when West Ham were the visitors, 2004

As an ex-Southampton player I'd normally have got stick, but in the circumstances I was seen as doing Pompey a favour. The supporters did sing 'We've got a Scummer in our goal', but with affection.
DAVE BEASANT, veteran goalkeeper, helping out Portsmouth during an injury crisis, 2003

They're very jealous of Portsmouth's history, both as a city and a club. What have they got? King Canute, who got his feet wet. The *Titanic,* which sank. Saints may have a nice new stadium at St Mary's, but there's a Pompey shirt buried under the centre circle. I know because I saw it put there.
MIKE HANCOCK MP, Liberal Democrat, 2003

Trying to explain why we hate Palace is like trying to explain why grass is green. We just do.
ATTILA THE STOCKBROKER, poet-ranter and Brighton fan, 1995

Everyone talks about what people like David Beckham and Graeme Le Saux have to put up with. But I can assure you it's far worse in the First Division than the Premiership. When a visiting player gets a red card, it's the highlight of the day for some home supporters. They jump up and down with delight as though they have just won the game.
IAN WRIGHT, former England striker, on life with Burnley, 2000

At the Worthington Cup final, when there was trouble on the pitch, with Robbie Savage involved, there was this guy behind me yelling: 'Savage, you cheating, long-haired, gypsy Welsh cunt.' I had to turn to him and say: 'Oi mate, less of the Welsh.'
PAUL WHITEHOUSE, comedian, actor and Welsh-born Tottenham fan, 1999

It'll be a good day for the burglars and one when the sheep will be left in peace.
DICK CAMPBELL, Brechin City manager, on the exodus of fans from the city (population 10,000) to Rangers for a Scottish Cup tie, 2001

The pub landlords in Walsall will be in the Bahamas in two weeks' time on the money they take tonight.
RAY GRAYDON, Walsall manager, after a derby win at Wolves, 1999

If it was one of our meat pies, it could have done more damage than a brick.

ANDY RITCHIE, Oldham manager, after food was thrown at the referee during an FA Cup match v Chelsea, 1999

Q: What's the craziest request you have ever had from a fan?
A: Can you do your brother's autograph?
CARL HODDLE, Barnet midfielder and brother of Glenn, answering a Sun questionnaire, 1995

Did I get any enjoyment from my visit to Marston Road? As a matter of fact I did. Guessing the contents of the liquid which came out of the tea urn fired my imagination for some time.
LETTER from a disaffected Stafford Rangers fan to the Staffordshire Newsletter, 1992

When Saturday comes, a hell of a lot of lads go home with a hard-on.
JULIE BURCHILL, writer and critic, claiming a homo-erotic motivation for male football fans in her book Burchill on Beckham, 2001

Show me a man who loves football and nine times out of 10 you'll be pointing at a really bad shag.
BURCHILL in Burchill on Beckham, 2001

Diehard football fans are much more optimistic about their sex appeal after a victory.
DR MIRIAM STOPPARD claiming football could induce hormonal change, 2002

You won't get me flicking on a [football] phone-in. I'd rather listen to a game of chess on the radio. Phone-ins are platforms for idiots.
JOE ROYLE, Manchester City manager, 2001

There's a new breed of flash young executives who think they've got the right to call to account anyone in the world.
RON GREENWOOD, England manager, after the Wembley crowd booed his team v Spain, 1981

Football's getting too polished and nice and trendy now. You get media people in London saying: 'Football's the new rock 'n' roll.' For all us working class, football's a way of life, always has been.
SEAN BEAN, actor and Sheffield United fan, 1996

I went with two friends to watch Forest's game at Barnsley. It cost over £60 to watch the football equivalent of what French farmers have been feeding their cattle.
LETTER to Nottingham's Football Post, 1999

Some people come to Old Trafford and I don't think they can spell football, let alone understand it. They have a few drinks and a prawn sandwich and don't realise what's going on out on the pitch.
ROY KEANE, Manchester United captain, on the club's corporate supporters, 2000

The man in the street has been pushed aside for the corporate fan.
MARTIN O'NEILL, Leicester manager, 1999

The average working lad can't understand or relate to the money involved in the game, but he'll go along with it if he believes it will make his team better.
ALEX FERGUSON in interview with Racing Post, 1999

They sit and admire the stadium, waiting to be entertained as if they were at a musical. We have lots of visitors for whom it's a weekend holiday, and that's no use to me or the players.
FERGUSON on Manchester United's changing support, 1997

There is an element of people coming to Old Trafford for the first time, looking around the place and forgetting there is a game on.
FERGUSON urging 'control' of corporate supporters, 1999

Some fans would prefer we went back to Plough Lane and played Third Division football. They aren't true supporters. They'll end up buying a season ticket for Fulham.
CHARLES KOPPEL, Wimbledon chairman, arguing for the club to relocate to Milton Keynes, 2001

If you listened to the fans you wouldn't have a club. I spend 40 per cent of my working life here for nothing. So I'm going to listen to someone who pays £15 on a Saturday? Leave it out.
BARRY HEARN, Leyton Orient chairman, 1999

Same old story. Lost 5–0. Sometimes I wonder why I couldn't have been born in Liverpool.
RICHARD O. SMITH writing in Boston United fanzine Behind Your Fences *about a game at Cheltenham, 1990*

Why hasn't anyone taken me to a soccer game? There must be some English boy who wants to take me, for God's sake. I'll just have to cry and hope that someone will take me.
GWYNETH PALTROW, American actress, 2000

I'm looking for a woman but I keep landing on the same big old bloke.
STUART PEARCE, Manchester City manager, after jumping into the crowd to celebrate a goal in the derby defeat of United, 2006

eleven

BOARDROOM

The most amazing men in football are the Premiership chairmen. Your heroes might be on the pitch. Mine are in the boardroom.
DAVID GOLD, co-owner of Birmingham City, to the press, 2002

I don't give a fuck about football protocol and the other club owners. They want me to sit and have lunch before the games. Fuck that. I don't go to football to drink Chardonnay in the boardroom with those tossers. I go to win games.
SIMON JORDAN, Crystal Palace chairman, 2004

I see other clubs' chairmen as the enemy. I want to go in there and beat them up.

JORDAN, 2006

A fortunate few clubs are richer than ever... All too often the source of this wealth is individuals with little or no history of interest in the game, who have happened upon football as a means of serving some hidden agenda. Having set foot in the sport, seemingly out of nowhere, they proceed to throw pornographic amounts of money at it.
SEPP BLATTER, president of FIFA, football's world governing body, 2005

Call me old-fashioned, but we don't need his money and we don't want his sort. They only see an opportunity to make money. They know sweet FA about our football, and we don't want these types involved.
PETER HILL-WOOD, Arsenal chairman, on reports of interest in the club by American businessman Stan Kroenke, 2007

I don't really believe that foreign billionaires get involved because of their love of English football.
DELIA SMITH, TV chef and majority shareholder in Norwich City, 2007

I couldn't have sold to a foreigner. I didn't want an ex-Siamese prime minister here, thank you very much. This is an English club.
SIR JACK HAYWARD, former Wolves owner-chairman, after selling to Liverpudlian Steve Morgan, 2007

The only sure way to make a small fortune from football is to start with a big one.
JEFF RANDALL, BBC business correspondent, 2003

Football is a shambolically run business, run by greedy and vain people who seem only to act in self-interest. And none of them seems to realise that if they carry on the way they are going, they will destroy the business.
TOM BOWER, investigative reporter, in his book Broken Dreams: Vanity, Greed and the Souring of British Football, *2003*

That was a nasty era in my life... I met some very horrible people in that industry and it made me very guarded and suspicious.
SIR ALAN SUGAR on his time as Tottenham owner, 2005

Time was when you couldn't name a football club chairman let alone recognise one in the street. They were grey-suited men who drank white wine in the bowels of the stand and watched unrecognised from the best seats. Nowadays there is an egotistical breed of chairman who think they know it all.
JIMMY GREAVES, former England striker, in his Sun *column, 2003*

[Roman] Abramovich knows nothing about football. I already have his sword sticking into me... Even if I win the European Cup, I'll be sacked.
CLAUDIO RANIERI, Chelsea manager, on the club's new Russian billionaire owner, 2004

Abramovich spat on Russia by buying Chelsea. He abandoned our teams, which need support.

YURI LUZHOV, Mayor of Moscow, 2003

If he [Abramovich] helped me in training we would be bottom of the league. And if I had had to work in his world of big business we would be bankrupt.
JOSE MOURINHO, Chelsea manager, 2005

We passed like ships in the night. He was a huge yacht, I was a little rowing boat.
GRAEME LE SAUX recalling leaving Chelsea as Abramovich arrived, 2006

Mr Abramovich is almost like one of the lads, if a billionaire can be.
JOHN TERRY, Chelsea captain, 2005

He's a real Chelsea fan. When we lose a difficult match, he's sulking and there are tears in his eyes.
BRUCE BUCK, Chelsea chairman, on Abramovich's 'devotion', 2007

Malcolm Glazer risks plunging [Manchester] United into a financial meltdown that would make what happened at Leeds look like the equivalent of missing an HP payment on the telly.
SEAN BONES, spokesman for Shareholders United, a group opposed to the American tycoon's takeover at Old Trafford, 2005

[Malcolm] Glazer is a guy who looks more like he should be propping up a bar somewhere, or perhaps a bar owner. I just hope he has the humility to let other people make the decisions. People who know about football.
ERIC CANTONA, former United player, 2005

Mr Lerner was pleasantly surprised that I knew some things about American football, though he may have suspected I'd done a bit of homework the night before.
MARTIN O'NEILL, Aston Villa manager, on the club's American chairman Randy Lerner, who also owned the Cleveland Browns gridiron franchise, 2007

It's not my club, it's the fans' club. I'm just here as the maintenance man.

MILAN MANDARIC, Portsmouth owner and chairman, 2004

If you made a lot of money selling biscuits, buy our club.
SONG by West Ham fans (to the tune of the Club biscuit advert), after Icelandic entrepreneur Eggert Magnusson bought into the club, 2006

The story of the most popular football club chairman ever.
SLOGAN on a video about Peter Ridsdale's reign at Leeds, 2001

All this home-grown talent we've nurtured means we want them to stay to win trophies with Leeds United. They are not for sale. We're a public company and my responsibility is to the shareholders. But the responsibility is also to win things.
PETER RIDSDALE as Leeds challenged for top place in the Premiership, 2000

I have no intention of running away. When I go I would like to think that Leeds will be flying again.
RIDSDALE on being barracked at what proved to be his last home game before resigning, 2003

We lived the dream.
RIDSDALE on the spending he sanctioned when David O'Leary was manager, 2003

Leeds United may have lived the dream, but I inherited the nightmare.
PROFESSOR JOHN McKENZIE, Ridsdale's successor, 2003

But whose dream was it? The fans bought it, of course, but the real dream was that the people behind Ridsdale thought they were going to make oodles of money. Football was never meant to be like that.
JOHNNY GILES, former Leeds player, after Ridsdale resigned, 2003

Had we not invested, we wouldn't have had five years of going to Madrid and Milan and Barcelona. The fans want a successful team. For five years we've delivered that, then got it wrong. Should we have spent so heavily? Probably not.
RIDSDALE, 2003

Peter has had a nice ride and been very well paid for his time at Leeds. It's not as if he's going to end up in a grotty little bedsit.
SIMON JOSE, co-founder of Leeds United Independent Fans' Association, on Ridsdale's departure from the plc and club boards, 2003

[Ridsdale] used to sign autographs like the players. I got sick of him jumping up and down in the directors' box, shouting instructions. He has been like a kid in a sweetie shop and he made himself sick.
HOWARD SYMONDS, businessman, resigning his £3,000-a-season seat in the Leeds directors' box after the sale of Jonathan Woodgate to Newcastle, 2003

The Leeds programme has a team-sheet so glossy that it is impossible to write on it. They should have given Peter Ridsdale chequebooks like that.
DAVID HOPPS, sports writer, reporting in the Guardian, 2005

There are no more goldfish. I ate them with my tuna sandwich at lunch.
GERALD KRASNER, Leeds chairman, 2004. The goldfish kept by Ridsdale became a symbol of Leeds's free-spending ways

I want to show people who criticise me that I can run a football club well. Leeds was a dream come true, but Barnsley's even more exciting.
RIDSDALE on taking control at the South Yorkshire club, 2003

When I left Leeds I had two options – to jump off the top of a tall building or to cope. I decided to cope.
RIDSDALE on succeeding Sam Hammam as Cardiff chairman, 2007

If I was in Ken Bates's shoes I would wake every morning praying to God and thanking him that Pini Zahavi put £19m in his pocket [by bringing Roman Abramovich to Chelsea]. He is history as far as English football is concerned.
PINI ZAHAVI, Israeli football agent, on the 'revolting character' Bates, 2005

When Ken Bates jumps in the water, the sharks jump out.
DAVE ALLEN, Sheffield Wednesday chairman, on the former Chelsea chairman's interest in taking over at Hillsborough, 2004

There's nothing else in life except soccer and a good woman. I've got a good woman so I need the soccer.
KEN BATES on why he bought control of Leeds United, 2005

It's better than lying in bed, drinking gin and tonic and waiting to die.

BATES on coping with the financial problems at Leeds, 2006

If I had my time over again, I'd be a general or a bishop.
BATES, 2005

Bates always had to be one up on you. If you told him you'd been to Tenerife, he'd say he'd been to Elevenerife.
DAVID SPEEDIE, former Chelsea striker, 2003

With Ken Bates it's par for the course. He says derogatory things about a lot of people. It's sad that he has to be like that.
CHRIS SUTTON, shortly before leaving Chelsea for Celtic, 2000

We see a lot of Ken Bates. He'll always have a laugh and a joke with you. At your expense, obviously.

GRAEME LE SAUX, Chelsea defender, 2000

Ken Bates here. I understand you're richer than I am, so we'd better get together.
BATES, Chelsea chairman, in call to wealthy supporter Matthew Harding, 1994. Harding put in £24m over the next two years

The difference is that Bates appears to think Chelsea is his club, while Harding's attitude is that it's our club.
ROSS FRASER, chairman of Chelsea Independent Supporters' Association, as the Bates-Harding rift worsened, 1995

When David Mellor is prepared to put money into the club – or even pay for his own tickets – he will be entitled to his opinion.
MATTHEW HARDING after Mellor, a Conservative MP, criticised him while hosting a radio phone-in, 1995

I'm off to my 300-acre farm. You lot can bugger off to your council houses.
BATES to the press after Chelsea's relegation, 1988

I'm not star-struck around players. How could I be? I'm the biggest star here.
BATES, 1997

Has any chairman since Mao had more faith in his own opinions than Ken Bates? If laying down the law was an Olympic sport, the Chelsea chief would be staggering under the weight of gold medals.
ALEX FERGUSON in his autobiography, 2000

Some fans said: 'We don't want a bloody Londoner running Leeds.' I said: 'You've got a problem then, haven't you? Nobody in bloody Leeds wants to run Leeds, do they?' I see all these bloody millionaires with money coming out of their ears. Talk about long pockets and short hands.
BATES after six months as Leeds chairman, 2005

Ninety-nine per cent of the letters and emails [from fans] are supporting us. That's as good as Saddam Hussein got – and he was fiddling the figures.
BATES after beating off other bidders to buy debt-ridden Leeds back from the administrators, 2007

Why have I bought Birmingham City? Because football is good for society.
DAVID SULLIVAN, Daily Sport publisher, 1993

When I used to watch Roy Rogers on his white horse, Trigger, he never lost. He always won because he was the good guy. The bloke on the black horse with the mask, the baddie who killed, raped and pillaged, always got beat. I want that to continue here.
DAVID GOLD, Birmingham chairman and Sullivan's co-owner, 2002

I played with Johnny Haynes. It was at snooker, but hey, I played with him.

GOLD on his spell as a Fulham youth player, 2002

The chairman, Doug Ellis, said he was right behind me. I told him I'd sooner have him in front of me where I could see him.
TOMMY DOCHERTY after being fired as Aston Villa manager, 1970

When Tommy [Docherty] does his rounds of after-dinner speaking, he uses me at every opportunity. Greavsie [Jimmy Greaves] calls me 'Deadly' and lads in the street shout: 'Oi, Deadly!' As long as Aston Villa's name is attached to it, I don't mind. If you operate at a high profile, you have to accept criticism.
DOUG ELLIS, Villa chairman, 1991

To be fair, although there's been 11 Villa managers in roughly 30 years, there's only been seven I've sacked.
ELLIS, 1999

Aston Villa is the reason I get up every day and the day I'm not mentally able to hold my own with all the young whipper-snappers in this business is when I'll call it a day.
ELLIS at 77 years old, 2000

This is my life. I kick every ball and sign every cheque.

ELLIS, 2000

The trouble with our chairman is that he's living in a time warp.
JOHN GREGORY, Villa manager, 2000. He later had to make a public apology to Ellis

They're building another stand at Villa Park. They're going to call it 'The Other Doug Ellis Stand'.
KEN BATES, Chelsea chairman, in Jason Tomas's book Soccer Czars, *1996*

Six months [after trying to buy Chelsea] he bought Fulham, having discovered that he was a lifelong Fulham supporter.
BATES on Mohamed Al Fayed buying control of Chelsea's neighbours, 2002

Fayed certainly didn't know anything about the game although he pretended he did. I asked him once if he'd played football as a boy and he replied, 'Of course.' I asked what position. He said: 'Captain.' He also insisted he'd supported Fulham for years and used to watch players called Jimmy Haynes and Bobby Robinson.
MAX CLIFFORD, PR guru, in his book Read All About It, *2005*

The trouble with Fayed is that he doesn't understand British traditions and institutions. I mean, he took over Fulham and made them successful.
ANDY HAMILTON, comedy writer, on BBC Radio 4's News Quiz, *1999*

It's ironic that it's left to me to save the England team when no one will let me have a UK passport.
FAYED after agreeing to let Fulham manager Kevin Keegan coach England part-time, 1999

This is a message for possibly the best supporters in the world. We need a 12th man. Where are you? Let's be 'avin' you!
DELIA SMITH, Norwich City co-owner, in an impromptu loudspeaker appeal to fans during half-time v Manchester City, 2005

Delia, back in the kitchen, luv.
POSTING on the BBC football message board after her outburst, 2005

A few weeks before I left Southampton, the team went clay-pigeon shooting. I was ready to fire, looking through the sight, when the chairman [Rupert Lowe] came into view. It was very tempting, I can tell you.
JIM MAGILTON, Ipswich midfielder, 2004

Swing Lowe
Swing Rupert Lowe
Swinging from the Itchen Bridge
SONG by Southampton fans, 2006

We will not be pushed around by a bunch of north London yobbos.

LOWE as Tottenham courted Southampton manager Glenn Hoddle, 2001

How much have I put in? I wouldn't get much change from £75m, but I'd only have given it to the government on my death. I might as well spend it and give the people of Wigan some pleasure while I'm at it.
DAVE WHELAN, Wigan chairman-owner, after the club completed their rise from the Northern Premier League to the Premiership, 2005

You can spend your life in smart restaurants, but I've done all that. To be honest, I'd rather have a burger and a cup of Bovril.
GREG DYKE, former director general of the BBC, before his first match as Brentford chairman, 2006

My mum rang up when she heard I wanted to take over the club and said: 'Oh son, don't.' Only an 11-year-old boy would want to get into something like this. You have to have that mixture of romantic and businessman. I know it's a risk, but I can't think of anything I'd risk more for.
BILL KENWRIGHT, theatre director, on his bid for control of Everton, 1998

I remain the father of Wimbledon and wanted to be their hero. I have a lot of love and happiness for AFC Wimbledon. We are together in mind.
SAM HAMMAM, former Wimbledon FC owner, on the fans' 'breakaway' club, 2003

We will serve sheep's testicles as a delicacy in the boardroom. There are plenty of sheep in Wales so it's right that they should make some representation at Ninian Park.
HAMMAM, having left Wimbledon and taken over at Cardiff City, 2000

Alex Ferguson told me I was mad buying Cardiff and gave me the address of a good psychiatrist.
HAMMAM, 2000

Sometimes you need to employ someone who is a poacher turned gamekeeper. They know how the hooligans think.
HAMMAM after it was revealed that the Cardiff chairman's bodyguard was a convicted 'football' hooligan, 2002

I'd rather die and have vultures eat my insides than merge with Crystal Palace.
HAMMAM, Wimbledon chairman, on reports of a possible merger of the two Selhurst Park-based clubs, 1992

I just hope I can grab the heart of this man [Kjell-Inge Rokke] and make him understand. The man lives in a world of accountants, not football. I must make him love us. We must show him our legs and cleavage to make him fancy us.
HAMMAM on Wimbledon's Norwegian co-owner, 1999

Every time we lose, I feel like running a warm bath and slashing my wrists.
SIR JACK HAYWARD, Wolves chairman, 2003

When my son [Jonathan, Wolves chairman] asks me for more money to buy another player, I tell him: 'This is blackmail.' He says: 'Do you want to get into the Premiership?' I say yes. Then he says: 'Do you want to win the FA Cup?' I say yes. Then I say: 'Oh, go and buy him then.'
SIR JACK, 1995

A friend has described me as the village vicar of football-club chairmen, which I rather liked, but I've discovered there are people in the game who would slit your throat for tuppence.
JONATHAN HAYWARD, Wolves chairman and Northumberland farmer, 1996

I don't want Wolves fans to think I'm off my trolley, but Dermot Reeve [Warwickshire's cricket captain] is the kind of character I'm looking for as manager.
JONATHAN HAYWARD, Wolves chairman, 1995

I've never taken a penny out of Wolves and never want to. I only want an emotional return, not a financial one. If I go and stay with the team on a Friday night, I settle my own bill. When I eat in Sir Jack's [restaurant at the ground], I pay. I don't take a salary like some chairmen and I don't draw any expenses. That's why I was upset by this fan's remark, though I have to say that the letter he handed me was nicely typed and obviously thought out.
SIR JACK HAYWARD, stung by a supporter's criticism, 2000

I only hope Tony Adams plays because he's the only name I know. All these Viallis, Vieiras and Viagras. I prefer old-fashioned names like Cullis and Wright.
SIR JACK before Wolves' FA Cup semi-final v Arsenal, 1998

They thought the Golden Tit – me – would go on for ever.
SIR JACK on his £60m outlay on players and ground improvements, 1997

My friends in America say I must love it [owning his home-town club] but unless we're 6–0 up with 15 minutes left I hate it.
SIR JACK after Wolves again failed to reach the Premiership, 2002

Elton John and myself developed a relationship – it's a bit dangerous saying that about us, isn't it? For a period I was his reality.
GRAHAM TAYLOR, Watford manager, on his pop-star chairman, 2000

'Candle In The Wind' remains one of my favourite songs. But Elton and I had this agreement that I would tell him nothing about music if he told me nothing about football, and it worked well.
GRAHAM TAYLOR, 1991

I used to have to tour when I didn't really want to, to be able to afford to buy a centre-forward.
ELTON JOHN on his days of bankrolling Watford, 1995

An overview of my career is usually: glasses, homosexuality, Watford Football Club, tantrums, flowers. But the music was pretty phenomenal.
SIR ELTON JOHN, 2007

Ron Noades is the Fidel Castro of football, an enlightened despot rather than a dictator.

STEVE COPPELL, Crystal Palace manager, on his chairman, 1992

Beware of the clever sharp men who are creeping into the game.
WILLIAM McGREGOR, founder of the Football League, in League Football and the Men Who Made It, *1909*

A man who gives himself up to football, body and soul, will take risks and get himself entangled in such a way as he would never consider in the conduct of his own business.
SIR FREDERICK WALL, FA secretary, in his book Fifty Years of Football, *1935*

We shall all be rich one day when we've got a BUPA hospital and a hotel on this ground.
ERNIE CLAY, Fulham chairman, 1979

I've still got my old school report. It says I was dyslexic, backward, mentally deficient and illiterate – all the qualifications you need to be a football club chairman.
GEORGE REYNOLDS, Darlington chairman, 2000

The ideal board of directors should comprise three men – two dead and the other dying.
TOMMY DOCHERTY, manager with numerous clubs, 1977

I'm drinking from a cup today. I'd like a mug but they're all in the boardroom.

DOCHERTY, 1988

The biggest fans in the world are the chairmen, not the blokes on the terraces. Real fans? What does 'real' mean? A real fan is someone who works really hard for nothing, gives up all his time for nothing, worries all the time, and on top of that lot, puts in his own money.
BARRY HEARN, Leyton Orient chairman-owner, 2001

I'd always thought of chairmen as tight bastards. Now I can only applaud them for the money they put in and the abuse they take.
BARRY FRY in praise of his Peterborough chairman, Peter Boizot, 2000

I had hair when I became chairman. Not any longer.
PETER HILL, Hereford chairman, on using his toupee 'to wipe away my tears' after relegation from the league, 1997

Nowadays chairmen seem to live in Spain. That bloke who was at Forest [Irving Scholar] lived in Monaco. I often wonder how people like that got into football. You can't love football and live abroad, because you miss the one thing you want to watch, your team.
BRIAN CLOUGH, former manager, 1999

I have spoken to more than one chairman who has told me the quality they look for on a manager's CV is an ability to affect the share price.
HOWARD WILKINSON, FA technical director, 1999

Football attracts a certain percentage of nobodies who want to be somebodies at a football club.
BRIAN CLOUGH, Nottingham Forest manager, 1979

Football hooligans? Well, there are the 92 club chairmen for a start.
CLOUGH, 1980

I've never been so insulted by anyone in football as this little upstart puppy.
DENIS HILL-WOOD, Arsenal chairman and Old Etonian, responding to Clough, 1980

I am struck by the parallels between the disorder which characterises the
approach of some football boardrooms and the disorderly behaviour of a
minority of the game's followers.
NEIL MACFARLANE MP, Conservative, Minister for Sport, 1983

Let club directors make a hash of the affairs of their own teams, but spare
England the catastrophe of their attentions.
*LEN SHACKLETON, journalist and former England player, on the committee of club directors
who selected the national team, 1958*

Have you ever had an octogenarian English comedian at training before –
apart from FA committee members?
NORMAN WISDOM, comic actor, to Sven-Göran Eriksson in Albania, 2001

Soccer is run by second-rate conmen. Petit bourgeois, frustrated small
businessmen. It's a tragedy, because football is very important socially.
EAMON DUNPHY, Republic of Ireland midfielder, 1973

Football chairmen are, almost to a man, butchers and sausage-meat
manufacturers, pork-pie impresarios, industrial and property moguls.
DAVID TRIESMAN, sociologist, in Seven Days socialist newspaper, 1973

We don't recognise any supporters' organisations... I never go to supporters'
dinners; it only costs a fiver or so, but then they think they own you. I never
accept money from supporters' organisations; they hand you a couple of
cheques for a few thousand and the next thing you know they are demanding
a seat on the board. My ambition is for the club to function completely
without any money coming through the turnstiles at all. That is the road
to Utopia.
BOB LORD, Burnley chairman and butcher in the town, 1974

One wonders today what some businesses would be like if they were run on
the same haphazard lines as most football clubs still are. The amateur director
has been kicked out of most industrial and commercial boardrooms. But not
in football.
DEREK DOUGAN, Wolves striker, in Football as a Profession, 1974

When I was a director of Sheffield United for six months, the chairman told me normal business standards didn't apply in football. It was the most stupid advice I ever had.
MIKE WATTERSON, Derby chairman, 1982

Normal business principles don't apply in football.
LIONEL PICKERING, publisher and Derby chairman-owner, 1992

Industries go to the wall every day... Football's a business, it's no different, and it is not going to be run by the blazer brigade any more. It needs to be run as a business by businessmen.
SIR JOHN HALL, Newcastle chairman and advocate of a closed-shop, two-division Premier League, 1995

Football is an emotional game and that's where it's different from your average major business.

DAVID SHEEPSHANKS, Ipswich chairman, 2001

I entered as just AN Other, a member of the board, simply to do a job, i.e. finance director. No loyalty or love, but a cold, clinical job. I ended up falling in love like the rest of you, which became the most expensive love life man can imagine.
REG BREALEY, Sheffield United chairman, in message to supporters, 1990

People tell me: 'You must have better things to spend your money on.' But I have no desire for huge yachts in Monte Carlo. I'm just a homely boy from East Northants who enjoys doing what I do.
MAX GRIGGS, chairman of Rushden and Diamonds and the Doc Martens footwear empire, on ploughing millions into the then non-league club, 1995

I went out to buy a car for the missus and came back with a football club that cost me £5m just to clear the debts.
GEORGE REYNOLDS, Darlington chairman, 1999.

Wolves, Derby, Blackburn: these fans with money pour it in, the club lights up, then it fizzles away. Doesn't work. End of story.
KEN BATES, Chelsea chairman, 1995

Football clubs are great community institutions, to which supporters feel a huge sense of belonging. But the reality is that they are owned by private businessmen, using the clubs for their own purposes, who can ride roughshod over them. And the authorities are absolutely incapable of monitoring the game.
PETER KILFOYLE MP, Labour, on the ownership of Everton, 1999

We're trying to get rid of the assumption that football clubs are the preserve of white, middle-class men in camel coats, sipping champagne and using the game as an extension of their own egos and virility.
DAVE HELLIWELL, leader of Calderdale Council, after it bought control of Halifax Town, 1990

I've heard claims that I'm using Mafia money. Soccer clubs are in such a mess right now that you could buy them out of Brownie funds.
ANTON JOHNSON on becoming Rotherham chairman, 1983

Football directors are nobody's friends except when there are Cup final tickets to give away.

ROY HATTERSLEY MP, Labour, Sheffield Wednesday supporter, in Goodbye to Yorkshire, *1976*

When I came to Manchester from the north-east aged 15, I didn't know what a director was or what he did. My dad would have explained it as someone who didn't work.
BOBBY CHARLTON on joining the Manchester United board, 1985

The Super League idea has about as much chance of getting through as there is of Arthur Scargill admitting he needs a wig.
ERNIE CLAY, Fulham chairman, a decade before the launch of the Premier League, 1982

A few of us want to discuss super leagues but all the rest can talk about is the price of meat pies.
DAVID MURRAY, Rangers chairman, on his Scottish League counterparts, 1992

Sir Harold Thompson, the chairman of the FA, treated me like an employee. These Arab sheikhs treat me like one of them.
DON REVIE, United Arab Emirates coach and former England manager, 1979

I flew to Paris for the Real Madrid final with the Liverpool directors, and a more disagreeable bunch of people I've rarely encountered. I'd sooner take my chances with a bunch of so-called hooligans. They talked about players as if they were below-stairs staff. Their attitude towards them was so patronising it was almost Victorian.
JOHN PEEL, disc jockey and Liverpool fan, 1987

[The board] was full of furniture removers, insurance brokers and clueless fogies, living in a Scotch-and-soda, curled-up-sandwiches world of self-congratulation.
ROBERT PLANT, Led Zeppelin singer and Wolves fan, on why he resisted attempts in the 1980s to lure him on to the Molineux board, 2002

You could put his knowledge of the game on a postage stamp. He wanted us to sign Salford Van Hire because he thought he was a Dutch international.
FRED EYRE, former assistant manager of Wigan Athletic, on a powerful director, 1981

When I asked Michael [Jackson] to become a director, he said: 'Oh wow, do you realise I know nothing about sport?' I said: 'You don't have to.'
URI GELLER, spoon-bending psychic and joint chairman of Exeter City, on trying to lure the American pop singer on to the board, 2002

The man who sacked me at Fulham was Sir Eric Miller, the property developer who shot himself. Shows how he reacted to pressure, doesn't it?
BOBBY ROBSON, Ipswich manager, 1981

Even I could manage this lot.

SAM LONGSON, Derby chairman, after the final parting with Brian Clough, 1973

Sacking a manager is as big an event in my life as drinking a glass of beer. I would hire 20 managers a year if I wanted to – 100 if necessary.
JESUS GIL, president of Atletico Madrid, 1989

One chairman told me his club had only had 23 managers since the war. I said: 'Why, man, the war's only been over four weeks.'
LAWRIE McMENEMY, England assistant manager, soon after the Gulf War, 1992

I don't walk past him every day and ask if I've got his full support. But the other night he bought me a sandwich at the reserves' match and that's a real show of affection from our chairman
STUART PEARCE, Manchester City manager, on his chairman John Wardle, 2007

When I arrived here the board said there would be no money and they have kept their promise.

DAVE BASSETT, Sheffield United manager, 1994

There just aren't enough raving lunatics out there with chequebooks.
MICHAEL KNIGHTON, Carlisle chairman-owner, on struggling to sell the club, 2000

For years I've been saying that football should be run by football people. Then along came Franny Lee at Manchester City. Oh well, back to the drawing board.
JIMMY GREAVES, former England striker, in his Sun column, 1995

I've played in the World Cup, sweated out multi-million-pound business deals, I've trained some good horses and I'm a father. But 90 minutes at Maine Road can make me feel like an old dish-rag.
FRANCIS LEE, Manchester City chairman, 1997

I've survived two heart attacks and Stan Flashman. And Stan was the worst of the three.
BARRY FRY, Birmingham manager, recalling a turbulent relationship with his former chairman at Barnet, 1995

I'm sick of people telling me to relax. They can stick my heart up their arses.
JESUS GIL, Atletico Madrid president, on seeing them lose to Villarreal soon after having a pacemaker fitted, 2003

Bill Bell: chairman and business entrepreneur, dedicated to making Port Vale the No. 1 team in the Potteries. Bill also wants to find the lost city of Atlantis, be the first man to walk the Channel, and skateboard up Mount Everest.
THE OATCAKE, Stoke City fanzine, derby-day edition, 1989

What entitles you to question Alex Ferguson on football matters?
QUESTION to chief executive Martin Edwards at a Manchester United plc meeting, 1999

United have begun to think 'class' is something that comes with big office suites and flash cars. That great club is slowly being destroyed. And I blame one family for the ruin. The Edwards family, the master butchers of Manchester.
HARRY GREGG, former United goalkeeper, after his sacking as a coach at the club, 1981

How can anyone praise Martin Edwards at Manchester United? He has twice tried to sell the club to the enemies of football, Robert Maxwell and Rupert Murdoch. How can he look anybody in the eye and say he loves the club when he has been trying to make 60 million quid selling it?
BRIAN CLOUGH, 1999

Even the most brilliant manager could not deal with Manchester United as long as the club is run from the chairman's [Martin Edwards] office the way it is.
MICHAEL CRICK and DAVID SMITH, authors, in the book Betrayal of a Legend, *1989*

Peter Swales wore a wig, a blazer with an England badge on it and high-heeled shoes. As a man he really impressed me.
MALCOLM ALLISON, ex-Manchester City manager, on the club's former chairman in Jeremy Novick, In a League of Their Own: Football's Maverick Managers, *1995*

Peter Swales likes publicity. He wears a card round his neck saying: 'In case of heart attack call a press conference.'
TOMMY DOCHERTY on the Manchester City chairman, 1982

I gave up football the day I went back to Maine Road and saw the chairman [Peter Swales] signing autographs.
MIKE SUMMERBEE, former City winger, 1988

The trouble was he had no repartee with the fans.
PETER SWALES, City chairman, after sacking Mel Machin as manager, 1989

My chairman, Robert Maxwell, they ought to let him run football.
JIM SMITH, Oxford United manager, 1983

I threatened to quit over the sale of Dean Saunders, but Maxwell sacked me. He told me: 'No one resigns on the Maxwells.'
MARK LAWRENSON on his time as Oxford United manager, 1993

Maxwell has the posture and manners of the dominant male.
DR DESMOND MORRIS, author of The Naked Ape *and co-director of Maxwell's at Oxford, 1983*

I have played football since I was a toddler. Left wing, as you would expect. I was very fast.
ROBERT MAXWELL, Oxford chairman, 1985

If a supporter asked me about that [lending £1.1m to Tottenham to buy Gary Lineker], I'd tell him to get stuffed. What I do with my money is my business. Haven't I already done enough for Derby? They were in the knacker's yard when I was invited to help them.
MAXWELL, by now Derby chairman, on the club's 'transfer freeze', 1990

There are still some things that baffle me about the bloke [Maxwell]. Like why he loves seeing his mug across the back pages, because Robert Redford he ain't.
BRIAN CLOUGH, Nottingham Forest manager, 1987

Robert Maxwell has just bought Brighton and Hove Albion, and he's furious to find out that it's only one club.
TOMMY DOCHERTY as Maxwell tried to add to his portfolio of clubs, 1988

I like a challenge. If I'd been a woman I would have been pregnant all the time because I can't say no.
ROBERT MAXWELL on his interest in 'saving' hard-up Tottenham, 1990

Robert Maxwell's record is exemplary… He has always been prepared to invest heavily in football at a time when others are turning their backs on the game. Some people seem to doubt him, but they don't know the man.
IRVING SCHOLAR, Tottenham chairman, on Maxwell's bid to take control, 1990

I feel like the guy who shot Bambi. I'm not an egotistical loony.

ALAN SUGAR, Tottenham chairman, on the fans' reaction to his attempt to sack Terry Venables as manager, 1993

It has been the ultimate roller-coaster ride, but I hope that whoever takes this club over has as much success as I enjoyed in my first five years here. Obviously I wouldn't wish the last three on anybody.
MICHAEL KNIGHTON, Carlisle chairman, on his plans to sell the club and their latest last-day escape from relegation out of the league, 2000

From parks football to Carlisle to Milan, we all aspire to The Dream. Robert Maxwell dubbed me a Walter Mitty figure, but that's fine because this is the industry of dreams and I'm the greatest dreamer alive.
KNIGHTON, Carlisle chairman and ex-Manchester United director, 1995

Q: How did you feel when Darlington got a wild-card entry back into the FA Cup?
A: I always felt we'd get it. I had a chat with Him upstairs the night before. Got through to him even though he's ex-directory.
GEORGE REYNOLDS, Darlington chairman, after his club were readmitted to the Cup following Manchester United's withdrawal, 1999

I'm a great believer in God. He has always been very kind to me. I say to him: 'Can you get your finger out and give us some help?'
REYNOLDS, 2000

I won't turn my back on this club, and we will be successful, we will be profitable. I will turn it around. But I won't be travelling to Exeter to watch a pile of shite.
REYNOLDS after his wife criticised the Darlington players at a public meeting, prompting them to walk out, 2002

At other clubs the directors probably get worried if things aren't going well, and they don't like people coming up to them criticising in pubs and at parties. That doesn't influence me at all. If people start telling me what's wrong with the team, I just say: 'Look, why don't you f*** awff?'
PATRICK COBBOLD, Ipswich chairman, 1981

You ask what constitutes a crisis here. Well, if we ran out of white wine in the boardroom.
COBBOLD, 1982

At Ipswich, the chairman drank a bottle of champagne when we won. When we lost he drank two bottles and thought we'd won.
SIR BOBBY ROBSON, Newcastle and former Ipswich manager, 2003

If eventually I'm kicked out, I'll just go back to buying a season ticket.
PETER RIDSDALE, Leeds chairman, 2001

A chairman's place is in the directors' box, not on the terraces.
DAVID WILLMAN, Merseyside police chief superintendent, after Ridsdale left his seat at Everton to confront Leeds fans chanting against coach Brian Kidd, 2002

I knew it was going to be a red-hot atmosphere when I looked up and saw everyone in the directors' box singing and jumping up and down.
GARY NEVILLE, Manchester United defender, after winning at Rangers in the Champions' League, 2003

I'd rather have a big crowd than the TV money. I know what it's like to be roared on.

NIALL QUINN, Sunderland chairman and ex-player, on spurning an offer to have their match v Derby on TV and sticking to a 3pm kick-off, 2007

I've been chairman of a soccer club. I know how to lose.

ELTON JOHN before the Oscars ceremony, 1996

Being part of this football club is the fullest experience you can have of being alive.

DELIA SMITH, TV chef and Norwich City director, 2002

I came down last week to watch United play Port Vale. By the time I got home I was chairman again and looking for a new manager. My wife said: 'I'm taking you to the hospital to get your head examined.'

DEREK DOOLEY on his surprise return to the boardroom at Sheffield United, 1999

The locals are starting to accept me. Maybe when we've delivered the Champions' League in 2026 they will say: 'He's all right.'

KEVIN HEANEY, multi-millionaire chairman of Truro City, on plans to take the Cornish club from the Toolstation Western League to the Football League in 10 years, 2007

twelve

REFEREES

You're out there with 22 multi-millionaires who you have to control with a whistle and two – sometimes three – cards.
GRAHAM POLL, English referee, on quitting the game, 2007. A year earlier Poll had been cut from the World Cup after cautioning Croatia's Josip Simunic three times

All the next season the crowds sang 'World Cup, and you fucked it up,' and they were right. That hurt. I heard it and it cut me every time.
POLL reflects on the Simunic error after retiring, 2007

Two more, he only gets two more.
SONG by Colchester fans as Poll showed a yellow card in his first game after the World Cup, 2007

Football is shit. Football is nothing. Your family is what matters and you're a really nice guy.
CARLOS SIMON, Brazilian referee, to Poll after his error in Stuttgart, 2006

More men have been on the moon than have refereed a World Cup final, yet I was there, in Japan last year, as the fourth official when Brazil beat Germany to win the tournament. That was utopia.
HUGH DALLAS, Scottish referee, 2003

I became a referee because I did not play football that well.
URS MEIER, Swiss referee at European Championship finals, 2004

It's almost like playing, but without the ability.
GRAHAM POLL before refereeing the FA Cup final, 2000

Refereeing is a very cut-throat business. A player can play in a cup final on the left or right of midfield. There's only one position for a referee.
JEFF WINTER, former Premiership referee, 2006

Who's the Bastard in the Black?
TITLE of Winter's autobiography, 2006

I'm back refereeing in the Argentine League and receiving as much shit as ever.
HORACIO ELIZONDO, World Cup final referee, denying he had been offered a job in the Argentinian government, 2006

The fourth official was my guardian angel.
ELIZONDO on Spanish official Luis Medina Cantalejo, who spotted and alerted him to the butt by Zinedine Zidane of France on Italy's Marco Materazzi, World Cup final, 2006

I was very pleased to see him [Elizondo] again. It was a great pleasure. He sent me off, sure, but he just did what he had to do.
ZINEDINE ZIDANE, retired France captain, on meeting Elizondo a year after the Argentine sent him off in Berlin, 2007

At Stoke once an elderly lady was waiting by the dressing room after the game. She said: 'Mr Knight, I'm 74 and a grandmother, and I'd just like to say you're the worst fucking referee I've ever seen.' Certainly put me in my place.
BARRY KNIGHT, Football League referee, 2005

Hijo de puta! (Son of a whore!)

DAVID BECKHAM to the referee's assistant who flagged for a penalty against Real Madrid at Murcia, 2004. He was sent off

I do get abuse. You get 'Oh fuck off' but 'Fuck you' is more common. I say 'Fuck you as well' and away we go.
GRAHAM POLL at the World Cup finals, 2006

[Graham Poll] is good for games like these because he makes so many mistakes that people get angry and it motivates them.
JOSE MOURINHO, Chelsea manager, on the plus side of 'a referee we have no luck with' after a match v Manchester United, 2007

[Marcus Merk] is always against us. He must have been let out of prison to referee this match.
MOURINHO, then Porto coach, on the German referee after a match v Deportivo La Coruna, 2004

We've got the drug-testers here today. I assume they'll ignore the players and go straight to the officials.
MICK McCARTHY, Wolves manager, after a controversial home defeat by Birmingham, 2007

Usually I like to get kissed before I get screwed.
McCARTHY, as above, 2007

Sir Alex Ferguson once complimented me on my handling of a game against Nottingham Forest. Three weeks later – after I'd refereed Manchester United v Fulham – he pulled me aside and said: 'Well, Jeff, back to normal. Fucking business as usual.'
JEFF WINTER, retired Premiership referee, 2004

The ref was a big-time homer, more interested in his rub-on suntan.
DAVID MOYES, Everton manager, on Winter, 2003

Anyone who craps in Graham Poll's toilet can't be all bad.

WINTER on Robbie Savage using the referee's toilet before a match at Leicester, 2004

I said to him [Poll]: 'I didn't know you were a Tottenham supporter.' He took exception.
GRAEME SOUNESS, Blackburn manager, on why he was 'sent off', 2003

I've no qualms about playing in Uriah's charity golf events, although I might be tempted to wrap my five-iron around his neck.
DAVE JONES, Wolves manager, on Uriah Rennie's 'diabolical' handling of a game v Bolton, 2004

How the mega-rich male model referee slipped out of Molineux in his luxury Mercedes after a day of mayhem
HEADLINE in Wolverhampton's Express & Star *after the Rennie controversy, 2004*

I feel like a hunted animal and I'm scared to let my children leave the house. I don't want to live like that. I won't even go out on a pitch again. I'm too frightened. It's not worth it. Unfortunately, that's the way football looks today.
ANDERS FRISK, Swedish referee, on quitting the sport after receiving threats following criticism by Chelsea manager Jose Mourinho, 2005

These are not highly paid people like the players. They are basically people who have another job. It's unfair to put them in a situation where they have to go into hiding.
WILLIAM GAILLARD, UEFA director of communications, on Frisk's resignation, 2005

Shame on the Swiss referee, the Emmental-eating appeasement monkey who ruined the lives of millions of honest yeomen bearing their simple flag.
JUSTIN CARTWRIGHT, novelist, after Urs Meier refused England a last-gasp winner over Portugal, European Championship finals, 2004

Urs cheated on me and it sounds like he has cheated on England.

FRANZISKA MEIER, former wife of Urs Meier, 2004

Ninety-five per cent of the people who've watched the replay know it's not a penalty. Unfortunately the referee is one of the other 5 per cent.
NEIL WARNOCK, Sheffield United manager, after Rob Styles awarded Liverpool a spot-kick, 2006

In rugby it's accepted that the referee is right even when he's wrong, that you don't argue. The old saying is true: rugby is a game for thugs played by gentlemen, whereas football is a gentlemen's game played by thugs.
GORDON MILES, president of Warwickshire Society of Rugby Union Referees, 2005

The FA has accepted dissent. Everyone, especially the media, has bought into this entertainment-at-the-expense-of-sportsmanship ethos. We've forgotten what the game is about. It's childlike.
TONY KENNEDY, rugby referee, on the round-ball game's disciplinary problems, 2005

In rugby, you prevent things happening by continually talking to players. They call us 'Sir', not 'Ref'. There's no backchat; they know they'll be penalised. In football, all the refs are prima donnas.
ALAN GOLD, secretary of the Essex Society of Rugby Union Referees, 2005

Don Revie used to tell us to go in hard with the first tackle, because the referee would never book you for the first one. We used to call it the freebie. I'd go in hard, pick 'em up, say sorry to the ref and sometimes you hardly saw that player again.
NORMAN HUNTER, former Leeds and England defender, 2004

By the time referees are finally experienced enough to understand the teams and what the players are trying to get away with, it's time for them to retire.
RAFAEL BENITEZ, Liverpool manager, 2004

You can buy vibrating socks and electronic flags, but you can't buy experience. You can learn from others, but if you try to copy, it will be a bad copy.
KIM MILTON NIELSEN, Danish international referee, 2005

I don't want to be remembered for sending off David Beckham. I'll always be the man that sent him off even though it was in 1998 and so much has happened since.
NIELSEN, 2005

My dad used to referee me when I was a kid. I remember him booking me – and asking my name.
KEVIN KYLE, Coventry striker, 2006

Referees should arrive by the back door and leave the same way.
ALAN HARDAKER, Football League secretary, 1964

The trouble with referees is that they know the rules but they don't know the game.
BILL SHANKLY, Liverpool manager, during a referees' 'clampdown', 1971

Next thing we'll be giving our handbags to the linesmen before we skip on to the field.
MIKE SUMMERBEE, Manchester City winger, 1971

A good ref is one that doesn't chicken out – who'll give a penalty against Liverpool in front of the Kop.

DAVID CROSS, Coventry striker, 1975

The basic training of referees is appalling. They tested my eyesight by getting me to stand at one end of a small room, facing a wall chart showing red, yellow and blue kits. Some guy pointed to one shirt and said: 'What colour's that?' I replied 'Red' and he said, 'You're in.'
GORDON HILL, Football League referee, in Give a Little Whistle, *1975*

I got the impression that few toilets were used more than those in the referee's room.

JACK TAYLOR, World Cup referee, in World Soccer Review, *1976*

Mr Martinez was slow to realise that the Dutch invented the clog.

DAVID LACEY, football writer, reporting in the Guardian *on the Holland v Italy match, 1978*

'Referee, what would you do if I called you a bastard?' one player enquired politely. 'I'd send you off,' I replied. 'What would you do if I thought you were a bastard?' was the next question. 'There's not a lot I could do,' I answered. 'In that case, ref, I think you're a bastard,' he said, turning smartly on his heel.

PAT PARTRIDGE, Football League referee, in Oh, Ref!, *1979*

The referee must have felt like the President of the United States at the time of the Cuban missile crisis.

HOWARD WILKINSON, Leeds manager, after a game v Manchester United was postponed because of a waterlogged pitch, 1992

It's getting to the stage where we hate referees and they dislike us.

KENNY SANSOM, Arsenal and England defender, 1983

There's no rapport with referees these days. If you say anything you get booked. If you don't they send you off for dumb insolence.

JACK CHARLTON, Sheffield Wednesday manager, 1983

People say we've got the best referees in the world. I shudder to think what the rest are like.

MARTIN BUCHAN, Manchester United defender, 1983

We had a Mauritian referee against Paraguay. Mauritius is a lovely island, but they don't play football.

EVARISTO MACEDA, Iraq coach, World Cup finals, 1986

There was a murderer on the pitch – the referee.

OMAR BARRAS, Uruguay manager, on the Italian official who sent off one of his players after 40 seconds against Scotland, World Cup finals, 1986

Then my eyesight started to go and I took up refereeing.
NEIL MIDGLEY, FA Cup final referee, 1987

We may be useless, but we are not cheats.

DAVID ELLERAY, referee, to Arsenal defender Tony Adams, who had called him a 'fucking cheat', 1989

The referee is available for Christmas pantomime or cabaret.
KEITH VALLE, tannoy announcer, as Bristol Rovers and Wigan players left the pitch, 1989

I have nothing against the visually handicapped as such, but I am surprised they are allowed to referee at this level.
THE SOUP, Kidderminster Harriers fanzine, 1989

We are stage managers, not performers.
ALAN GUNN, FA Cup final referee, 1990

I'll have to stop that. I don't think the Italian referees appreciated being patted on the head or the bum.
PAUL GASCOIGNE, early in his Lazio career, 1991

Thank God the referee and his linesmen are all out there together, otherwise they could have ruined three matches instead of one.
TOMMY DOCHERTY, working as a radio pundit at Old Trafford, 1992

It takes some believing for a ref to mix up two players as different as we are. I'm 5ft 8in and white, he's 6ft 4in and black.
TONY SPEARING, Plymouth Argyle defender, after he was booked in mistake for Tony Witter's foul, 1992

I'm 27 years old and yet the referee tells me I'm not allowed to swear.
VINNIE JONES, Wimbledon midfielder, after being dismissed for foul and abusive language, 1992

The referee has got me the sack. Thank him for that.
GRAHAM TAYLOR to a linesman and the FIFA official as England lost to the Netherlands and failed to qualify for the World Cup finals, 1993

The perfect referee does not exist. It's one man against 90,000 people and 22 actors, and a percentage of decisions will always be wrong.
GUIDO TOGNONI, FIFA spokesman, defending standards at the World Cup finals, 1994

The official today was a muppet.
IAN WRIGHT, Arsenal striker, after being booked at Norwich, 1994

In fairness, the referee had a complete cerebral failure.
RICK HOLDEN, Oldham winger, after defeat at Southend, 1995

My certain feeling is of being raped week in, week out, by referees and it just cannot go on.
SAM HAMMAM, Wimbledon owner, 1995

I do swear a lot, but having played abroad I can do it in a language different from the referee's.
JURGEN KLINSMANN, Tottenham and Germany striker, 1995

My wife, who was in the stand, told me that at one stage the entire row in front of her stood up and gave me the V sign. I asked her what she did and she said she didn't want them to know who she was so she stood up and joined in.
NEIL MIDGLEY, retired referee, recalling his First Division debut in Derick Allsop, The Game of Their Lives, *1995*

I've no objection to women referees provided they're good. My only concern is that a dishy referee will have players swarming round her and protesting against decisions.
JOHN RUDGE, Stoke City director of football, 2000

I've been told off for smiling when I show the red card.

WENDY TOMS, first woman to referee at Conference level, 1996

I saw someone eyeing me in the pub. I asked him: 'Do I know you?' He said: 'You should. You sent me off today.'
SONYA HOME, referee, 1995

I played full-back in rugby union, wicketkeeper in cricket and goalkeeper in football. The positions in which you stand out. Refereeing is like that. We're very much loners.
PHILIP DON, Premier League referee, 1995

Why should I allow a referee to do things which destroy my life? When managers make mistakes they get sacked. [David Elleray] is probably going home in his car now thinking about where's he going to referee next week.
JOE KINNEAR, Wimbledon manager, 1995

I've seen harder tackles in the half-time queue for meat pies than the ones punished in games.
GEORGE FULSTON, Falkirk chairman, 1995

I have to hand it to Manchester United. They have the best players – and the best referees.
SAM HAMMAM, Wimbledon owner, 1995

Most jobs get easier as you get more experienced. I've been a local government officer for 20 years and it's getting easier. This [refereeing] is getting harder. The pressure has increased, the pace is greater. There's so much money involved, so much at stake.
STEPHEN LODGE, Premier League referee, 1995

You can't think that one decision by you could be worth millions of pounds. If you think about the financial implications when you see a possible penalty, it will disturb your concentration and you may make a wrong call.
KIM MILTON NIELSEN, Danish World Cup referee, 2005

Can anyone tell me why they give referees a watch? It's certainly not for keeping the time.

ALEX FERGUSON after Graham Poll added 'only three minutes', Manchester United v Everton, 1996

In England the referees either shoot you down with a machine-gun or don't blow their whistle at all.
GIANLUCA VIALLI after his Premiership debut for Chelsea, 1996

My motto is 'perfect preparation prevents poor performance'.

MIKE RILEY, Premiership referee, 2007

I do like Selhurst Park. There's a Sainsbury's next to the ground so it's an ideal chance to get some weekend shopping out of the way.
DAVID ELLERAY, Premier League referee, 1996

I love my job. I get a buzz when I say 'Play on' and a goal results. I think: 'God, I made that.'
ALAN WILKIE, Premiership referee, 1998

I made the gesture [punching the air] because the referee loves to see the ball in the net after he has played an advantage. It proves he was right.
MIKE REED, Premiership referee, after appearing to celebrate Patrik Berger's goal for Liverpool v Leeds, 2000

If we're going to have sponsored referees, maybe we could approach Optrex or the Royal National Institute for the Blind.
PAUL DURKIN, Premiership referee, 1998

There are occasions when you say to yourself: 'I need to give a yellow card here and re-establish my authority.' That's when it gets like teaching. When it gets a bit lively, you need a sacrificial lamb.
DAVID ELLERAY, Premiership referee and Harrow School housemaster, 1998

This referee [Mike Reed] is so poor that I'd have been booked just getting off the bus.
NORMAN HUNTER, Radio Leeds summariser and former Leeds and England defender, 1998

Professional referees may help but it won't necessarily bring better positioning, better eyesight and more courage.
MARTIN O'NEILL, Leicester manager, 1998

I understand that [Everton manager] Walter Smith described the ref as diabolical. I didn't think he was as good as that.
JIM SMITH, Derby manager, 1999

There's no point asking a referee for an explanation of his action. You get that in the report a couple of weeks later, when everyone has got the right story. The boys in black have time to organise a story, make sure it's right and then send it out. Yet I have to try to give instant explanations.
GORDON STRACHAN, Coventry manager, alleging a conspiracy by match officials after defeat at Liverpool, 1999

I tried to talk to the ref but it's easier to get an audience with the Pope. If I'm in London again and I get mugged, I hope the same amount of people turn up – there were six police officers, four stewards and a UN peace-keeping observer.
STRACHAN after controversy at Arsenal shortly before resigning as Southampton manager, 2004

I don't know why they don't have the bookings before the start so that we can get on with the game. You know they are coming.
DAVID O'LEARY, Leeds manager, complaining of over-zealous refereeing by Mike Reed at Tottenham, 1999

I tried to have a word with him after the game but he wouldn't speak to me. He's untouchable. He should have been a policeman.
JOHN GREGORY, Aston Villa manager, on referee Jeff Winter after defeat at Leicester, 1999

Referees act almost like policemen, and the fourth officials are becoming jobsworths. They are reporting managers up and down the country for stepping outside the technical area.
GREGORY, 1999

It is a great profession being a referee. They are never wrong.
ARSENE WENGER, Arsenal manager, 1999

The referee was bobbins. If you need that translating, it means crap.
DAVE JONES, Southampton manager, 1999

That linesman is as dangerous as a monkey with two pistols. He always seems to ruin the show.
GREGORIO MANZANO, Real Mallorca coach, blaming a referee's assistant after two of his team were sent off in a 4–0 defeat v Barcelona, 2003

I don't think we should have shoot-outs. We should have a shoot-the-ref shoot-out. After that penalty, the referee should have been shot.
JOHN GREGORY, Aston Villa manager, after a last-minute penalty awarded to West Ham, 1999

Referees should be wired up to a couple of electrodes and they should be allowed to make three mistakes before you run 50,000 volts through their genitals.
GREGORY after David Elleray awarded a penalty against Villa at Sunderland, 1999

The ref was a disgrace. He got three things right – the kick-off, half-time and full-time.
ANDY RITCHIE, Oldham manager, 1999

It doesn't seem to matter how hard we try, we still get a slagging for trying to do the job as honestly as we can. It would be very interesting one Saturday if we decided not to turn up until 3.30pm.
PAUL DURKIN, Premiership referee, 1999

The radio link will be a great help once we get used to it, but I'm still not sure where to put my microphone.

STEVE DUNN, Premiership referee, after a trial run with an earpiece and microphone, 1999

Sometimes, privately, I say, 'The referee was crap today,' but not publicly. Managers have a responsibility to protect the referee. You have to believe he gives his best. Good and bad decisions even themselves out.
ARSENE WENGER, 1999

In the tunnel I say to David Elleray: 'You might as well book me now and get it over with.' He takes it pretty well but he still books me.
ROY KEANE, Manchester United captain, 2000

They were like a pack of wolves. I've never seen so much hatred on players' faces. It looked as though they were trying to put pressure on Andy D'Urso so that he wouldn't send off Jaap Stam as well as giving the penalty decision.
KEITH COOPER, referees assessor and ex-referee, after United players pursued Andy D'Urso, 2000

If the ref had stood still we wouldn't have had to chase him.

ROY KEANE, United captain, on the D'Urso incident, 2000

When linesmen come to check the nets when I'm warming up, I'll usually say: 'I'm a referee too, so I know what you've got to put up with.' Referees could do with more help from us; players could sometimes be more honest with officials.
STEVE HARPER, Newcastle goalkeeper and referee in the Peterlee & District League, 2000

The penalty decision put us back in the game. The player should have been sent off, but Mr Harris didn't know who the player was who had handled. The ref did get the minute's silence right before the game, though.
JOHN GREGORY, Aston Villa manager, after a controversial game v Tottenham, 2000

My players wouldn't take a throw-in for that sort of money.
GORDON STRACHAN, Coventry manager, on learning that Gerald Ashby's match fee was £200, 1998

I can't understand why the ref wasn't more sympathetic. After all, we used to go to the same bookies.
STEVE CLARIDGE, Portsmouth player-manager, after his team incurred two red cards v Fulham, 2001

[David] Elleray went around with his arms folded like a schoolteacher. Which, of course, he is.
SIMON JORDAN, Crystal Palace chairman, 2001

I've got no friends among the players. You're doing a job of work and so are they.

STEPHEN LODGE, *Premiership referee, 2001*

When Paolo Di Canio pushed over the referee [Paul Alcock], if the referee had been a player he'd have been booked for diving.
BARRY DAVIES, *TV commentator, recalling a 1998 match between Arsenal and Sheffield Wednesday, 2004*

I'd like to smash the ball into a referee at 200 miles an hour and see if he can get out of the way.
BOBBY ROBSON, *Newcastle manager, criticising Nolberto Solano's dismissal for handling, 2001*

You cheated us. It was impossible to miss that handball. You deserve to go and referee in Afghanistan. If you made the same mistake there, you'd get shot.
ROBERT NITA, *Rapid Bucharest player, picked up by the TV microphones after match v Arges in which Constantin Fratila denied his team two penalties, 2001*

What makes a sane and rational person subject himself to such humiliation? Why on earth does anyone want to become a Premiership referee?
LORD HATTERSLEY, *Sheffield Wednesday supporter, 2002*

I believe when the referees are enjoying their recreation on the sunbeds, or swimming up and down the pool and talking together in their free time, there is an agenda with Alan Smith. They all have their little chats and jump on him very, very quickly.
DAVID O'LEARY, *Leeds manager, after Andy D'Urso sent off Smith in an FA Cup tie at Cardiff, 2002*

This is what happens when you have village referees in the World Cup.
CHRISTIAN VIERI, *Italy striker, after England's Graham Poll and his assistants denied the Azzurri two goals v Croatia, World Cup finals, 2002*

We weren't lucky – it was the Irish who had a flower up their backsides. What the referee did makes you want to kill him. He crushed us. And as for the linesman, he's got a spring-loaded arm.
JOSE ANTONIO CAMACHO, Spain coach, on the Swedish referee after beating the Republic of Ireland on penalties, World Cup finals, 2002

We were unlucky that we ran into a referee who ought to be thinking more about his diet than his refereeing.
ALESSANDRO NESTA, Italy defender, on the Ecuadorian referee for their defeat by South Korea, World Cup finals, 2002

I never talk to the media after a match. Anything you say is on your head, and the media certainly aren't there to help referees.
MIKE RILEY, Premiership referee, 2007

People say a good referee is one the fans don't notice but that's a myth. If a referee has to give three penalties in a match, then he is going to be noticed. That doesn't mean he's not a good referee.
PIERLUIGI COLLINA, Italian referee, shortly before officiating in the World Cup final, 2002

Collina says: You're off...to Comet.
SLOGAN on an advert using the Signor Collina to promote the electrical store, 2004

It was like 20 mates at a holiday camp. We used to do Arthur Askey impressions. And nobody missed the bingo nights.
GRAHAM POLL on referees' conventions in his autobiography Seeing Red, *2007*

thirteen
WOMEN

If there's anyone luckier than a footballer, it's a footballer's wife. She has all the money and prestige but none of the pressure.
GORDON STRACHAN, Southampton manager, 2003

I got really glammed up. The whole Millwall team turned up. I felt like a proper footballer's wife then.
NATALIE RUDD, model and girlfriend of the Stoke and ex-Millwall player Peter Sweeney, recalling her 21st birthday party in Nuts magazine, 2005

Q: What do you set the video for?
A: It has to be *Footballers Wives.* I like the show's gritty realism.
IFFY ONURA, Sheffield United striker, in a programme questionnaire, 2003

We do have occasional pangs about those 80 or 90 little girls there must be running around playgrounds lumbered with the name Chardonnay.
BRIAN PARK, executive producer of the ITV drama series Footballers Wives, 2004

With this ring I thee WAG
HEADLINE in the Daily Mail as four England players prepared to marry on the same day, 2007. WAGs was the media acronym for the wives and girlfriends of the England squad at the 2006 World Cup

You undertake to John, Toni and *OK!* magazine that you will not photograph or otherwise record any part of the wedding and/or reception.
WORDING on the invitation to the wedding of John Terry and Toni Poole, 2007

I've sold my wedding pictures to The Kop *magazine for a pound.*
JAMIE CARRAGHER, Liverpool and England defender, on his marriage to Nicola, 2005

How can you tell the difference between the species of English woman and the majority of German women? They spend more cash on clothes in 10 minutes than ours do in a lifetime.
BILD ZEITUNG, German newspaper, on the England WAGs at the spa resort of Baden Baden, 2006

I think shopping is their favourite thing to do. And they enjoy the cafes and bars, too.

BRIGITTE GOERTZ-MEISSNER, *head of tourism in Baden Baden, 2006*

Apparently, more young women are getting into debt because they shop like a footballer's wife. If I heard of anyone doing that, I'd tell them to get a grip.
COLEEN McLOUGHLIN, *Wayne Rooney's partner and prolific shopper, 2006*

Priorities have changed for footballers and they are being dictated to by their wives and girlfriends... Greed will always be part of the game, but this side of it, with the women running the show, worries me.
ROY KEANE, *Sunderland manager, complaining he had missed out on signing certain players because their partners wanted to be near the big shopping cities, 2007*

Tell all the WAGs we've got a brand new shopping centre in Plymouth.
IAN HOLLOWAY, *Plymouth Argyle manager, 2007*

What kind of person wants to be pictured going out for a meal? They were annoying me, and they're not even my wife.
ROY KEANE, *Sunderland manager, 2006*

They're famous for doing nothing. They take advantage of their partner's position. I didn't seek out Darren because he's a footballer. I've got my own career.
JAMELIA, *pop singer and partner of Millwall striker Darren Byfield, on the World Cup WAGs, 2006*

I don't know what the fuss is about the England players' wives. They look ugly to me.
VRATISLAV LOKVENC, *Czech Republic striker, European Championship finals, 2004*

A team-mate at Marseilles once told me: 'Ah, English footballers, fantastic. But ugly wives.' I'm pleased to say we've caught up with the Continent. These days, players' lounges are like beauty pageants.
TONY CASCARINO, *former Republic of Ireland striker, in his* Times *column, 2005*

Wives of old were quiet, sensible girls next door. Now they're feisty, independent socialites... Most are fun-loving, bubbly and far smarter than the stereotype. It's an environment with shallow elements, certainly. The percentage who've had hair extensions, breast enlargements and so on is probably higher than the national average. The wives of the older pros see the younger girlfriends and don't want to be outshone.
CASCARINO, as above

At 9am on Saturday, he [Ray Parlour] called me. I told him I was in bed... He said: 'Kal, I'm leaving.' I said: 'What, Arsenal?' And he said: 'No, you.' I said: 'Let's talk about this – tell me why you're leaving.' He said coolly: 'I can't talk now. I'm at the hotel and I've got a game this afternoon and have to concentrate.'
KAREN PARLOUR, ex-wife of the then Arsenal midfielder, after being awarded a substantial divorce settlement, 2004

How [Garry Flitcroft] was naive enough to think he could pledge eternal love to a lap dancer without having the whistle blown to his wife escapes me.
VANESSA FELTZ, television personality, after Blackburn captain Flitcroft failed in a legal bid to prevent the press reporting his allegedly serial philandering, 2002

If we did get promoted there would be a tear in my eye and my wife would hammer me. I didn't cry at my wedding or the birth of my children and she has warned me not to cry or I'll be in trouble.
MARC BIRCHAM, Queens Park Rangers player, before losing to Cardiff in the Second Division play-off final, 2003

I have to use my maiden name for work. Sometimes I even pretend my husband does something else for a living. When I taught at the Law Society in Madrid, for example, I told my students I was married to a plumber.
VICTORIA McMANAMAN, wife of former England player Steve McManaman, 2006

When I was first with Steve as a teenager, people couldn't believe it when I wanted to go to university. They said, 'Go on, give it up, do nothing.'
VICTORIA McMANAMAN, 2006

If my husband made a brilliant save in Europe the headline would never read: 'Husband of artist makes fantastic save.' When I was short-listed from 300 to 30 artists from 22 countries and won a prestigious award, my headline was: 'Footballer's wife is good at art shocker.'
SUSAN GUNN, artist and wife of former Scotland goalkeeper Bryan Gunn, 2006

I told Cathy I had a match, but she wasn't having any of it. She said it was a friendly and that I had to help her to pack because we're moving house.
SIR ALEX FERGUSON on how his wife stopped him attending Manchester United's pre-season game at Dunfermline, 2007

Of course I didn't take my wife to watch Rochdale as an anniversary present. It was her birthday. Would I have got married during the football season? And anyway it wasn't Rochdale, it was Rochdale Reserves.
BILL SHANKLY, Liverpool manager, 1966

I take my wife Lesley to watch midweek matches. She's in the studio audience tonight. It's one of the rare times I've taken her out somewhere she doesn't need to wear an overcoat.
GORDON STRACHAN, Southampton manager, on BBC TV's Onside show, 2002

Basically, he [Bill Nicholson] doesn't think women have any place in football. I never saw him play for Spurs and I'm not allowed to go to see them now. I feel an outsider, really, as if I was a member of the opposition.
GRACE NICHOLSON, wife of the then Tottenham manager, in Hunter Davies's The Glory Game, 1972

When I lose I've got to talk about it. I go home and relive it with the wife. She just nods and says yes or no.
NORMAN HUNTER, Leeds and England defender, 1973

It takes a lot to get me excited. Ask my wife.

ROY KEANE, Sunderland manager, after they beat Tottenham on returning to the Premier League, 2007

I used to stand up and glare around when fans were giving Geoff stick. Norman Hunter's mum used to lash out with her handbag when people booed her Norman.
JUDITH HURST, wife of Geoff Hurst, in Brian James's book Journey to Wembley, 1977

Isn't one of the main features of football match attendance still that it enables men to get away from nagging wives?
FRANK BURROWS, Portsmouth manager, 1981

When I said that even my missus could save Derby from relegation, I was exaggerating.
PETER TAYLOR, Derby manager, 1982

My wife knows more about football than any other woman I know... Many occasions I have said to her: 'Come on, luv, I'll take you out for a meal,' and she'll look disappointed and say: 'You know that Wimbledon Reserves are playing.'
ALEC STOCK, former manager, in A Little Thing Called Pride, *1982*

My wife has been magic about it.
JOHN BOND when the story of his affair with a Manchester City employee broke following his resignation as manager, 1983

John Bond has blackened my name with his insinuations about the private lives of football managers. Both my wives are upset.
MALCOLM ALLISON, Bond's predecessor as Manchester City manager, 1983

Q: Most dangerous opponent? A: My ex-wife.

FRANK WORTHINGTON, England striker, in a magazine questionnaire, 1975

We hope to revive the old tradition of the husband going to football on Christmas Day, while the wife cooks the turkey.
ERIC WHITE, Brentford official, 1983

Only women and horses work for nothing.
DOUG ELLIS, Aston Villa chairman, 1983

My idea of relaxation: going somewhere away from the wife.
TERRY FENWICK, QPR captain, in a Match *magazine questionnaire, 1986*

My wife says it would be better if there was another woman. At least then she would know what she's up against. But she says: 'How can I compete with football?'
DON MACKAY, Blackburn manager, 1988

The only threats I've had this week have been from the wife for not doing the washing-up.
HARRY REDKNAPP, Southampton manager, before the derby against his previous club Portsmouth, 2005

Q: At home, when was the last time you ironed a shirt?
A: I pay my wife to do that.
MARK ROBINS, Leicester striker, in a programme questionnaire, 1995

John Hollins was a mistake. He has a very strong wife. It might have been better if I had made her manager.
KEN BATES, Chelsea chairman, 1995

The reason I'm back is that the wife wants me out of the house.
KENNY DALGLISH on returning to management with Blackburn, 1991

What does my wife think of me still being in management? She doesn't talk to me. Well, she does, but she knows it's pointless.
SIR BOBBY ROBSON answering questions by Dutch journalists about being a manager at the age of 71, 2004

My wife was hoping I'd get the sack so we could retire down to Cornwall with the children.
NEIL WARNOCK, Sheffield United manager, 2005

I married a girl who was very easily told: 'If you marry me, you're marrying football.'

GRAHAM TAYLOR, England manager, 1992

Whether or not we win against Germany, I will stay away from all of you for seven days. I have to sleep with my wife.
LUIZ FELIPE SCOLARI, Brazil coach, to the media on the eve of the World Cup final, 2002

I would rather my wife got injured than my players.
JEAN TIGANA, Fulham manager, 2002

You can tell how a team's doing by the state of the wives. Second Division wives always need roots touching up.
MRS MERTON, played by Caroline Hook, on TV's The Mrs Merton Show, 1995

If it wasn't for Tracy, I'd be an 18-stone alcoholic playing for Penicuik Athletic.
ANDY GORAM, Rangers and Scotland goalkeeper, paying tribute to his second wife, 1995

Football is all very well as a game for rough girls, but it is hardly suitable for delicate boys.
OSCAR WILDE, 1890s

Football reminds me of the Nuremberg Rally. It's so aggressive. Great men with bald heads, roaring and screaming. Why should anyone welcome that?
MICHELE HANSON, Guardian Women writer, in Match of the Day magazine, 1998

Women should be in the kitchen, the discotheque and the boutique, but not in football.
RON ATKINSON, Sheffield Wednesday manager, 1989

What are women doing here? It's just tokenism for politically correct idiots.

MIKE NEWELL, Luton manager, on referee's assistant Amy Rayner, 2006

Who's cooking your tea?
STAN TERNENT, Burnley manager, to referee's assistant Wendy Toms, quoted in his autobiography Stan the Man, 2003

The Italians are a gayer set of lads, who love life and their girlfriends...
They think the English boys are slightly mad putting sport before the ladies.
EDDIE FIRMANI on his move from Charlton to Sampdoria, in Football With the Millionaires, 1960

To score in front of 70,000 fans at San Siro is like finding a place in a woman's heart. No, it's better.
NICOLA BERTI, Inter Milan midfielder, 1988

I don't think my girlfriend would be too happy to hear I've been chasing Totti round Rome.
JONATHAN WOODGATE, teenage Leeds defender, on the prospect of facing Roma's Francesco Totti, 1998

Blimey, you're the first bird I've met with an FA coaching badge.
RON ATKINSON to a female journalist who asked about Sheffield Wednesday's long-ball game under his predecessors, 1989

If there really are men who prefer football to girls, I've never met any.
SHARON KNIGHT, 19-year-old Miss Stoke-on-Trent, 1990

I know it sounds awful but it just hit me halfway through my stag night that I'd rather be going to the match with the lads than marrying Nicola.
KEVIN McCALL, Hereford fan, quoted in press reports after cancelling his wedding to watch an FA Cup tie at Aylesbury, 1991

I hate football. I think most women do. It's not the sort of sport I'm interested in. I prefer the indoor sort of games.
CYNTHIA PAYNE, Streatham 'Madam', 1990

The Old Firm are like two old girls in Sauchiehall Street raising their skirts to any league that walks past.
KEITH WYNESS, Aberdeen chief executive, on the possibility of Rangers and Celtic quitting the Scottish League, 2002

If a woman suggested that the simplest way of brightening up football was by making the goals a bit bigger, they would say she didn't understand the game and why didn't she go off and practise her netball.
NIGELLA LAWSON in her Evening Standard column after FIFA president Joao Havelange suggested widening the goals, 1990

They are nice people with a part to play but at the end of the day they are tea ladies who do not understand the game.
TREVOR STEELE, Bradford Park Avenue chairman, resigning after two women directors were elected to the board, 1990

The only place for women in football is making the tea at half-time.

RODNEY MARSH, former England player, 1997

Doing well in football is like childbirth – it doesn't happen overnight.
BRIAN CLOUGH, Nottingham Forest manager, 1991

Q: What has been your biggest thrill in life?
A: When my wife Norma told me she was pregnant and signing for Newcastle.
ALBERT CRAIG, Partick Thistle midfielder, in a Sun questionnaire, 1994

Why not treat the wife to a weekend in London and let her go shopping on Saturday afternoon while you go and watch the Latics play West Ham?
OLDHAM ATHLETIC programme, 1991

I've always believed in treating the ball like a woman. Give it a cuddle, caress it a wee bit, take your time, and you'll get the desired response.
JIM BAXTER, Rangers and Scotland player of the 1960s, 1991

Leaving a club is like leaving a woman. When there's nothing left to say, you go.
ERIC CANTONA after leaving Leeds for Manchester United, 1992

Footballers are the worst gossips – they're worse than women.
LEE CHAPMAN, Leeds striker, 1992

We defended like women.
JOE ROYLE, Oldham manager, after 5–2 defeat by Wimbledon, 1992

Footballers are turning into women. You'd never have got away with anything like that when I was playing.
GORDON RAMSAY, TV chef and former Rangers youth-team player, on reports that top players were shaving their body hair, 2005

The strip was a bloody stupid colour. I think one of the directors' wives must have chosen it.
DAVID PLEAT, Luton manager, on the end of his club's tangerine and navy kit, 1992

Women run everything. The only thing I've done within my house in the past 20 years is recognise Angola as an independent state.
BRIAN CLOUGH, 1992

Every girl I ever went out with I took on the North Bank at least once. They never wanted to go twice.
LAURENCE MARKS, comedy writer and Arsenal fan, in Tom Watt, The End: 80 Years of Life on Arsenal's North Bank, *1993*

I loved football. I played in the morning and in the afternoon. Even when I went to bed with my wife I was training.
DIEGO MARADONA after his last match for Argentina, 1994

Our last Prime Minister was a woman. The head of the Royal Family is a woman. And the head of Birmingham City is a woman.
KARREN BRADY, Birmingham City managing director, on why she believed men and women 'receive equal treatment in society', 1993

I met much more [male] chauvinism working for the *Sport*. I've always had the 'I bet she's shagging the boss' remarks.
BRADY, 1995. Her 'boss' at the Sport *and Birmingham was David Sullivan*

I know everybody thinks I earned this job between the sheets, but I'm not bonking him.

BRADY on her relationship with Sullivan, 1994

I am probably more male than most men. I was brought up going to watch boxing and football.
BRADY, 1995

I will tell you straight away, before you ask me: I have never slept with a footballer, never gone to dinner with one and never seen one naked in the dressing room. OK. Now we can start.
PAOLA FERRERA, Italian TV football presenter, before being interviewed, 1994

I didn't get too many women running after me. It was their fucking husbands who'd be after me.
CHARLIE GEORGE, former Arsenal player, recalling his 1970s heyday, 1995

Q: What's the craziest request you've ever had from a fan?
A: A male fan once asked me for my wife's phone number and when my next away match was.
FRANCIS BENALI, Southampton player, in Sun *questionnaire, 1995*

Could you take Eric's sliding tackle from behind? Football. It's a girl's game.
DAILY STAR advertisement, 1995

Q: Who's your dream woman?
A: Jennifer Lopez with the personality of Kathy Burke.
JASON McATEER, Blackburn midfielder, in newspaper questionnaire, 2000

After all, this is not a game for little ladies.
PLACIDO DOMINGO, opera singer, defending Spain's rugged tackling during the World Cup finals, 1994

I need to find a woman who is strong, quick and athletic, like Venus Williams. It doesn't matter whether she can play football – she can learn that. Ideally it would be a very tall, blonde and beautiful Norwegian.
LUCIANO GAUCCI, president of Perugia, announcing the Italian club's desire to field a female player in Serie A, 2003

The more beautiful game.

SLOGAN on Football Association billboards at Women's European Championship finals, in England, 2005

The future is feminine.
SEPP BLATTER, general secretary of FIFA, football's world governing body, after the Women's World Cup, 1995

Some of the girls can do things men would find very difficult. When I coached at the Centre of Excellence, one girl had a trick I'd never seen any professional do. I tried to work it out and gave up after 10 minutes. And they're physical when they want to be. They'll have a dig in and kick people – they're just the same [as the men].
KEVIN KEEGAN, England (men's) manager, 2000

I don't care for women's football, especially when they distract me by running round in those tight shirts. I've watched it on TV and they're not suited to it. I like my women to be feminine, not sliding into tackles and covered in mud.
BRIAN CLOUGH, 2000

Women's football is a game that should only be played by consenting adults in private.
BRIAN GLANVILLE, journalist, 1990

I thought I would watch some of the ladies' football at the Olympics. What a disappointment. The game they played was 20 years out of date. They did not spit every two minutes. They did not dive. They did not feign injury. There was no arguing with the referee. There was no amateur dramatics. And no really nasty tackles.
LETTER to the Independent, 2004

Let the women play in more feminine clothes, like they do in volleyball. For example, they could wear tight shorts.
SEPP BLATTER, head of FIFA, the world game's ruling body, 2004

Men say things like: 'Oh, they're just a bunch of dykes.' I hate the fact that there are girls who would love to play but don't because the image of women's soccer is so bad.
JULIE FOUDY, United States captain, 1995

There's still the blinkered view that all women footballers have thighs like joints of ham and make rugby players look like Flake adverts.
MARIANNE SPACEY, Arsenal and England striker, 1995

When I go to functions I love glamming it up, putting a gown on. People do a double take and are like: 'Oh my God, it's you!' When I wear skirts they go: 'I didn't know you had legs.' What do they think I play football with every week?
SPACEY, now Fulham player-coach, 2003

Trollops on tour
SIGN on bus carrying the Manchester United ladies' team, 1996

The coach [Gaute Haugenes] told me at half-time that he was substituting me because it was against the rules to have 12 people on the pitch.
KATIE CHAPMAN, Fulham and England midfielder, on how news of her pregnancy was broken to team-mates, 2002

We just don't like the males and females playing together. Anyway, it's not natural.

TED CROKER, FA chief executive, 1988

The men under-perform but still keep their massive pay checks while the women's side has all its financial support stopped. The Charlton board continue to sit in their lovely Laura Ashley offices and drive their fast cars, but the little girls who dreamt of playing for Charlton and England are told the girls' section is no longer going to exist.
DANIELLE MURPHY, Charlton Athletic and England midfielder, after the London club closed their women's team following relegation for the men, 2007

Some referees in women's football are avuncular, enthusiastic and fair. Some use the game to prove that they can control women.
ALYSON RUDD, Leyton Orient Ladies striker and Times columnist, 1994

I knew it wasn't going to be our day when I arrived at Montrose to find we had a woman running the line. She should be at home making the tea or dinner for her man after he has been to the football.

PETER HETHERSTON, Albion Rovers manager, on Scotland's first female referee, Morag Pirie, 2003

The court said it was unusual for a husband to complain about his wife spending too much time on football.

WENDY TOMS, the first woman referee to reach the Football League's reserve list, after her divorce, 1991

Stick to playing netball.

CHANT by Kidderminster fans to Wendy Toms when she became the first woman to referee a senior match, 1999

I've played netball, but never football. I couldn't kick a ball to save my life.

AMY RAYNER, 21, on her rise from officiating in the Rugeley Boys League to being fourth official at First Division matches, 1999

I am not sexist but...how can they make accurate decisions if they have never been tackled from behind by a 14-stone centre-half, or elbowed in the ribs or even caught offside?

JOE ROYLE, Manchester City manager, attacking the appointment of Wendy Toms as an official for the Worthington Cup final as 'politically correct', 2000

It's bad enough with the incapable referees and linesmen we have, but if you start bringing in women you have a big problem. This is championship football. This is not park football.

MIKE NEWELL, Luton manager, criticising referee's assistant Amy Rayner, 2006

We are now getting PC decisions about promoting ladies. It does not matter whether they are ladies, men or Alsatian dogs. If they are not good enough to run the line then they should not get the job.

GORDON STRACHAN, Coventry manager, complaining about a female assistant referee, 1999

I love women. I prefer their company to men's. Men are boring arseholes with nothing to talk about apart from football, and I don't like football.
LEMMY, leader of the rock group Motorhead, 1998

Five minutes after a game, everything is all right. After the 1999 Champions' League final when Bayern lost to Manchester United, I had to comfort my girlfriend. She was much more upset than I was.
LOTHAR MATTHAUS, 2000

Where's the girls, then? Where do we find them? Where's the shag?
STAN COLLYMORE in Leicester City's hotel at La Manga, as quoted by a businessman guest, 2000

I love England, one reason being the magnificent breasts of English girls. Women are ultimately all that matters in life. Everything that we do is for them. We seek riches, power and glory, all in order to please them.
EMMANUEL PETIT, French midfielder, 1998

It's incredible that she has left me. Only recently I paid £7,000 to make her breasts bigger – and now this.
MO IDRISSOU, Hanover striker, on his ex-girlfriend, 2004

I know women are stronger than we are. But I play the football, I make the money.
DAVID GINOLA, Tottenham winger, 2000

When I first came to England I was amazed at the way women behave. From London to Newcastle to Leeds to Manchester, I saw women vomiting in streets. In France the women will drink only a little bit because they have to drive their husbands home.
GINOLA, 2003

I don't even understand offside so I'm not likely to understand a Manchester United contract.
VICTORIA BECKHAM as David renegotiated his deal with the club, 2002

What I love most about Norway is you ladies. Back home I'm used to fat and hairy women journalists.
DIEGO MARADONA in Oslo, 2006

fourteen

MEDIA & ARTS

My programme has been switched to accommodate David Beckham and his boyfriends chasing an inflated sheep's pancreas round some field in Portugal.
JEREMY CLARKSON, presenter, on the TV motoring show Top Gear, *2004*

There's too much football on TV. You don't want roast beef and Yorkshire pudding every night and twice on Sunday.
BRIAN CLOUGH, former TV pundit, 2003

For Arsenal, the sight is in end.
DAVID PLEAT, ITV summariser, at the Champions' League final, 2006

Cristiano Ronaldo has been compared to George Best. The incomparable George Best.
PLEAT summarising a Manchester United match, 2007

If it doesn't go right tonight, Wenger has another leg up his sleeve.
GLENN HODDLE, Sky TV pundit, during the first leg of Arsenal's Carling Cup semi-final v Spurs, 2007

Liverpool have literally come back from the grave!
CLIVE TYLDESLEY, ITV commentator, at the Champions' League final, 2005

There's nothing more horrible than a big galoot coming up your backside with no protection.
MATT LE TISSIER, Sky TV pundit, 2005

Hakan Yakin plays with Young Boys in Berne.
JONATHAN PEARCE, BBC TV commentator, World Cup finals, 2006

Ljungberg desperately wants to suck in Cocu.
ANDY TOWNSEND, ITV summariser, 2004

Ian Evatt has gone down easier than my daughter.
DAVE BASSETT, Sky pundit, 2006

Liverpool were all mishy-mashy. I know that's not a word, but it should be.
PAUL MERSON, Sky TV summariser, on Arsenal's 6–3 win in the Carling Cup, 2007

[Robin] Van Persie is the right player for them – he can open a can of worms.
MERSON on Sky, 2006

Too many players looked like fish on trees.
MERSON on England's performance in a defeat by Croatia, 2006

Joaquin scuffed that shot with his chocolate leg.
MICK McCARTHY, Sunderland manager, working as a TV pundit at Spain v Greece, European Championship finals, 2004

The Dutch have tasted both sides of the coin now.
ANDY TOWNSEND, ITV summariser, as the Netherlands beat Sweden in a shoot-out, European Championship finals, 2004

Colour-wise it's oranges v lemons, with the Dutch in all white.
CLIVE TYLDESLEY, ITV commentator, at Netherlands v Sweden, 2004

They're wearing the white of Real Madrid and that's like a red rag to a bull.
DAVID PLEAT, TV summariser, as Chelsea prepared to face Barcelona, 2006

Senegal will be kicking themselves because they've shot themselves in the foot.
EFAN EKOKU, TV pundit and former Premiership striker, 2006

Jamie Carragher there, looks like he has cramp in both groins.
ANDY TOWNSEND, ITV summariser, at Champions' League final, 2005

Alan Shearer has banged it through a gap that wasn't even there.
PAUL WALSH, Sky TV summariser, 2005

You could have driven a Midnight Express through that Turkish defence.
TERRY VENABLES, ITV summariser, 2003

These Iraqis don't take any prisoners.
RON ATKINSON for ITV at the World Cup as the Iran–Iraq war raged, 1986

And the German stormtroopers are arriving at the far post.
BARRY DAVIES, BBC TV commentator, 1992

2-0 is a cricket score in Italian football.
ALAN PARRY, ITV commentator, 1990

Viv Anderson has pissed a fatness test.
JOHN HELM, ITV commentator, 1991

Great striking partnerships come in pairs.
NIGEL SPACKMAN, Chelsea player, working as a Sky TV pundit, 1994

He'll be the most famous Greek for years, even though he's Argentinian.
RON ATKINSON, ITV pundit, after Panathinaikos, managed by Juan Rocha, beat Ajax, 1994

Shelbourne are obviously having trouble with Bohemians' five-man back four.
EAMONN GREGG, Irish TV analyst, 1995

And that's a priceless goal, worth millions of pounds.

ALAN PARRY, ITV commentator, on European Cup final, 1995

The Northampton striker went through Stoke's defence like a combine harvester on summer holiday.
BRIAN BEARD, Sky TV reporter, 2000

And Hyypiä rises like a giraffe to head the ball clear.
GEORGE HAMILTON, RTE (Dublin) commentator, 2001

The Belgians will play like their fellow Scandinavians, Denmark and Sweden.
ANDY TOWNSEND, ITV pundit, World Cup finals, 2002

You would think that if anybody could put up a decent wall it would be China.
TERRY VENABLES, ITV pundit, after Brazil scored from a free-kick which passed through China's defensive wall, World Cup finals, 2002.

Germany benefited there from a last-gasp hand-job on the line.
DAVID PLEAT, ITV summariser, after Torsten Frings handled the ball v United States, World Cup finals, 2002

GARY LINEKER: Trevor Brooking is in the Sapporo Bowl. What's it like, Trevor?
TREVOR BROOKING: Well, it's a bowl-shape, Gary.
EXCHANGE during BBC coverage of a World Cup match in Japan, 2002

PAUL GASCOIGNE: I've never heard of Senegal before.
DES LYNAM: I think you'll find they've been part of Africa for some time.
EXCHANGE on ITV after the Senegalese victory v France, World Cup finals, 2002

GARY LINEKER: Do you think Rio Ferdinand is a natural defender?
DAVID O'LEARY: He could grow into one.
EXCHANGE during BBC TV's World Cup coverage, 2002

I never liked pundits before I became one.

ALAN HANSEN on becoming a fixture on Match of the Day, 1994

You win nothing with kids.
HANSEN on Match of the Day after a youthful Manchester United lost 3–1 at Aston Villa on the season's opening day, 1995. United went on to win the Premiership

I should rather like the *Match of the Day* theme tune played at my funeral.
CARDINAL BASIL HUME, Newcastle fan, 1986

It was when old ladies who had been coming into my shop for years started talking about sweepers and creating space that I really understood the influence of television.
JACK TAYLOR, Wolverhampton butcher and World Cup referee, 1974

The governing body of football: television.
MIKE INGHAM, BBC radio football correspondent, 1991

It looks like a night of disappointment for Scotland, brought to you live by ITV in association with National Power.
BRIAN MOORE, ITV commentator, during Brazil v Scotland, World Cup finals, 1990

Poland v England, 7pm tonight, followed by Female Orgasm, 10.50pm tomorrow.
ADVERT for Channel 5, 1999

One old lady phoned to say that the fireworks made her cat bolt out of the door and she hadn't seen it since.
BRIAN TRUSCOTT, Southampton secretary, on BSkyB's pre-match extravaganza, 1992

There are already millions of camera angles showing everything, and referees even have things in their ears now. Pretty soon they'll be going out on to the pitch with a satellite dish stuck up their arses.
IAN WRIGHT, former England striker and TV presenter, 1999

For all my so-called obsession, I'm terribly conscious that football can start to eat you up a bit, and I try not to let it.
JOHN MOTSON, BBC TV commentator, 2002

Jimmy Hill is to football what King Herod was to babysitting.
TOMMY DOCHERTY, former manager, when Hill was a TV pundit, 1992

There! He blew the whistle! Norway has beaten England 2–1 at football and we are the best in the world! England, the home of the giants! Lord Nelson! Lord Beaverbrook! Sir Winston Churchill! Sir Anthony Eden! Clement Attlee! Henry Cooper! Lady Diana!
BJORGE LILLELIEN, Norwegian TV commentator, 1981

Maggie Thatcher, can you hear me? I have a message for you in your campaigning. We have beaten England in the World Cup! As they say in the boxing bars around Madison Square Gardens in New York, your boys took a hell of a beating!
LILLELIEN, 1981.

MIKE CHANNON: We've got to get bodies in the box. The French do it, the Italians do it, the Brazilians do it.
BRIAN CLOUGH: Even educated bees do it.
EXCHANGE on the ITV World Cup panel, 1986

They'll be dancing in the streets of Total Network Solutions.
JEFF STELLING, Sky TV presenter, in what became a catchphrase used after victories by Welsh Premier League club TNS, 2000s

You are not Manchester United. You are Dagenham.
SIMON COWELL, judge on ITV's Pop Idol show, to an auditioning singer, 2003

There are some people on the pitch. They think it's all over. It is now!
KENNETH WOLSTENHOLME, BBC TV commentator, as Geoff Hurst completed his hat-trick in England's win over West Germany, World Cup final, 1966

England are sizzling in Shizouka and after this the sausages will be sizzling back home.
JOHN MOTSON, commentating on Brazil v England, World Cup finals, 2002. Throughout the tournament Motson referred to what viewers might be having for breakfast

Actually, none of the players is wearing earrings. [Jacob] Kjeldberg, with his contact lenses, is the closest we can get.
EXTRACT of Motson commentary from his book, co-authored with Adam Ward, Motson's National Obsession: The Greatest Football Trivia Book Ever, *2004*

[John Motson] is a guffawing whining-voiced clown, anally obsessed with meaningless statistics.
TONY PARSONS, Daily Mirror columnist, 2006

One man's commentary is another man's pain in the arse.
BARRY DAVIES, BBC TV commentator, 1990s

[Alan] Hansen thinks every goal ever scored is a defensive error. When you don't understand football you can stop a tape anywhere running up to a goal and find a mistake. [Gary] Lineker goes: 'Oh, all right then.' [Mark] Lawrenson simply underlines or puts inverted commas round what Hansen says. It's all happy families. They need to be challenged.
MICHAEL ROBINSON, former Liverpool striker and Spanish TV summariser, on his 'comfy' BBC equivalents, 2005

They [the Belgian media] are filth. They smell of shit as they torture themselves. Fortunately their criticism is erased by the praise of international connoisseurs Gary Lineker and Alan Hansen.
ROBERT WASEIGE, Belgium coach, during the World Cup finals, 2002

When you've got the ball on one side of the pitch and you switch it, what happens to the defence? It has to move, and if they move, there's a hole. All you work on as a defender is shifting position. But imagine trying to explain that – or Dennis Bergkamp's psychological chemistry – on TV? They don't want that kind of technical analysis. They want all the usual cliches. I just thought: 'This is not for me.'
TONY ADAMS, former England captain, on why he decided against TV punditry, 2003

I want to stay in football. What else can I do? I do media and that farting around, but there's no passion there. Who wants to sit and commentate on Middlesbrough v Everton? Where's the job satisfaction in that?
STUART PEARCE, former England captain, facing retirement as a player, 2003

Peter Schmeichel is a BBC pundit, but they could put a parking meter next to Alan Hansen and I'd find it more interesting watching it click round.
RODNEY MARSH, talkSPORT and former Sky pundit, 2005

You could have got an ice-cream salesman from the street who supports Arsenal, dragged him from his van and put him on instead, and he'd have done a better job.
MARSH on the ITV panel of Michael Owen, Terry Venables and Gabby Logan, Liverpool v Chelsea, 2005

You won't see me in 20 or 30 years' time, sitting and slagging off an England performance. Shoot me if you do.
FRANK LAMPARD, England midfielder, on the TV panel's criticisms of the team at the World Cup, 2006

A Premiership manager said to me: 'If I lose my job, I think I'll do what you do.' That's the attitude. They think it's easy. It's not.
TONY CASCARINO, talkSPORT radio pundit, 2004

Ferguson refusing to speak to MUTV is like Joseph Stalin blanking Pravda.
DAVID LACEY, Guardian football writer, on Manchester United's defeat by Norwich, 2005

I'm trying to tell you the positive things. So I'm getting to the point where I might whack you over the head with a big stick, you bad, negative man.
GORDON STRACHAN, Southampton manager, to a Sky interviewer after a third successive defeat, 2004

Arsenal's touch and movement are amazing. I hope the listeners are watching this.
CHRIS WADDLE, BBC Radio 5 Live summariser, at Bolton v Arsenal, 2007

This World Cup has got a very international feel about it.
JIMMY ARMFIELD, 5 Live summariser, 2006

In technical terms, that's what I call a dinky-do.
ARMFIELD on 5 Live after Ruud Van Nistelrooy chipped a goal for Manchester United, 2004

The good people of Suffolk will be looking forward to this.
BOBBY GOULD, 5 Live summariser, before Norwich v Bayern Munich, 1993

I'm not saying he's going to field a weakened team. It just won't be as strong.
MARK LAWRENSON, 5 Live summariser, 2007

Most players would give their right arm for Jason Wilcox's left foot.
LAWRENSON on 5 Live, 1996

And Vegard Heggem, my word, he must have a Honda down his shorts.
TERRY BUTCHER, Radio 5 Live summariser, on Liverpool's Norwegian defender, Euro 2000

What a goal! One for the puritans.
COMMENTATOR on Capital Gold radio after Dennis Bergkamp scored for Arsenal v Newcastle, 2002

What I said to them at half-time would be unprintable on radio.
GERRY FRANCIS, Tottenham manager, to Radio 5 Live after his team came from behind to beat West Ham, 1995

Sorry, but I've had a really busy day today. I've been playing in a golf day for a boy seriously injured in a car accident. I had to drive like a lunatic to get here.
RAY HOUGHTON, talkSPORT radio pundit, apologising for being late on-air, 2004

I only hope that callers to Six-O-Six repeatedly ask David Mellor how he is on the off-chance that he will one day reply: 'Terminally ill.'
LETTER to When Saturday Comes magazine, 1999. Mellor, a former Conservative cabinet minister, hosted the 5 Live phone-in

Don't ever call me a bottler on the radio with all those thousands of people listening.
JAMIE CARRAGHER, Liverpool and England defender, calling a talkSPORT phone-in after the host questioned his appetite for continuing to play for his country, 2007

George from Sligo has rung to say that since most countries in Euro 2000 play in a colour that appears in their national flag, why do Italy play in blue? Well, George, I have to inform you that, as far as I know, the colours of the Italian flag are red, white and blue.

EAMON DUNPHY, media pundit and former Republic of Ireland player, hosting a radio phone-in, 2000

You're such nice people. Sometimes I wonder who writes all the articles.

SVEN-GÖRAN ERIKSSON to journalists at an FA get-together, 2004

A very nice bunch of bastards.

GRAHAM TAYLOR, England manager, describing the English press pack in Norway, 1993

I've always said there's a place for the tabloid press in football. They just haven't dug it yet.

TOMMY DOCHERTY, former manager, 2005

[Football journalists] are just about able to do joined-up writing.

SIR ALAN SUGAR, former Tottenham owner, 2005

How do I relax? I read the English newspapers.

CLAUDIO RANIERI, Chelsea manager, as media speculation intensified about his job security, 2004

When a dog three months old is the front page of a newspaper in this country, you cannot believe the things you read.

JOSE MOURINHO, Chelsea manager, after being arrested by police over the quarantine status of his Yorkshire terrier, 2007

I've had players arguing their worth based on the marks out of 10 they get in the *Sun*. The media and football live off and need each other. The papers get used by football people day after day. Circulation tarts that they are, they love it and beg for more.

SIMON JORDAN, Crystal Palace chairman, 2006

You fucking sell your papers and radio shows off the back of this club.

SIR ALEX FERGUSON banishing the press after reporters raised an issue he had insisted was off the agenda, 2003

They [the press] have a hatred of Manchester United. It's always been there. It goes with the territory.
FERGUSON on a press conference he curtailed after 74 seconds, 2005

You always feel with the press that they don't really want to know about the football side... There was a time when sports journalism was about what happened in the 20th minute, how the goal was scored, how good the final pass was. Now a team loses and it's another headline about the manager's future.
FERGUSON, 2004

The thing I don't enjoy [about English football] is the way the media talk about us. I feel as if the knives are being aimed in our direction while the flowers are in another.
JOSE MOURINHO in his first season at Chelsea, 2004

They say Alf Ramsey was hounded out by the press, but they were pussycats compared to now. It doesn't matter who you are, or what your character is, they're going to pick you to bits. With me it was tactics, with Don Revie it was too dour. He was a great guy but they didn't like him. Ron Greenwood was too nice. With Sven-Göran Eriksson it was what happened off the pitch. They will always find something.
KEVIN KEEGAN, former England manager, 2007

The worst opponent the England team has is the media... [Their] treatment makes certain players I know question the value of playing for their country. Is it really worth the hassle?
PETER SCHMEICHEL, former Denmark and Manchester United goalkeeper, 2001

Many Swedes think the English press is crazy. To instigate such a story, making such an effort and working for six months to set it up – what's the point? What Sven said was quite boring. It was a classic Sven moment.
ERIK NIVA, football writer with Swedish paper Aftonbladet, *on the 'fake sheikh' sting by the* News of the World, *2006*

There are 20 reporters outside my house now. If that is part of another culture, it isn't part of mine.
LUIZ FELIPE SCOLARI, Portugal and former Brazil coach, on why he turned down England, 2006

I'd love someone in America to write a story like that about me [Graeme Souness reputedly leaving Blackburn to manage Tottenham]. You don't sue for 10 thousand, you sue for 10 million. Press in England is fantasy, fiction, exaggeration.
BRAD FRIEDEL, Blackburn's American goalkeeper, 2004

The press in England make from a little mosquito a big elephant.
RUUD GULLIT at Chelsea, 1997

Not only the cows are mad in England. The English press is also infected.
EL MUNDO DEPORTIVO newspaper after 'Spain-bashing' stories before the European Championship quarter-final, 1996

As it was the media who had tipped us to win, I thought one or two of their jobs might be in jeopardy. Not likely. It was me they were after.
BOBBY ROBSON, former England manager, recalling failure in the 1988 European Championship finals in Against All Odds, *1990*

During Scotland's 1974 World Cup in Frankfurt, my English colleagues – remember, 'Britain' didn't qualify for that one – labelled us 'fans with typewriters'. Here's an update: the English Brat Pack are hooligans with computers.
JIM BLAIR, columnist in Scotland's Daily Record, *after press vitriol aimed at Graham Taylor, 1992*

Now, if you could just let us have your names and those of your newspapers, we'll know who to ban.
KEN BATES ending his first press conference as Leeds chairman, 2005

We've got crash-bang-wallop journalism now where you're either the best in the world or the worst. You have letter pages, phone-ins, websites and TV polls on football. Everyone thinks managing is fantasy football. They say 'I'll take him off' or 'I'll get him for £8m'.
JOE ROYLE, Manchester City manager, 2001

For the press, you're either brilliant or you're crap. We didn't win so it was crap. That's how they work.
TEDDY SHERINGHAM, England striker, after 0–0 draw v Croatia, 1996

The shrewdest players never take any notice whatsoever of good press or bad press.
MALCOLM ALLISON, Manchester City coach, 1971

A lot of people in football don't have much time for the press; they say they are amateurs. But I say: 'Noah built the Ark, but the *Titanic* was built by professionals.'
ALLISON, back as City manager, 1980

Reporters can make or break footballers. The reverse can rarely be said.

MALCOLM MACDONALD, Newcastle player, 1974

Mistrust of the press is a standard feature of any international footballer.
PETE DAVIES, author, All Played Out: The Full Story of Italia 90, *1990*

I have been let down so often, read so much that wasn't remotely true, that I now find it difficult to trust anyone who shows up with notebook and pen.
JOHN HOLLINS, Chelsea manager, 1988

People have perceptions on you and they're based on portrayals written by guys who've never had five minutes with you. Why get worked up about it?
SOL CAMPBELL, Arsenal and England defender, 2005

Theatre critics and film critics do know what the mechanics of a production are. Most football writers don't. So players tend to despise journalists. On the other hand players are flattered by their attention... So you have contempt and at the same time a slight awe at seeing your name in print.
EAMON DUNPHY in his book Only a Game?, *1976*

Players always get upset when old pros criticise them in the papers. You just think: 'What an old git. He doesn't know what he's talking about.'
ALAN SMITH, Daily Telegraph columnist and ex-Arsenal and England striker, 2004

I have to make a living just like you. I happen to make mine in a nice way. You make yours in a nasty way.
SIR ALF RAMSEY, England manager, to journalists, 1973

Reporters want a quick answer to something I might want all Saturday night and all Sunday to get somewhere near.
HOWARD WILKINSON, Sheffield Wednesday manager, 1983

I read the papers and they said we played badly last week. I thought we were fantastic, so it shows how much I know.
DAVID O'LEARY, Leeds manager, 1999

I've had enough of this bullshit. After every game some smart-ass journalist tells us what we've done wrong. The way you're reporting is an impudence. It's pure crap. We've played badly but you guys are sitting comfortably, having downed a few beers, and asking us why we haven't thrashed Iceland 5–0.
RUDI VOLLER, Germany coach, addressing the media after a 0–0 draw in Reykjavik, 2003

After that performance I have to say to you: I have a gun and a licence and I wouldn't mind blowing their brains out.
MICHAEL ADOLF ROTH, Nuremberg president, to reporters after defeat by Lubeck, 2003

This is the last day I speak to you. I never cared what you write anyway. You can say what you want about me as a player, but when you offend me as a person – well, I'm more of a man than all of you put together.
CHRISTIAN VIERI, Italy striker, to his country's media at the European Championship finals, 2004

You have to remember I have managed in Italy and it's much, much worse. In this country, the journalists want to kill you some of the time. In Italy, all of the time.
CLAUDIO RANIERI, Chelsea manager, on whether he felt 'pressure' from the media, 2004

You lot [the media] are amazing. You moan and claim we never say anything interesting. What on earth do you want? Of course we tell you we're behind the manager. Do you seriously expect us to say anything different?
LUIS ENRIQUE, Barcelona midfielder, after sacking of coach Louis Van Gaal, 2003

I am ashamed of the [French] press. I am dealing with dishonest, incompetent yobs. I hope the public can figure that out.
AIME JACQUET, France coach, after criticism of him and his team en route to winning the World Cup, 1998

You shouldn't be training your lenses on our bedroom windows. I don't think the French people care whether Fabien Barthez sleeps in boxer shorts or underpants.
WILLY SAGNOL, France defender, in a tirade against photographers at their base in Germany, World Cup finals, 2006

It's nice to be stabbed in the front for a change.

TERRY VENABLES, Australia coach, on the open antipathy of the media Down Under, 1997

I've always understood that criticism from the media is part of football. There is a simple answer to it. If you don't like it, don't read it. Nobody makes you look at it. I didn't realise for five days that I'd been called a turnip because I hadn't seen the *Sun.*
GRAHAM TAYLOR, sports journalist's son and former England manager, after goalkeeper David James was branded a donkey, 2004

You smell blood, don't you?
RUUD GULLIT to media before defeat at Southampton which provoked his dismissal by Newcastle, 1999

I never speak, according to the newspapers. I just storm and blast.
KEN BATES, Chelsea chairman, 1990

They were Rotherham feelers, writing in a Rotherham paper for other Rotherham feelers, so bugger impartiality.
BILL GRUNDY, television presenter, recalling his earlier career as a football reporter, 1975

Shame fills the heart of every right-thinking Englishman. How could our lads play like that? How could they let us down so badly?
LEADER in the Sun after England opened the World Cup with a draw v Republic of Ireland, 1990

They couldn't play, sneered the critics. They couldn't string two passes together. How wrong the world was.
LEADER in the Sun after England's semi-final exit v West Germany, 1990

Swedes 2 Turnips 1
HEADLINE in the Sun after England lost to Sweden, 1992

I'm beginning to wonder what the bloody national vegetable of Norway is.
GRAHAM TAYLOR, England manager, before game in Oslo, 1992

Swede 1 Beetroot 0
HEADLINE in The Times over pictures of Sven-Göran Eriksson and a red-faced Sir Alex Ferguson after City beat United in the Manchester derby, 2007

You lot got rid of [Neil] Kinnock. You must be able to do something about referees.
BOBBY GOULD, Coventry manager, to the press after match v Norwich, 1993

KRANKIES 0 KRANKL 2
HEADLINE in the Daily Record after Scotland lost to Hans Krankl's Austria, 2003

WE IN!
HEADLINE in Newsday, Trinidad & Tobago newspaper, after the Caribbean islands qualified for their first World Cup, 2005

Nil–Nil Desperandum
HEADLINE in the Independent on Sunday after England's barren draw v Macedonia, 2006

NORSE MANURE!
HEADLINE in the Scottish Sun after Scotland drew 0–0 in Norway, 1992

YES! WE'VE LOST!
HEADLINE in the Daily Mirror after England lost at home to Scotland but still qualified for Euro 2000, 1999

Queen in brawl at Palace
HEADLINE on match report in the Guardian, 1970. Crystal Palace had a player called Gerry Queen

I'll spill beans on Swindon
HEADLINE in Today newspaper about allegations of corruption, 1990

Yanks rate Arsenal as exciting as a slice of cold pizza
HEADLINE in Evening Standard story on Arsenal's impact in Miami tournament, 1989

Super Caley Go Ballistic, Celtic Are Atrocious
HEADLINE in the Scottish Sun *after Inverness Caledonian Thistle won at Celtic, 2000*

United supporter to be next Pope
HEADLINE in Newcastle's Evening Chronicle *on report that Cardinal Basil Hulme was likely to be elected to the Vatican, 1981*

Next week Newton Heath have to meet Burnley, and if both play to their ordinary style it will perhaps create an extra run of business for the undertakers.
REPORT in the Birmingham Daily Gazette, *1894. Newton Heath, soon to become Manchester United, sued for libel and won a farthing in damages*

The Quakers are likely to be without Greg Blundell tomorrow as the striker struggles with a dead calf.
STORY about Darlington in the Northern Echo, *2007*

I kept wondering which side had soiled their underpants more with the fear of making a mistake.
PAUL BREITNER, former West Germany captain, reporting on England 1 Germany 0, Bild *newspaper, at Euro 2000*

England star Rio Ferdinand has admitted he has no idea how he got his unusual name. But today the *Daily Mirror* can solve the mystery once and for all. The Leeds United centre-back is named after a river, the Rio Grande in Jamaica.
NEWS SECTION of the Daily Mirror, *11 June 2002*

Rio Ferdinand has revealed his ultimate World Cup dream – a showdown with Brazil. The England defender, named after the Brazilian city, has been a fan since he saw Brazil in the 1986 World Cup.
SPORTS SECTION of the Daily Mirror, *11 June 2002*

A mundane first half saw Everton nose in front thanks to a stunning strike from David Unsworth, whose swerving shot beat the despairing dive of keeper Patriot Fellatio.
REPORT in the News of the World *on Derby v Everton, 2002. The computer spell-check had corrupted the name of Patrick Filotti*

I'm not going to speculate on speculation.
DAVID PLEAT, acting Tottenham manager, on reports that Giovanni Trapattoni would be the club's next manager, 2003

What the fuck's a rhetorical question?
STEVE BRUCE, Birmingham manager, to a press conference, 2004

Strictly off the record, no comment.
COLIN MURPHY, Lincoln manager, 1983

How can you lie back and think of England
When you don't even know who's in the team?
BILLY BRAGG in his song 'Greetings To the New Brunette', 1986

It's coming home, it's coming home
It's coming, football's coming home.
OPENING of the England song 'Three Lions' by David Baddiel, Frank Skinner and the Lightning Seeds, 1996

Three lions on the shirt
Jules Rimet still gleaming
Thirty years of hurt
Never stopped me dreaming.
CHORUS of 'Three Lions', 1996

Ossie's going to Wembley
His knees have gone all trembly.

TOTTENHAM FA Cup final song, 1981

He's football crazy
He's football mad
And the football it has robbed him
Of the wee bit sense he had.
SONG by Scottish folk duo Robin Hall and Jimmy MacGregor, 1960

We're representing Britain
We've got to do or die
England cannae do it
Cos they didnae qualify.
ANDY CAMERON, comedian/singer, on the World Cup record 'Ally's Tartan Army', 1978

O-li O-la
O-li O-la
We're gonna bring that
World Cup home from over tha'.
ROD STEWART song for Scotland's World Cup campaign, 1978

All I want for Christmas is a Dukla Prague away strip.
TITLE of a song about Subbuteo by Half Man Half Biscuit, 1986

He looked into my eyes
Just as an airplane roared above.
Said something about football
But he never mentioned love.
KIRSTY MacCOLL, pop singer, in a song co-written with Jem Finer of the Pogues, 1991

'But I don't see what football has got to do with being mayor.' She
endeavoured to look like a serious politician. 'You are nothing but a cuckoo,'
Denry pleasantly informed her. 'Football has got to do with everything.'
ARNOLD BENNETT in his novel The Card, 1911

To say that these men paid their shillings to watch 22 hirelings kick a ball is
merely to say that a violin is wood and catgut, that Hamlet is so much paper and
ink. For a shilling the Bruddersford United AFC offered you conflict and art.
J.B. PRIESTLEY in the novel The Good Companions, 1929

I'm a schizofanatic, sad burrits true
One half of me's red, and the other half's blue
I can't make up my mind which team to support
Whether to lean to starboard or port
I'd be bisexual if I had time for sex
Cos it's Goodison one week and Anfield the next.
ROGER McGOUGH in 'The Football Poem', 1975

'Anything you say may be used in Everton against you,' said Harry. And it was.
JOHN LENNON in In His Own Write, 1964

And that, boys, is how to take a penalty. Look one way and kick the other.
BRIAN GLOVER, playing the games teacher Sugden in the film Kes, 1969

I could have been a footballer but I had a paper round.
YOSSER HUGHES, played by Bernard Hill, in Alan Bleasdale's television drama series Boys
From the Blackstuff, *1981*

The sturdie ploughman, lustie, strong and bold
Overcometh the winter with driving the foote-ball
Forgetting labour and many a grievous fall.
ALEXANDER BARCLAY in Fifth Eclogue, *1508*

Am I so round with you as you with me
That like a football you do spurn me thus?
WILLIAM SHAKESPEARE in Comedy of Errors, *1590*

LEAR: My lady's father! my lord's knave! you whoreson dog! you slave! you cur!
OSWALD: I am none of these, my lord; I beseech your pardon.
LEAR: Do you bandy looks with me, you rascal! (Striking him)
OSWALD: I'll not be strucken, my lord.
KENT: Nor tripped either, you base football player.
WILLIAM SHAKESPEARE in King Lear, *1608*

How the quoit
Wizz'd from the stripling's arm!
If touched by him
The inglorious football mounted to the pitch
Of the lark's flight, or shaped a rainbow curve
Aloft, in prospect of the shooting field.
WILLIAM WORDSWORTH in 'The Excursion', *1814*

Then strip lads and to it, though sharp be the weather
And if, by mischance, you should happen to fall
There are worse things in life than a tumble in the heather
And life itself is but a game of football.
SIR WALTER SCOTT on the occasion of a match between Ettrick and Selkirk, 1815

Then ye returned to your trinkets;
Then ye contented you souls
With the flannelled fools at the wicket
And the muddied oafs in the goals.
RUDYARD KIPLING in 'The Islanders', *1902*

fifteen

FAMOUS
LAST
WORDS

Never, never, never, never. Nothing, never, never, never. Not now. Not ever.
FLORENTINO PEREZ, Real Madrid president, denying his club's interest in Beckham shortly before signing him, 2003

I want to stay at United. There's been lots of stuff in the media about me and Real, but my feelings for Manchester, the club, the players, the fans and staff, are as strong as ever.
DAVID BECKHAM dismissing reports he would join Real, weeks before he did, 2003

Beckham will never play for this club again.
FABIO CAPELLO, Real Madrid coach, when Beckham set up a deal with Los Angeles Galaxy, 2007. Beckham won back his place and helped Capello's side win La Liga

The proof that our technical staff was correct not to retain [Beckham] has been borne out by every other technical staff in the world not wanting him, even though he was out of contract. He will be an average cinema actor living in Hollywood.
RAMON CALDERON, Real Madrid president, January 2007. By May he was calling Beckham 'a truly great professional' and exploring ways to prevent his leaving

I've never played in Spain and never will. This is my last contract.
THIERRY HENRY, Arsenal striker, rejecting Barcelona to re-sign for a further four years with the Gunners, 2006. He joined the Catalan club a year later

As long as he [Arsene Wenger] is here then I will be here – it's just as simple as that.
HENRY pledging allegiance to Arsenal in April, 2007. He left in June

Mr Chairman, I think that the second half will be a damage-limitation exercise for your team.
MICHEL PLATINI, UEFA president and former France captain, to Liverpool chairman David Moores when Milan led Liverpool 3–0 in the Champions' League final, 2005. Liverpool won the trophy on penalties

What I'm proposing is that I give you chapter and verse on her [Faria Alam] and Sven... Get her to do an interview to say she lied to everybody this week.
COLIN GIBSON, FA director of communications, to a News of the World *executive in an attempt to strike a deal to save the job of FA chief executive Mark Palios during the Faria Alam affair, 2004. Gibson and Palios left while Eriksson continued as England coach*

The bookies are offering odds that I'll be out before Christmas. I've told my mates to have a bet because there's no way I won't be here then.
PAUL GASCOIGNE on becoming manager of Kettering, 2005. He did not make it to Christmas

My heart, my head and my legs are fine. I've still got a bright and alert mind and I still have ambitions.
SIR BOBBY ROBSON shortly before he was sacked as Newcastle manager, 2004

You simply do not sack Bobby Robson.
FREDDY SHEPHERD, Newcastle chairman, 2004. Within days he dismissed the veteran manager, saying there was 'no room for sentiment'

I'm sick of every Tom, Dick and Harry getting linked with my job every day. Well ding dang doo. It's my job, I own it and it's up to anyone else to take it off me.
IAN HOLLOWAY, Queens Park Rangers manager, 2005. A month later he lost his job

I've just heard there's a lot of rubbish on Radio 5 that I'm walking out. I'm not leaving. I've got a job to do, especially for these fans. They're the best in the country.
HARRY REDKNAPP, Portsmouth manager, 2004. He promptly joined local rivals Southampton

The Blackburn job is just more speculation. I have no plans to leave the Wales post. I'm a Welshman, who is as proud today of being national team manager as he was on the day he was appointed.
MARK HUGHES, Wales manager, the day before taking over from Graeme Souness at Blackburn, 2004

Thank God there are people like Eric [Black]. He's been like a Messiah for the club.

MIKE McGINNITY, Coventry chairman, three weeks before firing Black as manager, 2004

If anyone ever hears that Kevin Keegan is coming back to football full-time, they can laugh as much as I will. It will never happen. That is certain.
KEVIN KEEGAN, later to become England manager, on going to live in Marbella, 1985

I'm not interested in the England job, so I hope no one has had a bet on me.
KEEGAN a week before being named interim national coach, 1999

If I am to lose this job they will have to take it away from me.

KEEGAN weeks before resigning as England manager, 2000

I'm not a person who goes into deep depression after a defeat. I try to remain upbeat. I'm realistic enough to know that results are often unpredictable and things don't always work out as one would wish.
KEEGAN in his programme notes before match v Germany, 2000. England lost 1–0 and Keegan resigned minutes later

Sven is staying until the end of the season. I shall not get tired of saying that.
SERGIO CRAGNOTTI, Lazio owner, giving a vote of confidence to the coach as the Italian champions struggled, 2000. Eriksson was named England manager within days

Good afternoon everyone, and yes, I am still here.
BRIAN TALBOT, West Bromwich Albion manager, in his programme column, December 1990. He was dismissed in January

At least you know you're alive and not half-dead from all the emotion. Now that it has all come good, it's a lovely feeling. See you all next season.
JIM RYAN, Luton Town manager, after his team's escape from relegation, 1991. The next day he was sacked

I must be barmy to think of leaving this club. I've got the best job in football. In the final analysis, I couldn't turn my back on people who have been so good to me.
RON ATKINSON, Sheffield Wednesday manager, after spurning Aston Villa's advances, 1991. He joined Villa within a week

I believe Big Ron to be one of the top three managers in the country.
DOUG ELLIS, Villa chairman, three weeks before sacking Atkinson, 1994

I wish to make it clear I will not be the next manager of Aston Villa. I've had no approach from them and have no idea what my plans are. It's time to do something different with my life.
BRIAN LITTLE, resigning as Leicester manager four days before being unveiled at Villa, 1994

I've never been tempted to walk away in frustration. It's a thing I would never do. I wouldn't turn my back on the players because they're still a fantastic bunch to work for. And I'm not interested in going to another club.
JOHN GREGORY, Villa manager, weeks before resigning and joining Derby, 2002

Let's kill off the rumours that Ossie Ardiles's job is on the line. If he ever leaves it will be of his own volition.
SIR JOHN HALL, Newcastle chairman, three days before dismissing the Argentinian, 1992

If Alan Sugar thinks he can just walk in and take West Bromwich Albion's manager, I'll be down that motorway in my car like an Exocet to blow up his bloody computers.
TREVOR SUMMERS, West Brom chairman, on Tottenham's interest in Ossie Ardiles, 1993. Ardiles duly became Spurs' manager

We hope Peter Reid will see this club through to the next century.

PETER SWALES, Manchester City chairman, after Reid signed a three-year contract, 1993. He was sacked within six months

George Graham will not go to Spurs. I spoke to him recently and he assured me he would not walk out on Leeds.
JOHN BARNWELL, chief executive of the League Managers' Association, days before Graham moved to White Hart Lane, 1998

Good managers give in when they want to, not when other people tell them to.
HOWARD WILKINSON before what proved to be his last match in charge of Leeds, 1996

I am a very happy man and every day I wake up with a smile because it is a thrill to go to work. I know one day I will be sacked. That is inevitable. But I won't cry – I'll just say I did my best and move on.
RUUD GULLIT shortly before his dismissal by Chelsea, which he disputed vehemently, 1997

Ideally, I'd like to pop my clogs punching the air while celebrating the Blues' winning goal at Wembley in the year 2130.
BARRY FRY, days before his sacking as manager of Birmingham, 1996

Now I'm a director, I can give myself a vote of confidence.
STEVE BRUCE, Huddersfield manager, 1999. He was sacked the following year

All the speculation surrounding Birmingham has been off-putting…. I'm extremely happy here. I want to manage in the Premiership and I'd love to take Crystal Palace there. End of story.
STEVE BRUCE, Palace manager, shortly before making Birmingham his fifth club in four years, 2001

Peter Taylor needs three or four seasons with us, then he can become the next England manager.
JOHN ELSOM, Leicester chairman, 2000. He sacked Taylor within a year

Ideally, I would like David O'Leary to be at this club for life.

PETER RIDSDALE, Leeds chairman, 2000. He fired the Irishman as manager within two years

Of all the great clubs I've worked with, none has had the infrastructure, commitment and potential of Leeds. The team have all the necessary qualities to become the country's best for years to come.
TERRY VENABLES on taking over as Leeds United manager, 2002. Leeds would finish the season selling off key players and narrowly avoiding relegation, Venables having already been sacked

I don't want to leave Leeds in the lurch and I fully intend to put things right. I've no intention of running away. When I go it will be when Leeds United are flying again.
PETER RIDSDALE, Leeds chairman, 2003. Within a fortnight he had quit

My team just played like spoilt children who think they are great players for whom the victories will simply arrive... Today, if I was the president, I would dismiss the coach and line the players up against a wall and give them all a kick up the backside.

MARCELLO LIPPI, Inter Milan coach, after his team lost at home, 2000. He was sacked within 48 hours

I congratulate the president for making the decision not to sack me.

LLORENC SERRA FERRER, Barcelona coach, after defeat by Liverpool in the UEFA Cup, 2001. He was fired within 48 hours

It's a question of me getting in and talking to the media about what's going on in the community, about the stadium, about disability. And about helping Paul Bracewell when you've got all these rumours that every manager in the world is taking his job, that they are all at Harrods having lunch with the chairman [Mohamed Al Fayed].

MAX CLIFFORD, public-relations consultant to Fulham, shortly before Fayed sacked Bracewell, 2000

It's the same crap week in, week out. The players may think they can just hang out for the last few weeks of the season, but they're in for the hardest month of their lives.

SCOTT FITZGERALD, Brentford manager, after relegation from League One, 2007. He was dismissed the next day

Rio Ferdinand is going nowhere. Where does he think he is going – into thin air?

PETER RIDSDALE, Leeds chairman, insisting they would never allow their captain to join Manchester United, 2002. The £29.1m deal went through within days

If someone wants to give you a bum steer on who we're after, then so be it. If you want to know, ask me because I have a list of players we want and Robbie Keane isn't on it.

GLENN HODDLE, Tottenham manager, shortly before paying Leeds £7m for Keane, 2002

I might even agree to become Rangers' first Catholic if they paid me £1m and bought me Stirling Castle. Let me spell out where I stand. I am a Celtic man through and through and so I dislike Rangers because they are a force in Scottish football and therefore a threat to the club I love. But more than that I hate the religious policy they maintain.
MAURICE JOHNSTON, then with Nantes, in Mo: An Autobiography, *1988. Within a year he had joined Rangers*

It's a complete fabrication. You can run that story for 10 years and it still wouldn't be true.

BILL McMURDO, Johnston's agent, ridiculing reports that Rangers wanted to sign his client, 1989. Within days he moved to Ibrox

I like Nottingham. It's a bit like Ireland. My heart is with this club. My present contract has another three years to go, and I did have another one of three years in mind, but now I fancy something a bit longer.
ROY KEANE professing allegiance to Forest, 1993. Six months later he was with Manchester United

I want to reassure fans that Luis Figo, with all the certainty in the world, will be at Nou Camp on 24 July to start the season.
LUIS FIGO, Portugal captain, a fortnight before forsaking Barcelona for their bitter rivals Real Madrid, 2000

Have you seen the size of the house he owns in Leicester? He owns half of Leicester and he's not going to want to leave that behind.
GORDON STRACHAN, Coventry manager, on why Gary McAllister would not be leaving the club, 2000. He soon joined Liverpool

There's only one way I will leave West Ham, and that is if the club kick me out. I feel the shirt like a second skin to my body.
PAOLO DI CANIO, 2001. The following year, when Manchester United tried to buy him, he declared his hope that the deal would go through

Everyone knows how important the West Ham shirt is to me. When I kiss the badge people say: 'It's because he wants a new contract.' If I wanted a contract I would come in here and lick the club's arse.
DI CANIO, 2003. He joined Charlton a few months later

There's no chance of Sol leaving for Arsenal. He's a Spurs fan and there's not a hope in hell of his playing in an Arsenal shirt.
DAVID BUCHLER, Tottenham chairman, weeks before Campbell defected to Highbury, 2001

It's hard to think of a bigger and better club to play for [than Manchester United], especially as I have no real desire to taste life in Italy or Spain.
JAAP STAM in Head to Head, *published days before United sold him to Lazio, 2001*

No matter what happens, I want to stay. It's easy for people to walk away when you've been relegated but it takes a better type of person to stay and say we're going to stick together and make sure the club gets back where it belongs. That would be my attitude.
ALAN SMITH, Leeds United striker, in 2003. Less than a year later, within days of Leeds going down, he joined Manchester United

The talk about Manchester United is an honour, but I'm happy at Fulham. I don't get angry about things. Life is too beautiful for that. And Chris Coleman is a great man. He's just perfect. I can't think of anybody who has impressed me more.
LOUIS SAHA shortly before he reputedly began not talking to Coleman, Fulham's manager, for refusing to let him talk to United, 2004. He soon moved to Old Trafford

I would not have signed a five-year contract with Charlton if I didn't think I could fulfil my ambitions here. Charlton's the best place for me – I love the lads and the fans. I owe them.
SCOTT PARKER, Charlton midfielder, before he became 'unsettled' by Chelsea's interest and joined them, 2004

I am saying 'Get lost, Abramovich' and I think that speaks for the rest of football. Someone has got to make a stand.
MARTIN SIMONS, Charlton chairman, refusing to sell Parker to Chelsea, 2004. Within weeks, the deal had been done

My son will not go to Chelsea. Over my dead body will he go there. Old Trafford is the only place he wants to play. If he can't play there he would rather stay at PSV and play in their reserves than join Chelsea.
HANS ROBBEN, father of Arjen Robben, a month before the PSV Eindhoven winger joined Chelsea for £13.5m, 2004

The [Michael] Essien case is closed. He will remain at Lyon. They behaved to us as if we were just country bumpkins with our berets and baguettes. England may have won the Olympics, but Chelsea will not get Essien.
JEAN-MICHEL AULAS, Lyon president, 10 days before selling the Ghanaian midfielder to Chelsea for £24.4m, 2005

Are you trying to tell me there's a bigger club than Everton? Do me a favour. Wayne Rooney is going nowhere.
BILL KENWRIGHT, Everton vice-chairman and owner, when asked whether Rooney might eventually join 'a bigger club', 2003. He moved to Manchester United within a year

I am desperate to be the first Brazilian to play for Manchester United. All the biggest stars – like Pele, Ronaldo, Roberto Carlos and Rivaldo – wanted to be the one. But now I know it's going to be me. When I close my eyes, my subconscious is red and I can't stop seeing myself as a Red Devil.
RONALDINHO, Brazil striker, days before spurning United in favour of Barcelona, 2003

AJ [Andrew Johnson] is our player, I paid for him and he'll have to be prised from my dead hand before he leaves here.
SIMON JORDAN, Crystal Palace chairman, after relegation from the Premiership, 2005. Johnson joined Everton in 2006

We'll probably get more fans than if we'd signed Ronaldo.

NEIL WARNOCK, Bury manager, expecting a rush of Asian spectators after signing Indian international Baichung Bhutia, 1999. His first appearance drew 3,603

I don't consider signing Stan a risk at all. He'll enhance the dressing-room spirit because he's a bright lad.
MARTIN O'NEILL, Leicester manager, a week before Collymore was prominent in the spraying of a Spanish hotel lobby with a fire extinguisher, 2000

I would lie in front of a tank for the guy [Alex Ferguson]. Now that I'm here they will have to chase me out with wild animals.
MARK BOSNICH, Manchester United goalkeeper, 2000. Within months, Ferguson gave him a free transfer

There's as much chance of [Frank] McAvennie moving as there is of Rangers beating us 5–1 tomorrow.
BILLY McNEILL, Celtic manager, 1988. Celtic lost 5–1 and McAvennie eventually left

What reputation do Holland have anyway? They didn't qualify for the last World Cup, and they're in the play-offs, so it's not a great record, is it?
JAMES McFADDEN, Scotland striker, before a two-leg play-off with the Dutch for a place in the European Championship finals, 2003. Scotland lost 6–1 on aggregate

Bergkamp? He's fucking scared, that guy. He won't get on a plane. Van Bronckhorst? How good is he? Get at him. Put him on his arse!
GRAHAM WESTLEY, Farnborough manager, to the Conference club's players as they prepared to face Arsenal in the FA Cup, 2003. Arsenal won 5–1

They are just another English club. It doesn't make any difference if we're playing Sheffield United or Manchester United. All English clubs play the same way.
RONALD KOEMAN, Barcelona and Netherlands sweeper, before the European Cup-Winners' Cup final v Manchester United, 1991. United won 3–1

Oh, it's OK, it's only Ray Parlour.

TIM LOVEJOY, Sky fanzone commentator and Chelsea supporter, seconds before Parlour's spectacular goal for Arsenal against his team, FA Cup final, 2002

I will wage my watch on Italy to beat France, and it's a gold Cartier. They will leave France by the wayside.
DIEGO MARADONA at the World Cup finals, 1986. France won 2–0

You can mark down the 25th June 1978 as the day Scottish football conquers the world.
ALLY MacLEOD, Scotland manager, before presiding over a shambolic first-round exit from the World Cup finals in Argentina, 1978

There is no limit to what this team can achieve. We will win the European Cup. European football is full of cowards and we will terrorise them with our power and attacking football.
MALCOLM ALLISON, Manchester City coach, 1968. City went out in the first round to unfancied Fenerbahce of Turkey

[Franz] Beckenbauer is like Humpty Dumpty, and the team are playing like a bunch of cucumbers.
ULLI STEIN, West Germany's third-choice goalkeeper, during the World Cup finals, 1986. Stein was duly sent home and the Germans reached the final

You can rest assured it will not happen again. Last year's defeat by Sutton United was our inoculation against that.
JOHN SILLETT, Coventry manager, the day before his team's FA Cup defeat by Fourth Division Northampton, 1990

Touch wood, I've never scored an own goal in 10 years as a professional.

DAVID MILLER, Stockport defender, before scoring Derby's last-minute winner in the FA Cup, 1993

Before City got their first we could have been 3–0 up. I turned to my physio and said: 'I think I'll have a cigar. If we keep this up we'll get double figures.'
MALCOLM MACDONALD, Huddersfield manager, after a 10–1 defeat at Manchester City, 1987

The players are under no pressure to get a result, so you never know what might happen.
TOMMY GEMMELL, Albion Rovers manager, before an 11–0 defeat by Partick Thistle, Scottish Cup, 1994

We will give it a real go at Norwich. People need to see shots, action and attacking football.
PAUL MERSON, Walsall caretaker-manager, on his first match, 2004. Walsall lost 6–0

If we were getting murdered every week, I'd be panicking. As it is, I'm not anxious.

DANNY WILSON, Sheffield Wednesday manager, before an 8–0 defeat at Newcastle, 1999

You don't get many opportunities in your career to have a real crack at the FA Cup, but we're at home, in the quarter-finals, so why not?
STEVE BRUCE, Birmingham manager, before a 7–0 home defeat by Liverpool, 2005

I don't think anyone can put their finger on Tony Parkes's success [as caretaker-manager] but he has got us all playing for him. We have team meetings but we never talk about the opposition.
ALAN KELLY, Blackburn goalkeeper, before a 5–1 defeat at Barnsley, 1999

I'm waiting for [Marcel] Desailly. I excel myself against blacks.
HRISTO STOICHKOV, Barcelona's Bulgarian striker, before European Cup final, 1994. Milan won 4–0 and Desailly scored

Whatever the result, the players, directors, staff and of course the supporters of Kidderminster will have had a terrific day out.
BIRMINGHAM CITY programme welcome to Kidderminster Harriers, FA Cup tie, 1994. The non-league side won 2–1

England fans will be talking about their 1–0 win for years.
CLIVE TYLDESLEY, ITV commentator, moments before France scored twice to win 2–1, European Championship finals, 2004

There's only one team that's going to win now and that's England. I hope I'm not tempting providence there.
KEVIN KEEGAN, working as an ITV summariser, moments before Dan Petrescu's winner for Romania, World Cup finals, 1998

After tonight, England v Argentina will be remembered for what a player did with his feet.
ADVERT by Adidas featuring David Beckham, who kicked Diego Simeone and was dismissed, World Cup finals, 1998

These days, our opponents are quaking in their boots when they look at our line-up.
WILLIAM GALLAS, France defender, the day before the World Cup finalists lost to Scotland, 2006

The bagpipes will scare the stupid bandana off David Beckham. I reckon there's one or two of their players that will crack under pressure. We've got more soul than England. They just take it for granted that they'll come up here, do the business and go away again. It's not like that for us.
JOHNNY MARR, Edinburgh Tartan Army, before England's 2–0 win over Scotland at Hampden Park, 1999

All that stuff about the foreigners and their superior technique is a media myth as far as I'm concerned. I was playing for England 10 years ago when we were getting all that, and we went to Spain and beat them 4–2.
TONY ADAMS, Arsenal captain, on the eve of 4–2 defeat by Barcelona, 1999

This could be the most boring cup final in history.

JOHAN CRUYFF, former Netherlands captain, before Liverpool beat Alaves of Spain 5–4 to win the UEFA Cup, 2001

I have no doubts whatsoever that Germany will thrash England and qualify easily for the World Cup. What could possibly go wrong? The English haven't beaten us in Munich for a hundred years. I'm convinced we're headed into another golden age of German soccer.
ULI HOENESS, former Germany player, on the eve of England's visit, 2001. England won 5–1

In remembrance of arrogant, clinical, penalty-scoring and downright bloody irritating German football…Oliver Kahn's gloves will be cremated and the ashes taken to England.
THE MIRROR after England's 5–1 win v Germany, 2001. Ten months later Germany contested the World Cup final, England having gone out in the quarter-finals

Apart from Oliver Kahn, if you put all the players in a sack and punched it, whoever you hit would deserve it.
FRANZ BECKENBAUER, former Germany captain and coach, in the early stages of the World Cup finals, 2002. Within a fortnight Germany had reached the final

Zidane and Vieira? They're only names. I think we can win this game.
BERTI VOGTS in Paris before his debut as Scotland manager, 2002. France won 5–0

My friends are coming over to Korea and Japan for the group stages but my
family are not planning to visit until the final week of the tournament.
*MARCEL DESAILLY, France defender, before his country's defence of the World Cup, 2002.
France did not survive the first round*

Sometimes in such a Herculean struggle an outside body can influence the
outcome. God, once again, will decide this match. And we will win it.
*JUAN SEBASTIAN VERON, Argentina midfielder, before the meeting with England in the
World Cup finals, 2002. England won*

I doubt this game will be a 0-0 draw. You don't see many goalless draws these
days. The way football is now, if you're not scoring at one end then you're
likely to be letting them in at the other.
KEVIN KEEGAN, Manchester City manager, before a 0–0 draw with Tottenham, 2003

We hope to surprise our Scottish friends on the playground.

*MART TARMAK, Estonian FA vice-president, welcoming Scotland in the programme
before 'the game that never was', 1996*

I think I've had only a couple of bookings in the last dozen games, which is
good for me. I had better not say any more or I'll probably be sent off
tonight.
ROY KEANE quoted in Dublin's Evening Herald *before being dismissed playing for the
Republic of Ireland v Russia, 1996*

I've never stopped learning since I came to Inter. When I was young, I was
a bit soft-headed, stupid sometimes. Having a family has settled me down.
The older you get, the more you learn to take it. I feel more in control.
PAUL INCE in Milan, 1996. He was sent off in his next match

I'm looking for a team that fights. No more nicey-nicey football.
*STEVE McMAHON before being sent off on his debut as Swindon player-manager for elbowing
an opponent, 1994*

Go out there and drop hand grenades.

KEVIN KEEGAN, England manager, to Paul Scholes before a match v Sweden, 1999.
Scholes was sent off

Loyalty and respect seem old-fashioned words nowadays. But, as far as professional football is concerned, these are still the most important values of all in my view.
DON REVIE, England manager, in the FA Book of Soccer, *1975. Two years later he suddenly took a lucrative post in the Middle East*

Bobby, of course, was twice a contender for the Chelsea managership, a job he always wanted. But on the principle that you can't have friends in partnership, there's no chance that he will ever become manager of Chelsea.
KEN BATES, Chelsea chairman, in Chelsea: My Year, *when Campbell was in charge of Portsmouth, 1984. Campbell eventually became manager at Stamford Bridge*

Arsenal and Spurs? No chance. The best two clubs in London are still Stringfellow's and the Hippodrome.
TERRY McDERMOTT, former Liverpool player, dismissing the capital's championship chances, 1988. Five months later, Arsenal took the title – at Liverpool

You have to be careful or you end up on the front page of the *Daily Record*.
DONALD FINDLAY QC, Rangers vice-chairman, on taking the stage at the Ibrox social club to sing sectarian songs, 1999. He resigned after being exposed by the Daily Record

I know now that the public and press are out there waiting for me to take responsibility and live differently.
JERMAINE PENNANT, Birmingham winger, 2005. The next day he was sent home from training after reputedly turning up drunk

Q: What's your favourite drink?
A: A couple of years ago the answer would have been 'everything'. But now I like Diet Coke.
GASCOIGNE interviewed by a Guardian *football website, 2005. A few days later alcohol was given as a reason for his losing the Kettering job, 2005*

Q: Favourite drink?
A: Beer. No, I mean Coke.
Q: Most prized possession?
A: My car.
EIRIK BAKKE, Leeds and Norway midfielder, in a programme interview, 2003. He was soon convicted of drink-driving

If you make a big mistake it will be your last game.

GRAHAM POLL, English referee, before the World Cup finals, 2006. He was sent home after giving Croatia's Josip Simunic three yellow cards, 2006

In a tournament like this my target is always the same – to make no mistakes. And when someone complains to you, it is better to pretend that you are deaf. For a referee it is always better to see things than to hear them.
URS MEIER, Swiss referee, before the European Championship, 2004. In the finals he controversially disallowed a potentially decisive goal for England v Portugal by Sol Campbell

If Roy has said he might play for Ireland again, someone must have caught him just after he'd had his Christmas pudding.
SIR ALEX FERGUSON, 2004. Within three months Keane announced his desire to resume playing for the Republic

Rooney is incredible, the best attacker in the world. Give him space and he will kill any defender. And the amazing thing about him is that he is never injured.
SVEN-GÖRAN ERIKSSON, England coach, before the European Championship finals, 2004. Rooney broke a foot early in the quarter-final

I was asked the other day who is going to be the top scorer [in the World Cup finals]. What a stupid question. Me!
MICHAEL OWEN before the tournament in Germany, 2006. The England striker's tournament ended early in serious injury

INDEX